PUBLICATIONS OF THE
NATIONAL BUREAU OF ECONOMIC RESEARCH, INC.

NUMBER 23

PRODUCTION TRENDS IN
THE UNITED STATES
SINCE 1870

PUBLICATIONS OF THE

NATIONAL BUREAU OF ECONOMIC RESEARCH

*1. INCOME IN THE UNITED STATES
   By WESLEY C. MITCHELL, WILLFORD I. KING, FREDERICK R. MACAULAY AND OSWALD W. KNAUTH
   Volume I (1921) Summary   152 pp.
*2. Volume II (1922) Details   440 pp.
3. DISTRIBUTION OF INCOME BY STATES IN 1919 (1922)
   By OSWALD W. KNAUTH   30 pp., $1.30
4. BUSINESS CYCLES AND UNEMPLOYMENT (1923)
   By the NATIONAL BUREAU STAFF and 16 COLLABORATORS   405 pp., $4.10
*5. EMPLOYMENT, HOURS AND EARNINGS IN PROSPERITY AND DEPRESSION, UNITED STATES, 1920–22 (1923)
   By WILLFORD I. KING   147 pp.
6. THE GROWTH OF AMERICAN TRADE UNIONS, 1880–1923 (1924)
   By LEO WOLMAN   170 pp., $2.50
7. INCOME IN THE VARIOUS STATES: ITS SOURCES AND DISTRIBUTION, 1919, 1920 AND 1921 (1925)
   By MAURICE LEVEN   306 pp., $3.50
8. BUSINESS ANNALS (1926)
   By WILLARD L. THORP, with an introductory chapter, Business Cycles as Revealed by Business Annals, by WESLEY C. MITCHELL
                                                380 pp., $2.50
9. MIGRATION AND BUSINESS CYCLES (1926)
   By HARRY JEROME   256 pp., $2.50
10. BUSINESS CYCLES: THE PROBLEM AND ITS SETTING (1927)
    By WESLEY C. MITCHELL   489 pp., $5.00
*11. THE BEHAVIOR OF PRICES (1927)
    By FREDERICK C. MILLS   598 pp.
12. TRENDS IN PHILANTHROPY (1928)
    By WILLFORD I. KING   78 pp., $1.00
13. RECENT ECONOMIC CHANGES (1929)
    By the NATIONAL BUREAU STAFF and 15 COLLABORATORS
                                        2 vol., 950 pp., per set, $7.50
14. INTERNATIONAL MIGRATIONS
    Volume I, Statistics (1929), compiled by IMRE FERENCZI of the International Labour Office, and edited by WALTER F. WILLCOX
                                                1,112 pp., $7.00
18. Volume II, Interpretations (1931), edited by WALTER F. WILLCOX
                                                 715 pp., $5.00
*15. THE NATIONAL INCOME AND ITS PURCHASING POWER (1930)
    By WILLFORD I. KING   394 pp.

* *Out of print.*

16. CORPORATION CONTRIBUTIONS TO ORGANIZED COMMUNITY WELFARE SERVICES (1930)
    By Pierce Williams and Frederick E. Croxton   347 pp., $2.00
17. PLANNING AND CONTROL OF PUBLIC WORKS (1930)
    By Leo Wolman   260 pp., $2.50
19. THE SMOOTHING OF TIME SERIES (1931)
    By Frederick R. Macaulay   172 pp., $2.00
20. THE PURCHASE OF MEDICAL CARE THROUGH FIXED PERIODIC PAYMENT (1932)
    By Pierce Williams   308 pp., $3.00
21. ECONOMIC TENDENCIES IN THE UNITED STATES: ASPECTS OF PRE-WAR AND POST-WAR CHANGES (1932)
    By Frederick C. Mills   639 pp., $5.00
22. SEASONAL VARIATIONS IN INDUSTRY AND TRADE (1933)
    By Simon Kuznets   455 pp., $4.00
23. PRODUCTION TRENDS IN THE UNITED STATES SINCE 1870 (1934)
    By Arthur F. Burns   363 pp., $3.50
24. STRATEGIC FACTORS IN BUSINESS CYCLES (1934)
    By John Maurice Clark   238 pp., $1.50

The National Bureau of Economic Research was organized in 1920 in response to a growing demand for scientific determination and impartial interpretation of facts bearing upon economic and social problems. Freedom from bias is sought by the constitution of its Board of Directors without whose approval no report may be published. Rigid provisions guard the National Bureau from becoming a source of profit to its members, directors or officers, or from becoming an agency for propaganda.

Officers

H. W. LAIDLER, *Ch. of the Board*   JOSEPH H. WILLITS, *Vice-Pres.*
OSWALD W. KNAUTH, *President*   GEORGE E. ROBERTS, *Treasurer*
CHARLES A. BLISS, *Executive Secretary*

Research Staff

WESLEY C. MITCHELL, *Director of Research*
ARTHUR F. BURNS   FREDERICK R. MACAULAY
SIMON KUZNETS   FREDERICK C. MILLS
LEO WOLMAN
EUGEN ALTSCHUL, *Associate*

Directors at Large

OSWALD W. KNAUTH   GEORGE O. MAY
H. W. LAIDLER   ELWOOD MEAD
SHEPARD MORGAN   GEORGE SOULE
L. C. MARSHALL   N. I. STONE
MATTHEW WOLL

Directors by University Appointment

EDWIN F. GAY, *Harvard*   HARRY ALVIN MILLIS, *Chicago*
WALTON H. HAMILTON, *Yale*   WESLEY C. MITCHELL, *Columbia*
HARRY JEROME, *Wisconsin*   JOSEPH H. WILLITS, *Pennsylvania*

Directors appointed by other Organizations

HUGH FRAYNE   GEORGE E. ROBERTS
American Federation of Labor   *American Bankers Association*
DAVID FRIDAY   M. C. RORTY
American Economic Association   *American Statistical Association*
LEE GALLOWAY   ARCH W. SHAW
American Management Association   *National Publishers Association*
ROBERT B. WOLF
American Engineering Council

PRODUCTION TRENDS IN THE UNITED STATES SINCE 1870

ARTHUR F. BURNS

NATIONAL BUREAU OF ECONOMIC RESEARCH

NEW YORK · 1934

COPYRIGHT, 1934, BY NATIONAL BUREAU OF ECONOMIC RESEARCH, INC.,
51 MADISON AVENUE, NEW YORK, N. Y. ALL RIGHTS RESERVED

DESIGN: ERNST REICHL
PRINTED AND BOUND IN THE UNITED STATES OF AMERICA
BY H. WOLFF, NEW YORK

RELATION OF THE DIRECTORS TO THE WORK OF THE NATIONAL BUREAU OF ECONOMIC RESEARCH

1. The object of the National Bureau of Economic Research is to ascertain and to present to the public important economic facts and their interpretation in a scientific and impartial manner. The Board of Directors is charged with the responsibility of ensuring that the work of the Bureau is carried on in strict conformity with this object.

2. To this end the Board of Directors shall appoint one or more Directors of Research.

3. The Director or Directors of Research shall submit to the members of the Board, or to its Executive Committee, for their formal adoption, all specific proposals concerning researches to be instituted.

4. No study shall be published until the Director or Directors of Research shall have submitted to the Board a summary report drawing attention to the character of the data and their utilization in the study, the nature and treatment of the problems involved, the main conclusions and such other information as in their opinion will serve to determine the suitability of the study for publication in accordance with the principles of the Bureau.

5. A copy of any manuscript proposed for publication shall also be submitted to each member of the Board. If publication is approved each member is entitled to have published also a memorandum of any dissent or reservation he may express, together with a brief statement of his reasons. The publication of a volume does not, however, imply that each member of the Board of Directors has read the manuscript and passed upon its validity in every detail.

6. The results of an inquiry shall not be published except with the approval of at least a majority of the entire Board and a two-thirds majority of all those members of the Board who shall have voted on the proposal within the time fixed for the receipt of votes on the publication proposed. The limit shall be forty-five days from the date of the submission of the synopsis and manuscript of the proposed publication unless the Board extends the limit; upon the request of any member the limit may be extended for not more than thirty days.

7. A copy of this resolution shall, unless otherwise determined by the Board, be printed in each copy of every Bureau publication.

(*Resolution of October 25, 1926, revised February 6, 1933*)

ACKNOWLEDGMENTS

In the course of this study I have received considerable assistance from friends and co-workers, to whom I am deeply grateful.

I am chiefly indebted to the staff of the National Bureau: to Dr. Wesley C. Mitchell for helpful comments on successive versions of the manuscript; Dr. Simon Kuznets for constructive assistance at almost every stage of the inquiry; Dr. F. R. Macaulay for assistance on several points in statistical theory; Dr. A. G. Silverman for stimulating criticisms of the manuscript; and Mr. H. G. Brunsman, formerly with the Bureau, for aid in numerous problems of statistical mechanics.

A number of research workers not connected with the National Bureau generously supplied me with various types of information—in a few cases, with unpublished data. I have tried in the text to acknowledge fully the more important assistance I have received in this manner.

Two of my former students, Mr. M. Friedman and Mr. L. Vass, offered detailed suggestions for improving the manuscript, and checked the accuracy of various mathematical statements.

The bulk of the computing work was done by Mr. Harold Rosen and Mr. Charles Wittmann. In a late revision of the manuscript I was assisted by Miss Dorothy Achilles, who is also responsible for the excellence of the charts.

A. F. B.

THE PROBLEM AND A SUMMARY
OF THE FINDINGS

By Wesley C. Mitchell

SINCE its beginning in 1920 the National Bureau of Economic Research has been exploring the wide and intricate realm of social changes. One set of its reports starts with important factors in economic life, such as national income, unemployment, migrations, or prices, and shows how these factors fluctuate through time. A second set of reports starts with significant periods in American history and shows how different economic factors have fluctuated within them. *Recent Economic Changes* and Dr. Mills' *Economic Tendencies* are examples of this approach. A third set of reports starts with recognized types of economic fluctuation and shows what forms they assume in different economic activities. Here belong the National Bureau's several volumes upon business cycles, Dr. Kuznets' study of seasonal variations and the present study of secular trends by Dr. Burns.

Each of these approaches to the study of social changes has its special uses and its limitations. Each has also its established place in men's efforts to understand their shifting economic fortunes. We are prone to identify the third approach with 'time-series analysis' and to think of it as a twentieth-century development. Certainly it has gained much in precision and effectiveness since 1900. But the current classification of economic changes runs back at least to the times of the classical economists, when 'commercial cycles' were recognized, when Ricardo speculated about the long-time trends of wages, rents and profits, when writers upon finance began discussing seasonal variations and when every economist abstracted from 'disturbing circumstances' for the same reason that analytic statisticians now seek to eliminate random perturbations. Indeed, we can borrow from John Stuart Mill's *Principles of Political Economy* a sweeping statement of the general problem, one phase of which is treated in the present volume.

"Production (wrote Mill) is not a fixed, but an increasing thing. When not kept back by bad institutions, or a low state of the arts of life, the produce of industry has usually tended to increase; stimulated not only by the desire of the producers to augment their means of consumption, but by the increasing number of the consumers. Nothing in political economy can be of more importance than to ascertain the law of this increase of production; the conditions to which it is subject: whether it has practically any limits, and what these are. There is also no subject in political economy which is popularly less understood, or on which the errors committed are of a character to produce, and do produce, greater mischief." [1]

Dr. Burns does not undertake 'to ascertain the law of increase of production' at large. His aim is more restricted, but more attainable. He studies the widely varying rates at which many American industries have grown from decade to decade since the 1870's, and seeks to ascertain what general features have characterized this sample of increase in production.

An investigator who essays such a task should begin by subjecting his materials to a rigid inspection and by providing himself with proper tools. The materials are statistical data; the tools are scientific concepts and mathematical procedures. Accordingly Dr. Burns devotes his first two chapters to formulating the basic concepts of 'production' and 'secular trend', describing the production series and methods of anal-

[1] Book I, chapter X, section 1, p. 155 of Sir William J. Ashley's edition.

A SUMMARY OF THE FINDINGS

ysis employed, and discussing the relations of the concepts to the data and technique.

The gentle reader who lends easy credit to any confident author and wishes quick repayment in definite information may feel impatient with the meticulous care lavished upon these preliminaries. But scientific work requires an investigator to know precisely what he is studying, to test his materials, to scrutinize his methods, and to make sure that concepts, materials and methods fit one another. Scientific work requires also that an investigator expose all his concepts, materials and methods to the critical scrutiny of his fellows. It is only by following these honest rules that progress in understanding can be achieved. On the other hand, it is not every reader's duty to share personally in assaying the metal of economic results. To those who will take much on faith the following summary of Dr. Burns' chapters may be helpful in showing what they wish to 'skip' and what they wish to read.

The production studied is the physical output of commodities and services as shown by annual statistics in the United States since the years 1870–85. One hundred and four series are used, 20 for agriculture, 3 for fisheries, 22 for mining, 45 for manufacturing, 2 for construction, 7 for transportation and 5 for trade. It is estimated that about two-fifths of the country's total production is covered by these series in 1925. Though the original data are subject to various defects, they constitute a sample sufficiently representative and reliable to justify analysis.

By 'secular trends' Dr. Burns means economic movements of longer duration than business cycles. He believes that such trends express the relatively long-run effects of forces making for change, and that they are economic realities as fit for systematic study as are the shorter cycles in business activity to which so much attention is given.

To measure production trends, he breaks each of his series into overlapping eleven-year segments (1870–80, 1875–85, 1880–90 and so on), adjusts these standard periods so that the end years in each segment of each series represent approximately the same phase of a cycle in production, fits exponential curves to the successive segments by the method of moments, and finally computes the average rate of growth during each segment. Thus Dr. Burns describes the trend of a series, not in the usual fashion by fitting a single curve to all the years covered by the data, but by using a number of curves fitted to brief periods with centers five years apart. In this way he is able to give a more faithful picture of the secular movements in production than if he had relied upon the customary technique.

As one would expect, the 'decade rates of growth' yielded by this method show changes of pace. 'Increase in production' is by no means regular even over periods long enough to include two or three business cycles. To take proper account of this fact, Dr. Burns elaborates his first concept of secular trend. "Lines of secular trend trace out paths more or less undulatory and also have an underlying general sweep; both types of movement are of interest and significance." The general sweep of the secular trends of a series is called its 'primary trend'.

The first use to which Dr. Burns puts his measurements in Chapter III is to make broad comparisons among the rates of growth in different branches of industry. For this purpose he reduces the several decade rates computed for each series to a single arithmetic mean. The figures show that "mining has grown at a spectacular rate, manufacture at a somewhat lower rate, and agriculture at a decidedly lower rate." The

A SUMMARY OF THE FINDINGS   xv

fisheries have declined in relative importance, while transportation and trade have gained. In general, the output of producers' goods has grown faster than the output of consumers' goods. When smaller divisions of production are considered, the most rapid growth is found among relatively new industries such as beet sugar, raisins, sulphur, Portland cement, aluminum and cigarettes, while the slowest growth is found among relatively old industries such as cane sugar, whaling, mercury, non-Portland cements and roofing slate.

Turning back from his general averages to the rates of growth for successive decades, Dr. Burns next shows that not a single industry in his list has grown at a constant rate. More than half of the 'basic' industries have undergone a shrinkage in at least one of the eleven-year periods. As measured by the differences between the decade rates, fisheries has had the least variable increase and sulphur the most variable. These extreme differences in the variability of the decade rates lie far apart (under 3 and over 100 per cent). About half of the series show ranges of more than 11 per cent between their slowest and their fastest rates of growth. Thus inconstancy of rate has been a universal characteristic of industrial expansion in the United States so far as our knowledge goes. Yet amidst the maze of variations one element of order stands out boldly: the rates of growth tend to decline as the decades pass.

This significant fact of retardation in industrial expansion is the theme of Chapter IV. From exponential curves fitted to the decade rates, Dr. Burns derives constants which measure retardation or acceleration in growth as shown by his data. To give an example of these measures: he finds the retardation in the growth of pig-iron production to be 1.2 per cent per decade; that is, the annual rate of growth at any given time averaged .988 of the annual rate of growth ten years earlier. Of the 104 continuous series analyzed, 92 show retardation; of 43 supplementary discontinuous series, 38 show retardation. In most series the rates of retardation are appreciable. The exceptions to the rule are mainly industries of secondary importance. Careful measurements thus bear out the first impression: retardation is a prevailing characteristic of industrial growth. To what is it due?

The gist of Dr. Burns' answer is that rapid growth in general production and decline in the rate of growth of individual industries go together. The latter is as characteristic of a progressive state as the former. The incessant introduction of new commodities restricts the increase in the demand for old commodities. The faster these new industries expand at first the greater is this restrictive influence, and the harder it is to sustain their own rates of growth for long. Doubling output each year may be feasible when a novel product wins favor; but a continuation of that rate of growth for a generation or two would mean the marketing of impossible quantities. Changes in methods also lead to retardation. For example: "The increasing replacement of farm work animals by automobiles and tractors has resulted in a rapid retardation in the production of horses and mules, has tended to retard the lumber industry, and has released millions of acres of crop land—which means that the increasing mechanization of agriculture has contributed to the retarded growth of certain of its branches, especially the production of oats and hay." Similarly, the coal industry is suffering from improved methods of combustion in railway locomotives and electric power plants. Reclamation of raw materials checks the increase in the demand for fresh production: between 1907 and 1929 the smelter output of primary copper increased at the rate of 2.5 per cent annually, that of secondary copper by 7.5 per cent. Further, new products and new processes exert a retarding influence upon other parts of the system by attracting to themselves portions of the capital, labor and materials which might have been used to sustain the growth of older industries. Perhaps the innovations augment the growth of capital; but they have not prevented a retardation in the growth of population, and they have contributed toward the necessity of resorting to inferior natural resources. Invention tends to offset deterioration in natural resources; but it has its limits. After Smeaton and Watt had reduced the coal consumption of steam engines from 30 pounds per horsepower hour to 9 pounds, no genius could make a further reduction of 21 pounds. Fundamental changes in industrial methods still keep occurring—for example, the introduction of the rotary kiln in making Portland cement, the Frasch process of mining sulphur, the use of rubber tires on vehicles. For a time such inventions may accelerate the rate of growth, but once the reorganization has been accomplished retardation reappears. Finally, industries which experience retardation are prone to organize in self-defence; in particular they resort to technical research and more intensive salesmanship. Insofar as these efforts prosper they increase the pressure upon all other industries, limiting the expansion of the latter's markets and so strengthening the forces tending toward retardation.

There seems no warrant for the common notion that industries grow until they approximate some maximum size and then maintain a stationary position indefinitely. No one of Dr. Burns' series shows a broad plateau at the apex; once an industry has ceased to advance it soon begins to decline. Several decadent industries appear in the original list of 104 series—cod and mackerel fishing, whaling, New York canal traffic, the production of non-Portland cements and mercury; several others appear in the supplementary list of 43 series— hemp raising, the production of maple sugar and walking plows. To these are added from other lists iron rails, anthracite pig iron, charcoal pig iron, cut nails and fine cut tobacco. The decadent industries reveal diverse fortunes, running all the way from the complete disappearance of iron rails and anthracite pig iron to the long decline of whaling. New York canal traffic even shows a notable revival since 1918, when the elaborate improvements made by the state were completed. There are some indications of retardation in decline corresponding to retardation in advance; but the materials do not justify a generalization.

Dr. Burns concludes his analysis of retardation by hazarding the suggestion that the life histories of industries are becoming shorter. A growing share of production is assuming the form of luxuries, superfluities and style goods; the demand for such products has no such stability as the demand for staples. Hence an increase in the birth-rate of new products means an increase in the death-rate among old products and a decline in the average life-span of individual industries.

Even more general than retardation is a second characteristic of production trends as Dr. Burns measures them—the undulatory movements spoken of above, 'trend-cycles' as they are called in Chapter V. Since the rate of secular growth is unstable in all the series analyzed, each series must show trend-cycles in the sense that it has alternations of more and less rapid growth. Granted the undulations, that is a matter of course which excites no interest. But it is a highly significant fact that the trend-cycles of different series tend to concur in time with one another.

Economic life in this country since the Civil War has been pervaded not only by the short-term rhythm of business cycles but also by a long-term rhythm of accelerated and retarded secular growth. These two rhythms are interconnected. Each time the national economy has experienced an exceptionally rapid secular advance, the production trends of different industries have diverged so widely as to suggest a partial loss of balance, and progress has been checked by a business depression of great severity.

To measure trend-cycles, Dr. Burns takes the successive rates of growth as plus or minus deviations from their primary trends. Ranking these deviations for all of his series at each of the eleven overlapping decades centered on the years 1875, 1880 and so on to 1925, he draws up a table of 'decils' which shows a high degree of concurrence among the trend cycles. (See Chart 5, p. 184). On repeating this procedure for several sub-groups of series, he gets similar results. The fact that the decil lines commonly rise and fall together indicates the prevalence of common movements among the 104 series. The parallelism of decil lines is most striking in 'basic nonagricultural' industries, and becomes nearly perfect when several dubious series are dropped from this group. (See Chart 8D, p. 189). The likelihood that these co-movements are due to chance is so remote that we seem bound to believe that the trend-cycles arise from common causes. But there is an important exception to the rule of similar movements of the trends. The leading crops trace out patterns of marked individuality. Few have more than a faint resemblance to the general pattern. Trend-cycles seem to be confined to nonagricultural production. These conclusions, including that concerning agriculture, reached by a study of individual series, are confirmed by a similar analysis of the leading index numbers of production.

Dr. Burns examines the trend-cycles of individual industries to see how regularly they conform to the general pattern and to find their relative amplitudes. His results for trend-cycles agree rather closely with those which the present writer is obtaining for business cycles. The erratic relationship of farm production to the fluctuations of general business activity appear as clearly in the latter investigation as in this one. In both cases most branches of production in which output is subject to close business control have high indexes of conformity to the movements of general business. In both cases again, the precious metals behave erratically, as do various manufactures of food products. Petroleum is an outlaw. In amplitude of fluctuation both of trend-cycles and of business cycles, crops rank low and mineral products relatively high. Also, the output of producers' goods undergoes larger cyclical fluctuations than that of consumers' goods, whether we take the long cycles or the short ones.

The chronology of the standard trend-cycles may be tabulated as follows:

'General Production' Shows Exceptionally

Rapid Growth in	Slow Growth in
1875–1885	1885 1895
1895–1905	1905–1915
1910–1920	1915–1925
1920–1929	

The overlapping of these periods since 1910 may indicate that the basic framework of eleven-year periods with centers separated by five years fits the actual tempo of change in trends less well in recent times than in the nineteenth century.

Concerning the causes of the standard trend-cycle, Dr. Burns must speak cautiously because his data cover only part of the economic system. But he brings out one highly significant fact. During the years when the increase in general production has been exceptionally rapid, the decade rates of growth shown by individual industries have drifted apart sharply. This 'dispersion' has regularly reached a maximum when the trend-cycles reached their peaks. On the other hand, the decade rates of growth drift closer together when the increase in general production declines; dispersion falls to a minimum in the troughs of the trend-cycles. The suggestion is that exceptionally rapid growth disrupts the 'balance' of the industrial system and so causes grave business difficulties, while the ensuing retardation of growth restores the balance and so paves the way for another phase of rapid growth. But the mechanism of this process and the part which random influences play in it remain to be worked out.

Business cycles from this viewpoint are short waves superimposed upon the long waves of trend-cycles. That there is a close connection between the two phenomena is suggested by theoretical analysis and the suggestion gets some support from chronology. The first peak in the trend-cycle pattern and in the divergence of production trends occurred in 1875–85; a severe depression occurred in 1882–85. The second peak in the trend-cycle comes in 1895–1905. This period of rapid growth was followed by the severe crisis of 1907. Similarly, the third peak of 1910–20 was followed by the severe depression of 1920–21, and the fourth peak of 1920–29 by the severe depression of 1929–33. In this list the great depression of 1893–94 is conspicuous by its absence, so that we cannot say that every severe depression has been preceded by the culmination of a trend-cycle. But we can say that each of the peaks in trend-cycles within the period covered has been accompanied or followed by a severe depression. If the arbitrarily centered decades of Dr. Burns' scheme were replaced by periods chosen to fit the problem of trend-cycles, a closer relation might appear between the chronologies of the long and short waves. Dr. Burns does not profess to settle the problem in this book; but he does state it in challenging fashion. Students of business cycles as well as students of secular trends must take account of his analysis. So, for that matter, should economic historians at large and the growing number of men who are seeking light upon the economic tendencies of today and tomorrow.

To this point Dr. Burns has dealt primarily with measurements of secular movements in individual industries. Retardation in growth and trend-cycles are found in most of the one hundred and four series with which the investigation started; also in most of the supplementary series introduced for special purposes. Both retardation and trend-cycles in individual industries indicate an orderly transformation in the pattern of national production. It remains to examine the increase in total production.

This task drives Dr. Burns back to a critique of the available statistics. Several attempts have been made to compile index numbers representing changes in the total output of American industry over considerable periods of time. How far can these indexes be trusted to show whether total production has grown at a steady, at a declining, or at an increasing rate?

Even if we waive aside the logical difficulties of interpreting an index number of 'physical' production made by applying fixed money weights to bales of cotton, ton-miles of transportation, numbers of locomotives and the like, Dr. Burns points out that the wide differences among the decade rates of growth found among industries make questionable the adequacy of any sample we can obtain for total production. Indeed, we know definitely that the best of our production indexes give inadequate representation to new industries, to services as compared with commodities, to 'secondary' production, to the utilization of by-products, and to improvements in the quality of products. All of these inadequacies tend to introduce a downward growth bias into the indexes. This bias is offset only in small part by the omission of industries which have ceased to exist and the under-

A SUMMARY OF THE FINDINGS xxiii

representation of decadent industries. Hence all the long-range production indexes now available, and probably the best long-range indexes which could be constructed from surviving records, are likely to understate the rate of growth in total production.

Taking the indexes as they stand, Dr. Burns finds that the least defective for his purpose are the Day-Persons and Warren-Pearson indexes. In 1870–1930 the first shows an average annual rate of growth of 3.7 per cent, while the second shows a rate of 3.8 per cent. The actual increase of total physical production has almost certainly been more rapid than these figures suggest—quite possibly a good deal more rapid.

Further, the two indexes named show rates of retardation amounting respectively to 0.5 and 0.6 per cent per decade. The higher of these rates is only half of that cited above for pig iron. Most individual industries, indeed, show higher rates of retardation than these indexes. Nor does that fact cast doubt upon either the indexes or the individual series; for declining percentage rates of growth in all industries taken one at a time would not be mathematically inconsistent with an increase in the percentage rate of growth of total production, and that quite apart from the birth of new industries. In view of the moderate retardation shown by the least defective indexes and of their inadequate representation of new industries, Dr. Burns concludes: "If there has been any decline in the rate of growth in the total physical production of this country, its extent has probably been slight and it is even mildly probable that the rate of growth may have been increasing somewhat."

While this general proposition must be stated in these cautious terms, two supplementary remarks can be made in bolder form. (1) Population has grown at a declining percentage rate. Hence production per capita has experienced retardation, if any, at a lower rate than total production. (2)

Despite their downward growth bias, the Day-Persons and the Warren-Pearson indexes show an increase on the average in the absolute yearly increments of total production.

A reader who grasps the import of Dr. Burns' conclusions concerning the growth of total production, concerning trend-cycles and retardation in the life histories of individual industries must ask himself whether these conclusions are really valid. If he takes this question seriously, he will read the book with the care it merits. For it is only by following Dr. Burns through his careful tests of the original data, his discussions of concepts and explanations of methods that one can appraise the results. These results contain many significant items not mentioned in this summary. While the reader will not find 'the law of increase of production' for which John Stuart Mill called, he will find the most important contribution to our knowledge of increase in production which has been made since Mill wrote.

CONTENTS

	Page
The Problem and a Summary of the Findings By Wesley C. Mitchell	xi
Foreword	3

CHAPTER I

Description of Production Statistics 5

    I. Measurement of Production 5
   II. List of Production Series 10
  III. Industrial Coverage of Production Data 17
  IV. Defects of Production Data 22
   V. Limitations Imposed by Data 28

CHAPTER II

Measurement and Analysis of Production Trends 30

    I. Concept of Secular Trend of Production 30
   II. Measurement of Production Trends 34
       1. Exponential Curves for Decade Periods .. 35
       2. Correction for the Cyclical Factor 38
       3. Method of Curve-Fitting 42
  III. Analysis of Production Trends 44

CHAPTER III

	Page
The Changing Pattern of Production	49
I. Divergence of Production Trends	49
1. Statistical Record of Divergence	50
2. Causes of Divergence	62
II. Inconstancy of Rates of Growth	69
III. Elements of Order in Secular Change	79

CHAPTER IV

Retardation in the Growth of Industries	96
I. Measurement of Retardation	97
II. The Statistical Evidence	104
III. The Explanation of Industrial Retardation	120
1. Retardation as Characteristic of a Progressive Economy	120
2. Forces Operating in the Markets for Goods	123
3. Forces Operating in the Workshops of the Economy	133
4. Impact of the Outside Economy	145
5. Cumulation of Retardation Forces	150
6. Influence of Structural Changes	153
7. Retardation and Industrial Decadence	158
8. Variation in the Rates of Retardation	162
IV. On a Law of Industrial Growth	169

CHAPTER V

Cycles in the Growth of Industries	174
I. Measurement of Trend-Cycles	175
II. A General Trend-Cycle in Production	179

CONTENTS

		Page
III.	Trend-Cycle Patterns of Individual Industries .	206
	1. Agricultural Industries	207
	2. Nonagricultural Industries	215
IV.	Trend-Cycle Amplitudes of Individual Industries	226
V.	The Explanation of Trend-Cycles	239
VI.	Relation of Trend-Cycles to Business Depressions	247

CHAPTER VI

The Growth of Total Production 253

I.	Measurement of Total Production	254
II.	Average Rate of Industrial Growth	262
III.	Change in the Rate of Industrial Growth	270

APPENDIX A

Supporting Statistical Data 283

APPENDIX B

Sources of Production Data 326

I.	Continuous Series	326
II.	Discontinuous Series	344

APPENDIX C

Notes on Measures for Production Series 347

I.	Average Rates of Growth	347
II.	Average Rates of Retardation	349
III.	Trend-Cycle Patterns	351

Index 355

TABLES

Table	Page
1. Production Series and Their Dates of Commencement	12
2. Estimates of the Coverage of Production Series, by Industrial Groups, in 1925	19
3. Frequency Distributions of Average Rates of Industrial Growth, during 1870-1929 and 1885-1929	52
4. Frequency Distributions of Average Rates of Growth during 1885-1929, for 'All' Series and Basic Series, by Industrial Groups	54
5. Rates of Growth of Industries: Agriculture and Fisheries	55
6. Rates of Growth of Industries: Mining	57
7. Rates of Growth of Industries: Manufactures and Construction	58
8. Rates of Growth of Industries: Transportation and Trade	61
9. Measures of Inconstancy of Growth of Industries	70
10. Frequency Distributions of Measures of Continuity of Growth, for 'All' Series and Basic Series, by Industrial Groups	75
11. Frequency Distribution of Ranges of Decade Rates, for 'All' Series	77
12. Frequency Distributions of Standard Deviations of Decade Rates, for 'All' Series and Basic Series, by Industrial Groups	78
13. Production Series Having Decade Rates of 10 Per Cent or More, and 0 or Less, by Decades Indicated by Their Central Years	81
14. Measures of the Relative Position of the Trend Movements of Basic Series, for 1885-1929	84
15. Coefficients of Correlation between Decade Rates	

Table	Page
of 38 Basic Series, for Pairs of Decades Indicated by Their Central Years	87
16. Coefficients of Correlation between Decade Rates of 57 Basic Series, for Pairs of Decades Indicated by Their Central Years	88
17. Coefficients of Correlation between Decade Rates of 44 Basic Nonagricultural Series, for Pairs of Decades Indicated by Their Central Years	89
18. Averages of the Coefficients of Correlation between Decade Rates	90
19. Frequency Distribution of Average Rates of Retardation, for 142 Production Series	106
20. Frequency Distribution of Measures of Continuity of Retardation, for 'All' Series	108
21. Frequency Distributions of Average Rates of Retardation, for 142 Production Series, by Industrial Groups	109
22. Retardation in the Growth of Industries: Agriculture, Fisheries, and Forestry	111
23. Retardation in the Growth of Industries: Mining	112
24. Retardation in the Growth of Industries: Manufactures and Construction	113
25. Retardation in the Growth of Industries: Transportation and Trade	117
26. Percentage of World Production of Certain Raw Materials Accounted for by Domestic Production	147
27. Percentage of Domestic Production of Certain Agricultural Products Exported	149
28. Frequency Distributions of Average Rates of Retardation, for 'All' Series and Basic Series	164
29. Coefficients of Correlation between Average Rates of Growth and Average Rates of Retardation, for Several Groups of Production Series	168

Table	Page
30. Medians of Trend-Cycle Observations at Central Decade Years, for Several Groups of Production Series	180
31. Types of Movement of Trend-Cycles between Successive Central Decade Years, for Several Groups of Production Series	197
32. Conformity of Trend-Cycles of Production Series to Standard Trend-Cycle: Agriculture and Fisheries	208
33. Conformity of Trend-Cycles of Crop Series to Trend-Cycle in Total Crop Production and to Standard Trend-Cycle	210
34. Conformity of Trend-Cycles of Acreages and Production Volumes of Eight Leading Crops to Standard Trend-Cycle	211
35. Conformity of Trend-Cycles of Production Series to Standard Trend-Cycle: Mining	216
36. Conformity of Trend-Cycles of Production Series to Standard Trend-Cycle: Manufactures and Construction	218
37. Conformity of Trend-Cycles of Production Series to Standard Trend-Cycle: Transportation and Trade	220
38. Frequency Distributions of Measures of Trend-Cycle Amplitude, for 'All' Series and Basic Series, by Industrial Groups	228
39. Measures of Trend-Cycle Amplitude	230
40. Coefficients of Correlation between Average Rates of Growth and Trend-Cycle Amplitudes, for Several Groups of Production Series	237
41. Rates of Growth Shown by Population and Indexes of Production	263

LIST OF CHARTS

Table		Page
42.	Measures of Inconstancy of Growth, for Indexes of Production	272
43.	Rates of Retardation Shown by Population and Indexes of Production	274
44.	Continuous Production Series: 1870–1929	284
45.	Decade Rates of Production Series	305
46.	Composition of Several Groups of Series Analyzed	309
47.	Trend-Cycles of Production Series	313
48.	Decils of Trend-Cycles of Several Groups of Production Series	318
49.	Medians of Trend-Cycles of Subgroups of Nonagricultural Series	321
50.	Trend-Cycles of Indexes of Production	322
51.	Trend-Cycles of Acreages and Acre-Yields of Eight Leading Crops	323
52.	Medians of Trend-Cycles of Two Groups of Manufactures	324
53.	Standard Trend-Cycle and Trend-Cycles of Several Non-Production Series	324
54.	Measures of Dispersion, and of Cycles in Dispersion, of Decade Rates	325

CHARTS

Chart		Page
1.	Frequency Distributions of Average Rates of Growth during 1870–1929 and 1885–1929	53
2.	Frequency Distribution of Average Rates of Retardation of 142 Production Series	107
3.	Frequency Distributions of Average Rates of Retardation of 'All' Series and Basic Series	165
4.	Medians of Trend-Cycles of Several Groups of Production Series	181
5.	Decils of Trend-Cycles of 'All' Series	184

Chart		Page
6.	Decils of Trend-Cycles of Nonagricultural Series.	185
7.	Decils of Trend-Cycles of Basic Series	186
8.	Decils of Trend-Cycles of Basic Nonagricultural Series	188
9.	Medians of Trend-Cycles of Subgroups of Nonagricultural Series, Varying in Their Amplitudes ..	193
10.	Medians of Trend-Cycles of Subgroups of Basic Nonagricultural Series, Varying in Their Amplitudes	195
11.	Trend-Cycles of Indexes of Total Production	201
12.	Trend-Cycles of Indexes of Production of Several Major Industrial Groups	205
13.	Trend-Cycles of Production of Eight Leading Crops	209
14.	Trend-Cycles of Acreages and Acre-Yields of Eight Leading Crops	214
15.	Trend-Cycles of Production of Eight Leading Minerals	217
16.	Medians of Trend-Cycles of Two Groups of Manufactures	219
17.	Trend-Cycles of Production of Iron, Steel, and Coke	221
18.	Trend-Cycles of Production Series Relating to Construction	222
19.	Trend-Cycles of Several Series Relating to Transportation and Trade	223
20.	Trend-Cycles of Processes Other than Production Compared with Standard Trend-Cycle	241
21.	Cycles of Dispersion of Decade Rates of Production Series Compared with Standard Trend-Cycle	243

PRODUCTION TRENDS IN
THE UNITED STATES
SINCE 1870

FOREWORD

THIS inquiry into economic change is restricted to one type of change, secular trends; to one aspect of the economic system, industrial production; to one geographic division, the United States; and to a portion of the economic history of that division, the period from approximately 1870 to 1930. The first three limitations are matters of choice, the last is virtually a matter of necessity.

The theme of the work is the industrial progress of the United States, but the approach is theoretical—not historical. The production trends of a large number of industries are analyzed with a view to discovering such elements of order as have characterized the rapid development and changing content of our national production of commodities and services. The first two chapters are devoted to a description of statistical data and technique. Chapter III presents a general picture of the changes in the qualitative composition of production, and suggests certain elements of order in these changes. These elements of order are investigated in some detail in Chapters IV and V. The final chapter passes from the changes in the pattern of production to the quantitative increase in total production, the principal aim being to determine whether there has been any regularity in the secular trend of total production.

The economist need not be reminded that an inquiry confined to secular changes in industrial production can give only a partial glimpse into secular changes in the economic system as a whole; that an inquiry into secular changes in the physical volume of production can give only a partial glimpse into secular changes in industrial production; and that an inquiry carried through largely in terms of data of the physical volume of production can give only a partial glimpse even into secular changes in the physical volume of production, since the production system does not have an independent existence. If some of our interpretations of statistical regularities in secular changes in the physical volume of production lack thoroughness, that is one of the 'costs' of a study aiming at general results, but based on a restricted range of statistical data.

Chapter I

DESCRIPTION OF PRODUCTION STATISTICS

AN INQUIRY into production trends cannot be better than its basic materials. Therefore, an attempt will be made in this chapter to indicate the meaning of production statistics, the extent to which long-range production series are available, and the degree of their correspondence with the quantities of which they purport to be measures. The production series analyzed in detail in this study go back at least to 1885 but no further than 1870. The series relate to the physical volume of production and cover a fairly large portion of the total production area. But the gaps in the data are numerous and important, and the series themselves are at times of uncertain quality. It is only proper that the reader be warned at the start that he may be asked to accept conclusions which do not always have as thorough a factual basis as he has a right to expect.[1]

1. MEASUREMENT OF PRODUCTION

In traditional economic theory, 'production' means the 'creation of valuable utilities'. But the things to which 'valuable utilities' are added by industry have attributes other than price. The output of any given commodity may be viewed not only in terms of monetary value (gross or net),

[1] This chapter is devoted to a general description of the production series which form the backbone of the analysis in Chapters III–V; the production indexes on which the analysis in Chapter VI rests are described in the introductory section of that chapter.

but also in terms of physical volume, in terms of the satisfactions (direct or indirect) of consumers, or from the standpoint of its social value. Let us suppose that one thousand cigars of a standard grade are made in one month and two thousand the next. The physical volume of production may then be said to have doubled. But the gross pecuniary volume of production may have changed in another ratio, depending on the price of cigars in the two months. The net pecuniary volume of production may have changed in still another ratio, depending not only on the price of cigars but also on the prices of the materials entering into the cigars. If the character of the consuming group remained the same over the two months, the volume of created utilities will have increased, though by less than one hundred per cent: if the character of the consuming group changed, the volume of utilities may have increased or decreased in almost any ratio; but in either case the exact change is indeterminate. Finally, the social value of the output of cigars may have changed in any ratio whatsoever, depending on the moral universe of the person or group concerned with the change. According as the production of cigars or any other good is viewed in one or another of these respective ways, a physical, pecuniary, utility, or normative concept of production is embraced. However, since the utility and normative concepts do not generally lead to objective measurements, the physical or pecuniary concepts must be employed, if a study of production is to convey more than the personal bias of an investigator.

The measurable aspects of the things to which valuable utilities are added by industry consist, speaking generally, of certain pecuniary and physical characteristics. The pecuniary characteristics are numerous: the gross value, net value, labor cost, materials cost, and so on. The physical characteristics are likewise numerous: we can express the physical volume of production of wheat in terms of units of weight (the ton), units of cubic content (the bushel), units of energy (the calorie), units of expended labor (the man-hour), and so on. Constant relations will hold between series of year-by-year measurements of divers pecuniary aspects of a produced commodity, if industrial technique remain constant and prices move in identical ratio; between measurements of divers physical aspects of the commodity other than the labor bestowed upon it, if the commodity be perfectly homogeneous; between measurements of all physical aspects of the commodity, if the commodity be perfectly homogeneous and industrial technique constant; and between measurements of all physical or pecuniary aspects of the commodity, if the commodity be perfectly homogeneous, industrial technique constant, and prices move in identical ratio. However, industrial technique and price changes are ordinarily dynamic; and, although certain commodities are homogeneous (as is true in high degree of copper since the widespread adoption of electrolytic refining, and of Portland cement since 1911), commodities are as a rule heterogeneous. Therefore, series of year-by-year measurements of divers physical or pecuniary aspects of the aggregate of some produced commodity will differ from one another in variable ratio. Granted minute knowledge of the distinguishable units (bushels) of the output of wheat (a heterogeneous product) over a series of years, we could express the production of wheat in terms of gross value, net value, tons, bushels, calories, or man-hours of labor; each of these sets of measurements would express precisely the quantity of that homogeneous attribute of which the particular measurement takes account; but the several sets of measurements would ordinarily bear a more or less inconstant relation to one another. Moreover, we would attain dollar sums, bushel sums, calorie sums, and so on, for a 'bundle' of closely related commodities called 'wheat', not for a unique commodity.

The significance of the various measurable aspects of things to which valuable utilities are added by industry differs, of course, with the purpose at hand. What is most important from the standpoint of farming enterprisers having different grades of wheat for sale, at least so far as their immediate economic status is concerned, is the gross value product; from the standpoint of the welfare of those attached to the wheat-farming industry, the net value product; from the standpoint of the technical branch of the transportation industry, the number of bushels of wheat and their tonnage; from the standpoint of the business branch of the transportation industry, the number of bushels of wheat, their tonnage, and their gross value. All of the measurements are important from a 'social' standpoint: calorific content, because the energy value of wheat is one of the elements entering into its want-satisfying power; the number of bushels of wheat, because of the calorific value of wheat, and even more, the preference of the population for this grain; the quantity of expended labor, because it expresses, when related to the number of bushels of wheat, the effectiveness of man in the mastery of his environment; the net value product, because it enters directly into the economic welfare of one important section of the population and indirectly into the economic welfare of the entire population; and the gross value product, because it bears some relation—however vague, inconstant, and erratic—to the satisfactions accruing to the domestic population from the consumption of wheat or from the consumption of other goods obtained from the outside economy in exchange for wheat.[2]

[2] One might argue that, from a 'social' standpoint, the gross value of a produced commodity is the most significant of its various measurable aspects; for the qualitative differences of, say, wheat are primarily important to the economist when they are attended by utility differentials, which, in turn, always enter into price differentials. This assumes that a series of wheat production expressed in terms of gross value will correspond more closely to utility differentials than will a series of wheat production expressed in some

In this study, our interest centers in the secular changes in the volume and forms of productive activity; to be more explicit, in the development of individual industries and of industry as a whole, and in changes in those economic customs which are expressed in the composition of the 'heap' of national production. In studying the things to which valuable utilities are added by industry, we should, therefore, make use of measurements of gross value, of net value, and of various physical attributes (these will differ, of course, from commodity to commodity). However, the only measurements of production available in reasonable abundance are of gross value, and of physical production as expressed in commercial units (bushels of wheat, number of locomotives, flasks of mercury). Practical limitations on the scope of this investigation make it impossible to utilize even these measurements. Price fluctuations, especially when violent and erratic, complicate the meaning of pecuniary measurements of production; these will therefore be left out of account in this restricted study. The long-term records of the physical volume of production of wheat, coal, cotton, and other commodities reveal more sharply the growth tendencies in specific types of industrial activity, and changes in the channels into which the industrial activity of the population flows.

To be sure, our data on the physical volume of production are expressed in units which are inconstant over time, and this detracts somewhat from the import of the measurements. Fortunately, however, the changes in the qualitative character of the units are generally very gradual.[3] For example, there has been a persistent improvement in the quality of

---

physical unit, say, bushels. It is not feasible to enter at this point into a discussion of the conditions under which this will be true or false. Suffice it to say, though, that it is altogether impossible to state whether the one or the other measure will generally correspond more closely to the volume of created utilities.

[3] See pp. 25-7.

rails and locomotives since the Civil War, but no sharp variation in quality from year to year. Even when the quality of products varies considerably from year to year, as in most agricultural produce, the trend in quality, whether upward, as in sugar beets, or downward, as in raw wool, is ordinarily gradual. The units of physical output change, as a rule, in a regular manner, especially in the case of raw materials and crude manufactures, which bulk large in the long-range production statistics available. To be sure, sudden and fairly comprehensive qualitative changes in the aggregate production of a commodity take place at times, either as a result of an outstanding technical discovery, as in the case of Goodyear rubber, or a legislative fiat, as in fermented liquors after the Prohibition Amendment. But really discrete and revolutionary changes in the aggregate output of a commodity are rare, and are never an important feature of the economic system as a whole.

II. LIST OF PRODUCTION SERIES

The production series on which the greater portion of this study is founded are listed in Table 1. These series constitute a fairly exhaustive record of the continuous data available for a study of production trends during the period since 1870–85.[4] All of the important series, taking value of product represented as an index of importance, are included, as are also a fairly large number of minor series. Some of the minor production series are used because they represent decadent industries, but the main reason for including such series is to compare the trend characteristics of major and minor industries. Economic theory suggests that the growth tendencies of minor industries will not be marked by the same degree of

[4] Series which do not extend back at least to 1885 are not included, because a shorter period would prove inadequate for the kind of analysis to which the data are subjected.

PRODUCTION STATISTICS

'stability' as major industries, and it therefore seems desirable to determine empirically such differences as may exist in the trend behavior of the two.

The series listed in Table 1 are arranged under conventional industrial categories,[5] and in the order of the length of period for which they are available. The number of series listed in Table 1 is 104, several of them being duplications

[5] The allocation of the individual series to the several industrial categories is in some instances arbitrary. A number of series which relate to manufactures (according to the usage of the Census Bureau) are placed under agriculture and mining, the purpose being to cover the raw materials group as thoroughly as possible. But this rule could not be followed uniformly. Thus, aluminum is not placed under mining, because its production in this country antedates that of bauxite, and foreign bauxite has played throughout an important rôle in the domestic aluminum manufacture. Nor is roofing slate placed under mining, the ground being that it accounts for only a portion of the output of slate quarries. A similar reason holds for several other series. Insofar as series technically relate to manufactures, but are not so classified in Table 1, they are distinguished in Table 7, being repeated there from tabulations for agriculture and mining. Several border-line cases remain, but there is no need to discuss them.

Another group of arbitrary allocations is found in the transportation and trade divisions. Thus, the series 'postage stamps' and 'postal money orders' are placed in the transportation division, on the view that the postal service is a communication industry. The series 'railway freight' is placed under trade, and 'railway ton-miles' under transportation, on the view that the actual volume of goods shipped is symptomatic of trade activity, and that a compound series of freight and distance is the real measure of the service rendered by the freight branch of the railway transportation industry. The series 'coastal trade' is placed under transportation, on the view that coastal shipping is a distinct branch of the transportation category. But plausible grounds could be advanced for assigning some of the series placed in the transportation category to the trade category, and vice versa.

The arbitrariness at various points of the classification of series in Table 1 is one reason for combining certain of the industrial categories in the substantive tabulations. Thus, trade and transportation series are generally treated together. The manufactures and construction categories are also joined in most of the substantive tabulations, but for another reason. Both manufacture and construction are elaborative industries, the only technical difference between them being that the seat of the activities of the latter is inconstant; this difference is of no significance from the standpoint of secular trends in industry. Finally, the agriculture and fisheries categories are generally joined in the tabulations, in part because they relate commonly to organic raw materials, but primarily on grounds of convenience.

Table 1
PRODUCTION SERIES AND THEIR DATES OF COMMENCEMENT

AGRICULTURE

1. Barley 1870
2. Beet sugar 1870
3. Buckwheat 1870
4. Cane sugar 1870
5. Corn 1870
6. Cotton 1870
7. Hay 1870
8. Molasses and sirup 1870
9. Oats 1870
10. Potatoes 1870
11. Rice 1870
12. Rye 1870
13. Tobacco, raw 1870
14. Wheat 1870
15. Wool 1870
16. Raisins 1872
17. Flaxseed 1879
18. Cattle 1880
19. Hogs 1880
20. Sheep 1880

FISHERIES

21. Cod and mackerel 1870
22. Whale 1870
23. Fish, total 1880

MINING

24. Anthracite coal 1870
25. Bituminous coal 1870
26. Coal, total 1870
27. Copper 1870
28. Gold 1870
29. Lead, domestic 1870
30. Mercury 1870
31. Petroleum 1870
32. Phosphate rock 1870
33. Silver 1870
34. Zinc 1870
35. Asphalt 1880
36. Cement, total 1880
37. Fluorspar 1880
38. Gypsum 1880
39. Iron ore 1880
40. Non-Portland cements .. 1880
41. Portland cement 1880
42. Pyrites 1880
43. Salt 1880
44. Sulphur 1880
45. Natural gas 1882

MANUFACTURES

46. Cocoa imports 1870
47. Coffee imports 1870
48. Cotton consumption ... 1870
49. Distilled spirits 1870
50. Fermented liquors 1870
51. Jute imports 1870
52. Lead consumption 1870
53. Lead, total 1870
54. Manila hemp imports .. 1870
55. Minor fiber imports ... 1870
56. Pig iron 1870
57. Rails 1870
58. Raw sugar consumption. 1870
59. Rubber imports 1870
60. Silk imports, raw 1870
61. Sisal imports 1870
62. Steel 1870
63. Superphosphate 1870
64. Tin imports 1870
65. Vessels 1870
66. Wool consumption 1870
67. Antimonial lead 1871
68. Tin-plate consumption.. 1871
69. Tobacco and snuff 1871
70. Cottonseed cake and meal 1872
71. Cottonseed oil 1872
72. Nails 1872
73. Zinc consumption 1873
74. Flaxseed consumption .. 1879
75. Roofing slate 1879
76. Cigarettes 1880
77. Cigars 1880
78. Coke 1880
79. Flour 1880
80. Gold consumption 1880
81. Locomotives 1880
82. Silver consumption ... 1880
83. Tobacco consumption .. 1880
84. Aluminum 1883
85. Copper consumption .. 1883
86. Silk imports, unmanufactured 1883
87. White lead 1884
88. Canned corn 1885
89. Canned tomatoes 1885

Table 1 (cont.)
PRODUCTION SERIES AND THEIR DATES OF COMMENCEMENT

MANUFACTURES (cont.)

90. Rolled iron and steel ... 1885

CONSTRUCTION

91. Rail consumption 1870
92. Building permits 1874

TRANSPORTATION

93. Coastal trade 1870
94. N. Y. canals traffic 1870
95. Postage stamps 1870

96. Postal money orders ... 1870
97. Railway ton-miles 1870
98. S. S. Marie canals traffic 1870
99. Railway passenger-miles. 1882

TRADE

100. Agricultural exports ... 1870
101. Deflated clearings 1870
102. Tonnage entered and cleared 1870
103. Shares traded 1875
104. Railway freight 1882

about which something will be said presently. With minor exceptions, all of the series are continuous annual records, continuity and annual availability being essential for the main tasks of this study. With minor exceptions again, all of the series are analyzed through 1929, so that the dates at which the series begin indicate the exact periods covered by the series in this study.[6]

A word may be said about the nomenclature of the series. When the name of a commodity is given without any further qualifying term, 'production' is almost always implied. The two most frequent qualifying terms are 'imports' and 'consumption'. The former is self-explanatory except that the imports are 'net'; the latter refers in each case to industrial

[6] While the analysis of most of the individual production series is extended through 1929 only, most of the production indexes covered in Chapter VI are analyzed through 1930. Two series, distilled spirits and fermented liquors, are not analyzed beyond 1918; the qualitative change in these commodities, at least so far as the statistically reported product is concerned, was so comprehensive that all that the products before and after this date have in common is their name. Two series, building permits and roofing slate, have a one-year gap (see Appendix B), but this was not deemed a bar to their utilization.

In addition to the series in Table 1, a fairly large number of discontinuous production series are available; they have been used as supplementary materials in one portion of the study where discontinuity of data did not matter much. See Tables 22, 24–25, and Appendix B, II.

consumption, that is, utilization by industrial units, not by final consumers. One of the consumption series, 'rail consumption', calls for special comment: it represents the apparent utilization of rails by railroads, and therefore offers an indication of the volume of railway construction, including repairs. The series 'minor fiber imports' is a composite of sisal, jute, and Manila hemp imports. The series 'coastal trade' measures the tonnage documented for the coastal trade and not the freight moved in coastwise commerce. Similarly, the series 'cod and mackerel' and 'whale' relate to the tonnage documented for these fisheries and not to the quantities of catch. The series 'railway freight' refers to the volume of freight transported over the various railroads, and includes such duplications as shipments moving over the lines of several roads may involve. The series 'lead, domestic' refers to the primary lead refined from domestic ores, while the series 'lead, total' relates to the primary lead refined from all ores or base bullion, irrespective of origin. The series 'cattle', 'sheep', and 'hogs' represent federally inspected slaughter or its estimated equivalent. The series 'silk imports, unmanufactured' differs from 'silk imports, raw' in that it includes cocoons and silk waste in addition to the silk fiber. These comments are confined to those series whose coverage is most vaguely indicated by the synoptic nomenclature of Table 1.[7] For the content of the various series, reference should be made to Appendix B and to the sources there listed.

[7] The use of the terms 'sisal', 'Manila hemp', and 'cocoa' is sanctioned by trade custom. Practically all of the so-called 'sisal' imports are really imports of 'henequen'. The correct name of 'Manila hemp' fiber is 'abacá'. The term 'cocoa' properly refers to the finished product only; the present statistics are for the crude product which, strictly speaking, goes by the name 'cacao'. However, the term 'superphosphate' has been used in preference to the more familiar name 'acid phosphate', in view of the official adoption of the former by fertilizer manufacturers in 1928. The term 'coastal trade', on the other hand, has been used instead of 'coasting trade', which is the preferred term in official reports.

Among the 104 series, there is a certain amount of duplication, that is, a given stage in the production of a commodity is in some cases represented by more than one series. Thus, there are two series for silk imports, varying only in the degree of their inclusiveness. There are series for the total production of coal and cement, and also separate series for the subdivisions of each. The imports of three minor fibers—jute, sisal, and Manila hemp—are covered separately and in combination. There is a series for all rolled iron and steel products and also for rails—a specific kind of rolled product. There are three series for manufactured tobacco products—cigarettes, cigars, and tobacco and snuff—and also a series for tobacco consumption which indirectly subsumes all of them. There is a series for all the fisheries, and also two series for certain divisions of the industry. The various duplications derive in part from the form in which the statistical materials are cast; for example, data of the output of all rolled iron and steel products are available back to 1885, but not for the individual products except rails; or to cite another example, a homogeneous record of unmanufactured silk imports extends back to 1883 only, while a consistent record of raw silk imports is available back to 1870. However, most of the duplications in the list of series result from our interest in the aggregate production of certain industries and also in certain of their subdivisions; though gaps in statistics and practical considerations imposed restrictions on the extent to which subgroups of industries are covered.

The fact that the series in Table 1 involve a certain amount of duplication suggests that the production data lack qualitative homogeneity. Actually, the qualitative differences among the series extend considerably beyond the duplicated areas. In referring to the various series, the term 'industry' is very frequently used in this study; that term, however, does not have a uniform signification,[8] since the series differ appreciably in the degree of generality of their industrial reference. Thus, several series are included for separate divisions of freight transportation by water, but the series for railways is comprehensive; Portland cement is treated separately, but all other cements are lumped together; there is only a single series for all distilled spirits, yet there is one series for all rolled iron and steel forms and another for a specific kind of rolled product; and the numerous materials consumption series are of a distinctly higher order of generality than the rest. These differences in the industrial dimension of the series result, in part, from practical exigencies which imposed limitations on the use of such materials as are available, but mainly, from the nature, that is, the quantity and quality, of the data which have come down to us. The heterogeneity of the underlying data is in a sense intellectually unsatisfactory; but the inelegancies in the list of series could not be wholly eliminated or even appreciably reduced without discarding a large portion of the usable statistical records of production. The wide differences in the industrial dimension of the series are allowed for in the later analysis, in part through separate treatment of 'basic' series, which include series representing industries of large importance and also series of wide industrial reference, and in part through comparisons of series of production and industrial consumption for identical commodities. It will be seen that the analysis gains in some ways from that very heterogeneity in the form of the data which appears at first sight an unmixed evil.

[8] Several fairly definite conceptions of a national industry which might be used are: (1) a given product turned out by all establishments by a given technical process, (2) a given product turned out by all establishments irrespective of type of technique, (3) related products turned out by all establishments irrespective of type of technique. But it would be difficult to employ strictly any of these conceptions.

III. INDUSTRIAL COVERAGE OF PRODUCTION DATA

Any one who examines the list of series carefully will not fail to note numerous inadequacies in the materials. A large portion of the field of 'service' production is completely unrepresented. To be sure, trade and transportation are covered after a fashion; but the services performed by these industries are mainly adjuncts of the process of producing tangible goods. There are glaring gaps even in the field of 'commodity' production. Among the industries producing raw materials, the mining group alone is covered with reasonable thoroughness. Forestry is not represented at all. The fisheries are completely represented, but by a single general series rather than by component series. No dairy products are included in the agricultural group, and very few fruits or vegetables. The gaps in the manufactures group are numerous and important: the paper, printing and publishing, lumber products, musical instruments, leather, petroleum refining, and machinery industries are untouched, and there are serious omissions in such divisions of manufacture as are represented. The construction industry is represented by the 'building permits' and 'rail consumption' series; but the permits figures, at best, serve as an indication of the volume of urban construction only, since they leave out of account rural and governmental construction. Clearly, the production series included in this study fall far short of a comprehensive coverage of the area of national production.

It is desirable to form a somewhat exact notion of the extent to which the production of the American economy is covered by the series listed. In Table 2 estimates are given of the coverage of the total output of various groups of industries and of all industries during 1925. These estimates are necessarily rough, and are intended merely to give some idea of the extent of the production area covered by the series.[9] It will be noticed that the coverage of mining, the fisheries, and trade is very high; that the coverage of agriculture, construction, and transportation is rather high; that the coverage of manufactures is low; and that many branches of the service industries are not covered at all. Our series account for about 60 per cent of the output of the seven industrial groups covered, and for about 40 per cent of total national production; but these global estimates are less revealing than estimates for certain

[9] Whenever possible, separate computations were made for 1925, 1926, and 1927, and the results averaged. The percentage coverage of agriculture was computed by expressing the gross farm value of the listed crops and animal products as a ratio to the gross value of total farm production; the data used are those given in *Farm Value, Gross Income, and Cash Income from Farm Production* (Department of Agriculture, 1930). The percentage coverage of mining was obtained by expressing the value of the listed mineral products as a ratio to the total value of mineral production; the data used are those given in *Mineral Resources of the United States* (Bureau of Mines). In view of the difference in the classification of the Bureau of Mines and that of Table 1, it was necessary to modify the latter so that it correspond with the former. It should be noted that the Bureau of Mines surveys of mining overlap in considerable part the field of manufactures; a stricter definition of mining would probably yield a higher estimate of the coverage. The percentage coverage of manufactures was determined by obtaining the 'value added' of the industries included, this requiring estimation in many cases, and then expressing this figure as a percentage of the 'value added' by all manufactures; the data used are those of the *Census of Manufactures*. In view of the difference in the classification practice of the Census Bureau and that in Table 1, it was necessary to modify the latter so that it correspond with the former. The estimate for manufactures is probably somewhat too high, for it was impossible completely to avoid indirect representation of industries. The percentage coverage of construction was determined by (1) subtracting the value of public and rural construction from total construction (the figures used for public and total construction are Wolman's estimates,—see his *Planning and Control of Public Works*, National Bureau of Economic Research, 1930, p. 126; the estimate of rural construction was made by multiplying the estimate of non-public construction by an estimate of the percentage—the basis being the Federal Trade Commission's *National Wealth and Income*, 1926, pp. 366–7—which rural construction constitutes of total non-public construction); and (2), expressing (1) as a percentage of the value of total construction. The percentage coverage of transportation was obtained by (1) adding King's estimates for 1925 of the realized income of steam railroads, the realized income of the water transportation industry, and the wages of postal service employees; (2) adding wages of postal employees to King's estimate of realized

Table 2
ESTIMATES OF THE COVERAGE OF PRODUCTION SERIES, BY INDUSTRIAL GROUPS, IN 1925

Industrial group	Per cent of product accounted for by series
(1) Agriculture	65
(2) Fisheries	100
(3) Mining	83
(4) Manufactures	22
(5) Construction	63
(6) Transportation	69
(7) Trade	100
Above industrial groups, (1) to (7)	60
Above and all other industrial groups	39
All commodity-producing industries	43
All service-producing industries	37
Above industrial groups, except (2), (5), and (7)	46
All industrial groups, except (2), (5), and (7)	26
All commodity-producing industries, except (2) and (5)	40
All service-producing industries, except (7)	15

of the industrial groups. Thus, the coverage of the commodity-producing industries is 43 per cent, a somewhat higher figure than for the service-producing industries. More significant estimates of the industrial coverage of the series are attained

---

income for the transportation industry; and (3), expressing (1) as a percentage of (2). (King's estimates are given in his *National Income and Its Purchasing Power*, National Bureau of Economic Research, 1930, pp. 95 and 364.) The percentage coverage of the fisheries is given as 100, in view of our use of a series of total fish catch. In the case of trade, the series included do not run in the desired form, that is, they fail to cover separately either distinct branches of trade or the trading transactions in distinct industries. In view of the generality of the series, a 100 per cent coverage is assumed; but because of the unsatisfactoriness of the form of the series, trade is omitted from some of the summary computations.

In order to determine the percentage coverage of all industry and the several combined industrial groups (the fishery was ignored because of its rela-

by excluding construction, trade, and the fisheries; for, although high percentages are recorded for these industrial groups, the series falling in the groups are either very indirect measurements of output or else defective in other ways—more so than the generality of series for other industries. With these omissions, the coverage of all industries drops to 26 per cent, and the gap between the 'commodity' and 'service' industries becomes more pronounced, their estimated coverage being 40 and 15 per cent, respectively. These estimates hold approximately for more recent years; but they are probably much too low for the early years of the period covered by this study. It must also be observed that the estimates do not make allowance for the indirect industrial representation of the series.

It has already been stated that although the series listed fail to cover a large portion of the production area, they constitute a fairly exhaustive record of the long-range production data available. The wide gaps in our historical records of production are, in considerable part, a legacy of the neglect of statistics in earlier days. The reluctance of producers to disclose

---

tive insignificance), more extensive use had to be made of King's estimates of the income created by various industries. His estimates for 1925 were used, this being the latest year for which full data are given. As a first step, the net value product of the various industries accounted for by the series included had to be estimated; this was done by applying the estimated percentages of coverage for agriculture, mining, manufactures, construction, and trade to King's estimates of income created by these industries; in the case of transportation, the estimate of net value product was yielded directly by the method earlier indicated. As a second step, minor adjustments were made in certain of King's estimates of income created by industries: (1) the figure for transportation was raised by the amount of wages paid to postal service employees; (2) the figure for government was lowered by the amount of pensions and gratuities, and by the amount paid to postal service employees; (3) income from foreign investments and imputed interest on durable consumption goods were excluded from the 'miscellaneous' category. From this point on, only totals had to be struck and compared. The commodity-producing industries group includes the following of King's groups: agriculture, mining, manufactures, construction, and a small portion of the 'miscellaneous' category. The service-producing industries group includes transportation, trade, government, banking, 'unclassified', and the bulk of the 'miscellaneous' category.

their output was formerly the most serious impediment to a system of national production statistics.[10] The consequences of statistical reticence are most conspicuous in monopolistic industries; for example, the aluminum industry, and the sulphur industry for some years. But such obstacles, originating in the vested interests of private enterprise, might easily have been overcome, had there been greater public appreciation of the importance of regular compilation of authoritative data on production. The extent of earlier public indifference to the recording of national progress is strikingly indicated by the fact that such long-range production series as are now available for other than agricultural and mineral industries are in very considerable part an accidental by-product of various branches of governmental administration—mainly the customs, postal system, internal revenue, and the waterways. Because of their origin, these statistics have a decidedly indiscriminate character as far as the significance of their industrial coverage is concerned, and rarely have the most desirable form for a study of production. In the case of crop production and mining, the government has served posterity more kindly. For these industries the statistical record is relatively ample, by virtue of the annual estimates of crop production which the Department of Agriculture initiated in 1862, and the annual canvasses of mineral production which the Geological Survey began in 1882. It is fortunate that government records do not constitute the only source of long-range production statistics. Data on the output of several industries—especially iron and steel, railway equipment and traffic, and sugar—have come down to us as a result of the diligence of certain private organizations. Moreover, by the use of government and other sources, students have recreated the statistical record of many

[10] Fortunately, that reluctance has diminished considerably; but it is still found—especially in declining industries.

industries—notably the production of certain classes of livestock, of superphosphate, flour, and natural gas.

But with new industries emerging and old industries vanishing, the pattern of national production continually undergoes modification, so that even an ideally complete set of long-range production series could embrace only that portion of the production area which is common to each of the years covered. In view of the considerable current importance of commodities such as automobiles, rayon, radio sets, washing machines, photographic materials, and electrical appliances of all sorts, a set of series reaching back to the 1870's or '80's must necessarily fall short of including important sections of contemporaneous productive activity. Even some of our industries producing raw materials are of rather recent origin: the first shipment of bauxite was made in 1889, and the discovery of Fuller's earth dates back only to 1893. So, the dynamic character of production, no less than the sparseness of statistical records, accounts for the incomplete coverage of the field of production by our long-range series.

IV. DEFECTS OF PRODUCTION DATA

Though the relative industrial coverage of the series listed in Table 1 falls far short of ideal requirements, a point had yet to be stretched in order to achieve this coverage. A number of series which do not report the volume of production directly are included. Several estimated series which have not as yet stood the test of critical review are also included. Moreover, even the production series which are commonly accepted as authoritative have a variety of defects. The defects of physical volume statistics derive, in part, from the dynamic character of production processes, and in part, from the statistical procedures of compiling agencies. Sundry references have already been made to inadequacies in the form of the

PRODUCTION STATISTICS

production data. It remains now to consider more systematically the nature of the inadequacies.

From a qualitative standpoint, the chief types of defects in the production series are as follows. First, a large number of the series are results of estimates rather than enumerations: practically all the figures of crop production [11] are in this form, and the data for many of the other series are also estimates—the materials consumption series requiring special mention since they are, generally, calculated series. Second, many of the series are indirect measurements of production: about twenty series relate to 'imports' or 'consumption', a few series really measure shipments, and a few volume of equipment. Third, several of the presumptive physical volume series are really pecuniary in form or origin: the series 'postage stamps' runs in dollar units, while the 'building permits' and 'deflated clearings' series are adjusted for changes in price levels. Fourth, the significance of the units in which certain of the series are expressed is open to doubt: this holds particularly for several of the indirect production series, for the series on animal slaughter, and in more or less degree for some other series. Fifth, the real content of the units of practically all of the series lacks temporal constancy: though less pronounced, this is as true of the series 'cattle' and 'copper' as of 'rails' and 'locomotives'. Sixth, the industrial coverage of several series is incomplete: this is true mainly of 'building permits' and of the series on animal slaughter. Seventh, the geographic coverage of some series exceeds or falls short of all of the contiguous areas of the United States: import series cover also some of the possessions, the production data for certain commodities are occasionally limited to the leading producing states, and at times a portion of the output of

---

[11] At present, the Division of Crop and Livestock Estimates of the Department of Agriculture is engaged in a comprehensive revision of the historical record of crop statistics.

bordering foreign countries is covered by the statistics. Eighth, the time reference of some series is not uniform, as when data are first given on a fiscal and later on a calendar year basis. Finally, a few of the series are spliced, and differences in the exact composition of the joined series may give rise to error: the most conspicuous instances are the several series on minor fiber imports, which relate first to 'imports entered for consumption' and later to 'general imports' minus 'foreign exports'.

This conspectus of the types of defects in production series might be elaborated upon to some advantage, were it not for the fact that certain of the defects are of little importance when the series are used to study production trends. Clearly, inaccuracies in the year-by-year figures will matter little, provided the general trend of the figures is unaffected. Since many of the estimated series rest on the support of census enumerations, their trends may be approximately accurate, even though year-by-year movements at times are not.[12] A constant error in the figures, irrespective of its direction, will exercise no influence on their trend. Lack of uniformity of time reference will affect the general trend but imperceptibly, as will also minor differences in geographic or industrial coverage. And many of the consumption series for metals, though undoubtedly in error for individual years because of insufficient account of stocks, are in all likelihood reasonably accurate in their general drift, being compounded from rather reliable data on production and foreign trade.

However, the series have a variety of defects even from the standpoint of an inquiry into production trends, though their exact importance will vary with the nature of such an inquiry. The limitations are clearest when the data are used to indi-

---

[12] There are often doubts, however, concerning the accuracy of the census base. See Joseph S. Davis, "Some Observations on Federal Agricultural Statistics," *Proceedings of the American Statistical Association*, March, 1928.

cate the average rates of growth of industries.[13] It will therefore be instructive to analyze the 'growth bias' of the series,—meaning by this a persistently increasing or a persistently decreasing percentage differential between the data and the 'real volume' of production throughout the period covered by the series or during some appreciable time segment.

One of the conditions under which a growth bias will arise in a production series is when the coverage of the series has an upward or downward trend. This may be due to a change in the efficiency of collecting the data: in the case of such series as are obtained by the enumerative method, there has probably been a slightly upward growth bias arising from increasing comprehensiveness of reporting. A trend in the relative coverage of a series may also be due to a change in the relative importance of the statistically covered area of an industrial process. Thus, the livestock slaughter series, being limited to federally inspected slaughter or its estimated equivalent, have an upward growth bias, as far as their representation of meat production is concerned, because of the relative decline of 'rural' slaughter. On the other hand, several of the metal production series, insofar as they are used to represent metallurgical rather than mining processes, have a downward growth bias because they are confined to 'primary' metal and exclude 'secondary' metal which is of increasing relative importance.

A growth bias is also likely to arise when an indirect production series has a trend of a somewhat different curvature than the real phenomenon which it is taken to represent. One of the outstanding consequences of technological advance (including improved management) in industry is the increasing yield of materials in the form of fabricated products. Hence, the numerous 'consumption' and 'import' series used in this

[13] When production series are used for other purposes, their defects are more difficult to appraise. See, however, pp. 99–100, note 4, and Appendix C.

study very probably have, on the whole, a downward growth bias, as far as their representation of production volumes is concerned. The same is true of the equipment series; for example, the series of tonnage documented for the cod and mackerel fisheries understates the trend of cod and mackerel catch, for fishing vessels and gear are being used with steadily greater effectiveness. The same factors are operative, but their statistical impact is opposite, when direct production series are used to represent production indirectly—a paradoxical procedure which at times has its advantages, as when cane sugar production is used to represent the production of sugar cane, and beet sugar to represent sugar beets, with a view to attaining a more rounded picture of agriculture. In these two cases, because of improved methods of extraction, the series used have an upward growth bias.

Finally, a growth bias will arise in a production series when the product covered has improved in quality. This may mean either that the quality of a product has been generally raised, or else that the high-quality portion of the output has increased in relative importance. It may be the result of increased care in the selection of seeds, as in crop production; or of breeding for desirable meat strains, as in animal husbandry; or of the development of alloys, as in the manufacture of steel. Observers of the industrial scene differ as to whether the quality of the total national output is improving or worsening. Doubts may be legitimate as far as a large portion of the field of elaborative manufactures is concerned. However, no one with even an elementary knowledge of the history of basic commodities can doubt that there has been, generally, a secular advance in their quality. Accordingly, a considerable number of the production series assembled for this study have a downward growth bias on this score.[14]

[14] It may be argued that the output of by-products associated with some fundamental commodity constitutes an additional source of growth bias when

PRODUCTION STATISTICS

The factors making for growth bias are compensatory in certain cases and cumulative in others. Thus, as an indicator of beef production, the series of cattle slaughter has an upward growth bias, arising from the increasing relative importance of federal slaughter and the declining weight of cattle at slaughter, but a downward growth bias because of the improving quality of beef. On the other hand, the series of copper consumption, when used as an indicator of the manufactures into which copper enters, has a downward growth bias which derives from the increasing importance of secondary copper, the increasing yield of copper in finished products, and the improving quality of the manufactures based on copper.[15] In most cases, the exact degree of growth bias cannot be ascertained, and the degree to which growth bias is cancelled or cumulated can be determined at best in a qualitative way only. For some industries, such as locomotive production, livestock slaughter, and a few others, auxiliary statistics are available which suggest the probable magnitude of the growth bias, at least as far as single determinants of bias are concerned.[16] Taking the production series as a whole, the one generalization which can safely be made is that their growth bias is in most instances downward.

---

the by-products grow at a different rate than the main product. The series of coke production, on this basis, has an appreciable downward growth bias. The problem is, in the last analysis, one of definition. It depends, specifically, on whether 'coke' or 'coke and its manufactures' is taken as the industrial unit.

[15] If a series of sugar beets were used to indicate the production of sugar beets, it would have a downward growth bias originating in the improved quality of beets; if a series of beet sugar were used to indicate the production of sugar beets, it would have an upward growth bias originating in the improved methods of sugar extraction; but, if a series of sugar beets were used to indicate the production of beet sugar, it would have a downward growth bias originating both in the improved quality of beets and in the improved methods of sugar extraction.

[16] See Appendix C, I.

V. LIMITATIONS IMPOSED BY DATA

It is evident that neither in point of quantity nor of quality are the listed long-range production series fully adequate for a serious inquiry into production trends, even when the scope of the inquiry is restricted to physical volume data. The restricted coverage of the production statistics imposes limitations on any generalizations which may be made concerning production trends as a whole. The qualitative deficiencies of the data impose restrictions even on such generalizations as may be limited to the series studied. In working with defective statistical materials, the economist finds himself, to use the apt words of Mr. Meeker, "in much the situation of a chemist compelled always to do his qualitative and quantitative analysis with leaky test-tubes and impure reagents." [17]

The aim of this chapter has been to set forth in general terms the nature of the underlying data of this study, not to impound their defects. In the substantive chapters, the propriety of passing from the specific results obtained to a generalization for the production system as a whole will be considered at each critical point. In some cases, generalization is possible with some assurance, despite the sundry inadequacies of the data. In other cases, an attempt to generalize on the basis of the available materials would be boldness bordering on folly.

The fact is that the inadequacies of the statistical data do not bear equally on all kinds of problems, and each particular question must therefore be settled on its own merits. For example, the statistics are grossly inadequate for the purpose of accurate measurement of the long-term trend of general production.[18] To attempt to achieve this is to tempt faith out of its proper channel. On the other hand, the statistical mate-

[17] J. E. Meeker, *Measuring the Stock Market* (pamphlet by New York Stock Exchange, 1931) sec. VII.
[18] See Ch. VI, sec. I.

rials are quite adequate for the purpose of determining whether industries have grown characteristically at a declining rate, whether a long-term rhythm has been pervasive in industry, and for still other purposes. In certain connections, statistical methods may be used to reduce biases which actually exist or may exist in the data.[19] Also, it is often possible to reckon appropriately, on the basis of general knowledge, with the inadequacies of the data. There is, indeed, no more important check on the validity of conclusions drawn from statistical materials than the reasonableness of the results. If they conform to a priori expectations, or if they admit of a rational explanation, some confidence, however tentative, must attach to them.

These remarks apply to statistical results of a general nature which alone are a matter of real concern in this work. The primary aim of the inquiry is to describe in general terms the trends of the production system as a whole, the interest in individual industries being merely incidental. If the specific numerical results for the individual series are at times in error, that need not detract from the general conclusions reached on the basis of the data taken in the mass. Though the data have been compiled with considerable care, a serious effort having been made to obtain the most authoritative figures, it may still be true that some of the results for individual series reflect faultiness of the data, or of the technique of their analysis, rather than the nature of the actual phenomena. Insofar as the interest of the reader may center in any of the individual results, he would therefore do well to acquaint himself with their full history. To help the reader who may become so engaged, the raw data are presented in Appendix A, Table 44; the sources of the data accompanied by brief comments are listed in Appendix B; and a detailed description of their elaborate treatment is presented in Chapter II and also in portions of the substantive chapters which follow.

[19] See pp. 242–3, note 54.

Chapter II

MEASUREMENT AND ANALYSIS OF PRODUCTION TRENDS

A STATISTICAL technique is to be adjudged in the light of the purpose it is made to serve and of the data on which it is put to work. The aim of this chapter, accordingly, is to describe our technique of measuring secular trends, in relation to the underlying concept of secular trend of production and to the raw data on production. The measurements of secular trends will be analyzed in detail in later chapters, the primary aim being to throw light on the elements of order in the secular changes in the pattern of production of the United States, and in the quantitative increase of its total production. The special techniques employed in the analysis of the measurements of secular trends will be described fully at the points where they are introduced; but their general nature will be discussed briefly in the closing section of this chapter.

1. CONCEPT OF SECULAR TREND OF PRODUCTION

There is probably no concept in the whole field of contemporary 'quantitative' economics that is vaguer than that of secular trend. However, what the most appropriate denotation of secular trend should be is perhaps less important than that the term have real economic content, a fairly unequivocal meaning, and a uniform use in any given investigation.

The term 'secular' is derived from 'saeculum'; etymology might therefore require that we refer to a century when we speak of the 'secular trend' of some economic element. But there is a firm tradition in economics, going back to Cournot, which justifies a looser use of the term. The secular trend of an industry's production may be considered as the persistent, underlying movement of its output over a period which is 'long' in relation to the changes associated with the 'business cycle'.[1] So viewed, the secular trend is irreversible within the periods of a business cycle, though it may be reversible within longer periods. The secular trend can be represented graphically by a curve and may be given algebraic expression by a mathematical equation. A set of secular trend lines for the component branches of a national productive system will register the rapidity of advance (or decline) and the changing pattern of the parts of the system.

This statement of the meaning of secular trends does not suffice for the purpose of measurement. From a statistical standpoint, it is more convenient to define secular trends negatively. Accordingly, secular trends of production may be considered, on the economic side, as the 'non-cyclical' movements of series, and on the statistical side, as curves which delineate these movements. This view of the secular trend of production will be definite in the degree to which the idea of a production 'cycle' has definiteness. Any number of cycles may be distinguished in long production series; but we shall view a cycle arbitrarily as a period containing a rise and a fall, the cycle being the shortest that can occur in annual data. Such a cycle will have a minimum period of two years, and although the maximum period is indefinite, it will generally be only a few years—especially when the year-

[1] This term is used in Professor Mitchell's sense. See his *Business Cycles: The Problem and Its Setting* (National Bureau of Economic Research, 1927), particularly pp. 468-9. See also, p. 247, note 55.

to-year variations of a series are taken in the form of first differences, as may justifiably be done when production rises with exceptional swiftness.[2] The idea of a cycle, then, can be made definite enough for our purpose, thus leaving the present concept of secular trend reasonably precise. Being merely denotative, this concept is free from the question-begging notion that secular trends are measures of the effects of causes independent of those generating the cyclical, seasonal, and random variations in production series. Furthermore, it is free from the notion that secular trends are equilibria paths which quantities 'strive' or 'tend' to approach, and the notion that secular trends cannot themselves have undulatory contours.

But if cycles are viewed in a purely statistical way, the derivative trend concept may seem equally formal. A trend concept resting on a statistical definition of cycles is itself statistical. Its economic significance may well be questioned, for statistical notions concerning trends and cycles have disturbing logical implications. If a cycle be nothing more than a rise followed by a decline or a decline followed by a rise, a considerable number of trends and cycles may be established for almost any long production series. What have been defined as secular trends will also exhibit cycles, in the sense of up and down movements, and will therefore give rise to new lines of trend, which may show statistical cycles once more, and so on. Yet it is only natural to think that such progressive refinement of time series, actuated by a statistical urge, is more likely to result in statistical curiosities than in anything of economic importance. And this doubt also casts a shadow on the significance of the concept of secular trend of production which has been explicated.

[2] Thus, Professor Mitchell distinguishes cycles of acceleration and retardation of increase, which he has found to be particularly important in certain cumulative banking series.

MEASUREMENT OF TRENDS

Fortunately, this is largely an unfounded scepticism, for the statistically defined cycles are also important economic realities. They have broad economic significance, inasmuch as the various production series trace out patterns of fluctuation which have considerable similarity. It is, in fact, the high degree of synchronism in the movements of the ensemble of production and other economic elements that makes their fluctuations a *general* economic phenomenon and leads us to speak of *the* business cycle. The cycles of the individual production series reveal fluctuations of the total national economy, and for this reason, their elucidation is a problem in general economic theory. If the cycles of various industries evidenced little of a common pattern, we could hardly speak of general economic cycles at all. The problem of their elucidation would then fall outside the province of general theory, and would belong rather to the history of specific industries. But once it is recognized that cycles are a generic economic phenomenon, secular trends of production conceived of as non-cyclical movements also take on economic significance. They thus constitute a distinct economic movement or, perhaps, congeries of movements.

This conclusion, however, flows from a characterization of cycles that is somewhat too simple. The 'business cycle' rhythm is not revealed uniformly in all production series. The series which conform perfectly to the general business cycle still contain random elements in their cyclical course: many series occasionally either trace out cycles not found at all in the progression of the business cycle or else skip certain of the business cycles; and some series, especially the class of agricultural crops, have cycles which show little of a systematic time relationship to the swing of the cycle in general business.[3] These erratic cycles and random elements in cycles

[3] This problem is being investigated with great thoroughness by Professor Mitchell, who has devised an ingenious method for comparing the 'specific cycle' patterns of series with their 'reference cycle' patterns, the latter being

are but remotely connected with the 'business cycle' rhythm of the national economy and arise largely from causes peculiar to individual industries. However, for reasons of convenience, the term 'cycle' has here been defined as a congeries of short-run economic movements, those connected with the business cycle and those of a random character. Secular trends, viewed as non-cyclical movements, refer therefore to economic movements of longer duration, expressing the relatively long-run effects of the forces making for change. In view of the inclusion of random movements under cycles, the secular trend of a series, defined as its non-cyclical movement, must not be considered as strictly bisecting successive cycles; it may, at times, have to be considered with reference to several cycles taken together, so that the movement underlying the ensemble of cycles may be properly exposed. Understood in this way, secular trends are not perfectly precise components of the total movements of production, but they are sufficiently precise for statistical purposes. They are economic realities which invite systematic investigation, quite as much as the short-run fluctuations which have inspired such extensive study in recent years.[4]

II. MEASUREMENT OF PRODUCTION TRENDS

Secular trends of production express the growth (including decadence under this term) of industries; and it is only because the growth of economic quantities is a question of large interest that secular trends are important. In delineating secular trends of production, what we really do is to measure growth. But the mere direction of trend lines does not suffice for effective comparisons of the growth tendencies of

---

determined on the basis of turning points in general business. The results of his researches will be incorporated in Volume II of his *Business Cycles*, a forthcoming publication of the National Bureau.

[4] For a further discussion of the concept of secular trend, see this chapter, sec. III.

MEASUREMENT OF TRENDS

different industries in given periods or of given industries in different periods. A common unit of the direction of trend lines is necessary; this cannot be given by the absolute rate of movement of trend lines, but it can be given by the logarithmic rate of movement of trend lines, or the percentage rate of movement. Of the various attributes of trend lines, the percentage rate of change provides the common unit which should prove most satisfactory in comparing the secular trends of industries.

1. Exponential Curves for Decade Periods

An excellent measure of the average percentage rate of change per time unit is yielded by a trend line of the simple exponential type.[5] However, when the periods of production series are long, exponential curves will ordinarily fail to embody the central notion concerning secular trends, explicated in the preceding section; for they will rarely trace

[5] Let the exponential function be written as $y = ab^x$, where y is production and x is time. Then, the average percentage rate of change per time unit is given by $100 \left(\dfrac{ab^{x+1} - ab^x}{ab^x} \right) = 100(b-1)$. The average percentage rate of change obtained from the equation of a simple exponential curve fitted to a production series gives a better indication of the average rate of growth than an average of percentage changes computed directly. An arithmetic mean of year-to-year percentage changes is defective because the theoretical scale of percentages is limited at one end but not at the other. A geometric mean of percentage changes is preferable to an arithmetic mean, since it is based on the logarithms of percentage changes (or rather link ratios), and therefore gives equal weight to changes of equal proportionate magnitude. The geometric mean of percentage changes has nevertheless a serious defect: it is absolutely conditioned by two items, the initial and final values, and these may of course be of 'accidental' magnitude. The geometric mean can report what happened from one time unit to another, but not what happened during the period marked off by them, and is therefore but poorly suited to yield the kind of information about growth that is here desired. Clearly, an exponential curve affords a better method of averaging year-to-year percentage changes: it embodies the essential idea of the geometric mean and, at the same time, takes full account of the internal structure of the historigram.

out the non-cyclical movements of the series accurately.[6] Hence, it has been deemed necessary to break up our series into segments, and to fit exponential curves to each of the segments. Such trend lines have an element of artificiality in that they are discontinuous. At times discontinuities in secular movements are real, as when a fundamental change takes place in the conditions underlying an industry's operation. But such changes do not occur frequently; and in order to approximate continuous trend lines for the various series and in that way obtain more faithful records of secular changes, exponential curves have been determined for two sets of successive segments for each series, one set overlapping the other.

Exponential curves have been fitted to intervals of about ten years, the length of the time segments being determined, however, only in part by logical considerations. It was desirable to make the periods fairly short in order to insure that the trend lines follow faithfully the paths of secular changes, but the periods had yet to be distinctly longer than the average duration of cycles in order to prevent a distortion of the trends by the cyclical factor. In pursuing our inquiry into secular movements, it was practically essential that the trends of the various series cover intervals of constant duration and identical calendar timing. In all, ten-year intervals of customary dating (1870–79, 1880–89, and so on) seemed satisfactory; but the circumstance of cyclical high points [7] in a fair number of production series at 1890, 1900, 1910, and

[6] To be sure, exponential curves give satisfactory fits in some cases, as in flaxseed consumption, fish catch, and cigarette production; but in the majority of cases, they afford inadequate fits; and occasionally, absurd fits, as in cane sugar or steel production. Even when an exponential curve yields a moderately good fit to a series taken as a whole, it may give an extremely poor fit to certain segments of the series, as when the fitted line of trend marches on imperiously at a rapid and uninterrupted pace, while the series shows a mild rise or even decline during some ten-year interval. A case in point is cigarette production, a very rapidly growing industry, which nevertheless experienced a declining trend during the decade 1895–1905.

[7] See below, pp. 38–40.

MEASUREMENT OF TRENDS

1920, and the desideratum of conveniently centered 'decades', led to the use of eleven-year periods bounded by round dates (1870–80, 1880–90, and so on).[8] These were supplemented by overlapping periods, shifted by five years from the first, to give another set of continuous time segments (1875–85, 1885–95, and so on). The term 'decade' is convenient and is used hereafter in referring to these periods.

Trend lines have been fitted to overlapping periods in order to establish a more detailed and faithful record of secular change than would otherwise have been had. In many series, a single set of successive decade trends would have left entirely unreported some significant change in the secular movement. The production of cottonseed cake and meal furnishes an instructive example. Starting with 1870, the output shows an upward trend in each decade. The same is true starting with 1875, except for the decade 1915–25. What happened is that cake and meal production rose more sharply in the first few years of the decade 1910–20 than it declined in the last few years, and rose more sharply in the last few years of the decade 1920–29 than it declined in the first few years. Clearly, what occurred during the decade 1915–25 is as much a part of the trend history of this industry as what happened during 1910–20 and 1920–29. To have worked with a single set of decades would have seriously restricted the validity of the further analysis to which the decade trends were subjected. The use of overlapping decade trends overcame—in a measure and, of course, implicitly—the difficulty of trend discontinuity.

In the substantive parts of this work, our interest will be confined to the average annual percentage rates of change which the exponential curves yield. These average annual percentage rates of change over decade intervals may be

[8] Since most of the series analyzed do not extend beyond 1929, the period 1920–29 is an exception.

briefly termed 'decade rates'. Before going further in the description of our technique of trend measurement, it is important that the exact significance of the decade rates for a given production series be fully understood. Each set of successive decade rates records the average annual rate at which production increased (or declined) decade after decade during the period covered by the series. The two sets of successive decade rates, taken separately, may show somewhat different patterns of growth; but this is only to be expected, first, because the full periods covered are not exactly the same, second, because secular trends may be reversible over periods longer than a business cycle. Once the two sets of decade rates are combined in a chronological sequence, the technical limitations of each are largely overcome, while the meaning of the now overlapping decade rates is in no way beclouded. For some purposes it is desirable to view them as rates at which production increased at the central dates of the decades, since the decade rates are but slope readings (speaking loosely) of the exponential curves.[9] Regarded from this standpoint, the decade rates constitute quinquennial observations on the slope of the secular trend. But it is often preferable to view the decade rates as applying to the full decade intervals. The fact that the decade rates of a given series refer to overlapping periods should not detract from their clear import of being equitemporal observations on the rate of growth of an industry.

2. Correction for the Cyclical Factor

It remains to describe the details of the technique of determining the decade rates. Clearly, a rigid use of calendar decades would have led to considerable error in the trend computations. Since decade intervals of production series only

---

[9] In speaking of the 'slope' of the secular trend, we shall mean the percentage rate at which the secular trend rises or declines.

MEASUREMENT OF TRENDS

infrequently contain an integral number of cycles, trends for such short intervals are likely to reflect the cyclical factor as well as the trend proper. For any given decade, the possible extent of trend distortion depends upon the relative magnitude of the cyclical swings with respect to the trend slope. When the slope is steep and the cyclical amplitude small, the distortion will be negligible; but in the case of a rather mild trend slope and sharply defined cycles, the distortion may be considerable.

In order to prevent an admixture of trend and cycle elements in the decade rate computations, the fixed calendar decades have been used as reference periods for the decade rates, but these rates themselves have been computed for periods of only approximate decade duration. Let us speak of the actual periods for which trend computations have been made as 'working decades', and the periods to which the computations are taken to refer as 'reference decades'. The boundary dates of a given working decade were chosen so that the end values were approximately at the same cyclical phase, and in this way a cyclical bias in the trend of the working decade was in large part prevented. Since the trend computations for the working decades were to apply to their respective reference decades, it was necessary to circumscribe the procedure of locating the boundary dates of working decades so as to insure as small a deviation from the reference decades as was compatible with the principle underlying the use of working decades. The observance of several mechanical rules [10] limiting the freedom of choosing boundary dates in-

[10] The rules used to limit the choice of boundary dates are as follows: (1) the working decades were allowed to vary from a minimum of nine years to a maximum of thirteen years, (2) the maximum leeway allowed on either side of the reference decade was two years, (3) at least nine years of the reference decade had to be included in the working decade. However, these rules were relaxed considerably in the computations for 1920–29 (several series extend to 1930) because: (1) the period is one year shorter than the others, (2) the finality of the closing year (the investigation was begun in 1930) made ac-

sured a close time union between the working and reference decades; at the same time, it gave sufficient flexibility to the technique of trend measurement to free the decade rate computations from the larger part of the cyclical bias.

This is the general method which has been used to reduce the influence of the cyclical factor on the decade trend computations. The exact procedure was more laborious. The first step was to select, for a given reference decade, that working decade [11] whose trend seemed to contain a minimum cyclical bias; when several working decades were equally acceptable, that one was chosen which conformed most closely in time position to the reference decade. The next step was to choose, for the same reference decade, that working decade which seemed best calculated to compensate for whatever cyclical bias there was in the trend of the first working decade; here again, the subsidiary canon of choice was closeness of time conformity to the reference decade. Quite frequently, still a third working decade was chosen to offset the net cyclical bias of the others.[12] These additional steps were necessary because an integral number of cycles does not in itself insure that the cyclical factor will not influence the trend computations.[13]

---

curate determination of boundary dates for working decades intrinsically more difficult than for other periods, and (3) it was desirable to limit the influence of the extreme cyclical trough in 1921 on the trend calculations for this decade. For special technical reasons, the rules for determining boundary dates were relaxed somewhat in a few cases for other periods.

[11] The rules for choosing working decades (see the preceding note) allowed nineteen sets of combination dates. The range of practical choice was of course very much smaller, since the aim was to choose working decades whose end values were approximately at the same cyclical phase.

[12] Moving decade trends might have been employed to a greater extent than they were, and had that been feasible, something would have been gained in the later analysis, especially in Chapter V. But the extent to which the apparatus of moving decade trends could be reasonably employed was limited by the technique of locating boundary dates for working decades. Only a single set of overlapping reference decades, separated by a five-year span, seemed at all practicable, and this was used.

[13] When cyclical crests or troughs at the boundary dates are not of the same magnitude, the cyclical factor will still enter into the computations of trends;

With the rates of growth for two or three working decades for a given reference decade at hand, an arithmetic mean was struck to give the 'final decade rate'. It is submitted that these final decade rates, generally referred to hereafter simply as 'decade rates', are the best measures that can be achieved of the average annual rates at which the trends of production advanced during the reference decades. The decade rates for the series listed in Table 1 are presented in Appendix A, Table 45.

Of course, the procedure of determining the decade rates involves considerable arbitrariness, and is not 'objective' in one of the many senses of this ambiguous term. But there is no reason to suppose that a careful and intelligent use of the technique by another investigator would lead to results which would differ sufficiently to place any class of facts in a different light. There is a tendency to overrate the value of 'objectivity' in statistical methods. The fact that two or more persons may go through the same standardized technique and obtain the same results is no recommendation, as such, either for the technique or for the results. Certainly, a mechanical method is as arbitrary as any other, but the arbitrariness is fixed and therefore frequently overlooked. Judgment must always play a dominating rôle in the choice of statistical techniques, and the only question that really matters is whether the judgment is 'good' or 'bad'. It should be self-evident that the final decade rates computed from working decades have much better claim to significance and representativeness with re-

---

and when cyclical crests or troughs of extreme size occur at or near the boundary dates, they may, in fact, dominate the trend. Even with all the precautions taken to restrict the influence of the cyclical factor, no more can be claimed for our method than that it generally reduced the cyclical bias to small proportions. It was not always easy to achieve a nice balance between the cyclical biases of the working decades of a reference decade. But this was most difficult in those cases where the residual cyclical bias was relatively small; and here, of course, it made little difference whether or not the most suitable working decades were chosen.

42   PRODUCTION TRENDS

spect to the reference decades than rates computed directly for such reference decades. It is only because the rates computed for calendar decades would tell a spurious story in many instances about production trends during these decades that a much more laborious, and non-mechanical procedure has been used.

3. Method of Curve-Fitting

Exponential curves are most commonly fitted by the method of 'least squares', the criterion of least squares being applied to the deviations of the logarithms of observation data from a straight line fitted to the logarithms. Exponential curves may also be fitted by the method of 'moments', the criteria of moments being applied directly to the observation data. The results obtained by the two methods will differ significantly only when there are cyclical extremes at either end of the period for which an average rate of growth [14] is computed. Because the method of least squares involves the use of logarithms, a low cyclical extreme exercises a larger influence on a rate of growth computed by this method than on a rate of growth computed by the method of moments; the opposite is true when the cyclical extreme is a high point. Offhand, it might seem that, if the reduction of the influence of extreme cases is desired, there is little to choose between the two methods. But it is known empirically that a downward cyclical movement generally proceeds at a faster rate than an upward movement in practically all industries outside of agriculture; this is another way of saying that extreme cyclical troughs in production are more numerous than extreme peaks. There is, then, some theoretical basis for preferring the method of moments,[15] and this method has been

[14] Except where otherwise stated, 'average rate of growth' or just 'rate of growth' is taken to mean 100 (b—1), the constant b being derived from the function $y = ab^x$, in which y is production and x time expressed in years.

[15] A minor advantage of the method of moments is that it may be used

MEASUREMENT OF TRENDS

used in the fitting of exponential curves to our series. The device of multiple working decades in itself tended to preclude cyclical distortion of the rates of growth calculated,[16] but trend-fitting by the method of moments contributed further to this end.

The method of moments was preferred also on practical grounds. With the aid of Glover's 'mean value table', exponential curves may be fitted quite expeditiously by the method of moments.[17] The burden of computation was further reduced by the aid of a device which made it unnecessary to compute independently the rates of growth for the various segments of each production series. Preliminary to any of the calculations of rates of growth, a basic table was set up which contained, first, the original data, second, progressive cumulatives of the data, and third, cumulatives of the first set of cumulatives. It was then possible to compute from this basic table the average rate of growth for any period by going through a few simple arithmetic steps.[18] The routine burden involved in the determination of the considerable set of rates of growth for each series was smaller than, say, the computing work in fitting a 'least squares' second degree

---

when there are zeroes among the observation data; of course, this is impossible in the least squares method. This fact is of some practical import; for example, no sulphur output was reported during a few scattered years in the period surveyed.

[16] Were it not for this, it would have been desirable to use the method of least squares when high cyclical extremes occurred, and the method of moments when low cyclical extremes occurred.

[17] See J. W. Glover, *Tables of Applied Mathematics in Finance, Insurance, Statistics* (George Wahr, 1923), pp. 468–81. Except where otherwise stated, this method has been used also in all supplementary calculations of average rates of growth. As Glover's table does not go beyond increases of 10 per cent per time unit, it was necessary to extend the table in order to calculate values above this point.

[18] This simplification is a product of the ingenuity of Mr. Howard G. Brunsman, now of Ohio State University. Considerations of space make a description of the method impractical; this is also unnecessary, as Mr. Brunsman plans to publish the method in connection with a larger subject.

parabola to the logarithms of a sixty-year series by the customary method.

III. ANALYSIS OF PRODUCTION TRENDS

The decade rates, already described, constitute a set of fundamental measurements of the secular trends of industries. An inquiry into the behavior similarities of the production trends of individual industries, and into the elements of regularity in the trend of total production, is carried through in the following chapters on the basis of these measurements. It is no part of our aim to survey at this point the substantive problems of this study, or to describe the various statistical techniques which are employed in the course of their exploration. Such matters are best treated as they come up. But there are certain general aspects of the later statistical analysis, which may well be noted in this place.

Granting our definition of secular trends, the form of the secular trend line of a production series, in any particular period, is largely independent of varying predilections of statisticians, and of the full period to which a line of secular trend may be fitted; that is to say, it is possible to measure secular trends with fair 'precision'. But the secular trends of industries are complex in their nature, and must be analyzed from various angles in order to be grasped fully. Lines of secular trend trace out paths more or less undulatory and also have an underlying general sweep; both types of movement are of interest and significance.

It is convenient to refer to the general sweep of the secular trend of a series as its 'primary trend'.[19] A line of primary

[19] This term is used in a broader sense than by Professor Kuznets. See his *Secular Movements in Production and Prices* (Houghton Mifflin, 1930), pp. 70–2. The term 'trend' is used frequently in this work without qualification: ordinarily, 'trend' refers to 'secular trend'; at times, it refers to 'primary trend'; and in some cases, as in the title of the work, it refers generically to 'secular trend' and 'primary trend'. However, the meaning should be clear

MEASUREMENT OF TRENDS

trend will trace out synoptically and elegantly the general secular movement, without giving much heed to the details of the movement. If the secular trend has already been determined, the primary trend may be established by fitting a simple mathematical curve to the ordinates of secular trend; this may be done irrespective of whether the line of secular trend is continuous or discontinuous.[20] If the secular trend has not yet been determined, the primary trend may be established by fitting a simple mathematical curve directly to the data. In either case, the line of primary trend will generalize movements of longer duration than those generalized by a line of secular trend.

While the secular trend, as we have defined it, can be measured with a fair degree of 'precision', the primary trend cannot. There is considerable latitude for judgment in choosing a curve to represent the primary trend; and its exact form is not independent of the period covered, even with a given type of curve. However, if the primary trend be viewed instrumentally, a degree of certainty can be attained in its measurement. The nature of the problem leading to the measurement will then determine whatever definiteness and significance the primary trend will have.[21] Thus, if there is little point in inquiring about the average annual rate of increase in the world output of wheat since 1500, a primary trend embodying an answer to this question will also lack significance. On the other hand, if there is some point in inquiring about the average annual rate of increase of wheat pro-

---

from the context, since qualifying terms have been added where the sense might be ambiguous.

[20] In the case of our measurements of secular trends by 'decade rates', discontinuous lines of trend are only implicit; but they can be made explicit by the use of the criterion of the zero moment. See Ch. IV, sec. I, for another approach.

[21] Professor Mitchell has pointed out the serious limitations which attach to an empirical approach to trends; see his *Business Cycles,* cited above, pp. 212–26. Kuznets' *Secular Movements,* previously cited, is an example of an inquiry into production trends guided by the light of theory.

duction in the United States since 1870, a primary trend embodying an answer to this question will also have some significance. But the form of the primary trend will still be indefinite, since it may be either a straight line or an exponential curve, according as average annual rate of increase is regarded in absolute or percentage terms; the problem will therefore have to be defined more specifically before the primary trend can be determined with assurance. Or take another problem, which brings out more forcefully the correspondence between questions concerning long-range movements and the primary trends to which they lead. Suppose that growth at a declining percentage rate is considered as the outstanding characteristic of the history of pig-iron production in the United States, and that it is desired to give mathematical expression to this characteristic. In this case, the choice of a mathematical curve to represent the primary trend is limited to functions—such as the simple logistic, the Gompertz equation, or the 'logarithmic' parabola—which possess the characteristic of advance at a declining percentage rate. Suppose, now, that the aim is not only to indicate the presence of decline in the percentage rate of growth of pig-iron production, but also to measure the average rate of retardation per time unit over the period covered. In this case, a parabola fitted to the logarithms of the production data is the proper mathematical curve to represent the primary trend; for only this function can answer directly the question which has been asked.

Two conceptions of primary trend form the basis of much of the later statistical analysis: that defined by the average percentage rate of growth, and that defined by the average percentage rate of retardation. The former is investigated in section I of Chapter III and section II of Chapter VI, the latter in Chapter IV and section III of Chapter VI. It goes without saying that the full significance of the specific ques-

MEASUREMENT OF TRENDS

tions implicit in these measurements of primary trends can be clearly seen only in the light of the more general purposes which those questions subserve. If a summary of the progress of the iron industry were confined to two formulations of primary trend, one yielding an average rate of growth and the other an average rate of retardation, their significance might be small. But when measurements of the primary trends of this industry are taken together with similar measurements for many industries, as is done in this study, they acquire considerable significance; for the ensemble of primary trends serves to indicate certain general characteristics of national progress.

The detailed course of the secular movement of an industry may be investigated by a variety of methods. If the aim of these methods be summarization, they will have the common feature of measuring the undulatory movement of the secular trend—that is, its instability. There are various aspects of the instability of the secular trend of a series, which different methods will seek to ascertain. If interest center in the continuity of growth of an industry, the degree of uniformity with which its secular trend has an upward direction will be determined; if in the persistence of growth of an industry, the frequency with which its secular trend changes from an upward to a downward direction, and vice versa; if in the variability in the rate of growth of an industry, the degree of variation in the slopes of its secular trend at different periods. Similar questions concerning instability may arise with respect to retardation of growth, and they may be similarly resolved. Finally, the instability of the secular trend of an industry may be considered from the standpoint of the amplitude of its oscillatory movement, the primary trend, appropriately measured, having first been eliminated. The more important of these aspects of the instability of secular trends are considered in the following chapters—chiefly in section II of Chapter III, section II of Chapter IV, Chapter V, and section III of Chapter VI.

Measures of the detailed course of the secular trend may or may not prove useful summaries in the case of any one industry. But when a large number of industries is covered, such measures become powerful instruments in the description of the general characteristics of industrial progress. For this purpose, however, detailed measurements of the oscillatory movements of the secular trends of industries, an adjustment having been made for their primary trends, are probably more significant than any summary measures of the instability of secular trends; for a large degree of industrial concurrence in such oscillatory movements—we may speak of them conveniently as 'trend-cycles', that is, cycles in secular trends—would indicate that a long-term rhythm was pervasive in the economy. If the trend-cycles of individual industries were uncorrelated, they would be of little importance except for an understanding of the histories of specific industries. On the other hand, if they synchronized to a considerable degree, they would indicate the existence of a general trend-cycle in the economic system. They would furnish, therefore, an important datum for the acumen of the theorist. The oscillatory movements of production trends are investigated in detail in Chapter V.

Chapter III

THE CHANGING PATTERN OF PRODUCTION

THE outstanding characteristics of the economic progress in the United States since the Civil War have been increase and change in wants and activities. The total volume of national production has increased rapidly, as has the volume of production of major industrial groups. But the rate of advance has been uneven in the various individual industries, and in any one industry at various times. The growth of general production has therefore been accompanied by a continual transformation of its pattern. With the incessant introduction of new commodities and services, disappearance of old commodities, and shifts in the relative importance of continuing products, vast changes have occurred in the qualitative composition of national industry. The aim of this chapter is to present, so far as our limited list of production series will permit, a general description of these changes.

1. DIVERGENCE OF PRODUCTION TRENDS

Two methods might be used in presenting a statistical picture of changes in the pattern of production. One is to determine at given dates the relative contribution of the various individual industries to the aggregate of national output. The other is to compare the rates of growth of the individual industries either at given dates or over given periods of time—more precisely, to compare the instantaneous or average percentage rates of advance of the secular trends of the various industries. The first method presupposes the possibility of commensurating the outputs of different industries;[1] however, since any commensuration must be executed in terms of a single attribute of the produced goods, it will inevitably be, in some degree, unsatisfactory. The first method presupposes also that statistical records of the outputs which are to be commensurated are available in sufficient abundance to yield significant aggregates of production, but statistical data fall short considerably of this desideratum. It is practically impossible, then, to determine the changing contribution of individual industries to the total stream of production; though this might be done for that portion of the total production which is covered by the statistics, or for the production of certain industrial groups. With data restricted in quantity and not admitting of satisfactory general commensuration, it is preferable to use the second and theoretically inferior method, that of comparison of rates of industrial growth.

1. Statistical Record of Divergence

A telescopic view of the changes in the pattern of national industry will be obtained by comparing the average rates of advance of our series during the period investigated. The average annual rate of growth of each industry has been determined by taking an arithmetic mean of its decade rates.[2]

[1] General commensuration of 'produced' goods can be accomplished in terms of value or of expended labor; these are the only measurable aspects possessed by all 'produced' goods. However, partial commensuration, that is, for limited branches of industry, can be accomplished in other units: for the class of commodities, in terms of weight or cubic content; for the subclass of foods, in terms of calories (or British thermal units)—such a study covering a considerable number of years is now contemplated by Dr. Baker of the Department of Agriculture; for the subclass of fuels, also in terms of calories (or British thermal units)—such a study is reported in *Mineral Resources*, 1929, Part II, p. 699. See Ch. I, sec. I, and Ch. VI, sec. I.

[2] An average calculated in this way is influenced to a smaller extent by erratic values than an average yielded by an exponential curve fitted to the full period of the series, though the two methods lead generally to closely similar results. Theoretically, an arithmetic mean of decade rates is inferior

PATTERN OF PRODUCTION 51

Average rates have been computed for the period 1885–1929 which is covered by all the series,[3] in order to achieve strict comparability among them; and additional averages have been struck for whatever periods the individual series embrace, in order to utilize the statistical records to the full. The degree of divergence in these average rates of advance will serve to indicate the extent to which the pattern of production has undergone modification. It must be noted, however, that even if the ratios of all inter-industry physical outputs remained constant, which would be the case if the physical outputs of all industries grew at the same percentage rate, the relative contributions of the different industries to the stream of production might still be inconstant from the standpoint of some such measure of output as 'net value product'.

A summary of the average rates of industrial growth is presented in Table 3 and Chart 1. Two frequency distributions are given, one comprising the rates [4] of advance of 64 production series over the period 1870–1929, and the other the rates of advance of 99 production series over the period 1885–1929.[5] This summary shows that the rates of increase of the

---

to a geometric mean: first, because an arithmetic mean of percentages has an 'upward bias'; second, because only a geometric mean of the 'slopes' of a number of spliced exponential curves can yield trend values at the first and last dates of the entire period, which are identical with the trend values, defined by the subperiod exponential curves, at those dates. However, the second advantage is nominal since the decade rates refer to overlapping periods; and apart from the overlapping, the exponential curves, implicit in the decade rates, are not spliced (see Ch. II, sec. II, 2). The first advantage is of slight importance in view of the restricted range of variation of the decade rates (in the averaging process, the decade rates are, essentially, taken in ratio form, that is, as 1.054, 1.047, and so on, not as 5.4 per cent, 4.7 per cent, and so on). The arithmetic mean of decade rates therefore recommends itself on grounds of simplicity in computation.

[3] Except fermented liquors and distilled spirits, which terminate in 1918.

[4] The term 'rate' is used synonymously with 'average rate', 'average annual rate', and 'average annual percentage rate', throughout this chapter and also in section II of Chapter VI.

[5] Though a few of the 64 series do not extend to 1870, all go back sufficiently far to allow the computation of 'decade rates' for 1870–80. This group

Table 3
FREQUENCY DISTRIBUTIONS OF AVERAGE RATES OF INDUSTRIAL GROWTH, DURING 1870–1929 AND 1885–1929

Average annual rate of growth (per cent)	1870–1929		1885–1929	
	Number of series	Percentage of series	Number of series	Percentage of series
−5.0 to −3.1	1	1.6	1	1.0
−3.0 to −1.1	3	4.7	4	4.0
−1.0 to 0.9	3	4.7	9	9.1
1.0 to 2.9	24	37.5	29	29.3
3.0 to 4.9	6	9.4	28	28.3
5.0 to 6.9	13	20.3	15	15.2
7.0 to 8.9	10	15.6	7	7.1
9.0 to 10.9	2	3.1	2	2.0
11.0 to 12.9	..	...	..	...
13.0 to 14.9	..	...	..	...
15.0 to 16.9	2	3.1	1	1.0
17.0 to 18.9	..	...	1	1.0
19.0 to 20.9	..	...	..	...
21.0 to 22.9	..	...	..	...
23.0 to 24.9	..	...	2	2.0
Total	64	100.0	99	100.0

various industries have been sharply divergent during the period covered. The middle half of the rates of the 64 series covering the period since 1870 fall within the range from 2.0 to 6.5 per cent. How great a transformation this indicates in the structure of American industry may be gathered from the fact that if two industries had each 100 units of output in 1870, but one grew at a constant annual rate of 6.5 per cent and the other at a rate of 2.0 per cent, the first would be

---

does not include certain duplicative series which go back to 1870—total coal, and minor fiber imports. The group of 99 series contains all of the series listed in Table 1, except for five duplicative series. This group will be referred to as the 'all' series group without further qualification. The exact composition of the two groups is stated in Appendix A, Table 46, columns *a* and *e*.

producing over thirteen times as many units as the second by 1929. And as a matter of fact, the change in the pattern of our national industry has probably been very much greater than the frequency distributions suggest; for they are restricted to continuing industries, and exclude completely the new industries which have appeared and the old industries which have vanished—that is, the most dynamic portions of the production system.

Chart 1
FREQUENCY DISTRIBUTIONS OF AVERAGE RATES OF GROWTH DURING 1870-1929 AND 1885-1929

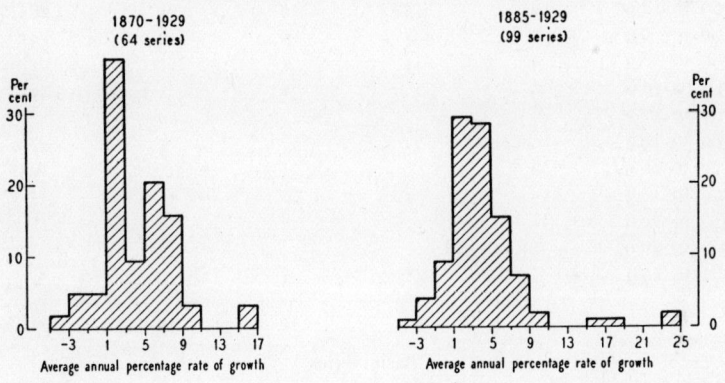

The detailed record of the variations among the rates of industrial growth is presented in Tables 4–8. These tables do not exhaust the range of industry; inadequate data account for the omission of forestry and the various professional and personal service industries. In the upper portion of Table 4, the rates of increase since 1885 of 'all' series are summarized according to various resource groups of industries. Taken by itself, this summary is of doubtful meaning, because the production series differ very considerably in the degree of generality of their industrial reference and in the significance of

Table 4
FREQUENCY DISTRIBUTIONS OF AVERAGE RATES OF GROWTH DURING 1885–1929, FOR 'ALL' SERIES AND BASIC SERIES, BY INDUSTRIAL GROUPS

Average annual rate of growth (per cent)	Agriculture and fisheries	Mining	Manufactures and construction	Transportation and trade	All industries
'All' series					
−5.0 to −3.1	1	..	..	..	1
−3.0 to −1.1	1	2	..	1	4
−1.0 to 0.9	4	1	4	..	9
1.0 to 2.9	13	2	12	2	29
3.0 to 4.9	1	5	17	5	28
5.0 to 6.9	1	4	6	4	15
7.0 to 8.9	1	4	2	..	7
9.0 to 10.9	..	..	2	..	2
11.0 to 12.9	..	..	..	..	..
13.0 to 14.9	..	..	..	..	..
15.0 to 16.9	1	..	..	..	1
17.0 to 18.9	..	1	..	..	1
19.0 to 20.9	..	..	..	..	..
21.0 to 22.9	..	..	..	..	..
23.0 to 24.9	..	1	1	..	2
Total	23	20	44	12	99
Basic series					
−1.0 to 0.9	2	1	..	..	3
1.0 to 2.9	10	2	7	1	20
3.0 to 4.9	1	4	13	5	23
5.0 to 6.9	..	3	4	1	8
7.0 to 8.9	..	2	2	..	4
9.0 to 10.9	..	..	1	..	1
Total	13	12	27	7	59

their industrial coverage. For this reason, the summary is restricted in the lower portion of the table to 59 basic series,[6]

[6] Though the criterion of basicity was not formulated in precise terms, the points are few at which doubts are likely to arise as to the propriety of the

Table 5
RATES OF GROWTH OF INDUSTRIES: AGRICULTURE AND FISHERIES
(Unit: one per cent)

Group and series	Period covered by series	Average annual rate of growth	
		In period covered	1885–1929
Agriculture			
FOOD CROPS			
Beet sugar	1870–1929	16.0	16.8
Raisins	1872–1929	15.9	8.1
Rice	1870–1929	5.0	5.0
Potatoes	1870–1929	2.1	1.7
Rye	1870–1929	2.0	1.5
Wheat	1870–1930	1.5	1.1
Molasses and sirup	1870–1929	2.0	1.0
Buckwheat	1870–1929	0.5	−0.1
Cane sugar	1870–1929	1.0	−0.6
FEED CROPS			
Barley	1870–1929	4.0	3.4
Oats	1870–1930	2.8	1.6
Hay	1870–1930	2.0	1.2
Corn	1870–1929	1.6	0.9
INDUSTRIAL CROPS			
Tobacco, raw	1870–1929	2.7	2.4
Flaxseed	1879–1929	2.2	2.0
Cotton	1870–1929	2.6	1.9
ANIMAL PRODUCTS			
Cattle	1880–1929	3.0	2.4
Sheep	1880–1929	2.5	2.4
Hogs	1880–1929	2.4	2.3
Wool	1870–1929	1.3	0.3
Fisheries			
Fish, total	1880–1929	0.9	1.0
Cod and mackerel	1870–1929	−1.7	−1.9
Whale	1870–1929	−4.2	−3.7

these constituting a relatively homogeneous group. Average rates of increase of each of the production series are presented in Tables 5–8 according to the industrial divisions of Table 4 and also various subdivisions.[7] These average rates serve to indicate, first, certain major shifts in the structure of the several industrial groups, and second, shifts in the relative importance of these groups in the total production system.

The one common feature of the several industrial groups is the very much smaller degree of divergence of production trends among basic than non-basic industries. Since the rates of advance of the basic series are at a medium level, the extremes on the growth scale of the 'all' series group are obviously accounted for by non-basic series. At the upper end of the growth scale are found such industries as beet sugar, raisins, sulphur, Portland cement, aluminum, and cigarettes—all of which are relatively new industries. At the lower end of the growth scale are found such industries as cane sugar, whaling, mercury, non-Portland cements, and roofing slate—all of which are relatively old industries.

Within the several industrial divisions, the divergence of production trends is rather moderate in the agriculture and fisheries division, but very extensive in the divisions of mining, manufactures and construction, and transportation and trade. Since the outstanding agricultural staples show a fair degree of similarity in their rates of growth, a goodly portion of the shifts in agriculture is traceable to the introduction of

---

classification; see, however, p. 183, note 10. The judgment was made with reference to the period covered rather than the present. With minor exceptions, the basic series are drawn from the 'all' series group. The 59 basic series—they are listed in Appendix A, Table 46, column f—will be referred to as the basic series group without further qualification.

[7] In view of the method used in determining the decade rates (see pp. 39–41), the measures refer to, but are not always based exactly on, the periods stated in the tables. This holds for all other tables as well.

Table 6
RATES OF GROWTH OF INDUSTRIES: MINING
(Unit: one per cent)

Group and series	Period covered by series	Average annual rate of growth	
		In period covered	1885–1929
FUELS			
Petroleum	1870–1929	9.0	8.5
Natural gas	1882–1929	8.6	5.1
Bituminous coal	1870–1929	5.4	4.3
Coal, total	1870–1929	4.7	3.7
Anthracite coal	1870–1929	2.2	1.2
INDUSTRIAL METALS			
Zinc	1870–1929	7.4	6.0
Copper	1870–1929	7.5	5.4
Iron ore	1880–1929	4.9	4.4
Lead, domestic	1870–1929	5.5	3.7
PRECIOUS METALS			
Gold	1870–1929	0.4	1.0
Silver	1870–1929	1.8	0.7
BUILDING MATERIALS			
Portland cement	1880–1929	18.8	18.5
Gypsum	1880–1929	8.6	8.7
Cement, total	1880–1929	9.1	8.6
Asphalt	1880–1929	13.4	8.0
Non-Portland cements	1880–1929	0.1	−1.5
CHEMICAL MATERIALS			
Sulphur	1880–1929	22.1	24.6
Fluorspar	1880–1929	7.6	7.4
Phosphate rock	1870–1929	7.4	5.4
Salt	1880–1929	4.8	4.9
Pyrites	1880–1929	5.7	3.3
Mercury	1870–1929	−2.0	−1.7

PRODUCTION TRENDS

Table 7

RATES OF GROWTH OF INDUSTRIES: MANUFACTURES AND CONSTRUCTION

(Unit: one per cent)

Group and series	Period covered by series	Average annual rate of growth	
		In period covered	1885–1929
FOODS, FEEDS, AND BEVERAGES			
*Beet sugar	1870–1929	16.0	16.8
Cocoa imports	1870–1929	8.8	8.4
Cottonseed cake and meal	1872–1929	8.9	5.5
Canned corn	1885–1929	4.9	4.9
*Salt	1880–1929	4.8	4.9
Cottonseed oil	1872–1929	8.3	4.7
Canned tomatoes	1885–1929	3.8	3.8
Distilled spirits	1870–1918	2.9	3.3
Fermented liquors	1870–1918	4.4	3.1
Raw sugar consumption	1870–1930	3.4	3.0
Coffee imports	1870–1929	2.8	2.5
*Cattle	1880–1929	3.0	2.4
*Sheep	1880–1929	2.5	2.4
*Hogs	1880–1929	2.4	2.3
Flour	1880–1929	1.3	1.1
*Cane sugar	1870–1929	1.0	−0.6
TOBACCO PRODUCTS			
Cigarettes	1880–1929	11.6	10.5
Tobacco consumption	1880–1929	2.5	2.3
Tobacco and snuff	1871–1929	2.3	1.4
Cigars	1880–1929	1.6	1.3
TEXTILE PRODUCTS			
Silk imports, raw	1870–1929	8.0	6.9
Silk imports, unmanufactured	1883–1929	6.8	6.8
Cotton consumption	1870–1929	3.5	3.0
Sisal imports	1870–1929	6.3	2.9
Manila hemp imports	1870–1929	2.1	2.1
Minor fiber imports	1870–1929	2.7	1.1
Wool consumption	1870–1930	1.7	1.0
Jute imports	1870–1929	1.3	−0.6

PATTERN OF PRODUCTION

Table 7 (cont.)
RATES OF GROWTH OF INDUSTRIES: MANUFACTURES AND CONSTRUCTION
(Unit: one per cent)

Group and series	Period covered by series	Average annual rate of growth	
		In period covered	1885–1929
IRON, STEEL, AND COKE			
Steel	1870–1929	10.4	7.2
Rolled iron and steel	1885–1929	5.0	5.0
Coke	1880–1929	5.4	4.6
Pig iron	1870–1929	5.4	4.4
NONFERROUS INDUSTRIAL METALS AND THEIR PRODUCTS			
Aluminum	1883–1929	24.3	24.3
*Zinc	1870–1929	7.4	6.0
Copper consumption	1883–1929	6.0	6.0
Zinc consumption	1873–1929	6.5	5.8
*Copper	1870–1929	7.5	5.4
Tin-plate consumption........	1871–1929	5.6	4.4
Antimonial lead	1871–1929	6.9	4.3
Lead, total	1870–1929	5.7	4.1
Tin imports	1870–1929	5.0	4.1
Lead consumption	1870–1929	3.9	3.7
PRECIOUS METALS AND THEIR PRODUCTS			
Silver consumption	1880–1929	5.1	4.8
Gold consumption...........	1880–1929	3.6	3.4
*Gold	1870–1929	0.4	1.0
*Silver	1870–1929	1.8	0.7
BUILDING MATERIALS AND CONSTRUCTION			
*Portland cement	1880–1929	18.8	18.5
*Cement, total	1880–1929	9.1	8.6
Flaxseed consumption	1879–1929	3.3	3.2
Building permits	1874–1929	4.2	2.6
White lead	1884–1929	1.8	1.8
Rails	1870–1929	2.3	1.4
Nails	1872–1929	2.2	1.3
Rail consumption	1870–1929	1.5	1.0

Table 7 (cont.)
RATES OF GROWTH OF INDUSTRIES: MANUFACTURES
AND CONSTRUCTION
(Unit: one per cent)

Group and series	Period covered by series	Average annual rate of growth	
		In period covered	1885–1929
Roofing slate	1879–1929	0.0	−0.8
*Non-Portland cements	1880–1929	0.1	−1.5
TRANSPORTATION EQUIPMENT			
Vessels	1870–1929	−0.2	0.5
Locomotives...................	1880–1929	0.0	−0.1
MISCELLANEOUS			
Rubber imports...............	1870–1929	8.5	9.1
Superphosphate...............	1870–1929	6.8	5.0

*These series are repeated from Tables 5–6.

new crops, such as sugar beets, raisins, and various vegetables, and to the decline of pasture, as reflected in the trend of wool production. In contrast to the agricultural industries, the minerals evidence very considerable variability. The series of manufactures resemble the minerals in the striking diversity of their rates of advance. Their variability would doubtless be appreciably greater if the list of series contained a larger number of specific and minor commodities; for "a growing share of our manufacturing product now consists of unessentials—man's toys and playthings," the demand for which is "determined largely by fashion and caprice." [8] Finally, though the transportation and trade series show only a moderate degree of divergence in their trends, the shifts in the pattern

[8] V. S. Clark, *History of Manufactures in the United States, 1860–1914* (Carnegie Institution of Washington, Publication No. 215B, Vol. II, 1928), p. 836.

Table 8
RATES OF GROWTH OF INDUSTRIES: TRANSPORTATION AND TRADE
(Unit: one per cent)

Series	Period covered by series	Average annual rate of growth — In period covered	Average annual rate of growth — 1885–1929
Transportation			
S. S. Marie canals traffic	1870–1929	8.9	6.9
Postage stamps	1870–1929	6.3	6.6
Postal money orders	1870–1929	7.9	6.5
Railway ton-miles	1870–1929	6.0	4.9
Railway passenger-miles	1882–1929	3.5	3.2
Coastal trade	1870–1929	2.2	2.7
N. Y. canals traffic	1870–1929	−1.1	−1.3
Trade			
Shares traded	1875–1929	5.0	5.7
Deflated clearings	1870–1929	5.2	4.6
Railway freight	1882–1929	4.3	3.9
Tonnage entered and cleared	1870–1929	3.5	3.8
Agricultural exports	1870–1929	2.0	1.0

of this industrial division have, as a matter of fact, been very extensive. One reason why they are not disclosed adequately is that certain new transport agencies,—the telephone, wireless, automobile, pipe line, and airplane,—which have grown at extremely rapid rates, are not covered in our list of series. Another reason is that most of the series in the trade and transportation group are of exceptionally broad industrial scope.[9]

A close inspection of Tables 4–8 will suggest, and additional evidence is presented in Chapter VI, that the various

[9] Concerning defects in the original series, which are reflected in the measures of their average rates of growth, see Appendix C, I.

major industrial groups have themselves grown at widely unequal rates.[10] Among the major branches of commodity production, mining has grown at a spectacular rate, manufacture at a somewhat lower rate, and agriculture at a decidedly lower rate. Some fifty to sixty years ago, agriculture was dominant, mining of relative insignificance, and manufactures were only beginning to step into their stride. At present, the elaborative industries are the dominating form of economic activity, and the mineral industries occupy the key position in our mechanized industrial system. The only other industrial groups covered in this survey are the fisheries, transportation, and trade. Though the fisheries industry has been mildly progressive, it has declined sharply in relative importance. Transportation and trade have increased in relative importance. As for forestry and the various personal service industries, which are not included in our survey, the former has declined in relative importance, while the relative trend of the latter has increased.

2. Causes of Divergence

Of late, a number of economists, most notably Cassel, have explicated the notion of a progressive economy, characterized by a rate of advance constant over time and uniform for all goods and agents of production including population. Whatever the merits of this conception may be for some problems in economic theory, it is certainly misleading to term such a hypothetical economy 'progressive'. For when all intercommodity relations of sequence, complementariness, and joint production are assumed to be constant, as is the number and kind of commodities, and the responsiveness of nature to man's

[10] See pp. 264–8. See also P. K. Whelpton, "Occupational Groups in the United States, 1820–1920," *Journal of the American Statistical Association*, September, 1926; A. R. Eckler, "Occupational Changes in the United States, 1850–1920," *Review of Economic Statistics*, May, 1930; and R. G. Hurlin and M. B. Givens, "Shifting Occupational Patterns" (Ch. VI of *Recent Social Trends in the United States*, Vol. I, McGraw-Hill, 1933).

PATTERN OF PRODUCTION

efforts, practically everything 'progressive' is omitted from the economy so termed. Industrial changes which we consider 'progressive' comprise revisions of productive techniques, conservation in the use of raw materials, changes in the number and kind of commodities produced, and so on. Such changes take place incessantly, and as their impact on various industries is unequal, they lead to divergent production trends. A progressive economy is always characterized by differences in the rates of development of its individual industries.

The very causes which have determined the rapid advance of general production in this country since the Civil War have also determined the divergence in the trends of its separate industries. Progress in the general economy has been marked by the invention of new commodities, development of new raw materials, and discovery of new mineral resources; by changes in the methods of production, transformation of industrial equipment, recovery of waste products, and changes in the forms of industrial organization; by an increase in the number of uses to which given raw materials are put, and in the number of materials put to given uses; and by an emergence of a variety of luxury products and style goods. These changes have resulted in an increasing divergence of production trends, for they have served to stimulate or depress, but to an unequal extent, the development of the various industries. Taking the economic system as a whole, the consequence has been that intercommodity relations of sequence, complementariness, and joint production have tended to become increasingly flexible; or to put it differently, those technical relations among commodities which make for similarity in rates of industrial growth have tended to diminish in importance.

The rates of industrial growth presented in Tables 5–8 illustrate abundantly the results of progressive developments, the differential extent of these developments in the various industries, and the impact of changes in the outside economy —all of which have made for divergence of production trends and, consequently, for shifts in the pattern of our national industry. For example, the trend towards more effective working of natural deposits is reflected in the rapid growth of the sulphur, copper, and petroleum industries; the trend towards increasing reclamation of waste products, in the rapid growth of the cottonseed products industries; towards reuse of materials, in the more rapid advance of steel than pig iron; towards better utilization of materials, in the respective rates of advance of feed crops and meat products;[11] towards increasing roundaboutness in the methods of production, in the generally more rapid growth of producers' goods than consumers' goods industries; towards improvement in agricultural technique, in the rapid growth of the phosphate industries; towards improvement in the quality of production, in the downward trend of the number of locomotives manufactured; and towards industrial diversification, in the sharp contrast between the rates of growth of such commodities as Portland and non-Portland cements, petroleum and coal, and cigarettes and other tobacco products. The resistance of nature to progressive developments is reflected conspicuously in the trends of the whaling, mercury, gold, and anthracite coal industries. The impact of changes in the outside economy on the de-

[11] The rates of increase of the animal slaughter series are higher than the rates of growth of any of the feed crops except barley, which is not a feed crop of outstanding importance. This contrast is more striking in the light of the decline in pasture acreage, which averaged 3 million acres per year between 1880 and 1920 (*Yearbook of Agriculture,* 1923, p. 317). A large portion of the difference between the two groups of series is accounted for by the defective statistical constitution of the animal slaughter series (see Appendix C, I). But several economic factors have conduced to the difference: the increasing efficiency of animals in converting feed into live weight, the recent decline in the population of work animals, the declining use of the so-called feed crops for purposes of human consumption, and the rapid growth of several minor feed crops (not included in Table 5) and certain manufactured feeds. Probably, the net exports of feed crops have also tended to decline relative to their total output (see p. 149).

velopment of domestic industries is reflected, for example, in the trend of jute imports, and in the discrepancy between the rates of production and consumption of wool, flaxseed, cotton, and copper. Finally, the growth of general welfare and change in methods of living are reflected in the sharp rates of advance of silk,[12] rubber, and cocoa imports, in the higher rate of growth of the sugar than the flour industry, and in the rapid advance of canned foodstuffs. Considerable divergence of production trends is, then, one of the essential features of a progressive economy. The more rapid the rate of general progress, the greater is the divergence of individual production trends likely to be; and some statistical evidence is presented later to show that the divergence of production trends has actually varied with the degree of progressiveness of our economy.[13]

Sharp discrepancies among rates of industrial growth are not, however, characteristic of a progressive economic system alone; they may also be found in a retrogressive economy. What distinguishes a progressive from a retrogressive system is the type of skewness, not the dispersion, of a distribution of rates of industrial change. In a progressive economy, as we know it, new industries are continually started, and occasionally, old industries are rejuvenated. The rate of growth of such industries is, generally, excitingly rapid; and this factor, quite apart from others working in the same direction, tends to produce a decided 'positive' skewness. When the rates of industrial growth are skewed towards the higher values, the indications are that the forces making for growth in the eco-

---

[12] It must be noted that our series of silk imports, though fair indicators of the growth of the domestic silk manufacture, cannot be used to indicate the trend in domestic consumption of silk products. While imports of manufactured silk are at present dwarfed by the domestic output, such imports were much more extensive than the domestic output during the 'seventies. See F. W. Taussig, *Some Aspects of the Tariff Question* (3d ed., Harvard University Press, 1931), pp. 221, 408.

[13] See pp. 242–3.

nomic system are in the ascendent over the forces making for decline. In a retrogressive economy, on the other hand, there will be few industries growing at a rapid rate, but many will be declining, a number of them at a rapid rate, and some —perhaps the pivotal ones exercising a downward pull on the system—at a very rapid rate. A distribution of rates of industrial change will therefore tend to be skewed 'negatively' in a retrogressive economy; and the skewness towards the lower values will reflect the dominance of the forces making for decline in the system over the forces making for growth. Despite their restricted industrial scope, the frequency distributions of Chart 1 show definitely a positive skewness. While they do not (and could not) reveal accurately the specific outlines of an ensemble of the rates of growth of all industries, they possess that general form which one would anticipate a priori.[14]

We noted in our statistical survey that the primary trends of production (as expressed in long-range average rates of growth) of basic industries are less divergent than of non-basic industries, and of agricultural industries than of min-

[14] The analysis would not be changed materially for weighted frequency distributions of rates of industrial change, weights being assigned to the various industries according to some index of their importance; for, the importance of industries is correlated with their rates of growth, the more important industries being characterized by medial rates of growth, and the less important by extreme rates. If anything, the degree of 'positive' skewness would probably be somewhat accentuated in the case of a weighted frequency distribution of rates of industrial change in a progressive economy; for there is some tendency for industries with extremely high rates of growth to be, on the whole, of greater importance than industries with extremely low rates of (algebraic) growth. The opposite is probably true of a retrogressive economy. It should be carefully noted, however, that our various statements concerning a retrogressive economy proceed on the implicit assumption that, since retrogression is the opposite of progress, a frequency distribution of rates of industrial change in a retrogressive economy will be the antithesis of a distribution for a progressive economy—a plausible assumption, to be sure, but one which might easily be invalid, if only because our knowledge of a progressive economy is confined to what may be merely a single type of progressive economy, and our knowledge of even that is not very great. See Ch. IV, sec. III, 1.

erals or manufactures. The smaller divergence of the production trends of basic than of non-basic industries derives, in part, from the closer technical ties uniting them, and in part, from their considerable size, which makes sharp rates of advance or decline unlikely. The rather moderate divergence of production trends in agriculture is due chiefly to the gradualness of change in the relative demand for agricultural products, itself a result in large part of the considerable extent to which they are substitutive in production and consumption; but it is due also to the interlocked character of much of agricultural production, as of feed crops and animal products, and to the similarity of foreign influences on individual agricultural industries, especially the various food products. The considerably greater divergence of production trends in the mining and manufacturing industries is due principally to the fact that their products serve, on the whole, more distinctive uses than do those of agriculture; that mineral products and manufactures, especially the latter, are subject to sharper changes in consumption habits, when long periods are considered; that they reflect the increasing roundaboutness and mechanization of all industry, including agriculture; and that their productive resources, especially in mining, while varying widely in quality, are highly specialized and so do not admit of the mobility possible in agriculture.

But these several divisions of commodity production have themselves grown at unequal rates. This is traceable to differences in the type of demand for, and in the comparative advantage of this country in the production of, their respective products. As agriculture yields mainly foodstuffs and textile materials, the demand for which is fairly inelastic, its output has tended to grow at a rate not very much faster than population. The growth of manufactures has been much greater, since the increasing prosperity of the nation has expressed itself in increasing wants for and increasing variety of elaborative products. The rapid growth of manufacture and transportation and their increasing mechanization have served to make the rate of growth of the mining industry exceed that of the other branches of commodity production.

However, the changing comparative advantage of the United States in the production of agricultural and nonagricultural commodities has been, perhaps, of even greater importance than the difference in the conditions underlying the demand for these two classes of products. Between the close of the Civil War and the turn of the century, our agriculture expanded at a rapid rate, while agricultural exports were so extensive that the United States came to be known as the 'granary of Europe'. But beginning with 1900 or so, our export of foodstuffs has declined steadily, except for the War and immediate post-War years; and though our export of cotton and tobacco continued to increase after that date, the advance has been relatively small. As a nation we might of course have continued after the turn of the century to devote our industrial energies to agriculture in relatively the same degree as formerly, utilize our surplus productive powers in the feeding of other nations, and obtain in return a variety of manufactures. This did not happen because we found it more advantageous to devote an increasing portion of our energies to nonagricultural pursuits. On the one side, mechanized industry was making tremendous headway in the United States. Our mineral resources were exploited energetically, if only for the reason that "in no other country can the mineral raw materials as a whole be delivered to manufacturing industry at lower prices." [15] And as increasing progress was made in the standardization, mechanization, and mass production of commodities, the United States ad-

[15] F. G. Tryon and L. Mann, "Mineral Resources for Future Populations" (Ch. VIII of *Population Problems in the United States and Canada*, ed. by L. I. Dublin; Pollak Foundation for Economic Research, 1926), p. 112.

PATTERN OF PRODUCTION

vanced to the front rank among manufacturing nations. On the other side, the agricultural map of the world was changing. While the decline in virgin lands was beginning to revise agricultural costs in this country, certain other regions which were experiencing the first flush of agricultural expansion—Argentina, Australia, Canada, Russia, and India—were offering severe competition to our products in foreign markets. The changing position of the United States in the production of agricultural commodities was reflected, during the decade or two before the World War, in a relative rise of agricultural prices with respect to both manufactures in this country and agricultural commodities abroad.[16]

II. INCONSTANCY OF RATES OF GROWTH

Changes in the pattern of national industry are disclosed in only the most general way by a set of long-term average rates of growth. Such rates imply trends of production of a simple exponential type; but as a matter of fact, few industries have traced out such trends over the past half-century or so.[17] They imply further that the relations among industrial trends have changed in a constant manner, but these relations have actually been inconstant from decade to decade. They might be interpreted to mean that industries having the same average rates of growth have also the same secular trends, but identical averages at times result from widely differing secular trends. Not only has the pattern of production undergone tremendous shifts, but these shifts themselves have not followed any simple plan. Or to put it differently, marked variations in the rates of growth of given industries over time have been superadded to differences in rates of industrial growth at any one time.

A glimpse into the inconstancy of the rates of growth of

[16] See pp. 149–50, and E. G. Nourse, *American Agriculture and the European Market* (McGraw-Hill, 1924), Ch. I and Appendix B.
[17] See p. 36, note 6.

Table 9
MEASURES OF INCONSTANCY OF GROWTH OF INDUSTRIES

Series	Period covered by series	Standard deviation of decade rates	Range of decade rates	Measure of continuity of growth
		(Unit: one per cent)		
Agriculture and fisheries				
Beet sugar	1870–1929	14.4	49.3	1.00
Raisins	1872–1929	14.2	37.5	1.00
Rice	1870–1929	5.1	19.1	.82
Cane sugar	1870–1929	5.1	17.1	.27
Flaxseed	1879–1929	5.1	15.1	.33
Rye	1870–1929	4.3	18.9	.82
Whale	1870–1929	3.9	15.2	−.82
Molasses and sirup	1870–1929	3.9	13.1	.64
Barley	1870–1929	2.8	10.1	.82
Cattle	1880–1929	2.8	8.5	.78
Oats	1870–1930	2.4	7.7	.64
Sheep	1880–1929	2.3	8.3	.78
Cotton	1870–1929	2.2	7.9	.64
Tobacco, raw	1870–1929	2.2	7.1	.82
Buckwheat	1870–1929	2.1	7.2	.36
Wool	1870–1929	2.1	6.8	.36
Hay	1870–1930	1.8	7.0	.64
Corn	1870–1929	1.8	6.5	.64
Cod and mackerel	1870–1929	1.7	6.4	−.55
Wheat	1870–1930	1.7	6.3	.64
Potatoes	1870–1929	1.5	4.8	.64
Hogs	1880–1929	1.0	3.7	1.00
Fish, total	1880–1929	0.8	2.9	.67
Mining				
Sulphur	1880–1929	31.8	108.4	1.00
Asphalt	1880–1929	18.0	58.6	.56
Portland cement	1880–1929	14.0	43.9	1.00
Non-Portland cements	1880–1929	11.5	35.5	.11
Natural gas	1882–1929	10.8	40.8	.78
Pyrites	1880–1929	8.6	35.3	.78
Fluorspar	1880–1929	7.6	28.4	.56

PATTERN OF PRODUCTION

Table 9 (cont.)
MEASURES OF INCONSTANCY OF GROWTH OF INDUSTRIES

Series	Period covered by series	Standard deviation of decade rates	Range of decade rates	Measure of continuity of growth
		(Unit: one per cent)		
Mining (cont.)				
Mercury	1870–1929	6.7	24.7	–.09
Gypsum	1880–1929	5.4	18.9	1.00
Gold	1870–1929	4.8	18.4	–.09
Copper	1870–1929	4.8	18.1	.82
Phosphate rock	1870–1929	4.7	16.3	.82
Cement, total	1880–1929	4.6	16.0	1.00
Lead, domestic	1870–1929	4.1	15.2	1.00
Zinc	1870–1929	3.6	14.8	.82
Petroleum	1870–1929	3.6	14.5	1.00
Iron ore	1880–1929	3.5	12.7	.78
Bituminous coal	1870–1929	3.5	12.5	.91
Coal, total	1870–1929	3.0	10.7	.64
Anthracite coal	1870–1929	2.6	9.7	.64
Silver	1870–1929	2.3	6.8	.36
Salt	1880–1929	2.2	7.0	1.00
Manufactures and construction				
Aluminum	1883–1929	21.3	64.5	1.00
Vessels	1870–1929	16.8	76.8	–.09
Locomotives	1880–1929	7.5	29.2	.33
Sisal imports	1870–1929	7.5	27.3	.64
Steel	1870–1929	7.3	29.1	1.00
Cottonseed oil	1872–1929	7.2	23.0	.82
Antimonial lead	1871–1929	7.0	29.0	.82
Cottonseed cake and meal ...	1872–1929	7.0	23.8	.82
Cigarettes	1880–1929	6.5	20.6	.78
Building permits	1874–1929	6.0	20.8	.40
Rubber imports	1870–1929	5.6	20.3	1.00
Roofing slate	1879–1929	5.1	16.4	.11
Superphosphate	1870–1929	4.5	16.0	1.00
Lead, total	1870–1929	4.1	15.2	1.00
Rail consumption	1870–1929	4.1	14.4	.45

Table 9 (cont.)
MEASURES OF INCONSTANCY OF GROWTH OF INDUSTRIES

Series	Period covered by series	Standard deviation of decade rates	Range of decade rates	Measure of continuity of growth
		(Unit: one per cent)		
Manufactures and construction (cont.)				
Canned corn	1885–1929	3.6	12.1	1.00
Jute imports	1870–1929	3.6	11.9	.09
Rails	1870–1929	3.5	12.4	.45
Coke	1880–1929	3.5	11.6	.78
Minor fiber imports	1870–1929	3.4	12.6	.64
Gold consumption	1880–1929	3.3	11.8	.78
Silver consumption	1880–1929	3.3	10.8	1.00
Canned tomatoes	1885–1929	3.0	9.7	.75
Cocoa imports	1870–1929	2.9	9.5	1.00
Pig iron	1870–1929	2.8	9.5	.82
Copper consumption	1883–1929	2.7	9.9	1.00
Rolled iron and steel	1885–1929	2.7	9.6	1.00
Tin-plate consumption	1871–1929	2.5	9.5	1.00
Fermented liquors	1870–1918	2.5	8.5	.78
Zinc consumption	1873–1929	2.5	8.4	1.00
Flaxseed consumption	1879–1929	2.4	7.6	.78
Distilled spirits	1870–1918	2.3	8.6	.78
Silk imports, raw	1870–1929	2.2	7.3	1.00
Cigars	1880–1929	2.2	7.3	.56
Tin imports	1870–1929	2.2	6.4	1.00
Wool consumption	1870–1930	2.1	8.4	.82
Nails	1872–1929	2.1	7.2	.73
Tobacco and snuff	1871–1929	2.1	7.0	.64
Manila hemp imports	1870–1929	2.0	8.1	.82
White lead	1884–1929	1.9	5.1	.50
Coffee imports	1870–1929	1.7	5.5	1.00
Cotton consumption	1870–1929	1.5	5.4	.91
Silk imports, unmanufactured	1883–1929	1.3	4.2	1.00
Raw sugar consumption	1870–1930	1.2	3.7	1.00
Lead consumption	1870–1929	1.1	4.0	1.00
Tobacco consumption	1880–1929	1.0	3.1	1.00
Flour	1880–1929	1.0	3.0	.78

Table 9 (cont.)
MEASURES OF INCONSTANCY OF GROWTH OF INDUSTRIES

Series	Period covered by series	Standard deviation of decade rates	Range of decade rates	Measure of continuity of growth
		(Unit: one per cent)		
Transportation and trade				
Shares traded	1875–1929	8.6	30.3	.40
S. S. Marie canals traffic.....	1870–1929	6.2	20.9	.82
N. Y. canals traffic..........	1870–1929	4.7	19.5	−.45
Agricultural exports.........	1870–1929	3.1	11.7	.45
Railway passenger-miles.....	1882–1929	3.1	10.3	.78
Railway ton-miles	1870–1929	2.7	9.2	1.00
Postal money orders.........	1870–1929	2.7	8.2	1.00
Railway freight..............	1882–1929	2.4	7.3	1.00
Coastal trade	1870–1929	1.8	5.2	.64
Tonnage entered and cleared.	1870–1929	1.6	5.8	.82
Deflated clearings...........	1870–1929	1.5	4.7	1.00
Postage stamps..............	1870–1929	1.0	3.8	1.00

individual industries may be obtained by comparing their rates of advance, detailed in Tables 5–8, during the period 1885–1929 and such longer periods as are covered by the statistical records. It will be noticed that the two rates for each series are practically never identical, and that the differential between them varies considerably. A far more comprehensive view of the extent of the inconstancy in the rates of growth of the various industries is afforded by Table 9, which presents three measures of inconstancy of growth for each series. The first measure is the standard deviation of the decade rates, and thus measures the 'average' extent of the variation of the decade rates of a given series.[18] The second

---

[18] When the standard deviation (or average deviation) of the decade rates is measured from their mean, the degree of uniformity in the 'slope' of the secular trend is ascertained with reference to the 'slope' of a primary trend of the type of a simple exponential curve. The chief ground for preferring the

measure states the range of the decade rates, that is, the difference between the highest and lowest of the decade rates of a given series. The third is a measure of the continuity of growth; it expresses the excess of the number of positive over negative decade rates of a given series as a ratio to the number of its decade rates.[19] This measure has a theoretical range from $+1$ to -1: the limits indicate respectively that growth has been continuous throughout in the sense that the trend has been upward in each decade, and that decline has been continuous throughout in the sense that the trend has been downward in each decade. The three measures are designed to reveal different aspects of the inconstancy in the trend movements of given industries over time. The measures relate to such periods as the series cover.[20]

The measures of continuity of growth for the ensemble of series are summarized in Table 10.[21] Being positive and high for the most part, they bear witness to the strong

---

standard deviation to the average deviation is that variability is later measured also from a line defining the drift of the decade rates (see Ch. V, sec. IV); in such a case the standard deviation does, while the average deviation does not, insure formally consistent results, in the sense that the variability about a 'trend line' must be lower than or equal to the variability about the arithmetic mean.

It is frequently argued that the standard deviation gives a larger weight to extreme items than the average deviation. Apparently, this criticism means (otherwise it seems pointless) that the average deviation of a given series containing an extreme item in relation to the others, will differ by a smaller percentage from the average deviation of the given series with the extreme item excluded, than would the standard deviation of the given series containing the extreme item from the standard deviation of the series with the extreme item excluded. But no such general mathematical rule can be proved.

[19] Decade rates of zero were ignored in determining the numerator of the ratio; this is tantamount to counting zeroes as half-positive and half-negative.

[20] The comparability of the ranges and also of the standard deviations of the decade rates, as among the various series, is impaired somewhat by the non-uniformity of their periods; for, as Chapter IV shows, retardation in industrial growth has been a systematically operative factor.

[21] Concerning the composition of the several groups of series in Tables 10–12, see p. 52, note, and p. 56, note 6. The group of nonagricultural industries in Table 10 excludes both agricultural and fisheries series.

Table 10
FREQUENCY DISTRIBUTIONS OF MEASURES OF CONTINUITY OF GROWTH, FOR 'ALL' SERIES AND BASIC SERIES, BY INDUSTRIAL GROUPS

Measure of continuity of growth	Agriculture and fisheries (1)	Nonagricultural industries (2)	All industries (1) + (2)
\multicolumn{4}{c}{'All' series}			
−.99 to −.80	1	..	1
−.79 to −.60	..	..	..
−.59 to −.40	1	1	2
−.39 to −.20	..	..	..
−.19 to .00	..	3	3
.01 to .20	..	3	3
.21 to .40	4	4	8
.41 to .60	..	7	7
.61 to .80	10	17	27
.81 to 1.00	7	41	48
Total	23	76	99
Below 1.00	20	48	68
1.00	3	28	31
Total	23	76	99
\multicolumn{4}{c}{Basic series}			
−.19 to .00	..	1	1
.01 to .20	..	..	..
.21 to .40	1	2	3
.41 to .60	..	1	1
.61 to .80	9	11	20
.81 to 1.00	3	31	34
Total	13	46	59
Below 1.00	12	24	36
1.00	1	22	23
Total	13	46	59

secular forces of progressiveness which have been operating in the economy. As might be expected, the measures of continuity of growth of industries are fairly closely correlated with their average rates of growth. But even the industries which have grown at an exceptionally rapid rate do not always evidence perfect continuity of growth. This is true especially of industries which fall outside of the 'basic' category; for when large stocks are customary, as in fluorspar, or foreign competition is considerable, as in pyrites, or another and more important industry shares in the market, as is the case of native asphalt which is dwarfed by manufactured asphalt, secular trends are likely to be sharply undulatory. Though non-basic series account for a relatively greater proportion of the measures of continuity which fall short of unity than do basic series, it is yet worth noting that less than 40 per cent of the basic series have experienced an uninterrupted upward secular movement. It is also of some significance that agricultural series have, on the average, somewhat lower measures of continuity than the nonagricultural; only three agricultural industries—beet sugar, raisins, and hog production—have had consistently an upward trend.

The measure of continuity of growth takes cognizance of the signs of the decade rates, but not of their absolute magnitudes. It therefore serves to reveal the degree of uniformity in the type of direction of the secular trend of a series, but not the degree of uniformity in the 'slope' of the secular trend. Series having given measures of continuity of growth may and do differ considerably from the standpoint of the variability of their decade rates. And the presence of some series with measures of continuity of 1.00 among those evidencing the extremest variability in their decade rates indicates that the measures of continuity may understate the degree of inconstancy in the secular movements of industries over

Table 11
FREQUENCY DISTRIBUTION OF RANGES OF DECADE RATES, FOR 'ALL' SERIES

Range of decade rates (per cent)	Number of series
2.0 to 4.9	9
5.0 to 7.9	22
8.0 to 10.9	19
11.0 to 13.9	9
14.0 to 16.9	10
17.0 to 19.9	7
20.0 to 22.9	4
23.0 to 25.9	3
26.0 to 28.9	2
29.0 to 31.9	4
32.0 to 34.9	..
35.0 to 37.9	3
38.0 to 40.9	1
41.0 to 43.9	1
44.0 to 46.9	..
47.0 and over *	5
Total	99

* The items in this class are: 49.3, 58.6, 64.5, 76.8, and 108.4.

time. The range depicts that inconstancy most graphically, the standard deviation with greater fidelity to the individual decade rates. A general summary of the ranges is given in Table 11, and a detailed analytic summary of the standard deviations in Table 12.

The outstanding features of the measures of variability of decade rates consist in the large difference among them and their generally high level. The smallest of the ranges is 2.9 per cent for fish, and the largest over 100 per cent for sulphur. About half of the series have ranges of over 11 per cent, about a quarter over 20 per cent, and about a tenth over 35 per cent. The standard deviations are closely

Table 12
FREQUENCY DISTRIBUTIONS OF STANDARD DEVIATIONS OF DECADE RATES, FOR 'ALL' SERIES AND BASIC SERIES, BY INDUSTRIAL GROUPS

Standard deviation of decade rates (per cent)	Agriculture and fisheries	Mining	Manufactures and construction	Transportation and trade	All industries
\multicolumn{6}{c}{'All' series}					
0.0 to 0.9	1	..	..	..	1
1.0 to 1.9	6	..	7	4	17
2.0 to 2.9	8	3	15	3	29
3.0 to 3.9	2	4	7	2	15
4.0 to 4.9	1	4	3	1	9
5.0 to 5.9	3	1	2	..	6
6.0 to 6.9	..	1	2	1	4
7.0 to 7.9	..	1	6	..	7
8.0 to 8.9	..	1	..	1	2
9.0 to 9.9	..	..	..	..	..
10.0 to 10.9	..	1	..	..	1
11.0 to 11.9	..	1	..	..	1
12.0 to 12.9	..	..	..	..	..
13.0 to 13.9	..	..	..	..	..
14.0 to 14.9	2	1	..	..	3
15.0 and over *	..	2	2	..	4
Total	23	20	44	12	99
\multicolumn{6}{c}{Basic series}					
0.0 to 0.9	1	..	..	..	1
1.0 to 1.9	5	..	7	4	16
2.0 to 2.9	7	3	11	2	23
3.0 to 3.9	..	4	4	1	9
4.0 to 4.9	..	5	1	..	6
5.0 to 5.9	..	..	1	..	1
6.0 to 6.9	..	..	1	..	1
7.0 to 7.9	..	..	2	..	2
Total	13	12	27	7	59

* The items in this class are: mining, 18.0 and 31.8 per cent; manufactures and construction, 16.8 and 21.3 per cent.

PATTERN OF PRODUCTION

correlated with the ranges. About half are above 3 per cent, and about a tenth above 10 per cent. The largest of the standard deviations are accounted for by non-basic series, and the standard deviations of the agricultural series are generally lower than of the nonagricultural. These industrial differences correspond to those which were found to hold for average rates of growth.[22]

III. ELEMENTS OF ORDER IN SECULAR CHANGE

The inconstancy in the rates of growth of the individual industries over time creates the impression that the secular changes in the pattern of general production have taken place in an irregular and unsystematic manner. But this impression is tempered by the threads of order and continuity which analysis discloses in the maze of industrial changes. Though irregular in large part, the secular shifts in the pattern of national industry have also been systematic to a considerable extent. The remaining portion of this chapter serves to introduce, and the following two chapters attempt to trace in detail, the elements of order in the process of secular change.

We have previously emphasized the irregularity in the differentials between the two average rates of growth given for each series in Tables 5–8, but careful scrutiny of the differentials suggests an underlying similarity in the behavior of the trends of the various industries. Though the differential between the two rates varies from series to series, its direction is on the whole remarkably systematic: all but four of the series of agriculture and fisheries show higher rates of growth when their full statistical history since 1870 is considered than for the period since 1885, and so do all but five

[22] The variability of the decade rates is investigated more thoroughly, though from a different angle, at a later point; see Ch. V, sec. IV.

of the mineral series, all but four series of manufactures and construction, and all but four series of transportation and trade.[23] The systematic direction of the differential indicates that the rates of growth of the industries covered were generally higher during 1870–85 than in the following years, and suggests that dominating causes common to the various industries were operative. Certainly, the class of agricultural industries received a considerable impetus during the period 1870–85 from the liberal homestead policy of the federal government, the westward extension of railroads, and the introduction of new machinery. But the differential in the average rates of growth suggests that other major forces have been at work,—forces which have extended over the entire range of industry and found expression in a declining rate of growth in the generality of individual industries. This is

[23] There are, then, seventeen exceptions in all, two of them—rice production and Manila hemp imports—having the same average rate for each period. Few of the exceptions have much significance. Several series commence as late as 1880; this makes the present comparison inapt. In the case of beet sugar, sulphur, rubber imports, and vessels, peculiar circumstances explain the higher rates of growth during the shorter period. Technological factors were dominant in the beet sugar industry: before 1890 the industry was virtually in an experimental stage, its output being quite negligible (see *Yearbook of Agriculture*, 1923, p. 156). The revolutionary change shortly after 1900 in the technical conditions of the sulphur industry renders almost meaningless any long-term average for this industry (see pp. 156–7). In the case of rubber imports, long-term comparisons are misleading because of the recent advent of the automobile (see pp. 154–5). The present comparison is pointless for vessels, in view of the influence of the extraordinary War-time boom in shipbuilding on its average rate of growth. As for the rice industry (which has the same average rate for the two periods), its underlying mechanism was changed towards the end of the 'eighties by a technical revolution in methods of cultivation; the scope of the transformation can be inferred from the fact that during 1895–1905 rice production expanded at the extraordinary pace of something like 19 per cent per year (see p. 157).

A word may be added about the series for which the same average rates of growth are recorded in the columns 'in period covered' and '1885–1929' (Tables 5–8). Except in the cases of rice production and Manila hemp imports, already mentioned, these averages are based on identical sets of decade rates, the minor differences in the periods stated having no meaning for the present comparison; see pp. 39–41, and p. 56, note 7.

also intimated by Table 13, which shows that extremely high rates of growth occurred with very much greater frequency in the early than in the late decades, and that the number of industries having downward trends has been very much greater in recent than in remote decades.

Table 13

PRODUCTION SERIES HAVING DECADE RATES OF 10 PER CENT OR MORE, AND 0 OR LESS, BY DECADES INDICATED BY THEIR CENTRAL YEARS

Central decade year	Total number of series covered	Rates of 10 per cent or over		Rates of 0 or less	
		Number of series	Percentage of series covered	Number of series	Percentage of series covered
1875	66	16	24.2	6	9.1
1880	69	20	29.0	5	7.2
1885	97	17	17.5	8	8.2
1890	104	11	10.6	10	9.6
1895	104	10	9.6	8	7.7
1900	104	21	20.2	8	7.7
1905	104	8	7.7	11	10.6
1910	104	4	3.8	17	16.3
1915	104	9	8.7	22	21.2
1920	102	5	4.9	43	42.2
1925	102	6	5.9	26	25.5

For the present, these indications concerning the tendency of industries to grow at a declining rate will have to suffice, as this subject is investigated in considerable detail in the next chapter. But it is important to note that insofar as individual industries grow at declining rates, the pattern of production will tend to undergo modification in a somewhat regular manner. If total production grew, for example, at a constant percentage rate while individual industries (their number being fixed or increasing) grew at declining rates, the percentage contributions of the individual industries to the production aggregate would be steadily diminishing over time, or else increasing but at a diminishing percentage rate.

When we take full account of the decade rates of the series, further evidence emerges of regularity in changes in the pattern of the production system. Table 14 aims to disclose through two measures the degree of stability in the relations of the trend movements of the various series, during the eight overlapping decade periods, separated by a five-year span, since 1885. The table is restricted to basic series,[24] 57 in all, because the rates of increase of the other series fluctuate within a wider range over time and a common analysis of all series would therefore impart an artificial instability to the relative trend movements of the more important series. The first measure in the table states the average rank of each series: this measure is an arithmetic mean of the ranks of the eight decade rates of each series, the decade rates of the series having been ranked at each date on the principle of assigning a rank of 1 to the highest decade rate and a rank of 57 to the lowest decade rate. The second measure states the average deviation of the ranks of each series: this measure is an arithmetic mean of the deviations (signs ignored) of the eight ranks for each series, the deviations being measured from the arithmetic mean of the two middle-sized ranks. While the first measure states the average position of the trend advance of each industry in relation to the others, the second measure states the con-

[24] The composition of the group is that given in Appendix A, Table 46, column *f*, except for the two beverage series—fermented liquors and distilled spirits—which were dropped because they do not cover the full period through 1929. Comparisons of the relative position of trend movements are strictly valid for only the group of 57 series included. But in view of the substantial portion of the basic production area covered by these series, such a limited study should also throw considerable light on the stability in the relations of trend movements of basic industries in general.

PATTERN OF PRODUCTION

sistency of the position of the trend advance of each industry in relation to the others.

These two measures impose a severe test on our data. The relative ranks of the trend movements of many industries have undergone a persistent change over the period since 1885: the trend advances of bituminous-coal, steel, coke, and cottonseed-oil production have declined relatively to the trend advances of other industries; the trend advances of petroleum production, silk imports, and tobacco consumption have increased relatively; and there have been other secular shifts in relative trend movements.[25] Secular shifts in the relative ranks of industries, no less than oscillatory shifts, make for increasing similarity in the average ranks of the various series and for increasing variability in the several ranks of each of the individual series. It is all the more remarkable, therefore, that the average ranks of the series show wide dissimilarity: the average deviation (measured from the median) of the average ranks of our series is 10.1, which compares with a maximum possible average deviation of average ranks of 14.2.[26] And it is further notable that the average deviations of the ranks of the individual series are, speaking generally, not very high: as many as 51 out of 57 series have average deviations below 14.2, which is the most probable average deviation under random conditions—that is, if each series had the same chance of having any one rank at each date as any other series. The statistical indications are, then, that there has been a fair degree of stability in the relative trend movements of industries even when we consider a period of a half-century during which many in-

[25] The ranks of relative trend advances of industries should not be confused with ranks in industrial importance—as measured by such yardsticks as value of product, number employed, etc.

[26] The clearest case of a maximum is when the ranks for each date constitute a perfect arithmetic progression, and when the average rank of each of the 57 series is identical with its rank at each date.

84 PRODUCTION TRENDS

Table 14
MEASURES OF THE RELATIVE POSITION OF THE TREND MOVEMENTS OF BASIC SERIES, FOR 1885–1929

Series	Average rank	Average deviation of ranks
Cocoa imports	7.4	5.1
Petroleum	8.2	5.7
Steel	9.7	5.2
Cement, total	10.1	7.1
Silk imports, unmanufactured	10.8	6.8
Postage stamps	11.7	6.7
Copper consumption	13.3	6.3
Zinc consumption	13.6	5.6
Zinc	14.9	8.2
Rubber imports	15.8	14.2
Copper	17.4	9.5
Rolled iron and steel	18.9	7.3
Phosphate rock	19.0	11.4
Railway ton-miles	19.3	4.9
Salt	20.7	8.4
Deflated clearings	21.1	7.7
Silver consumption	21.8	9.6
Coke	22.2	9.6
Pig iron	22.6	5.6
Tin-plate consumption	23.0	9.7
Bituminous coal	23.4	9.3
Iron ore	24.1	9.9
Cottonseed oil	24.3	15.9
Tin imports	24.4	7.9
Tonnage entered and cleared	26.1	6.7
Railway freight	26.5	5.9
Lead, domestic	26.7	6.3
Lead consumption	27.0	6.2
Railway passenger-miles	29.3	12.7
Cotton consumption	31.0	4.7
Barley	31.2	12.5
Gold consumption	31.7	17.6
Raw sugar consumption	32.3	9.6
Flaxseed consumption	32.9	13.6
Coastal trade	33.9	10.9

Table 14 (cont.)

MEASURES OF THE RELATIVE POSITION OF THE TREND MOVEMENTS OF BASIC SERIES, FOR 1885–1929

Series	Average rank	Average deviation of ranks
Tobacco, raw	34.2	13.4
Sheep	34.9	12.7
Building permits	35.1	17.9
Coffee imports	35.2	11.9
Hogs	36.5	8.7
Cattle	36.5	9.2
Tobacco consumption	37.1	7.1
Rail consumption	37.9	17.6
Cotton	38.7	9.1
Gold	39.9	14.7
Potatoes	41.1	5.2
Oats	42.2	7.0
Minor fiber imports	43.9	6.2
Anthracite coal	44.2	5.7
Wheat	44.4	8.0
Wool consumption	45.1	6.9
Hay	45.4	3.6
Flour	45.6	4.1
Silver	46.4	7.9
Corn	46.6	5.3
Fish, total	47.2	4.6
Wool	48.4	6.1

dustries experienced persistent shifts in the relative ranks of their trend advances. Examining the measures of Table 14 in detail, we find that they correspond roughly to distinct industrial groups, and this is the best evidence that the stability indicated by the ensemble of measures cannot be a 'chance' result, that it reflects the influence of systematic economic forces. On the whole, series of industrial metals and their derivatives, and luxury goods have the lowest average ranks, indicating the primacy of their rates of advance; series of food and textile staples have the highest average ranks; and series indicative of construction, transportation, and trade have the medium ranks. On the whole again, series of foods, textiles, industrial metals and their derivatives, transportation, and trade have rather low average deviations of ranks, while series relating to construction and to the precious metals have rather high average deviations.

The statistical measures just considered run in terms of averages for a period of a half-century. If we are to learn more about stability in the relations of industrial trend advances, it is necessary to pass to the evidence of the decade-by-decade movements of industrial trends; this may be done by correlating the average rates of growth during one decade with the average rates of growth during other decades. If an interdecade correlation be positive, it will mean that the industries with relatively high rates of growth during one decade tended to have relatively high rates of growth during the other decade. If an interdecade correlation be negative, it will mean that the industries with relatively high rates of growth during one decade tended to have relatively low rates of growth during the other decade. A high coefficient of correlation will indicate considerable regularity in the changes in the pattern of production, while a low coefficient will indicate only mild regularity. Moreover, insofar as the coefficients of correlation are fairly high and positive, they will help to explain the relatively large variation in the average ranks of trend movements of the basic series group and the moderately low variation in the ranks of the decade rates of the individual basic series. It must be noted, however, that correlation technique can measure the degree of stability in the relative trend advances of only those industries which are common to the periods compared. In a rapidly moving economy, old commodities are constantly

PATTERN OF PRODUCTION 87

falling into desuetude while new commodities are emerging. This portion of the production area is most unstable, and it completely eludes measurement in correlation analysis. Hence, even if the statistical materials encompassed fully that portion of the production area which is common to the periods compared, the coefficients of correlation would still understate the instability in the relative trend advances of the system of industries.

A record of the coefficients of correlation between average rates of growth of given decades and all other decades is presented in Tables 15–17, which relate respectively to 38

Table 15

COEFFICIENTS OF CORRELATION BETWEEN DECADE RATES OF 38 BASIC SERIES, FOR PAIRS OF DECADES INDICATED BY THEIR CENTRAL YEARS

Central decade year	1875	1880	1885	1890	1895	1900	1905	1910	1915	1920	1925
1875			.63		.58		.49		.20		.33
1880				.64		.60		.49		.18	
1885	.63				.59		.54		.36		.38
1890		.64				.52		.50		.09	
1895	.58		.59				.45		.08		.15
1900		.60		.52				.48		.29	
1905	.49		.54		.45				.52		.60
1910		.49		.50		.48				.54	
1915	.20		.36		.08		.52				.44
1920		.18		.09		.29		.54			
1925	.33		.38		.15		.60		.44		

Table 16
COEFFICIENTS OF CORRELATION BETWEEN DECADE RATES OF 57 BASIC SERIES, FOR PAIRS OF DECADES INDICATED BY THEIR CENTRAL YEARS

Central decade year	1890	1895	1900	1905	1910	1915	1920	1925
1890			.44		.46		.01	
1895				.44		.16		.22
1900	.44				.51		.23	
1905		.44				.39		.53
1910	.46		.51				.32	
1915		.16		.39				.29
1920	.01		.23		.32			
1925		.22		.53		.29		

basic production series covering the period since 1870, 57 basic series covering the period since 1885, and 44 basic nonagricultural series covering the same period.[27] A double entry is made in the tables for each of the decade combinations so as to facilitate reference. The outstanding feature of the record of correlations is that the coefficients are fairly high for contiguous decades, but become progressively lower as

[27] For purposes of simplicity, the correlations are confined to decades removed by ten-year steps or multiples thereof. The reasons for limiting the study to basic series are those set forth on p. 82. Except for the exclusion of fermented liquors and distilled spirits, the composition of the 38 basic series group, the 57 basic series group, and the 44 basic nonagricultural series group, is as listed in columns b, f, and h, respectively, of Table 46 in Appendix A. The group of 44 basic nonagricultural series differs from the group of 57 basic series in that it excludes the series of fish catch and the twelve agricultural series listed on p. 91, note 30.

Table 17

COEFFICIENTS OF CORRELATION BETWEEN DECADE RATES OF 44 BASIC NONAGRICULTURAL SERIES, FOR PAIRS OF DECADES INDICATED BY THEIR CENTRAL YEARS

Central decade year	1890	1895	1900	1905	1910	1915	1920	1925
1890			.36		.48		−.08	
1895				.37		.10		.17
1900	.36				.45		.13	
1905		.37				.36		.49
1910	.48		.45				.29	
1915		.10		.36				.31
1920	−.08		.13		.29			
1925		.17		.49		.31		

increasingly remote periods are correlated.[28] This is apparent from a careful reading of Tables 15–17, and it stands out conspicuously in Table 18 which presents arithmetic means of the coefficients for similarly spaced decades. The fact that the coefficients of correlation between the rates of growth of contiguous decades are fairly high indicates that there has been moderate regularity in the relations of the trend advances of industries during contiguous decades; this subject is investigated with more refined tools of analysis in Chapter V. The fact that the correlation tends to vanish as the periods compared become increasingly distant

[28] The coefficients of correlation were obtained by the Pearsonian method. They were checked by the method of rank correlation, which yielded about the same results. The term 'coefficient of correlation', as used throughout this work, refers to the Pearsonian coefficient.

Table 18
AVERAGES OF THE COEFFICIENTS OF CORRELATION BETWEEN DECADE RATES

Group	Number of cases	Average of coefficients
38 Basic series		
Contiguous decades	9	.53
Decades separated by ten years	7	.46
Decades separated by twenty years	5	.32
Decades separated by thirty years	3	.25
57 Basic series		
Contiguous decades	6	.40
Decades separated by ten years	4	.34
Decades separated by twenty years	2	.11
44 Basic nonagricultural series		
Contiguous decades	6	.36
Decades separated by ten years	4	.30
Decades separated by twenty years	2	.04

bears witness to the rapidity of change in the relations of industrial trend advances and, therefore, in the pattern of general industry.[29] These statistical results accord with a priori anticipations.

It will be noticed that the coefficients of correlation for basic nonagricultural series (Table 17) are lower than the

[29] If the degree of shift in the relative trend movements of industries followed any simple plan, that would be sharply reflected in the patterns formed by the coefficients of correlation in the several tables. If the degree of shift in the relative trend movements of industries were identical from decade to decade, the coefficients for contiguous decades would be constant; if, in addition, there were little tendency to revert to an earlier pattern of growth, the coefficients for separated decades would tend to decline as the intervening period increased, and the averages of the coefficients in successive columns (or rows) would therefore rise towards the center of the period and then decline. On the other hand, if the degree of shift increased rapidly, the coefficients for contiguous decades would have a sharp downward drift; if, in addition, there were little tendency to revert to an earlier pattern of growth, the averages of coefficients in successive columns (or rows) would tend to decline with time. Other patterns of coefficients may easily be imagined.

PATTERN OF PRODUCTION

corresponding coefficients for basic series (Table 16) in ten of the twelve interdecade combinations. This systematic difference suggests that the coefficients for the basic series group may partly reflect a systematic differential between the average rates of growth of agricultural and nonagricultural industries; for, since agricultural industries have generally grown at lower rates than nonagricultural industries, a fair degree of correlation between interdecade rates might be evidenced by a composite of the two groups, even if there were little correlation in either group taken separately. While fairly high coefficients of correlation would not be without significance under such conditions, their meaning would be simply that the class of nonagricultural industries persistently grew more rapidly than the class of agricultural industries. The fact is that the 12 basic agricultural series,[30] taken by

---

There are two aspects of the patterns actually formed by the coefficients of correlation in Tables 15–17 which are worthy of notice. By far the more important is the decline in the coefficients as successively remote periods are correlated. This has been emphasized in the text, but it will bear additional statistical comment. Taking the coefficients in the three tables *en masse*, we find that coefficients for 'decades$_a$' with 'decades$_b$', where b is later than a but may or may not be contiguous to a, are higher than coefficients for 'decades$_a$' with 'decades$_{b+1}$' in most cases (18 out of 28); higher than coefficients for 'decades$_a$' with 'decades$_{b+2}$' in all cases (13 out of 13); and higher than coefficients for 'decades$_a$' with 'decades$_{b+3}$' or for 'decades$_a$' with 'decades$_{b+4}$' in all cases (5 out of 5).

Another aspect of the patterns actually formed by the coefficients of correlation in the several tables is something of a downward drift in the coefficients for contiguous decades. This suggests that the degree of stability in the relations of the trend advances of industries, and therefore in the changes in the pattern of production, has been declining. The indication of increasing instability is, however, of uncertain significance. Part of the drift in the coefficients reflects merely the drastic shift in the pattern of production during the decade including the War-period: the tables disclose the striking fact that the correlation between the rates of growth during 1910–20 and other decades is lower in every instance than the correlation between the rates of growth during 1920–29 (a remoter period) and corresponding decades. Moreover, the drift in the coefficients may arise from the decreasing statistical representation of the production area, which results unavoidably from the use of a fixed list of production series in the analysis of a progressive economy.

[30] The numbers of the series are: 1, 5–7, 9–10, 13–15, 18–20. (The most

themselves, show on the whole little correlation: the arithmetic mean of their coefficients for contiguous decades (6 cases) is .03, for decades separated by ten years (4 cases) .01, and decades separated by twenty years (2 cases) −.01. The paradoxical result of excluding the agricultural series (which themselves show little correlation) from the basic group is a reduction in the size of the coefficients for the remaining series, that is, the basic nonagricultural group; but this result confirms the hypothesis of heterogeneity in the behavior of industrial trends. While the coefficients for the basic nonagricultural series are somewhat lower than for the larger group including agriculture, they are still fairly high and statistically significant in the case of contiguous decades: they relate to a group which is roughly homogeneous from the standpoint of the average rates of growth in its major industrial divisions and which covers a very substantial portion of what may be considered as the area of basic nonagricultural industry.

The above observations indicate that agricultural and nonagricultural industries have differed considerably in the degree of stability of their respective relative trend movements. The same difference may be noted between agriculture and mining, an important subdivision of the nonagricultural group and the second great source of raw materials. While

---

convenient reference to the numbers of the series, quoted extensively in later footnotes, is provided in Table 1; though a key accompanies also Tables 44–47.) Even though these series cover a substantial portion of agricultural industry, coefficients of correlation for such a small number of items are of limited significance. But the 'errors' in the coefficients are likely to be compensatory in part, and averages of coefficients of the same time dimension are therefore of greater significance than individual coefficients. The coefficients between decades indicated by their central years are given in parentheses: 1890 and 1900 (.55), 1890 and 1910 (−.18), 1890 and 1920 (.01), 1895 and 1905 (.11), 1895 and 1915 (.09), 1895 and 1925 (−.03), 1900 and 1910 (−.01), 1900 and 1920 (−.30), 1905 and 1915 (−.05), 1905 and 1925 (.43), 1910 and 1920 (−.14), and 1915 and 1925 (−.27). It may be noted parenthetically that the 6 coefficients for contiguous decades show a marked and continuous decline over time. This may be merely a 'chance' result; see, however, the preceding note.

PATTERN OF PRODUCTION

the agricultural series show practically no stability in their relative trend movements, mineral series show a fair degree of stability, as may be gathered from the coefficients for 12 basic mineral industries: [31] the arithmetic mean of their coefficients for contiguous decades (6 cases) is .49, for decades separated by ten years (4 cases) .39, and decades separated by twenty years (2 cases) .27.

The differences among major industrial divisions, in the relations of the advances of the secular trends of their individual industries, reflect differences in the underlying framework of their operation. The virtual absence of stability, speaking generally, in the relations of the trend movements of agricultural industries is due, in part, to the unspecialized character, and consequently, mobility, of a substantial portion of agricultural resources; in part, to the practice of substitution in the use of agricultural products; and finally, to the random impact of extrahuman factors which occasionally prove dominant, even though they are generally subsidiary to the factor of planning over intervals of some ten years or more. On the other hand, the relatively high stability in the relations of the trend advances of mineral industries is due, in part, to the specialized character, and consequently, immobility, of the factors of mineral production; [32] and in part, to the fair continuity in the relative trends of consumption of the industrial metals, fuels, and construction

[31] The numbers of these series are: 24–5, 27–9, 31–4, 36, 39, and 43. The coefficients between decades indicated by their central years are given in parentheses: 1890 and 1900 (.31), 1890 and 1910 (.42), 1890 and 1920 (.46), 1895 and 1905 (.29), 1895 and 1915 (−.25), 1895 and 1925 (.09), 1900 and 1910 (.67), 1900 and 1920 (.54), 1905 and 1915 (.38), 1905 and 1925 (.84), 1910 and 1920 (.79), 1915 and 1925 (.53). Concerning the interpretation of these individual coefficients, see the preceding note.

[32] Mineral resources admit of relatively unique uses only. To be sure, some discretion may be used in extracting ores which yield more of one metal than another, metallurgical treatment of ore admits of some variations in yield, more or less of natural gas may be recovered, and so on; but these are minor exceptions.

materials, which mines yield. Similar factors account for the moderate stability in the relative trend advances of other basic nonagricultural industries,[33] though the immobility of their resources is generally smaller than in mining.[34] Outside of the range of those nonagricultural industries which are basic, especially in the field of elaborative manufactures, the factor of substitution in consumptive use becomes of paramount importance: though the technical conditions of production conduce to stability in the relative trend advances of manufactures, their influence may be overriden easily by the volatile character of consumers' markets.

This analysis of the interdecade correlations of rates of industrial growth, the analysis of the relative positions of the trend movements of industries during 1885–1929, and the analysis of the differentials between the rates of industrial growth during 1885–1929 and such longer periods as the series cover, have yielded an inkling of the elements of order that have characterized the vast and rapid transformation in the industrial pattern of our national economy. What has been merely glimpsed in this chapter is illuminated in considerable detail in the two following chapters. Though accident has played no unimportant role in the changes in the

[33] Excluding the 12 mineral series from the basic nonagricultural group of 44 series (see p. 88, note 27, and p. 93, note 31) we have 32 series falling in the categories of manufacture, construction, transportation, and trade. The coefficients of correlation for this group for pairs of decades indicated by their central years are as follows: 1890 and 1900 (.38), 1890 and 1910 (.50), 1890 and 1920 (–.21), 1895 and 1905 (.36), 1895 and 1915 (.25), 1895 and 1925 (.25), 1900 and 1910 (.38), 1900 and 1920 (–.08), 1905 and 1915 (.48), 1905 and 1925 (.27), 1910 and 1920 (.14), 1915 and 1925 (.25). The arithmetic mean of these coefficients for contiguous decades (6 cases) is .33, for decades separated by ten years (4 cases) .23, and decades separated by twenty years (2 cases) .02.

[34] The forces which make for absence of stability in the relative advances of the secular trends of agricultural industries are, in large part, the same as those which make for only mild divergence in their primary trends; while the forces which make for moderate stability in the relative advances of the secular trends of nonagricultural industries are, in large part, the same as those which make for sharp divergence in their primary trends. See p. 67.

PATTERN OF PRODUCTION 95

industrial composition of our rapidly developing economy, we shall find that there are clear and unmistakable threads of regularity in these changes, that the production trends of individual industries manifest remarkable behavior similarities.

Chapter IV

RETARDATION IN THE GROWTH OF INDUSTRIES

FOR some time, the notion has been commonly held that the percentage rates of growth of individual industries tend to decline as their age increases.[1] Some statistical support for this notion has already been given in the course of the analysis in the last chapter. Our aim now is to inquire more closely, and with the aid of sharper statistical tools, into the experiential foundations of the general doctrine of retardation in industrial growth. Accordingly, a comprehensive statistical test of this doctrine will be made, insofar as the data for this country since 1870 permit; and the statistical analysis will be followed by an inquiry into the causes of the drifts which the *rates* of growth of individual industries tend to exhibit. It will be seen that growth and decline in the rate of growth, so far as individual industries are concerned, go hand in hand in a progressive economy; that they jointly reflect the operation of forces which determine the growth of the total national dividend; that the theory of decline in the rates of growth of individual industries calls

[1] Tarde, Ogburn, and Chapin have explicated such a conception about the growth of 'inventions', or cultural units—among which industries are surely an important single form. See G. Tarde, *The Laws of Imitation* (translation by E. C. Parsons; Henry Holt, 1903), Ch. IV, especially pp. 115 and 127; W. F. Ogburn, *Social Change* (B. W. Huebsch, 1922), pp. 112–3; F. S. Chapin, *Cultural Change* (Century, 1928), Part IV. For statistical studies of industrial retardation, see Kuznets, *Secular Movements*, cited above, Chs. I–III; R. Prescott, "Law of Growth in Forecasting Demand," *Journal of the American Statistical Association*, December, 1922; and C. Snyder, *Business Cycles and Business Measurements* (Macmillan, 1927), Ch. II.

for merely an amplification of the theory of divergence in the long-term rates of growth; that several of the instances of acceleration in industrial growth reduce to retardation upon proper analysis; and that such instances of acceleration as are reliably established are indicative of the slackening of progressive forces.

I. MEASUREMENT OF RETARDATION

Whether an industry has been growing at a rising or declining percentage rate may, in most instances, be ascertained readily from a graph of its production, the quantities being plotted on a logarithmic scale and time on a natural scale. In all cases, a mathematical description of retardation can be obtained by fitting a curve—such as the simple logistic, the Gompertz, or the 'logarithmic' parabola—which will reveal a decrescent rate of growth. Our present purpose calls for a method sufficiently flexible to describe either retardation or acceleration in the growth of individual industries, and so constituted as to yield measures of the extent of the retardation or acceleration. These conditions are fulfilled admirably by the logarithmic parabola; this function may be either concave or convex, and the antilog of its second derivative expresses the average rate of retardation or acceleration. If the primary trends of production are now viewed in a different way than in the preceding chapter, that is only because a different problem is being investigated.[2]

The logarithmic parabola, that is, $\log y = c + (\log a) x + (\frac{\log b}{2})x^2$, reports directly through $\log b$ (which is the second derivative of $\log y$ with respect to x) the degree of retardation (or acceleration). A parabola fitted to logarithms of annual production data (x referring to years and y to production) reports through the constant $\log b$ the

[2] See Ch. II, sec. III, and Ch. III, sec. I.

average annual rate of retardation (or acceleration) of the logarithms of the production data; it gives an average in the sense that a parabola fitted to data generalizes or 'averages' the course of the series. The average annual percentage rate of retardation of the production data may now be obtained from the formula: $100(b-1)$. That this is the correct expression may be shown easily: Differentiating log y with respect to x, we get $\log Y = \log a + (\log b)x$. Taking antilogs, we have $Y = ab^x$. Since log b is at the same time the first derivative of the straight line and the second derivative of the parabola, the annual percentage rate of retardation is given by $100 \left(\dfrac{ab^{x+1} - ab^x}{ab^x} \right)$, which reduces to $100(b-1)$.

A logarithmic parabola may be fitted to production data by various methods. Though the method of least squares is most commonly used, another method was deemed preferable for this study. If we (1) view the decade rates of a given production series as observations at quinquennial dates on the rate of growth of that series, (2) write the decade rates in ratio form (for example, as 1.054 and not 5.4 per cent, and so on), (3) fit a straight line to the logarithms of these decade rates, the equation being $\log Y = \log a + (\log b)x$, where Y refers to the decade rates centered at quinquennial dates and x to quinquennial dates, and (4) integrate the equation (or, to express it roughly, cumulate the ordinates) of this straight line; we obtain the equation of a parabola fitted to the logarithms of the original data, except for the constant of integration which can be determined readily by invoking the criterion of the zero moment. However, since the average rate of retardation is given by the antilog of the second derivative of a logarithmic parabola, or by the antilog of the first derivative of the first derivative of the parabola, we can obtain this average rate directly from the antilog of the first derivative of the straight line fitted to the

RETARDATION IN GROWTH

logarithms of the decade rates. Furthermore, since the antilog of log b, where log b is the first derivative of the above straight line, is equivalent to the term b in the exponential function $Y = ab^x$, our method of determining the average rate of retardation of a series consisted simply in calculating the value of the constant b in the exponential function $Y = ab^x$ (x referring to quinquennial dates and Y to decade rates centered at quinquennial dates), this type of curve being fitted by the method of moments [3] to the decade rates taken in ratio form.[4]

---

[3] See pp. 42–3.

[4] This method of measuring the average rate of retardation has three advantages. First, if we take the least squares method as a criterion, our method errs on the side of understatement of retardation; but as the backbone of the argument of this chapter stresses generality of actual retardation, a method of measurement which yields understatements of the extent of retardation lends firmer support to the conclusions reached. Second, the criterion of fit in our method is applied to the decade rates, while the criterion of fit in the method of least squares is applied to the logarithms of the original data. The consequence is that erratic movements in the original data exercise a smaller influence on an average rate of retardation calculated by our method than on one calculated by the least squares method. Third, the method adopted is much less laborious than the least squares method. With the decade rates at hand, it is a very simple matter to fit an exponential curve to them, especially when the method of moments, which does not involve the use of logarithms, is used. And as a matter of fact, it is not even necessary to determine in full the equation of the fitted exponential curve, for the constant which gives the rate of change suffices for our purpose.

A theoretical point remains to be noted. Let us assume that both actual production and production as observed through an empirical series trace out primary trends of the type of a 'logarithmic' parabola. Then, our method of measuring the rate of retardation will tend to 'compensate' for a downward retardation bias in production series, meaning by a downward retardation bias an overstatement by an empirical production series of the true retardation in actual production. On the other hand, the least squares method of measuring the rate of retardation will tend to 'compensate' for an upward retardation bias, meaning by that an understatement by the series of the true retardation. Hence, were it possible to appraise concretely our production series from the standpoint of their retardation bias, we could employ in each particular series that method which would compensate for the retardation bias in the original series. However, we are unable to appraise our series, from the standpoint of their retardation bias, with any assurance. It has, indeed, been possible to analyze our series in a general way from the standpoint of their growth bias (see pp. 25–7); but it is extremely hazardous to pass from the conclusions

The average rates of retardation (or acceleration) calculated for the various industries have been expressed in percentage form and on a decade basis. The decade rates being centered at quinquennial dates, the average percentage rate of retardation per decade is given by the formula: $100 \left(\dfrac{ab^{x+2} - ab^x}{ab^x} \right)$, which reduces to $100 (b^2 - 1)$. The average rate of retardation in the rate of growth of pig-iron production, for example, is recorded as -1.2 per cent per decade. The exact meaning of this is that the annual percentage rate of growth of the primary trend of pig-iron production had a downward drift such that the annual rate of growth (this is more conveniently expressed in ratio form) at any one time was .988 of the annual rate of growth ten years earlier. Thus the annual rate of advance of the primary trend of pig-iron output was 8.5 per cent in 1875, but only 7.2 per cent (determined from 1.085 × .988) in 1885, and 5.9 per cent (determined from 1.085 × .988 × .988) in 1895, and so on. As the decade rates of most industries are not very high, it is not necessary to observe these niceties of interpretation. The exponential curves fitted to the decade rates of growth approach straight lines very closely in a preponderant number of the series. Hence, a rate of retardation of, let us say, -1.0 per cent may be interpreted to mean that the rate of advance of the primary trend of the given industry was, say, 5.0 per cent per year during one decade,

---

reached concerning their growth bias to inferences concerning their retardation bias. All that we know with certainty is that if a series had a downward growth bias, at all points past or future, it would also have, at all points past or future, a downward retardation bias (or no retardation bias). This means that a production series having a downward growth bias during the period investigated will have of necessity also a downward retardation bias (or no retardation bias) during the period investigated, provided it is certain that the production series will continue to have a downward growth bias in the indefinite future. Obviously, this compass cannot be used with much assurance in seeking the theoretically preferable method of measuring the rate of retardation.

RETARDATION IN GROWTH

4.0 per cent per year during the next decade, 3.0 per cent during the next, and so on.

It should be observed that in the above examples of retardation, a negative sign is attached to the measures. This implies that a positive sign will be taken to denote acceleration. The present sign convention accords with mathematical usage, but is somewhat inconsistent with the name 'retardation' of the characteristic of production trends which is being investigated. In mathematical terms, we are throughout really measuring acceleration, positive or negative. All the same, the term retardation will be used generically to cover both retardation proper and acceleration, just as the term growth was used previously to cover both growth proper and decline. The justification of this terminology lies in the economic facts considered—that is, the generality of the phenomena of actual growth, and of actual decline in the rate of growth. Whether the term retardation is used generically or merely to cover the cases of actual decline in the rate of growth will be clear in each particular instance.

The average rates of retardation have been supplemented by another set of measures, which serve, first, to make clearer the graphic meaning of the rates of retardation,[5] and second, to indicate the stage reached in the development of the various industries. These supplementary measures are, in effect, the dates at which 'logarithmic' parabolas fitted to the original production data pass through maxima. In our method of procedure, it was necessary merely to find the dates at which the ordinates of the exponential curves fitted to the decade rates of the individual series are equal to unity.[6] These dates may, of course, define either maxima or

[5] The term 'rate of retardation' is used synonymously with 'average rate of 'retardation' throughout this chapter, and also in section III of Chapter VI. Similarly, the phrases 'retardation in growth' and 'decline in the rate of growth' are used synonymously.

[6] The value of x which will maximize the function $\log y = c + (\log a)x$

minima; but the dates have been computed only when they defined maxima—that is, they have been restricted to the series which show actual retardation in their growth. The dates of parabolic maxima will be referred to as measures of the stage of retardation. If the rate of retardation of one industry is −2.0 per cent per decade, and of another −1.0 per cent, but both have parabolic maxima in 1940, there is some ground for considering their relative stages of development to be the same, even though the rate of retardation of the one is twice that of the other.

The calculated parabolic turning dates are descriptions based on particular segments of economic history, as are the measures of the average rate of retardation, which the parabolic turning dates supplement.[7] The parabolic turning dates are not to be interpreted as predictions when industries will cease to grow, or as statements that they have already passed their zenith. Of course, the implications of the measures extend beyond the specific periods studied, but that is quite another thing from attaching significance to any extrapolations of specific numerical results. To guard against any misuse of the calculated parabolic turning dates, they are presented in the form of deviations from the year 1930. Thus, the measure of the stage of retardation of pig-iron production

---

$+ (\frac{\log b}{2}) x^2$ may be obtained by equating its first derivative to 0. Doing this, we have $\log Y = \log a + (\log b)x = 0$. Or, taking antilogs, $Y = ab^x = 1$. Of course, the dates of parabolic maxima obtained from exponential curves fitted to the decade rates are not necessarily identical with those which would be yielded by parabolas fitted directly to the logarithms of the original data by the method of least squares.

[7] The average rates of retardation hold strictly for only the specific periods covered by the series. It goes without saying that the measures may differ considerably, if somewhat different periods are analyzed. Thus, the rate of retardation of total coal production is −1.4 per cent per decade for 1870–1929, −0.9 per cent for 1850–1929, and −1.7 per cent for 1820–1929. Rates of retardation are generally cited in later pages as so many 'per cent', but they are always to be understood as so many 'per cent per decade'.

RETARDATION IN GROWTH

is stated to be 13 years, which means that the date of its parabolic maximum is 1943; and the measure of the stage of retardation of roofing slate is stated to be −25, which means that the date of its parabolic maximum is 1905.

The descriptive significance of measures of the rate and stage of retardation of a given production series is conditioned by the adequacy with which an exponential curve fits the decade rates of the series.[8] If a satisfactory fit is obtained, the measure of stage of retardation will also be satisfactory. However, though an average rate of retardation will gain in significance when the fit is satisfactory, its true significance depends further on the degree of continuity in the march of retardation. Accordingly, a measure of the continuity of retardation has been determined for each series. This measure expresses the excess of positive over negative first differences of the decade rates of a series as a ratio to the number of first differences,[9] and therefore has a theoretical range from −1 to +1: it will be −1 when retardation is continuous, that is, when each decade rate is lower than the preceding one; it will be +1 when acceleration is continuous, that is, when each decade rate is higher than the preceding one; it will be 0 when the number of decade rates higher than those preceding them is exactly the same as the number of decade rates lower than those preceding them. To cite two examples,

[8] Satisfactory fits were obtained in a preponderant number of series, but not in all series. Perhaps the most conspicuous of the poor 'fits' are those for the production of sulphur and of non-Portland cements, whose measures of retardation are therefore largely nominal.

[9] The decade rates were taken as centered at successive quinquennial dates. Since the decade rates are imperfect measures (see pp. 40–1, note 13), the range of error in the first differences of the decade rates will be greater than in the decade rates proper. Even though the measure of continuity takes account of only the signs of the first differences, it may still be unreliable when the decade rates of a series are highly similar. First differences of zero were ignored in determining the numerator of the ratio in the measure of continuity; this is tantamount to counting zeroes as half-positive and half-negative.

the measure of continuity of retardation is —.30 for pig iron, and —.25 for roofing slate.

Our measures of industrial retardation comprise, then, the average rate of retardation, the stage of retardation, and the continuity of retardation. These measures have been determined for the full period covered by each series. The primary reason for having the several measures of retardation cover the longest interval possible, within the limits of the period investigated, is that the distorting influence of trend-cycles on the measures is in this way reduced. In the preceding chapter, average rates of growth were presented for the period 1885–1929, which the series cover in common, as well as for the full period covered by each series, for the reason that the existence of a drift in the decade rates of the individual series would have seriously affected any comparisons of average rates of growth over periods of variable duration. But there is no such compelling reason for clinging to the same time interval for each series in a study of retardation. Moreover, as the series analyzed run over intervals varying from 45 to 60 years, all falling within the period since about 1870, their time reference is sufficiently similar to insure ample comparability for the present purpose.

II. THE STATISTICAL EVIDENCE

The first part of the inquiry in this chapter is a statistical report which attempts to answer the questions: To what extent is a decrescent rate of growth of individual industries a general phenomenon? How rapid is retardation generally? To what extent is retardation continuous in the individual industries? In seeking to establish the facts, average rates of retardation were determined for the 104 continuous series considered in the preceding chapter, and for 43 additional series of discontinuous data; measures of continuity of retardation were determined for all of the continuous series;

RETARDATION IN GROWTH

and measures of stage of retardation, for those continuous series which show actual retardation. The several measures of retardation for the individual series are recorded in Tables 22–25, which give also the periods covered by the series.

The rates of retardation of 142 production series are summarized in Table 19 and Chart 2.[10] A mere glance at the chart or table will suffice to reveal that a preponderant number of the industries have grown at a declining rate. Furthermore, though the rates of retardation vary considerably, their general level is fairly high. Of the 142 series included in Table 19, as many as 122 have rates of retardation in excess of –0.2 per cent per decade, which is the average rate of retardation in the population growth of this country since 1870.[11] It is difficult to escape the conclusion that retardation in the growth of production has been almost universal among the industries covered, and that the rapidity of retardation has been, on the whole, quite appreciable.

Measures of the stage of retardation, recorded in Tables

[10] This group of 142 series consists of 99 continuous series (the 'all' series group,—see Appendix A, Table 46, column *e*) and 43 discontinuous series (these are starred in Tables 22–25). Although discontinuous series cannot be used generally in analyzing the characteristics of production trends, they satisfy in most instances the purpose of indicating the presence or absence of retardation and its approximate extent; so, by using these series, it has been possible to extend considerably the range of industrial observation. In order to insure comparability, the rates of retardation for the discontinuous series were determined by the same method as the rates for the continuous series, except that the preliminary 'decade rates' were determined for successive decades only. Various makeshifts were necessary, of course, in applying the method. Thus, in the case of data available for decennial dates only, geometric average annual rates of growth were calculated, and similarly, when data were given at quinquennial intervals. When data were available at more frequent intervals, Glover's 'mean value table' was used for annual, biennial, or triennial data, according to the fullness of the record. Whenever possible, corrections were made for the cyclical factor. The exact procedure differed from series to series and little would be gained by detailing what was done in each case. Once approximations to 'decade rates' were reached, exponential curves were fitted to them to yield measures of retardation. For the sources of the discontinuous series and brief descriptive notes, see Appendix B, II.

[11] See p. 262, note 11, concerning data on population, and this chapter, note 10, concerning method of measuring its retardation.

22–25, bear further witness to the magnitude of retardation in the industries covered. Of the 104 continuous series, 92 show abatement in their rates of growth; and of these 92

Table 19

FREQUENCY DISTRIBUTION OF AVERAGE RATES OF RETARDATION, FOR 142 PRODUCTION SERIES

Average rate of retardation (per cent per decade)	Number of series	Percentage of series
Below –6.2 *	1	0.7
–6.2 to –5.8	3	2.1
–5.7 to –5.3	..	...
–5.2 to –4.8	3	2.1
–4.7 to –4.3	..	...
–4.2 to –3.8	4	2.8
–3.7 to –3.3	6	4.2
–3.2 to –2.8	3	2.1
–2.7 to –2.3	11	7.7
–2.2 to –1.8	13	9.2
–1.7 to –1.3	16	11.3
–1.2 to –0.8	37	26.1
–0.7 to –0.3	25	17.6
–0.2 to 0.2	5	3.5
0.3 to 0.7	8	5.6
0.8 to 1.2	4	2.8
1.3 to 1.7	1	0.7
1.8 to 2.2	1	0.7
2.3 to 2.7	..	...
2.8 to 3.2	1	0.7
Total	142	100.0

* The item in this class is –11.5.

series, 9 have parabolic maxima in 1910 or earlier, 21 in 1920 or earlier, and 45 in 1930 or earlier. Of course, not all of these industries can be considered to have actually passed their apex, but it is equally likely that certain others have already done so.[12] Speaking very roughly, the industries

[12] Thus, the summits of aluminum and steel production are probably in the

which have experienced the most rapid rates of retardation are also in the most advanced stages of retardation. Thus, all but 4 of the 15 series having the highest rates of retardation have parabolic maxima before 1930, while all but 3 of the 15 series having the lowest rates of retardation have parabolic maxima some time after 1930. The measures of stage of retardation suggest that a considerable number of the industries surveyed have already passed their zenith. In this sense, they corroborate the evidence of the rates of retardation, which are generally of a rather high order of magnitude.

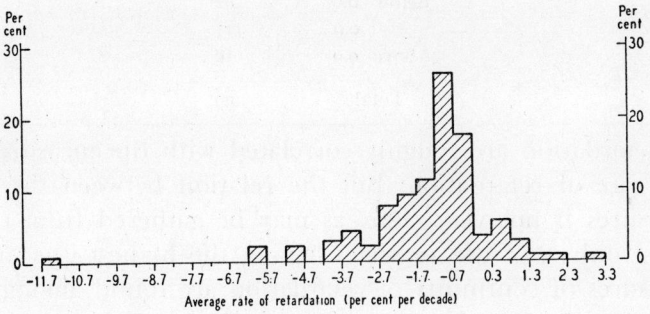

Chart 2

FREQUENCY DISTRIBUTION OF AVERAGE RATES OF RETARDATION OF 142 PRODUCTION SERIES

But though retardation has been a general phenomenon and its intensity fairly marked, its march has not been continuous, as Table 20 shows, in any of the industries surveyed. However, most of the measures of continuity of retardation are negative in sign; this indicates that retardation has dominated over acceleration in the decade-by-decade movements of the individual series, and lends support to the rates of retardation. As is to be expected, the measures of continuity

---

distant future; but the actual peaks of rail consumption and railway passenger traffic come earlier than their dates of parabolic maxima, and it is improbable that these peaks will be surpassed in the reckonable future.

Table 20
FREQUENCY DISTRIBUTION OF MEASURES OF CONTINUITY OF RETARDATION, FOR 'ALL' SERIES

Measure of continuity of retardation	Number of series
−.89 to −.70	3
−.69 to −.50	13
−.49 to −.30	18
−.29 to −.10	28
−.09 to .10	27
.11 to .30	4
.31 to .50	6
Total	99
Below 0.0	62
0.0	27
Above 0.0	10
Total	99

of retardation are roughly correlated with the measures of the rate of retardation. But the relation between the two measures is not very close, as may be gathered from these facts: only 3 of the 12 series having the highest (negative) measures of continuity of retardation are found among the 12 series having the highest rates of retardation, and the signs of the two measures are reversed in as many as 9 series. The inconstancy of retardation, registered in the measures of continuity of retardation, arises from the undulatory movements of production trends, which are analyzed in the next chapter.

The details of the statistical evidence of industrial retardation are in some ways more interesting than the general tenor of the evidence. Attention will be confined in the remaining portions of this section to the average rates of retardation, which may be significantly approached from the

Table 21
FREQUENCY DISTRIBUTIONS OF AVERAGE RATES OF RETARDATION, FOR 142 PRODUCTION SERIES, BY INDUSTRIAL GROUPS

Average rate of retardation (per cent per decade)	(1) Agriculture, fisheries, and forestry	(2) Mining	(3) Manufactures and construction	(4) Transportation and trade	(5) Nonagricultural industries (2)+(3)+(4)	(6) All industries (1)+(5)
Below −6.2 *	..	..	1	..	1	1
−6.2 to −5.8	1	1	1	..	2	3
−5.7 to −5.3	..	..	..	..	..	..
−5.2 to −4.8	..	1	2	..	3	3
−4.7 to −4.3	..	..	..	..	..	..
−4.2 to −3.8	..	1	3	..	4	4
−3.7 to −3.3	1	..	5	..	5	6
−3.2 to −2.8	1	..	2	..	2	3
−2.7 to −2.3	..	3	7	1	11	11
−2.2 to −1.8	2	3	8	..	11	13
−1.7 to −1.3	1	4	7	4	15	16
−1.2 to −0.8	12	4	19	2	25	37
−0.7 to −0.3	10	2	12	1	15	25
−0.2 to 0.2	2	1	1	1	3	5
0.3 to 0.7	1	..	5	2	7	8
0.8 to 1.2	1	..	2	1	3	4
1.3 to 1.7	..	..	1	..	1	1
1.8 to 2.2	..	..	..	1	1	1
2.3 to 2.7	..	..	..	..	..	..
2.8 to 3.2	..	..	1	..	1	1
Total	32	20	77	13	110	142

* The item in this class is −11.5.

standpoint of different resource groups of industries. The rates of retardation of the 142 production series earlier considered are distributed in Table 21 into four main divisions. It will be noticed that the series of organic materials (agriculture, fisheries, and forestry) do not exhibit, on the average, such extensive retardation as do the series in the other divisions, except transportation and trade. The rates of retardation of the organic materials are also more definitely concentrated within a narrow range than the rates of the series in any of the other divisions: approximately two-thirds of the organic materials series, but only about two-fifths of the series in each of the other industrial divisions, are included in the one per cent interval of greatest concentration on the several scales of retardation. The distinctive character of the frequency distribution of the rates of retardation of organic materials is revealed most sharply when it is contrasted with the corresponding distribution of the 'nonagricultural' group, which is a combination of the divisions of mining, manufactures and construction, and transportation and trade.

The rates of retardation of the individual series of organic raw materials and inorganic raw materials are stated respectively in Tables 22 and 23. The record of the minerals group is quite striking, as the production of each of the minerals has grown at a decrescent rate. Three series in the organic materials group evidence acceleration, but these series are of minor importance; and it is also of some interest that two of them—cod and mackerel tonnage, and whale tonnage—relate to decadent industries, their acceleration meaning a decline in the rate of decadence. The more important mineral and agricultural products generally have medial rates of retardation, though there are such conspicuous exceptions as petroleum and Portland cement. What is most significant now is that a tendency towards abatement in the rate of growth is evidenced almost without exception by the rather extensive production records of individual raw materials. This generalization may be safely extended to the class of individual raw materials, since a very large portion of the entire field of raw material production is covered by our statistics.

The rates of retardation of the series of manufactures are set forth in Table 24, the two construction series—building

Table 22
RETARDATION IN THE GROWTH OF INDUSTRIES: AGRICULTURE, FISHERIES, AND FORESTRY

Series	Period covered by series	Measures of retardation		
		Average rate (per cent per decade)	Continuity	Stage (years from 1930)
Raisins...............	1872–1929	−6.2	−.20	− 7
Beet sugar............	1870–1929	−3.4	−.40	14
Cane sugar...........	1870–1929	−2.8	−.40	−27
Molasses and sirup.....	1870–1929	−1.8	−.20	−19
*Hemp...............	1869–1929	−1.8	...	...
Cattle................	1880–1929	−1.7	−.25	− 6
Oats.................	1870–1930	−1.2	−.10	− 7
Buckwheat............	1870–1929	−1.1	.00	−26
Sheep................	1880–1929	−1.1	.00	− 4
*Broom corn..........	1879–1929	−1.1	...	...
Corn.................	1870–1929	−1.0	−.70	−14
Hay	1870–1930	−1.0	−.30	−10
*Honey...............	1869–1929	−1.0	...	...
Rye	1870–1929	−0.9	−.20	− 6
*Lumber..............	1869–1929	−0.9	...	...
*Sweet potatoes	1869–1930	−0.9	...	...
Cotton...............	1870–1929	−0.8	.00	2
Wool	1870–1929	−0.8	.20	−14
Potatoes..............	1870–1929	−0.7	−.40	− 4
Barley	1870–1929	−0.7	−.20	19
Flaxseed..............	1879–1929	−0.6	.00	11
*Maple sugar	1869–1930	−0.6	...	...
Wheat	1870–1930	−0.5	−.40	− 5
*Butter	1879–1929	−0.5	...	...
*Hops	1869–1929	−0.5	...	...
Hogs	1880–1929	−0.4	−.50	35
Rice	1870–1929	−0.4	−.40	93
Tobacco, raw	1870–1929	−0.3	−.30	36
Fish, total	1880–1929	−0.1	.50	143
Cod and mackerel	1870–1929	0.1	.00	...
*Beans, dry, edible	1879–1929	0.4	...	...
Whale	1870–1929	0.8	.00	...

*The data are discontinuous.

Table 23
RETARDATION IN THE GROWTH OF INDUSTRIES: MINING

Series	Period covered by series	Measures of retardation		
		Average rate (per cent per decade)	Continuity	Stage (years from 1930)
Portland cement.......	1880–1929	−5.9	−.50	3
Pyrites	1880–1929	−4.9	−.25	−14
Asphalt	1880–1929	−4.1	−.50	5
Phosphate rock........	1870–1929	−2.5	−.50	− 3
Fluorspar............	1880–1929	−2.3	.00	8
Sulphur	1880–1929	−2.3	.00	58
Copper	1870–1929	−2.2	−.60	3
Natural gas	1882–1929	−2.1	.00	13
Iron ore.............	1880–1929	−1.9	−.25	− 1
Zinc.................	1870–1929	−1.7	−.60	10
Bituminous coal	1870–1929	−1.6	−.40	3
Lead, domestic........	1870–1929	−1.6	.00	3
Coal, total...........	1870–1929	−1.4	−.60	2
Anthracite coal........	1870–1929	−1.4	−.40	−14
Cement, total	1880–1929	−1.3	.00	37
Silver	1870–1929	−1.1	−.20	−12
Salt..................	1880–1929	−1.0	.00	22
Gypsum.............	1880–1929	−0.9	−.25	57
Gold.................	1870–1929	−0.9	−.20	−26
Mercury.............	1870–1929	−0.5	.00	−63
Petroleum	1870–1929	−0.3	−.10	186
Non-Portland cements..	1880–1929	−0.2	−.25	−20

permits and rail consumption—being included along with the manufactures. The rates of retardation of the manufactures are even more variable than the rates of the minerals. The antipodal positions are occupied by two rather new industries, each of which has experienced remarkable expansion: aluminum production has the highest rate of retardation, and light petroleum distillates the highest rate of acceleration. The industries whose rates of growth have

Table 24
RETARDATION IN THE GROWTH OF INDUSTRIES: MANUFACTURES AND CONSTRUCTION

Series	Period covered by series	Measures of retardation		
		Average rate (per cent per decade)	Continuity	Stage (years from 1930)
Aluminum............	1883–1929	−11.5	−.43	− 6
*Wood pulp	1869–1929	− 5.9	...	...
*Paraffin oils	1879–1929	− 4.9	...	...
*Paraffin wax.........	1879–1929	− 4.8	...	...
Cottonseed oil........	1872–1929	− 3.8	−.60	−10
Cottonseed cake and meal...............	1872–1929	− 3.8	−.60	− 8
Sisal imports..........	1870–1929	− 3.8	−.20	−15
*Harrows, other than disk................	1869–1929	− 3.5	...	...
Steel.................	1870–1929	− 3.4	−.60	− 1
*Broad silks...........	1869–1929	− 3.4	...	...
*Shirts and drawers, knit	1869–1929	− 3.4	...	...
*Gloves and mittens, knit	1869–1929	− 3.3	...	...
Locomotives..........	1880–1929	− 3.1	.00	−28
*Plate glass, polished...	1879–1929	− 3.0	...	...
Roofing slate..........	1879–1929	− 2.7	−.25	−25
*Mowers..............	1869–1929	− 2.7	...	...
Antimonial lead	1871–1929	− 2.6	−.40	− 4
Canned tomatoes......	1885–1929	− 2.3	−.71	− 7
*Boards paper	1879–1929	− 2.3	...	...
*Fertilizers	1869–1929	− 2.3	...	...
*Shingles.............	1869–1929	− 2.3	...	...
Coke.................	1880–1929	− 2.2	−.25	− 1
*Newsprint and book paper...............	1879–1929	− 2.1	...	...
Superphosphate	1870–1929	− 2.0	−.40	3
*Condensed and evaporated milk	1879–1929	− 2.0	...	...
*Sulphuric acid	1879–1929	− 2.0	...	...
*Structural shapes	1879–1929	− 1.9	...	...
Minor fiber imports....	1870–1929	− 1.8	.00	−15
Lead, total	1870–1929	− 1.8	.00	1
Canned corn..........	1885–1929	− 1.8	.29	4

Table 24 (cont.)
RETARDATION IN THE GROWTH OF INDUSTRIES: MANUFACTURES AND CONSTRUCTION

Series	Period covered by series	Measures of retardation		
		Average rate (per cent per decade)	Continuity	Stage (years from 1930)
Silver consumption	1880–1929	− 1.7	−.25	3
Jute imports	1870–1929	− 1.7	−.20	−23
Fermented liquors	1870–1918	− 1.5	−.25	− 8
Copper consumption ...	1883–1929	− 1.4	.14	19
*Common brick	1869–1929	− 1.4	...	...
Cigars	1880–1929	− 1.3	−.37	−14
*Hay rakes	1869–1929	− 1.3	...	...
Pig iron	1870–1929	− 1.2	−.30	13
*Laths	1869–1929	− 1.2	...	...
*Walking plows	1869–1929	− 1.2	...	...
Tobacco and snuff.....	1871–1929	− 1.1	−.40	− 7
Tin imports...........	1870–1929	− 1.1	−.20	10
White lead............	1884–1929	− 1.1	−.14	− 4
Vessels	1870–1929	− 1.1	.00	−32
*Zinc oxide...........	1880–1929	− 1.1	...	...
Zinc consumption	1873–1929	− 1.0	−.56	35
Rails.................	1870–1929	− 1.0	−.20	− 7
*Hosiery	1869–1929	− 1.0	...	...
Nails.................	1872–1929	− 0.9	−.60	− 3
Building permits.......	1874–1929	− 0.9	−.33	24
*Lumber consumption .	1869–1929	− 0.9	...	...
*Window glass	1879–1929	− 0.9	...	...
Tin-plate consumption .	1871–1929	− 0.8	.00	38
Cocoa imports	1870–1929	− 0.8	.00	75
Wool consumption	1870–1930	− 0.8	.40	− 9
*Wrapping paper......	1879–1929	− 0.8	...	...
Gold consumption	1880–1929	− 0.7	−.50	35
Rolled iron and steel ...	1885–1929	− 0.7	−.14	38
Flour	1880–1929	− 0.7	.00	− 4
Silk imports, raw	1870–1929	− 0.7	.00	99
Cotton consumption ...	1870–1929	− 0.6	−.20	28
*Grain drills	1869–1929	− 0.6	...	...
Coffee imports	1870–1929	− 0.5	−.20	40
Manila hemp imports ..	1870–1929	− 0.5	.00	4
*Boots and shoes	1869–1929	− 0.5	...	...
*Cotton, woven goods..	1879–1929	− 0.4	...	...
Raw sugar consumption	1870–1930	− 0.3	.40	54

Table 24 (cont.)
RETARDATION IN THE GROWTH OF INDUSTRIES: MANUFACTURES AND CONSTRUCTION

Series	Period covered by series	Measures of retardation		
		Average rate (per cent per decade)	Continuity	Stage (years from 1930)
Lead consumption	1870–1929	− 0.3	.40	163
*Fine paper	1879–1929	− 0.3	...	...
Tobacco consumption	1880–1929	− 0.2	−.50	97
Rail consumption	1870–1929	− 0.2	.00	46
Cigarettes	1880–1929	0.3	−.25	...
Flaxseed consumption	1879–1929	0.3	.00	...
*Face brick	1879–1929	0.5	...	...
Distilled spirits	1870–1918	0.6	.00	...
Silk imports, unmanufactured	1883–1929	0.6	.43	...
*Burning oils	1879–1929	0.8	...	...
*Hay loaders	1879–1929	1.0	...	...
Rubber imports	1870–1929	1.6	.20	...
*Light petroleum distillates	1879–1929	3.1	...	...

*The data are discontinuous.

declined most rapidly are, in many instances, rather specific manufactures. Series representative of broad classes of manufacture—for example, zinc consumption, copper consumption, lead consumption, tin imports, cotton consumption, tobacco consumption, and rolled iron and steel—are not found among those with extreme rates of retardation. There is some tendency for the rates of retardation of industries producing consumers' goods to cluster at the bottom of the list, but there is not nearly the same tendency for the rates of retardation of producers' goods series to cluster in the upper portion of the list. Only nine series of manufactures evidence accelerated growth; but the present cases are found among progressive industries, some of which are also of great importance. While several[13] of these instances of acceleration are traceable to economic causes of profound importance, others [14] are of doubtful reliability.

Certainly, most of our series of manufactures disclose declining rates of growth. But the important question is whether or not it is proper to extend this generalization for our series to the class of individual manufactures. According to our estimate, the coverage of the continuous series of manufactures amounts to only about 22 per cent of the output of all manufactures in 1925; and even with the industrial coverage of the discontinuous series added, the representation of manufactures is only about 32 per cent.[15] These figures, however, are somewhat misleading; for they ignore the considerable indirect representation of the series, understate the coverage for early years, and are not restricted to that portion of the production area which is common to the entire period surveyed.[16] The series which have been analyzed relate to widely varying branches of manufacture, some refer to groups of commodities and others to fairly specific products, some to commodities of large industrial importance and others to products of very minor consequence: the extent and the variety of the series create a strong presumption that a generalization holding for them will hold for individual manufactures as a class.

The measures of retardation for such series as are indicative of transportation and trade are assembled in Table 25. As five of the thirteen series in this group show acceleration, it might possibly appear that retardation has been less general in this industrial division than in the others. However,

[13] Cigarettes, face brick, burning oils, rubber imports, and light petroleum distillates; see pp. 154–5.
[14] See Appendix C, II.
[15] For the estimates of the coverage of the continuous series, see pp. 18–20. The coverage of the discontinuous series has been estimated by the same method as the coverage of the continuous series.
[16] In a sense, the really important comparison is between the industries

Table 25
RETARDATION IN THE GROWTH OF INDUSTRIES: TRANSPORTATION AND TRADE

Series	Period covered by series	Measures of retardation		
		Average rate (per cent per decade)	Continuity	Stage (years from 1930)
S. S. Marie canals traffic	1870–1929	−2.7	−.40	0
Railway ton-miles	1870–1929	−1.4	−.40	12
Railway freight	1882–1929	−1.4	.00	5
Railway passenger-miles	1882–1929	−1.3	−.75	−1
Agricultural exports	1870–1929	−1.3	.00	−16
Postal money orders	1870–1929	−1.2	−.60	33
*Snyder's index of trade	1870–1930	−0.8	...	...
Deflated clearings	1870–1929	−0.3	−.20	96
Tonnage entered and cleared	1870–1929	0.1	.00	...
Postage stamps	1870–1929	0.3	−.10	...
Coastal trade	1870–1929	0.4	.00	...
N. Y. canals traffic	1870–1929	0.8	.00	...
Shares traded	1875–1929	2.2	.33	...

*The data are discontinuous.

the acceleration is limited to series which are statistically defective,[17] or of minor industrial importance, or both. One of the minor series—New York canals traffic—is of special interest because it provides an additional instance of a de-

---

covered and those which could have been covered. It would be extremely difficult to estimate this ratio; but it is obvious that the ratio must be considerably higher than the estimate of the industrial coverage of our series. Then again, certain industries whose statistical (and occasionally, economic) history does not go back to 1885—oleomargarine, electricity, railway passenger and freight cars, motor vehicles, rayon, and a few others—also disclose declining rates of growth. But the statistical records of some of these industries are too short to yield reliable results: short series for new industries, even when they extend back to the very nascence of the industries, may have a retardation which is more arithmetic than economic in significance (see p. 120); while short series for old industries may reflect little more than a dominant phase of their trend-cycles (see Ch. V).

[17] See Appendix C, II.

clining industry showing algebraically a rising rate of growth. It is probably true that most of the individual industries performing transport or trade functions have grown at a decrescent rate, but such a generalization cannot confidently be drawn from the series covered.

This much, then, can be said in summary about the industrial incidence of retardation during the period since 1870 or so. Retardation has taken place in a preponderant number of the industries covered in our survey;[18] its extent in the individual industries has been on the whole rather high; but its march has not been continuous, because of the 'interference' of cycles in the secular trends with the downward drift of the rates of growth. There is considerable evi-

[18] It has already been pointed out that several accelerative series are defective from the standpoint of the use to which they are put in this chapter (some evidence is presented in Appendix C, II), and that certain other accelerative series express the influence of profound economic causes (see pp. 153–5). All the same, the question is of some interest whether the seventeen series (among the 147 distributed through Tables 22–25) showing acceleration would continue to do so if the period of observation were extended.

It is possible to carry back the statistical records of only eight of the accelerative series: New York canals traffic, tonnage entered and cleared, coastal trade, postage stamps, cod and mackerel tonnage, whale tonnage, production of dry beans, and cigarette production. (The series of cigarette production used in this study begins in 1880; but estimates of cigarette production, made by W. W. Young, *The Story of the Cigarette*, Appleton, 1916, p. 115, on the basis of tax receipts, are available for 1869–79. The series 'dry beans' used in this study begins in 1879; but estimates for census years back to 1849 have been made by Warren and Pearson, *The Physical Volume of Production in the United States*, Cornell University Agricultural Experiment Station, Memoir 144, p. 40. Though the estimates for these two series are too uncertain to warrant general use, they are adequate for the purpose of a splicing whose aim is to indicate whether or not retardation has been present. All the other series which are extended are carried back of 1870, their initial date in this work. Data for distilled spirits can also be carried back, but only to 1863; this is too small an extension to be worth making.)

So far as New York canals traffic, the cod and mackerel fisheries, and the whale 'fishery' are concerned, it is altogether superfluous to resort to quantitative measurements. The summit of these industries has long been passed: the peak of New York canals traffic was reached around 1870, in the mackerel fishery in the early 'eighties, probably somewhat earlier in the cod fishery, and about 1850 in the whale 'fishery'. It goes without saying that if the record of

dence that most of the individual industries in agriculture, mining, and manufacture have experienced abatement in their rates of growth. In all likelihood, this is true as well of the individual branches of forestry, the fisheries, construction, transportation, and trade. Little is known about other industrial divisions, such as banking, and the various professional and personal services, except that these fields of productive endeavor have greatly expanded. No attempt has been made to determine whether or not the individual branches of these service industries have grown at declining rates, as practically no statistics of their production are available, except the very indirect and not altogether comparable data contained in the federal censuses of occupations.[19]

these industries were carried back of the dates of their highest development, very considerable retardation in their growth would become evident. The five remaining series—tonnage entered and cleared, coastal trade, postage stamps, dry beans, and cigarettes—represent progressive industrial activities. Four of these series evidence a declining rate of growth, when their full statistical history is analyzed: for the period 1869–1929, 'cigarettes' show a rate of retardation of –3.6 per cent (see p. 155); for 1852–1929, 'postage stamps', –1.0 per cent; for 1821–1929, 'tonnage entered and cleared', –0.2 per cent; and for 1790–1929, 'coastal trade', –0.3 per cent. The series 'dry beans' shows a rate of acceleration of 0.4 per cent for 1879–1929, but only 0.1 per cent for 1849–1929. There are, then, some statistical indications that when the period under observation is extended, the various instances of acceleration reduce to retardation. Incidentally, the extensions show how careful one must be in interpreting the rates of retardation, which are in the nature of averages for specific time intervals.

It is not proper to carry back the statistical records of only those industries which evidence acceleration. Obviously enough, if the records of the industries showing retardation were also carried back, it might develop that some of them show acceleration for the longer period. In order to test for this possibility, the statistics of lead, copper, zinc, pig iron, petroleum, rails, vessels, total coal, railway ton-miles, and cotton consumption were extended back of 1870 (there are very few other series which go back of 1870). Each of these series discloses a declining rate of growth, when the entire period of its statistical history is investigated.

[19] Such data do show retardation; see Hurlin and Givens, cited above, pp. 271–304. For a further statistical analysis of retardation in individual industries, see pp. 163–9. Concerning the problem of retardation in the growth of total production, see Ch. VI, sec. III.

III. THE EXPLANATION OF INDUSTRIAL RETARDATION

The foregoing statistical conclusions accord nicely with common intuitions about the course of industrial development. That industries rise and decline is a matter of familiar knowledge. Retardation in the growth of individual industries is to be expected in a world of scarce resources: not only is it ordinarily more difficult to double a large output of some commodity than a small one, but an increase in production at a uniform or increasing rate for a long period implies an aggregate prodigious beyond comprehension. In one way at least, the generalization of industrial retardation is little short of an arithmetic truism: nothing can compare with the percentage rate of growth of the initial output of an industry.[20]

1. Retardation as Characteristic of a Progressive Economy

We must seek, however, a more reasoned view of the causes of industrial retardation. Before attempting a detailed analysis, it is desirable to approach the problem from an a priori standpoint. Let us assume, then, that the total production of some economy is increasing at a uniform percentage rate over a period of sizable duration. Further, let us assume explicitly that this economy possesses certain progressive characteristics—many new industries are being started while some old industries are disappearing, labor-saving devices are being introduced, various economies are being effected in the utilization of raw materials, and so on. Since the ratio of manufactured output per unit of raw material consumed will be increasing, the aggregate output of raw materials

[20] The statistical records of several industries start almost at the stage of their commercial inception. If this were true of the bulk of the series analyzed, and if the retardation were confined to the early stage of development, the problem of retardation in industrial growth would be simple and unimportant.

will increase at a lower percentage rate than total production; but within the limits of this restriction, the aggregate output of raw materials may grow at a declining, constant, or increasing percentage rate. If the aggregate output of raw materials grow at a declining rate, the aggregate output of manufactures will also grow at a declining rate throughout, or else will at first grow at an increasing rate and later at a declining rate; while if the aggregate output of raw materials grow at a constant or increasing rate, the aggregate output of manufactures will grow throughout at a declining rate. If the aggregate output of raw materials increase at a declining rate, the rates of growth of individual raw materials will tend to decline more rapidly, even when their number remains fixed;[21] and they are virtually certain to decline more rapidly when their number increases, which is our original assumption. Similarly, if the aggregate output of raw materials increase at a constant rate, the tendency will be for the rates of growth of individual raw materials to decline. Finally, even if the aggregate output of raw materials increase at an increasing rate, the tendency will still be for the rates of growth of individual raw materials to decline,—provided there is a fair degree of divergence between the rates of growth of the raw materials, and their number increases at all rapidly. Similar relations hold between the rate of growth of the aggregate of manufactures and the rates of growth of individual manufactures. It follows, therefore, that the host of individual industries will grow at a declining rate, some of them declining absolutely. Some industries may, indeed, grow at an increasing rate for a considerable period, but they will form exceptions to the general rule. Within the limits of the assumptions which have been made, retardation in the growth of the generality

[21] See pp. 273–8.

of individual industries is an essential characteristic of a progressive industrial system.

It is important to observe that these assumptions hold with a reasonable degree of accuracy for the American economy during the period under survey. Industrial diversification and conservation in the use of raw materials are outstanding among the consequences of the technical progress characteristic of this period. The assumption of a uniform rate of growth probably does not conform exactly to what has actually happened, but it is practically certain that total production has not grown at a rapidly increasing rate, and only under the last condition, though not necessarily even then, would the above analysis be invalid.[22] It appears, then, that retardation in the growth of individual industries is linked to the sort of economic progress which the United States has experienced since the Civil War. And this view of retardation lends added significance to the statistical evidence already presented. It will be noticed that the frequency distribution of the rates of retardation (Chart 2) is skewed 'negatively', contrasting with the distributions of average rates of growth, presented in the preceding chapter (Chart 1), which are skewed 'positively'. Apparently, just as the forces making for growth of individual industries have dominated in the American system over the forces making for decline, so have the forces making for retardation in the growth of individual industries dominated in the system over the forces making for acceleration.[23]

The main thesis to be supported in the following pages is that retardation in the growth of individual industries is one of the expressions of the progressiveness of American industry.[24] With this end in view, we shall analyze succes-

[22] See Ch. VI, sec. III.
[23] See pp. 65–6.
[24] The suggestion may be ventured (see, however, p. 66, note 14) that increasing rates of growth (speaking algebraically) of individual industries are

sively the forces making for retardation which have been operative in the domestic markets for goods, the more fundamental forces which have been operative in the workshops of our national economy, the forces deriving from the impact of the outside economy, and the process whereby the various forces promoting retardation tend to cumulate in strength through their indirect effects. Next, we shall analyze the influence of structural changes on rates of industrial growth, and the forces making for different types of drift in the rates of growth of decadent industries. Finally, we shall attempt to interpret in general terms the variations in the actual rates of retardation of our statistical series.

2. Forces Operating in the Markets for Goods

In tracing the forces making for retardation which have been at work in the markets for goods, the major factors to be considered are technical progress, change in industrial organization, and population growth. We may start with population growth, probably the least important of these factors.

It is a familiar fact that the population of this country increased at a fairly uniform rate from about 1790 to 1860, but at a declining rate since then. In the current literature on production trends, reference is frequently made to the decrescent rate of population growth; and at times it is even argued that the declining rates of growth of various individual industries merely reflect the trend of population. This common theory doubtless contains an important element of truth; but it can scarcely be claimed with any seriousness that the trend of population can alone, or even largely, explain the abatement in the rates of growth of any

---

probably characteristic of the late stage of a retrogressive economy. This, at any rate, is suggested by an analysis of retrogressive industries (see pp. 160–2). The point, of course, is mainly of academic interest.

considerable number of individual industries. If that were true, the trends of production of individual industries would resemble closely the trend of population. But as a matter of fact, the primary trends of industries, as expressed in their rates of growth and rates of retardation, differ very considerably among themselves, and few are of the same magnitude as population. Such statistics as are available suggest that most commodities have definite trends both in their consumption per capita and in their net foreign trade per capita.

However, any general influence of population growth on the trends of individual industries is obscured when they are considered separately, since the trends of individual industries reflect chiefly the variety of special influences impinging on them. It appears that the trend of the aggregate production of at least one important group of products, consumers' staples, has been dominated by the trend of population. All the indexes of production of principal crops trace out trends which resemble closely, especially since 1880, the trend of population, even though the trends of most of the individual crops do not. Such statistics on consumption as are available indicate that, while the dietary of the American population has changed considerably during the past few decades, the total food consumption [25] has varied rather closely with the increase of numbers. At most, a slight decline in the per-capita consumption of foodstuffs may have taken place.

The apparent domination of the trend of aggregate production of foodstuffs by the trend of population cannot,

[25] See "The Decline in Per Capita Consumption of Flour in the United States" (Food Research Institute, *Wheat Studies*, Vol. II, No. 8, July, 1926); and O. E. Baker, "The Trend of Agricultural Production in North America and Its Relation to Europe and Asia" (contained in *Population*, giving the Lectures in 1929 on the Harris Foundation; University of Chicago Press, 1930), pp. 222–37.

however, be interpreted to mean that the latter has been an independent factor which has generated, so to speak, the former. The relation of population to production is one of interdependence. On the one hand, ignoring foreign trade, the size of population determines at any one time the aggregate production of consumers' staples. Even over a period of fair duration, the increase in the production of consumers' staples cannot be very different from the increase in population, provided the level of well-being in the economy is considerably above bare subsistence; for physiological laws set limits to the consumption of foodstuffs. In this sense, the declining rate of increase of population may be considered an 'ultimate' cause of the retardation which has taken place in the growth of production of foodstuffs. However, the size of population is itself closely related to the increase of national production. Our increasing material prosperity has tended to reduce the death rate, as it has promoted sanitation, medical knowledge, and medical care. The advance in material well-being has influenced also the trend of birth rates: it has improved the possibilities of increased parenthood and so has released forces working in that direction, but it has also made people more mindful of their improved standard of living and so has tended to promote limitation of the size of families (the indications are that the strength of the first influence has been declining and that of the second increasing). Finally, the advance in material prosperity has tended to stimulate migration: until very recent years, when rigid immigration bars were set up, the flow of migrants to this country varied directly, speaking broadly, with the state of national prosperity. Thus, the various factors back of the trend of population have been linked with the progress of our national industry, the decline in the rate of population growth being as deeply enmeshed in the industrial progress of the nation as the decline in the rates of growth of individual industries. For this reason, the fact that population has been growing at a declining rate is only of small help in explaining industrial retardation.

A more important factor is technical progress which has been incessantly operative in the American economy, releasing influences which have tended powerfully to retard the growth of individual industries. One of the ways in which technical progress has expressed itself is in the introduction of new goods. Our rising standards of living and increasing education have served as stimuli to industrial innovations, which have been carried forward rapidly by technical ingenuity, the advancing state of the arts, and venturesome business enterprise. Basic wants for food, clothing, transport, and recreation have come to be satisfied through an increasing number of media. The diversification of production has been most conspicuous in the case of elaborative manufactures, especially in the chemical industries; [26] but diversification has also extended to basic materials—beet sugar, bauxite, and natural gas are relatively new industries in this country. The new products have acted as substitutes for old, though the replacement of the latter has rarely been complete. With the increase of diversification, interindustrial competition has become more intense.[27] As every new product involves an absolute or relative shift of purchasing power from an old product, the increase in the number of goods has

[26] See *Chemical and Metallurgical Engineering*, January, 1931. This issue treats exhaustively of the problems of intercommodity and interprocess competition in the chemical industries.

[27] Of course, there are certain things that interindustrial competition, increasingly fostered by the growing variety of production, does not mean. For one, competition among goods is general and is not limited to the things which are directly substitutive—in the sense that they satisfy approximately the same specific want. Secondly, it is rarely true that an increasing number of directly competing goods have to share a fixed market or one growing at some natural rate.

RETARDATION IN GROWTH 127

tended to retard the growth in the production of old goods.[28]

The process whereby a new product diverts purchasing power to itself is generally as follows. A potential market of some size awaits almost every plausible commodity at its inception: there are always some people who clamor for novelties and are eager to seize any new opportunity to shift their outlays; and there are also others who habitually approach new commodities in a cautious but enterprisingly experimental spirit. So, new commodities which prove technically superior or satisfy important psychological wants are ready to march forward to success. As their production advances, they stimulate the industries with which they are technically (sequentially and complementarily) connected, while they encumber the industries to which they are competitively related. But the new industries themselves soon encounter resistance to a continuation of their earlier rates of development; for the custom of the more conservative members of the community, tied by inveterate practice or sentiment to old products, is gained only with increasing difficulty. Resistance from this side becomes greater with every fresh advance, except when a commodity becomes an object of competitive ostentation; though this too is self-limiting, for the wider the use of a commodity, the less does its possession become a mark of peculiar prestige. In part, the expanding production tends to overcome consumer resistance, for production on a quantity basis is conducive to various economies and improvements, which are reflected in

[28] The actual curve traced out by the production of any given industry is the net resultant of certain factors making for growth in production and others making for decline. Irrespective of the slope of the curve at any date, if a new force making for growth is added in the next date to the numerous forces impinging on the industry at the first date, the individual effect of this force will be to make for an increase in the rate of increase of the curve (that is, acceleration); and if the added force makes for decline, its individual effect will be to make for a decline in the rate of increase of the curve (that is, retardation).

falling prices. But, in the meantime, new commodities emerge: these come to exercise a restrictive influence on those which were only recently new: and the restrictive influence felt in any one industry is transmitted to the various industries which are technically related to it.

Industrial diversification has expressed itself not only in the production of an increasing number of commodities, but also in the production of given commodities by an increasing number of technical processes. Thus, wood pulp, a relatively recent product, is now the most important material in paper manufacture; aluminum-alloys have recently been added to the long list of structural materials; from the cottonseed now come many products obtained also in other ways; and the progress of chemistry has yielded synthetic camphor, indigo, resins, and still other synthetic products. An outstanding consequence of our technical progress is that given raw materials are being put to an increasing variety of uses. With the multiplication of technical methods for achieving given ends, industrial competition has tended to become intensified; for different technical methods generally involve the use of different materials, or the same materials in different proportions. As old commodities have been put to new uses, the rate of growth in the production of these commodities has tended to increase; but at the same time, the rate of growth in the production of the replaced commodities has tended to decline.

Practically every new commodity involves the use of new industrial equipment; and every substantial revision of industrial technique involves either a change in industrial equipment or the initial introduction of labor-saving devices. The substitution of machinery for hand-labor has tended to accelerate the progress of the machine-building, metal, and fuel industries; but labor-saving devices have often resulted in a saving of space, and so have tended to check the development of certain of the industries furnishing materials. Labor-saving devices and changes in the forms of industrial equipment have frequently made possible economies in the use of materials, and in this way have released forces making for retardation. Though various changes in the forms of industrial equipment have tended to stimulate the development of some industries, they have tended at the same time to restrict the development of others. For example, the increasing use of steel instead of wood in the construction of vessels has tended to retard the growth of the lumber industry. The increasing use of Diesel engines instead of steam engines has tended to retard the growth of the coal industry. The increasing replacement of farm work animals by automobiles and tractors has resulted in a rapid retardation in the production of horses and mules, has tended to retard the lumber industry, and has released millions of acres of crop land—which means that the increasing mechanization of agriculture has contributed to the retarded growth of certain of its branches, especially the production of oats and hay.[29]

Many revisions of technical processes are inspired primarily by the aim of, or incidentally result in, industrial conservation—using this term to indicate increased yield of raw materials in finished products, reclamation of used products, and recovery of waste products. The economic consequences of industrial conservation are similar, irrespective of whether they originate in new techniques for achieving given ends, in mechanical improvements of existing techniques, or in managerial improvements in the use of existing techniques.

[29] It has been estimated that 25 million acres of crop land were released between 1918 and 1930 on account of the automobile and tractor; this constitutes about 30 per cent of the acreage required for the sustenance of work animals at the earlier date. See O. E. Baker, "The Outlook for Land Utilization in the United States," *Journal of Farm Economics*, April, 1931, p. 214; and the same author's "The Trend of Agricultural Production," cited above, pp. 251–2.

When the ratio of manufactured output per unit of raw material consumed rises, or when used products are reclaimed, the demand for raw materials tends to decline; important forces are therefore released which make for retardation in the development of the industries producing raw materials. When the recovery of waste products takes the form of increased production of some commodity previously made, the aggregate output of that commodity tends to be accelerated; but its production by the older processes tends to be retarded, and this comes to be reflected in the production of the goods on which the older processes rest. When waste products are recovered and transformed into entirely new commodities,—the cottonseed products industry is rich in illustrations,—forces are set in motion which make for industrial retardation through the agencies of competition and substitution; this point has already been discussed and need not be further considered.

Industrial conservation has made tremendous headway in the United States. More effective utilization of raw materials has been rather general in industry. In animal husbandry, feeds have come to be converted with increasing efficiency into meat and milk; [30] and these economies have exercised a retarding influence on the production of feed crops and the various manufactured feeds. In the field of manufactures, improving ratios of output per unit of raw material used have been quite common: familiar examples are provided by the beet sugar, coke, head rice, and cottonseed industries. But perhaps the most remarkable instances of economies in the utilization of materials are afforded by the fuels, and some data are useful for illustrative purposes. In electric public utility power plants, 6.4 pounds of coal (or coal equivalent) were used in 1902 per kilowatt-hour generated, but only 1.68 pounds in 1929. In 1916, locomotives on Class

[30] See *ibid.*, pp. 261–6.

I steam railroads consumed 169 pounds of coal (or coal equivalent) per 1,000 gross ton-miles of freight service, and 18.5 pounds of coal per passenger-train car-mile; but in 1929 the corresponding consumption per unit of freight service was only 125 pounds, and per unit of passenger service 14.9 pounds. In the petroleum refining industry, the treatment of one barrel of crude oil required 860,000 B.t.u. in 1909, and 643,000 in 1928. In the cement industry, the consumption of coal (or coal equivalent) per barrel of output was 200 pounds in 1909, but only 158 pounds in 1928. In the iron and steel industry, 2.01 tons of coal (or coal equivalent) were used per ton of product in 1904, but only 1.41 tons in 1927. It has been estimated that the energy consumption per unit of output in the combined manufacturing and railway transportation industries declined as much as 33 per cent between 1909 and 1929.[31] It need hardly be stated that the remarkable advances in fuel efficiency have tended to retard the growth of the fuel industries, especially coal. Every improvement in industrial technique making possible a more effective utilization of a raw material has served to retard the growth in the production of that material.

The reclamation of used products has been practically as general as increasing yield of materials in finished products. The volume of 'secondary' production of many commodities has grown more rapidly than the volume of their 'primary' production. A few examples will indicate the increasing importance of 'secondary' production. Waste paper constituted in 1889 only 9 per cent of the weight of raw materials consumed in paper manufacture, but as much as 28 per cent in 1919, and 31 per cent in 1929. In 1909 the tonnage of scrap iron and steel consumed by steel works and rolling

---

[31] The figures are taken from F. G. Tryon and H. O. Rogers, "Statistical Studies of Progress in Fuel Efficiency," *Transactions of Second World Power Conference*, Berlin, 1930, Vol. VI; and from *Mineral Resources*, 1930, Part II, pp. 678–81.

mills was 52 per cent of the tonnage of pig iron consumed; the percentage rose to 61 in 1914, 67 in 1919, and 85 in 1929.[32] Between 1907 and 1929, refined lead produced from domestic ore increased at an average rate of 3.0 per cent per year, while secondary lead production increased at a rate of 11.0 per cent. During the same period, the smelter production of primary zinc increased at a rate of 3.7 per cent per year, but secondary zinc at a rate of 6.1 per cent; the smelter output of copper from domestic ore increased at a rate of 2.5 per cent, but secondary copper at a rate of 7.5 per cent. Between 1913 and 1929, the production of primary aluminum increased at a rate of 6.0 per cent, but secondary aluminum at a rate of 13.5 per cent.[33] Obviously enough, the relatively more rapid development of secondary than of virgin production in a number of industries has tended to retard the growth of the latter. Industrial reuse, then, has been an important factor in the declining rate of progress of many industries.

Technical progress—that is, mechanical innovations and betterments, and managerial improvements—has expressed itself in changes in the content and methods of production; and these changes have worked potently towards inducing retardation in the growth of individual industries. Along with the technical changes have gone changes in industrial organization, which have released myriad, though less powerful, influences making for retardation. An industry's organization comprises the geographic distribution of its producing units, their scale of operation, their interrelations of

[32] The above figures are based on data in the *Census of Manufactures*.

[33] In 1929 the ratio of secondary to primary output was .29 for zinc, .46 for copper, .40 for lead, and .43 for aluminum. While the figures of primary output entering into these ratios are for the smelter or refined products derived from both domestic and foreign ores, the trend computations (stated in the text) for primary copper and lead do not include metal of foreign origin. The sources of the data on primary production are stated in Appendix B, I; the data on secondary production are from *Mineral Resources*.

ownership and control, and their relation to the state. To the extent that industries have been relocated closer to the source of their raw materials, checks have become operative on the growth of transportation, and these have been transmitted to the metal, fuel, and allied industries. Similar consequences have ensued from horizontal combinations of the establishments of given industries. When the combination movement has taken the form of vertical integration, checks have become operative on the growth of trading. Insofar as enterprises have grown in size as a result of natural development, the consequences have frequently been the same as those arising from combination.[34] Industries founding trade associations have frequently been able to invade the markets and check the growth of competing industries functioning under a 'backward' form of organization. Finally, changes in the relation of given industries to the state have often released forces making for retardation.[35] These various types of change in industrial organization have operated incessantly during the period considered, and their influence on the rates of growth of individual industries has been considerable.

3. Forces Operating in the Workshops of the Economy

The introduction of new commodities, changes in the

---

[34] Changes in the scale of operation of the producing units of an industry, or in the ownership and control interrelations of these units, often lead to technical betterments; this factor, irrespective of its origin, has already been discussed.

[35] Of course, governmental action may tend to accelerate as well as retard the growth of given industries. In modern times the government has played a less obtrusive role in industrial affairs than formerly; but with the development of a philosophy of 'social control', the trend is now changing. The Prohibition Amendment is reminiscent of the general proscriptions of important industries practiced several centuries ago in various European countries. More frequently the government influences industrial trends by less drastic tools. The customary weapons are taxes, regulation of working conditions, regulation of business practices, and so on.

technical processes of making old commodities, and changes in industrial organization do not suffice to explain the generality of industrial retardation. For, if technical progress and change in industrial organization have released powerful influences making for retardation in the growth of some industries, they have at the same time released powerful influences making for acceleration in others. It remains to establish why the forces making for retardation have dominated in the generality of cases over the forces making for acceleration. To do this we must turn to the fundamental forces operating in the workshops of the economy. In the scarcity of productive resources we have a clue not only to the forces making for retardation operative in the workshops of the economy, but also to those operative in the markets for goods, for the latter originate largely in the necessity to conserve resources.

The introduction of new industries has tended to retard the development of old industries through the channels of competition for the factors of production, as well as through the channel of competition for custom. The flow of capital into new industries means an absolute or else a relative diversion of capital from other industries. Many new industries, a case in point is the airplane industry,[36] acquire abundant quantities of capital within a short period of their inception. The ability of a new industry to attract capital rests in large part on the expectation, at times actually realized as in the automobile and rayon industries,[37] that prodigious profits are to be made. A new industry may also divert capital to itself by promising stable rather than high

[36] See M. W. Watkins, "The Aviation Industry," *Journal of Political Economy*, February, 1931, pp. 57–60.
[37] See R. C. Epstein, *The Automobile Industry* (A. W. Shaw, 1928), Ch. IX; L. H. Seltzer, *A Financial History of the American Automobile Industry* (Houghton Mifflin, 1928); and M. H. Avram, *The Rayon Industry* (2d ed., London, 1930), Ch. V.

profits. For instance, the founding of the cotton manufacture in New Bedford created a safer outlet for investment funds than was provided by whaling and therefore led some of the wealthy citizens of the town to shift their funds from whaling.[38] The command by new industries over capital is not limited to the free capital (money) that they are able to attract; by bidding higher for the services of existing capital instruments, they are able to divert the uses of these instruments to themselves and in this way to acquire, in effect, command over the capital which these uses represent. The automobile industry furnishes a notable instance of a new industry which depended largely during its period of infancy on the capital facilities of other industries.[39] What is now chiefly important, however, is the fact and not the process of capital diversion. As capital flows into new industries, the quantity available for the old industries tends to be reduced, and this exercises a restrictive influence on their capacity for expansion. At the same time, the increase in the capital resources of the new industries enlarges the scale of their operations, lowers costs, and thereby strengthens their competitive power in the markets for intermediate and final goods.

One of the outlets of free capital is the labor market. In order to attract labor, new industries often have to outbid the older industries.[40] Thus, by offering high wages, the air-

[38] W. S. Tower, *A History of the American Whale Fishery* (Publications of the University of Pennsylvania, Series in Political Economy and Public Law, No. 20), pp. 75–6.

[39] The early automobile manufacturers did little more than assemble the parts furnished by wood- and metal-working enterprises, the 'bodies' furnished by carriage-makers, and so on. See Seltzer, *Financial History*, cited above, especially Ch. VI; also, his "The Mobility of Capital," *Quarterly Journal of Economics*, May, 1932.

[40] New units of established industries also tend to bid higher for labor than old units. It is quite probable that the shift of labor from old to new industries and from old to new concerns within given industries has been important among the mechanisms through which a rise in the general level of wages

plane industry has been able to draw on the working forces of the automobile and furniture trades.[41] A more spectacular instance of diversion through the lure of high rewards is provided by the motion picture industry, whose personnel has been recruited in large part from the legitimate theatre. In order to attract a labor force, a new industry need not always offer a higher remuneration per unit of labor than the going rate for similar grades of work. It may offer instead earnings which are low on the average, but prodigious in exceptional cases. Thus, when gold was discovered in California, there was a rush of labor from all over the country to the gold fields, the whaling industry being among the chief sufferers.[42] Of course, the flow of labor into new industries may mean a relative rather than an absolute diversion of labor from old industries, and the former is of more frequent occurrence in a progressive country. In either event, as a new industry acquires command over increasing quantities of labor, its competitive strength in the markets for goods tends to improve, while the capacity of the older industries to expand tends to be restricted.

The new industries compete with the old also for supplies of various sorts, and ultimately, if not directly, for raw materials. The bidding by the new industries against the old industries will tend to effect a relative if not an absolute diversion of raw materials to the new industries. As the prices of raw materials rise, their production tends to be stimulated. But natural resources are scarce: lands of high fertility and rich ores of easy accessibility are available in

---

has been brought about. The conspicuously high average level of wages in the western states is interesting in this connection. See P. F. Brissenden, *Earnings of Factory Workers, 1899 to 1927* (Bureau of the Census, Census Monographs, No. X), pp. 95, 138–42.

[41] M. Coleman, "Rank and File of the Air," *Survey Graphic*, October, 1928, p. 7.

[42] Tower, cited above, p. 74.

restricted quantities. As soils are worked more intensively and poorer lands come under the plough, increased expenditures of capital and labor are generally necessary to achieve given amounts of produce. And the resort to poorer mineral deposits means that the depth of mining must be increased, or ores of lower quality extracted, or more distant mines worked. In most branches of raw material production, technical advances have more than offset the tendency of natural resources to yield diminishing returns to applications of capital and labor; but in a few instances, as in anthracite mining and in whaling, diminishing returns have been for some time a thing of actual experience and not merely an operative tendency. The fact that technical improvements may counterbalance the increasing niggardliness of nature does not make the restrictive influence of natural resources any less significant. The retarding force is there, and tends to be diffused from the extractive branches of industry throughout the production system.

The insistence of the demand for industrial raw materials has involved, of course, the use of inferior resources. In many regions the quality of arable and pasture has deteriorated as a consequence of their being 'mined'. A good deal of the westward expansion of crop acreage in recent decades has meant a resort to lands of inferior quality, and consequently, lower yields. More conspicuous has been the resort to inferior mineral resources. The grade of dry and siliceous ore treated for gold has been declining for some years, as has the grade of siliceous ore treated for silver. The quality of copper ore has been worsening rapidly: before 1870 copper ores frequently yielded from 20 to 50 per cent in copper, but the average yield was only 2.50 per cent in 1906 and 1.41 per cent in 1928.[43] The yield of crude ores in the form of mercury

[43] F. E. Richter, "The Copper-Mining Industry in the United States, 1845–1925," *Quarterly Journal of Economics*, February, 1927, pp. 242–51; *Mineral*

has been declining persistently.[44] Though improved technology and new mineral discoveries have generally served to reduce 'real costs' more than inferior resources have served to increase them, the latter have prevailed in at least one mining industry of major importance, the anthracite coal industry, as may be gathered from the fact that the secular trend in the price of anthracite coal has been generally upward since the Civil War, and the secular trend in the productivity of anthracite miners downward since about 1900.

The competition for capital, labor, and materials has been viewed as taking place between new and old industries; and in this way it has become apparent how the continual accession of new industries comes to exercise a retarding influence on the older industries. But the competition for the factors of production is pervasive through industry: all industries, new and old, compete with one another for the use of productive resources, and the scarcity of these resources tends to exercise a restrictive influence on the growth of all industries. The retarding impulses are greatest when the available quantities of productive resources least admit of increase. As land area, considered with reference to both general and (at a given state of the arts) many special uses, is virtually fixed in quantity, the restrictive influence of its scarcity on the various land-using industries may be discerned with exceptional clearness. Thus, the decline of the lumbering industry is traceable chiefly to the pressure of the cropping and grazing industries. The decline of wool growing and the abated rate of progress of the sheep and beef-cattle industries are accounted for in large part by the encroachment of homesteading on pasture. The growing of

---

Resources, 1919, Part I, p. 556; *ibid.*, 1929, Part I, p. 546. Of the 12 major copper districts, 6 appear to have passed their zenith. See L. C. Graton, "Some Aspects of the Copper Industry," *Proceedings of the Mining and Metallurgical Society of America*, January, 1930, p. 11.

[44] *Mineral Resources*, 1925, Part I, p. 35; *ibid.*, 1927, Part I, pp. 62-3.

sugar cane has been checked by the fact that it is necessarily confined to the southern area and even in this region is grown beyond its natural climatic zone. And the rate of development of the corn industry has been checked by the difficulties of westward expansion, due to the semi-arid condition of the Great Plains, and of northward expansion, due to the shortness of the growing season.

However, the scarcity of productive resources is practically never absolute in any significant sense. Though it is at times convenient to speak of them quantitatively, their true economic meaning runs in terms of 'effectiveness' or 'productivity', which is a compound, most often inseparable, of their quantity and quality. More important than the size of the working population or the size of the land area under crops is the 'productivity' of the one and the other. The moral quality of a population enters significantly into the productivity of its labor, and the bounty with which its natural agents are endowed, into their productivity; but whether a given agricultural area or mine yields much or little to a given application of labor depends fundamentally on the technical competence with which labor is applied. Though the generosity of nature and the industrial qualities of the population may condition the state of technical knowledge, they are at any one time completely subordinate to it, for only through it can they be expressed. In this sense, the state of technical knowledge in a community is the chief 'cause' of its productivity. Every advance in technology means a decrease in the refractoriness of nature, an increase in the effectiveness of productive resources, and a decline in the scarcity of productive resources: it means, therefore, an increase in the possibilities of industrial growth.[45] The quan-

---

[45] Accurate appraisal of technical progress (viewed broadly, so as to include also improvements in the quality of labor and management), from an economic rather than an engineering standpoint, is most difficult. The available guides are given by price, 'net value product' per unit of output, and labor produc-

tities of the factors of production might remain fixed or even diminish; but if technical knowledge proceeded at a sufficiently rapid pace, the restrictions on the growth of industries arising from limited resources would be overcome; and the physical possibility would exist of continued growth, even at an undiminished pace, of the individual industries even of an economy whose pattern of production was becoming increasingly diversified.

But technical progress has served to reduce, not to eliminate, the restrictions of productive resources. As their influence remains, the extent to which a given industry can obtain a share of the available factors of production depends on its relative competitive power, which in turn rests in large part on its rate of technical progress in relation to other industries. Technical progress is Janus-faced: while improvements in any given industry, or in those technically related to it, always tend to stimulate its development, improvements in competing industries always tend to check its development. As variations take place in the technical progress of given industries in relation to their competing industries, changes tend to take place also in their relative competitive strengths in the markets for final goods and for productive factors. Thus, an old industry may be able to check the invasion of its markets by new industries if extraordinary improvements are effected in its technical methods. And a large technical improvement in an industry producing some raw material may enable it to reduce costs sufficiently to stimulate consumption even more than economies in the use of the material, originating in the technical improvements of

---

tivity. The first two are defective because of changes in the monetary factor; their meaning is further complicated when industries are wholly or partly monopolistic; finally, they reflect not only technical change but also 'diminishing returns'. Similarly, labor productivity measures the joint result of technical progress and refractoriness of nature. Further difficulties arise when the product is not uniform.

RETARDATION IN GROWTH

other industries, had served to reduce it.

Ordinarily, however, technical progress contributes more to the competitive power of the new than of the old industries, for technical progress is ordinarily more rapid in the early than in the late stages of the development of industries.[46] Technical progress tends to proceed at a declining rate because the possibilities of progress within any given industry are limited: the greater the improvements effected in an industry's technical basis, the less is left to be improved, and betterments tend, therefore, to decline in importance.[47] Thus, so far as progress in fuel efficiency is concerned, nothing can compare with the inventions made by Smeaton and Watt between 1769 and 1778; they reduced the coal consumption of atmospheric engines from 30 pounds per horsepower hour to 9 pounds, and therefore left a shorter road to travel than that already traversed.[48] Or take the influence of transportation methods on the 'real costs' of transporting: no matter how spectacular improvements in the future may be from an engineering standpoint, they can-

---

[46] This thesis has been argued brilliantly by Julius Wolf in his *Die Volkswirtschaft der Gegenwart und Zukunft* (Leipzig, 1912), Ch. VI. But it is to be observed that Wolf was concerned with the problem of retardation in general economic progress. To him, the 'law of limited technico-economic development' (das Gesetz der technisch-ökonomischen Entwicklungsgrenze) in individual industries was one of several 'laws' which pointed to a declining rate of general progress in the future. See below, Ch. VI, sec. III.

[47] The rate of mineral discoveries has characteristics similar to the rate of technical progress; and the two are, in a sense, substantially of the same significance, since the economic importance of each is expressed primarily in price. Every new mineral discovery reduces by so much the possibility of further discoveries, and for this reason a declining rate of mineral discoveries is to be expected. Apparently, the discovery of mineral deposits has actually been proceeding at a declining rate. There has not been an important discovery of iron ore in the United States since the Lake Superior ranges were opened up, a major lead discovery since 1886, a major gold discovery in twenty-five years. With the exception of oil, a major source of minerals has not been discovered in this country since 1910. See C. K. Leith, *World Minerals and World Politics* (McGraw-Hill, 1931), p. 26.

[48] See Tryon and Rogers, cited above, pp. 360–3.

not possibly reduce costs to the same absolute extent as did the steamboat and railway. Professor Kuznets found in his survey [49] of the technological histories of the cotton, woolen and worsted, iron and steel, boot and shoe, paper, and copper industries, that the rate of technical progress in each of these, except copper, has been slackening; and there are good grounds for questioning whether copper is any longer a real exception.[50]

It must be observed, however, that, restricting the point of view to something less than the entire histories of industries, the technical progress in a given industry tends to proceed at a declining rate only so long as the improvements effected do not alter the fundamental character of the industry's technique. Changes in the basic technological framework of an industry do take place occasionally—as in the glass industry during the last quarter of the nineteenth century with the coming of mechanization, in the rice industry during the decade of the 1880's with the adoption of implements employed in wheat-farming, in the Portland cement industry around 1890 with the introduction of the rotary kiln, and in the sulphur industry around 1900 with the application of the new Frasch process. In such cases, it will generally be found that the rate of technical progress has abated definitely in the period subsequent to the date when the fundamental transforming 'invention' took place; though

---

[49] Kuznets regards the tendency towards abatement in the rates of technical progress in individual industries as the most important cause of retardation in their growth. See his *Secular Movements*, cited above, Ch. I.

[50] According to F. S. Butler, "there is indubitably a law of diminishing returns applying to further technologic advances in copper production, because the aggregate losses in its treatment have become relatively slight and the maximum benefits of large tonnage production are probably already generally realized in mining, milling, and smelting practice" (*Mineral Resources*, 1928, Part I, p. 713). Professor L. C. Graton expresses (in a letter to the writer) assent to the above statement, except that he would prefer to say that "there is a tendency toward diminishing returns applying to further technologic advances . . . . etc."

when the period of observation is extended back of that date, the length of the period encompassed will alone determine whether the rate of technical progress may be considered as having abated. It is true, then, that old industries may experience technical changes comparable in magnitude with those ordinarily experienced by new industries; but the important fact is that revolutionary changes in the technologies of industries are rare—centuries elapsed between the invention of the mariners' compass and the steamboat. The basic technological framework of most industries has remained the same since the 'industrial revolution' took place in them; and in view of the persistence of the basic framework of industries, the generalization that technical progress tends to abate as the age of an industry increases is, in practice, no less significant for its being restricted to the period within which that framework continues.[51]

Though old industries are able to replenish their vigor from technology, they are generally unable to do this sufficiently to offset the check to their rates of development, which comes from the more rapid technical progress of competing new industries. Being special beneficiaries of technical progress, new industries tend to reduce the prices of their products more than old industries, and therefore tend generally to increase the markets for their products more rapidly. Apart from the stimulus derived from falling prices, the markets for new products tend to grow swiftly for a time because of the customary receptivity of some buyers to new products. The general result is that the old industries find the markets for their products dwindling relatively if not

[51] It may be argued that when the basic technological framework changes, what we really have is a cessation of one and the inception of another industry. Wolf's generalization becomes almost universally true on the basis of such a conception of industry. However, were it not for the fact that the basic technological framework of industries changes very infrequently, Wolf's generalization would be of little importance.

absolutely; and when they attempt to recapture their markets by cutting prices, in the expectation that they may be able to transfer the burden to the factors of production, they find themselves foiled by the new industries which, favored by expanding markets and inflow of capital, are bidding up the prices of productive agents. What is true of 'old' industries soon becomes true of the 'new'; for in the very periods of their adolescence, they are already obstructed by younger and more vigorous industries.

Thus, as the American economy has progressed, abatement has been experienced in the rates of development of its individual industries. The declining rate of population growth has been, if at all, an 'ultimate' cause of the retarded growth of only the aggregate production of foodstuffs and certain other consumers' staples. More important factors are industrial diversification and industrial conservation, operating in a world of scarce productive resources; and the tendency of technical progress, of whatever sort, to take place in individual industries at a diminishing rate. The number of commodities produced has been increasing rapidly in the face of scarce resources; and although improvements in our many-sided technology have served to diminish the restrictions imposed by scarce resources, they have not sufficed to permit the growing number of individual industries to advance at an undiminished rate. Industrial conservation has made extensive headway and has potently promoted retardation in the industries producing raw materials; and while industrial conservation, like other forms of technical progress, has served to increase the extent to which productive resources will go, it has not done this sufficiently to enable individual industries, including the raw materials or even excluding them, to advance at an undiminished rate in the face of increasing industrial diversification. Finally, the rate of progress in the technical processes of our individual industries, whose number has been steadily increasing, has been uneven: it has been more rapid in the new than in the old industries, and it has therefore made for a more rapid rate of growth in the new than in the old industries and for a more rapid rate of growth in the early than in the late stage of given industries.

4. Impact of the Outside Economy

The forces making for retardation have operated unceasingly, but without regard to political boundary lines. They have been operative in the markets and workshops of the outside economy as well as in our own: new mineral discoveries, new branches of manufacture, changes in industrial organization, and new or improved industrial techniques in foreign countries have influenced the production trends of our industries in much the same way as have economic changes in this country. Those of our industries which produce commodities that move in foreign trade are branches of world industries, and are therefore immediately affected by any changes in the outside economy; and those of our industries which produce solely for the domestic market are related by commercial and technical bonds to those producing partly or wholly for the foreign market, so that the influences exerted on the latter tend to be transmitted to the former. The foreign branch of a world industry may experience growth because of improvements in its technology, general industrial environment, or organization (particularly, its relation to the state, as expressed in tariffs, bounties, and so on); but irrespective of what the causes making for the growth of the foreign industry may be, they will exercise a retarding influence on the domestic industry, and this influence will tend to be reflected in the industries related to it. Similarly, the forces making for a decline in the foreign branch of a world industry, provided they arise out of the internal economy of the industry rather than its industrial environment, will exercise an accelerative influence on the domestic industry.

While the impact of the outside economy on domestic production cannot be measured statistically, it can be detected roughly in statistics of the changing contribution of the United States to the world output of various commodities. Such data might be presented for a fairly large number of commodities; but this is unnecessary, and the few figures in Table 26 will suffice for illustrative purposes. The table records the percentage of the world production of certain important materials which has been accounted for by the output of the United States, by decades from 1870 to 1910, and quinquennia since then. These percentages are crisp summaries of the effects of the myriad factors impinging on the development of the American and foreign branches of certain world industries. When the forces making for the growth of an industry producing an 'international' commodity are more potent in the outside economy, the domestic percentage of the world output will decline, and the converse will hold when progressive forces are more potent in the domestic economy. Table 26 is limited to commodities in the production of practically all of which the United States has had of late, if not for some time, a declining share in the world total; but the table is not intended to convey, and it would be wildly inept if it did, any inferences concerning the trend of American production as a whole in relation to world production.

Bearing in mind the limited scope of the data and their illustrative function, they are amply illuminating; for they indicate that the development of the outside economy has been an important force making for a declining rate of growth of many domestic industries. The commodities listed in Table 26 fall into three groups. First, come gold, silver,

Table 26

PERCENTAGE OF WORLD PRODUCTION OF CERTAIN RAW MATERIALS ACCOUNTED FOR BY DOMESTIC PRODUCTION*

Period	Gold	Silver	Cotton	Wheat	Petroleum	Coal	Pig iron	Steel	Copper	Lead	Zinc
1870–1879	37.4	41.5	73.9	21.3	86.8	18.0	15.5	20.7	14.8	14.8	7.3
1880–1889	31.2	42.4	79.7	22.5	66.7	25.3	23.7	30.2	32.9	26.2	12.8
1890–1899	23.8	35.9	68.4	24.5	51.8	29.3	31.5	36.0	51.2	23.1	20.0
1900–1909	24.0	31.3	66.4	21.5	56.2	35.9	40.0	42.6	56.0	28.8	27.4
1910–1914	20.6	30.2	66.1	19.6	64.2	38.6	39.8	41.6	56.3	32.9	31.8
1915–1919	19.4	37.4	63.5	23.4	67.4	43.0	55.6	54.3	60.6	43.7	59.7
1920–1924	14.6	29.2	60.7	23.3	67.2	40.7	52.8	53.4	52.7	40.2	48.1
1925–1929	11.7	24.3	62.1	19.1	69.6	37.9	45.8	48.4	50.6	35.8	41.7

*SOURCES: These figures are based on data from a variety of sources, of which only the more important will be indicated. (A) World production figures: gold and silver—*Annual Report of the Director of the Mint*, 1930, p. 263; cotton—Latham, Alexander & Company, *Cotton Movement and Fluctuations* (20th ed.), p. 147, and the Department of Agriculture (see *Yearbook of Agriculture*, 1931, p. 562, for graph); wheat—*Cincinnati Price Current*, April 18, 1901, p. 251, and Food Research Institute, *Wheat Studies*, April, 1933, p. 264 (the figures of the *Cincinnati Price Current* were adjusted to the level of the figures in *Wheat Studies* on the basis of the overlap for 1885–90); petroleum—*Mineral Resources*, 1920, Part II, p. 471; coal—American Iron and Steel Association, *Annual Report*, 1911, Part II, p. 63, and *Mineral Resources*, 1929, Part II, p. 801; pig iron and steel—M. Meisner, *Die Versorgung der Weltwirtschaft mit Bergwerkserzeugnissen*, Vol. I, 1860–1926, Part II, pp. 84 and 86, and Verein deutscher Eisenhüttenleute, *Gemeinfassliche Darstellung des Eisenhüttenwesens*, 9th, 12th, and 13th ed.; copper—Bureau of Mines, *Economic Paper* 1, pp. 3, 5; lead—Bureau of Mines, *Economic Paper* 5, p. 5; zinc—Bureau of Mines, *Economic Paper* 2, p. 5. (B) Domestic production figures: The series used are those given in Appendix A, Table 44, and described in Appendix B, except for cotton, its source being the *Yearbook of Agriculture*, 1931, p. 672. (The series 'lead, domestic' was used for lead.)

COMMENTS: The figures in the table give calculations from sources which are often inexact, and the single decimal is no indication of the order of accuracy. In the case of zinc, the figures for 1870–79 refer to 1871–79 only; copper, 1871–80; and wheat, 1873–79. The figures for copper for 1880–89 refer to 1881–90. The figures for cotton for 1890–99 refer to 1891–99. The coal production figures include lignite. China is explicitly excluded from the figures on world production of cotton for the years from 1891 on; China and southwestern Asia are explicitly excluded from the figures on world production of wheat from 1885 on.

cotton, and wheat; these commodities are of the type in which America's relative contribution to the world total has been declining fairly persistently for a rather long period.[52] Petroleum stands by itself; the American percentage declined for some years, but it has risen of late, and during the last decade the percentage was higher than during any other except the first. The remaining commodities are mineral products of major importance—coal, pig iron, steel, copper, zinc, and lead. They tell an astonishingly uniform story: for some time their production forged ahead more rapidly in the United States than in the rest of the world; a peak was reached during the War period; and since then the outside economy has definitely outstripped the United States. The American output of these mineral products increased disproportionately during the period of War stress, so that a relative decline was to be expected once Europe's productive capacity was restored. However, the drift of the percentages for certain of the commodities, most notably copper, suggests that the War merely accentuated a peak which was already impending.

The impact of the development of the outside economy on the fortunes of individual industries in the American economy may also be detected in figures of the fraction of the domestic output of various commodities which has been exported. Such statistics are not nearly so informative as the data already presented: the relative exports of a commodity may be constant while the relative contribution of the domestic product to the world total is declining, for domestic production may grow at the same rate as domestic consumption but at a lower rate than world production: or the relative export of a commodity may be declining while the relative contribution of the domestic product to the world

---

[52] Except for wheat, which rose during the War and immediate post-War years.

total is increasing, for the domestic economy may be outstripping the foreign economy in both production and consumption, but to a greater extent in the latter. All the same, the figures in Table 27, restricted to agricultural staples of large contemporary interest, are of some significance; for they strengthen the common impression that the competitive power of American agriculture in world markets has been declining for some time. It will be noticed that the trend in

Table 27

PERCENTAGE OF DOMESTIC PRODUCTION OF CERTAIN AGRICULTURAL PRODUCTS EXPORTED *

Period	Corn	Cottton	Tobacco	All meats	Wheat	Oats	Barley
1870–1879	4.6	69.3	69.5	...	21.3	0.5	2.5
1880–1889	3.5	67.1	47.2	...	24.7	0.6	1.5
1890–1899	5.7	67.4	48.9	...	26.6	3.0	8.4
1900–1909	3.1	64.4	38.0	10.8	21.0	1.4	5.6
1910–1919	1.4	52.5	33.8	9.7	22.9	4.8	10.6
1920–1929	1.8	50.5	33.7	7.4	23.6	1.3	14.7

* SOURCES: (A) Production figures: The data used are those given in Appendix A, Table 44, and described in Appendix B. The figures for 'all meats' are taken from Department of Agriculture, *Statistics of Meat Production, Consumption and Foreign Trade of the United States, 1900–1930* (mimeographed). (B) Figures of exports: The data are taken from *Yearbook of Agriculture,* except for meats, their source being *Statistics of Meat Production.*

COMMENTS: Figures of exports relate to 'net exports'; this includes total exports (domestic plus foreign) minus total imports. In 'all meats' are included beef, veal, lamb, mutton, pork, and lard. There are no data for meats prior to 1900.

relative exports has been sharply downward in cotton and tobacco, the two major crops of which the largest percentage of the domestic output is exported; that the trend has been definitely downward in corn, and meat products; slightly downward in wheat;[53] and upward, though sharply so, in barley only. Various statistics indicate that the proportion of

[53] According to the figures of the Department of Agriculture, the trend in the relative export of wheat has been pronouncedly downward. The wheat production figures used in Table 27 are estimates of the Food Research Institute.

our aggregate agricultural output exported has been declining decisively,[54] and that even the general trend of the volume of agricultural exports has of late been downward. For a time the War afforded a buoyant interlude to agricultural exports, but there has been little else to check their decline. In part, the decline is accounted for by increasing domestic consumption, but the competitive advantage of certain new agricultural areas in foreign countries has been an important contributory factor.[55] The decline in agricultural exports has tended to restrict the rate of growth in the production of agricultural staples in this country.

5. Cumulation of Retardation Forces

Though we are concerned in this inquiry with the causes of industrial retardation, not with its consequences, certain of the effects of retardation are important in promoting further retardation, and account must therefore be taken of them. Once a decline in the rate of growth has become marked, it is rarely accepted fatalistically by an industry. The leading firms will strenuously set about to improve their product, acquaint the public with its merits, or extend its possible uses. Such activities being in the interest of the industry as a whole, they are best pursued in concert through some central agency. Thus, retardation of industrial growth promotes industrial consciousness, perhaps more so than any other factor; and when a feeling of common interest has be-

[54] Beginning with 1895, the decade rates of the series 'agricultural exports' (a rather comprehensive index of the physical volume of agricultural exports) are consistently below, except for 1910–20, the decade rates of any of the indexes of production of major crops. Also, the retardation indicated by agricultural exports is −1.3 per cent, while the various crop indexes show a retardation of about −0.8 per cent. The coverage of the indexes of crop production is not the same as of the index of agricultural exports, but the difference between their rates of growth would probably be larger if the indexes of crop production had as large a coverage as the index of agricultural exports. See pp. 264–5.

[55] See pp. 68–9.

come sufficiently crystallized, it is often given concrete form in a national trade association. The main object of such a body is to promote the group interest; that is, to aid its members in obtaining the largest possible fraction of the total national income.

Technical research is one weapon employed by an industry experiencing a declining rate of growth. It is conducted, in part, cooperatively through a trade association binding the enterprises of the industry together,[56] and in part, individually by the strategic establishments of the industry. The general aims of technical research are to lower costs, improve the industry's product and the products complementary to it, and develop new uses for the product. But technical research, especially when conducted by private enterprises, is often inspired by a still higher aim: the development of new commodities which may prove marketable, attain considerable vogue, and become industrial prodigies. Systematic industrial research is a powerful weapon [57] of industrial defense and offense: in the degree to which it is wielded successfully by an industry, old markets are regained and new markets won.

The fundamental objective of any industry is to maintain and extend its markets. At least over short periods of time, this objective may be realized with considerable success, even when the product of the industry is technically defective. Technical betterments themselves are sought primarily for the gains they may bring in the markets for goods. Hence, an industry experiencing retardation is even more likely to resort to increased selling activity than to technical research; and when it does resort to the latter, it will almost always also resort to the former. There is a strong tendency for the

---

[56] See *Cooperative Industrial Research* (U. S. Chamber of Commerce, Department of Manufacture, Publication No. 1019).

[57] See T. M. Switz, "An Economic Appraisal of Intercommodity Competition," *Chemical and Metallurgical Engineering*, January, 1931.

trade association of such an industry to become active in the promotion of sales: to conduct market analyses with the aim of discovering latent sources of purchasing power; engage in publicity campaigns intended to acquaint the public with neglected merits of its product; bring its product before the public through the medium of symbolic advertising; attempt to stimulate legislation calculated to prove beneficial to the industry, or else detrimental to competing industries; and try to foster 'friendly relations' with the general public —especially when there is any danger of governmental interference with the wonted course of the industry. Quite apart from the efforts expended by the trade association, the strategic firms persistently pursue sales activities on their own account: they advertise, publicize, and devise ingenious schemes of financing and service. In a variety of ways, then, the sum of salesmanship is fostered. Instances of striking originality in the technique of salesmanship are to be found in all kinds of industries, but they are most likely to be found in hard-pressed industries fighting for their very existence. And perseverance and ingenuity in marketing are frequently rewarded by new markets.

Industries as yet undisturbed by retardation will often wield technical research and salesmanship, the two weapons of interindustrial competition, quite as militantly as industries experiencing sharp retardation; for they will attack today in order to be better able to defend tomorrow. The numerous industries wielding these weapons have done so with varying diligence and proficiency, and success has been unevenly distributed. Taken as a whole, the conquests to be imputed to them are very large, and much of our industrial history would be different were it not for their operation. But only this is now important: the industries which succeed in maintaining or extending their markets, through the pursuit of technical research and large-scale salesmanship, intensify by the very fact of their success the difficulties of other industries. As technical research and salesmanship are cultivated more intensively, the tempo of industrial change is increased. Every technical betterment or marketing gesture releases fresh forces making for retardation in the growth of individual industries. So, the forces making for retardation, earlier analyzed, are seen to cumulate in strength; once released, they are not soon spent, but rather gain momentum as they work themselves out through some of their effects.

6. Influence of Structural Changes

We have argued that the forces making for retardation in the industries of an advancing economy tend to dominate, in the generality of cases, over the forces making for acceleration. Except for casual mention that abrupt and revolutionary changes occasionally take place in the technologies of industries, the argument has implicitly assumed that economic changes operate in a continuous and regular way— that is to say, that their impact on a given industry at any one date is closely correlated with their impact at any preceding date. This is doubtless the case in the generality of individual industries; were it otherwise, production records would ordinarily show 'breaks' and 'discontinuities'. However, such 'breaks', though rare, are found occasionally: they may be caused by a comprehensive transformation of an industry's technology,[58] a new invention which revolutionizes the market for an old industry's product, a discovery of a mineral deposit overshadowing known deposits, or a revolution in fashion. When some such cause impinges on an industry, one epoch in its history has really come to a close and another begun. A single trend line fitted to portions of both epochs is likely to be misleading. It may show an in-

[58] See pp. 142–3.

creasing rate of growth; but when the acceleration is traceable to a discrete, fundamental change in the conditions underlying the industry's operation, it cannot be interpreted as a reflection of continuously operating forces. Such a trend line may conceal the decline in the rate of growth up to the time when the revolutionizing change took place, and also the retardation subsequent to that change. A number of the instances of acceleration which our statistical survey has disclosed—rubber imports, light petroleum distillates, burning oils, cigarettes, and face brick—are of just this character.

Thus, the growth of the automobile industry revolutionized the demand for the products of the rubber, and petroleum refining industries. Previous to 1910 or thereabouts, the growth of rubber imports reflected the manufacture of such things as boots and shoes, raincoats, and medical supplies; but since 1910 rubber imports have been increasingly dominated by the demand coming from manufacturers of automobile tires, casings, and tubes.[59] Similarly, prior to about 1910, products of the petroleum refining industry found their chief uses as illuminants and lubricants; since then, gasoline—the driving fuel of the internal combustion engine—has become the most important product of petroleum refining. The output of other derivatives of crude petroleum has also increased rapidly, though as a consequence very largely of their joint production with gasoline. It is true enough that the rubber and petroleum refining industries show acceleration in our measurements, but the period since 1870 has not been 'homogeneous' for these industries, and when it is broken down into economic subperiods, the rule of retardation is actually found to hold. The data of rubber imports show a break in trend some time

[59] See R. B. Prescott, *Analysis and Forecast of the World's Crude Rubber Consumption* (pamphlet by Rubber Association of America, May, 1924), pp. 9–10.

RETARDATION IN GROWTH

around 1910—more particularly, a declining rate of growth up to about 1910, and a declining rate of growth once more, though along a steeper trend, since then. Data on the production of light petroleum distillates [60] tell almost exactly the same story; and so do the data on burning oils, but not with quite the same distinctness.[61]

Other industries whose underlying conditions changed radically at some time during the period under survey are cigarette production and face brick production. A new stimulus of large magnitude was imparted to the cigarette industry during the War, when the cigarette became the smoking favorite of soldiers, and this stimulus has been carried forward by the widespread adoption of the cigarette by women. Despite the acceleration indicated for the period taken as a whole, the period up to about 1915 shows distinct retardation, and so does the period since that date.[62] In the face brick industry, a strenuous advertising campaign has apparently resulted in lifting the level of output of the industry in the period since 1920. Again, despite the acceleration indicated for the period as a whole, the period up to about 1920 shows retardation, as does the period since then, though along a much steeper trend than previously.[63]

[60] This series includes more than the production of gasoline; see Appendix B, II. But if a record of gasoline production alone were available, it would probably have the same trend characteristics.

[61] Rubber imports show an acceleration of 1.6 per cent for the period 1870–1929, but a retardation of –0.5 per cent for 1870–1910. Light petroleum distillates show an acceleration of 3.1 per cent for 1879–1929, but a retardation of –0.7 per cent for 1879–1909. Burning oils show acceleration not only for the period 1879–1929 but also for 1879–1909; but the gaps in data for the early period are greater than for the later period, and the relations of the figures for 1879, 1889, 1904 and 1909 appear somewhat irregular. Each of the three series shows unmistakable retardation for the period since 1910; this period is too short to warrant the computing of retardation measures.

[62] Cigarette production shows an acceleration of 0.3 per cent for the period 1880–1929, but a retardation of –1.1 per cent for 1880–1915. It is to be observed, however, that there is no very definite 'break' in the trend of this industry at 1915 or thereabouts. See p. 119, note.

[63] Face brick production shows an acceleration of 0.5 per cent for the period

Fundamental changes in the conditions of industrial operation have not been limited to industries in the group evidencing acceleration. It is partly an accident of the periods covered that our measures show declining rates of growth for certain of the other industries affected by revolutionary changes—particularly petroleum, rice, and sulphur. It has already been observed that beginning with about 1910, the automobile provided a great stimulus to the rubber and petroleum refining industries. The technical conditions of extracting petroleum permitted a large expansion in these industries. So, while petroleum production evidences moderate retardation for the period 1870–1929, it shows considerably greater retardation for the period 1870–1910.[64]

The sulphur industry is instructive because it furnishes an instance of a 'break' in trend originating in a technical invention which made tremendous deposits of a coveted mineral commercially available. Prior to about 1900 the American sulphur industry was of negligible importance, most of the sulphur used in the country coming from Sicily. Though extensive and pure sulphur deposits were known to exist in Louisiana, they could not be mined in the ordinary way, as they were overlain with quicksand impregnated with hydrogen sulphide gas. In 1901 mining was started through a method, invented by Herman Frasch, whereby sulphur was melted underground and then pumped to the surface.[65] With the leading technical problem solved, the production of sul-

---

1879–1929, but a retardation of –1.5 per cent for 1879–1920. The retardation would not be quite so high for the latter period were the War-years excluded.

[64] The measure of retardation is –0.3 per cent for the period 1870–1929, but –0.9 per cent for 1870–1910. (However, the 'break' in the trend of petroleum seems to come somewhat earlier than 1910.) Petroleum production does not show any retardation since 1910.

[65] H. Wigglesworth, "Chemical Industries" (Ch. IV in *Representative Industries in the United States*, ed. by H. T. Warshow; Henry Holt, 1928), pp. 135–6. The Louisiana deposits have since been exhausted, mining operations having been suspended in 1924. But large deposits have been found in Texas, and the industry has continued to grow.

phur began to mount: it rose from 5,000 tons in 1902 to 85,000 tons in 1904 and to 364,000 tons in 1908; by 1917 output exceeded one million tons, and in 1929 it reached the stupendous aggregate of 2,362,000 tons. While sulphur production shows a declining rate of growth for the period 1880–1929, its rate of retardation for the period since 1900 is very much greater.[66]

Finally, the rice industry provides an instance of a break in trend originating in mechanization. Though the American rice industry dates back to colonial days, its present mechanized technique goes back to only about 1890. The transformation in the technology of this agricultural industry was carried through in very short time. During 1884 and 1885 the Louisiana prairies were settled by a group of farmers from the northwestern prairie states. Some one among them conceived the brilliant idea of transferring the implements employed in wheat farming to rice cultivation. "In place of the old hand-sowing, hand-hoeing, and hand-harvesting, now came the gang-plow, the broadcast-seeder and drill, and disc harrow, and the twine-binder and harvester." [67] A sharp break in the trend of rice production can be discerned during the decade of the 'nineties. While rice production is credited with only a mild rate of retardation in our measures, the actual rate of retardation was rather considerable during the economic subperiods bounded approximately by the year 1895.[68]

The instances of abrupt change in the conditions of industrial operation which have been cited indicate that the assumption of continuity in economic change, on which our

---

[66] The measure of retardation is −2.3 per cent for the period 1880–1929, and −7.5 per cent for 1900–29.

[67] A. H. Cole, "The American Rice-Growing Industry: A Study of Comparative Advantages," *Quarterly Journal of Economics*, August, 1927, p. 605.

[68] The measure of retardation is −0.4 per cent for the period 1870–1929, but −3.5 per cent for 1870–95 and −5.5 per cent for 1895–1929.

general analysis of the causes of industrial retardation has mainly proceeded, does not conform to the actual events in the histories of some of the industries; but the instances of discrete change indicate no more than this. A vitalizing force of large magnitude occasionally impinges on an industry and quickly transforms its status in the economic system. When a fundamental change in the underlying conditions of an industry takes place within a short period, a 'break' in its trend will generally be discernible. A measure of retardation encompassing portions of the period preceding and following the fundamental change will understate the true retardation, and at times will show even acceleration.[69] But the rule of retardation seems to hold when industrially homogeneous subperiods are analyzed separately.

7. Retardation and Industrial Decadence

For a time the forces making for retardation may be more than offset or just offset by those making for acceleration. But in a progressive economy the forces conducing to retardation operate with great effectiveness: many industries soon find that not only has their growth been retarded, but that it has been retarded so extensively that they have actually entered the phase of decadence. In some cases the forces making for retardation continue to press relentlessly until the industry reaches extinction. In other cases, the forces making for retardation relent: an industry may continue to shrink, but at a declining rate, or it may even experience a favorable structural change and become revitalized; such industries will show an increasing rate of growth in an algebraic sense.

[69] We have considered only such breaks in trend as mark industrial revitalization, this being the one type revealed by our series. A case of sudden collapse is afforded by the mackerel industry, which experienced an almost perpendicular decline in output during the middle 'eighties. See *Outlook for the Mackerel Fishery in 1931* (Bureau of Fisheries, Fishery Circular No. 4), p. 4.

The drift in the rates of decline of decadent industries is in some ways more puzzling than the drift in the rates of growth of progressive industries. It is therefore regrettable that the available statistical record of decadent industries is seriously inadequate. Viewed from the standpoint of both the duration and the intensity of their decline, only the following of our series show pronounced decadence: cod and mackerel, whale, hemp, New York canals traffic, maple sugar, walking plows, non-Portland cements, and mercury. With a view to obtaining a larger grasp of decadent industries, we may add several series hitherto unanalyzed—iron rails, anthracite pig iron, charcoal pig iron, cut nails, and fine cut tobacco.[70] Even so, the number of decadent industries remains small; but since the data available do not enable us to go further, they will have to serve our purpose.

Two groups or types of decadent industries raise no new questions. The first comprises industries which have vanished completely—such as iron rails and anthracite pig iron.[71] The forces making for retardation have pressed insistently in such industries, not relenting until the industries disappeared. Necessarily, their rates of decline increased rapidly, at least during the last phase of retrogression. The second group comprises 'decadent' industries whose decline has been checked as a result of some structural change. A case in point is New York canals traffic which has experienced a notable revival since 1918, when the elaborate canal improvements, under way for many years, reached completion. If we confine our observation of New York canals traffic to the period prior to about 1920, a very considerable retardation is evi-

[70] Figures on the production of fine cut tobacco are given in the *Annual Reports of the Commissioner of Internal Revenue*. Figures for the other supplementary series are given in the *Annual Statistical Reports of the American Iron and Steel Institute*.

[71] Iron rails have not been produced since 1911. No pig iron has been smelted with anthracite alone since 1914, and none with an anthracite-coke mixture since 1923.

denced, even though the full period through 1929 shows acceleration in our measures.[72] There is little difference between this instance of industrial rejuvenation and those cited earlier.

The case of decadent industries which are still with us and whose decline has not been interrupted by a structural change is more difficult to comprehend. The statistical records we have for industries of this type suggest that once their trend has turned definitely downward, the rate of decline increases for some time, but later begins to abate. The duration of the period over which the decline is accelerative varies from industry to industry. It appears to have been rather brief in the production of non-Portland cements and cut nails, but rather long in the whale 'fishery'. In certain industries—for example, the production of hemp, mercury, charcoal pig iron, maple sugar, fine cut tobacco, and walking plows—the phase of abatement in the rate of decline does not appear to have been reached even yet; and there is no telling whether it ever will be. Those decadent industries which have entered the phase of abatement in their rate of decline are very likely to show acceleration in our measurements.

The fundamental question which decadent industries raise is why some of them show abatement in their rates of decline after a certain period of decadence. The fact of abatement means that the resistance offered by the declining industry to further inroads on its markets increases. The smaller the output of a declining industry, the greater is such resistance likely to be; for, with a small output, the industry comes to satisfy fairly tenacious and impregnable wants. The decadent industry may produce an altogether inferior product; but the ignorance or inertia of small

---

[72] An acceleration of 0.8 per cent is indicated for the period 1870–1929, but a retardation of −1.6 per cent for 1870–1920.

groups may enable the industry to linger on. Or else a declining industry may produce a commodity, which has, or is believed to have, special merits for certain uses; and as the amount required in these residual uses approaches more closely the total consumption of the commodity, the rate of decline of the industry will tend to abate. Thus, the cut nail has been increasingly supplanted by the wire nail, which is easier to handle, more attractive in appearance, and for which automatic nailing machines have been devised. But the use of cut nails has continued in hardwood flooring and paneling, in part because blunt-pointed nails tend to prevent splitting, and in part because there is a belief in the trade (not wholly justified) that cut nails have greater holding power. About 90 per cent of the current output of cut nails goes into flooring and paneling; and the persistence of the demand for these uses has checked the rate of decline of the cut nail industry.[73]

Then again, if the demand for one of a group of commodities produced by a joint process is sharply curtailed, the continuing demand for another of the joint products may tend to check the rate of the industry's decline. Such abatement in the rate of decline may take place even in the face of rapidly diminishing resources. Thus, the American whaling industry suffered a severe setback when whale oil and sperm oil gave way to kerosene and paraffin wax; and even the persisting demand for whalebone did not suffice to check the rate of decline.[74] When, some time later, the demand for whalebone was practically eliminated as a consequence of change in dress fashions and of the development of substitutes for the costly whalebone, the whaling industry was operating at a very low level, and only a small stimulus

---

[73] The writer is indebted for information concerning cut nails to Mr. R. W. Thompson of the Reading Iron Company and Mr. J. A. Newlin of the Forest Service of the Department of Agriculture.

[74] W. S. Tower, cited above, Chs. VIII–IX.

was needed to check its rate of decline. This was supplied by an increased demand for whale oil originating with soap fabricators. This new change in the current of demand has apparently been sufficient to check the rate of decline of the whaling industry; though neither the revived esteem in which whale oil is now held, nor the new technology of whaling,[75] has sufficed to impart a fillip to the American branch of this industry—now virtually extinct. Whaling has passed largely into the hands of Norwegians, who in recent years have had remarkable success in the Antarctic regions where whales are still found in great abundance.

The cases of acceleration among lingering decadent industries are theoretically more important than those among progressive industries. As we have seen, the latter, when statistically reliable, generally reduce to retardation, the moment our measurements take account of structural changes in the status of industries.[76] However, the acceleration found in decadent industries whose decline has not been interrupted by a structural change cannot be resolved in this fashion. These cases of acceleration are 'real', and they are indicative of the slackening of progressive forces. For, if the pressure of technical or market factors did not relent, industries which had begun to decline would continue to do so and soon reach extinction; or else, as progressive forces within the industry continued to press, a structural change might take place in the declining industry, which—once rejuvenated—would embark on a new career of rapid growth and retardation.

8. Variation in the Rates of Retardation

Our earlier statistical survey disclosed, but left uninterpreted, the quantitative differences among the rates of re-

[75] See C. H. Townsend, "Twentieth Century Whaling," *Bulletin New York Zoological Society*, January-February, 1930.
[76] See pp. 154–5, and Appendix C. II.

RETARDATION IN GROWTH

tardation of the individual industries; for that survey was virtually restricted to the one purpose of establishing the generality, rapidity, and continuity of retardation in the ensemble of industries. Now that our analysis of the causes of retardation is completed, it is desirable to examine some of the general variations in the actual rates of retardation. Our sketch of the causes of retardation furnishes clues for interpreting these variations, and that sketch itself will gain support from a quantitative study of industrial differences. This study will be confined mainly to the continuous production series.

The rates of retardation of two groups of series earlier distinguished—'all' series and basic series, the first group including practically all of the second—are summarized in Table 28 and Chart 3. It will be observed that, on the average, the rates of retardation of the basic series are distinctly lower and more nearly uniform than the rates of retardation of the non-basic series.[77] These differences accord with what the general analysis of industrial retardation suggests. The series classed as 'basic' represent industries of considerable importance and of extensive reference, and in such industries strong tendencies are at work towards cancellation of the forces making for retardation by the forces making for acceleration. For instance, retardation in the consumption of a leading raw material by old industries, originating in either a retardation of their output or increased conserva-

[77] The difference between the basic and non-basic groups is greater than the frequency distributions may suggest, for the 'all' series group includes practically all of the basic group. A direct comparison of the rates of retardation for 59 basic series and 41 non-basic series shows the following: arithmetic mean for basic series, −0.9 per cent, for non-basic series, −2.0 per cent; median for basic series, −0.9 per cent, for non-basic series, −1.7 per cent. The measures of stage of retardation confirm the difference found between basic and non-basic series. (The composition of the various groups, except the non-basic, is set forth in Appendix A, Table 46, columns e and f. The numbers of the non-basic series are: 2–4, 8, 11–2, 16–7, 21–2, 30, 35, 37–8, 40–2, 44–5, 51, 54, 57, 61, 63, 65, 67, 69–70, 72, 75–7, 81, 84, 87–9, 94, 96, 98, and 103.)

Table 28
FREQUENCY DISTRIBUTIONS OF AVERAGE RATES OF RETARDATION, FOR 'ALL' SERIES AND BASIC SERIES

Average rate of retardation (per cent per decade)	'All' series		Basic series	
	Number	Percentage	Number	Percentage
Below −6.2*	1	1.0	..	...
−6.2 to −5.8	2	2.0	..	...
−5.7 to −5.3	..	...	..	...
−5.2 to −4.8	1	1.0	..	...
−4.7 to −4.3	..	...	..	...
−4.2 to −3.8	4	4.0	1	1.7
−3.7 to −3.3	2	2.0	1	1.7
−3.2 to −2.8	2	2.0	..	...
−2.7 to −2.3	7	7.1	1	1.7
−2.2 to −1.8	8	8.1	4	6.8
−1.7 to −1.3	14	14.1	12	20.3
−1.2 to −0.8	25	25.3	16	27.1
−0.7 to −0.3	18	18.2	14	23.7
−0.2 to 0.2	5	5.1	4	6.8
0.3 to 0.7	6	6.1	5	8.5
0.8 to 1.2	2	2.0	..	...
1.3 to 1.7	1	1.0	1	1.7
1.8 to 2.2	1	1.0	..	...
Total	99	100.0	59	100.0

*The item in this class is −11.5.

tion in the use of the material, will tend to be counteracted in considerable measure by the demand for the raw material originating with the 'new' and vigorously growing industries. The consequence is that the rates of retardation of the basic series are only moderately high in their general level and in the degree of their dispersion. The non-basic series, on the other hand, include a number of rather new industries, whose spectacular rates of growth in the early decades have since been sharply curtailed, so that their rates of retardation are very high. They include several retrogressive industries, decadent for some time, which have experienced abatement in their rates of decline, so that their rates of retardation are low. They include also several industries which only recently have entered the phase of decadence, so that their rates of retardation are high. On the whole, the non-basic series represent industrial activities whose growth has been subject to a smaller degree of counteraction of the

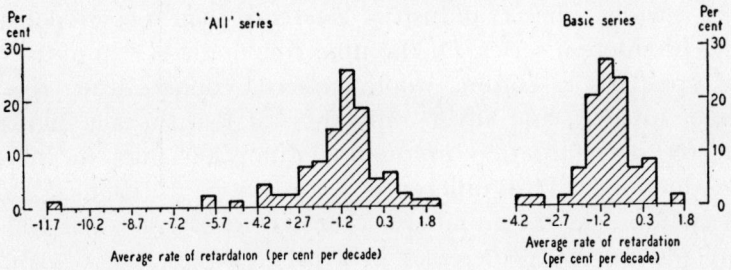

Chart 3

FREQUENCY DISTRIBUTIONS OF AVERAGE RATES OF RETARDATION OF 'ALL' SERIES AND BASIC SERIES

forces making for retardation by those making for acceleration than is found in basic series; for a restricted number of factors ordinarily dominate the impulses impinging on the development of individual non-basic industries—as when the demand for a raw material arises in few sources, or the demand for a finished product is subject to vagaries of fashion, or a commodity is produced under conditions of rapidly diminishing resources. The consequence is that the rates of retardation of the non-basic series, while higher in their general level than the rates of the basic series, show greater dispersion.

It is apparent from the comparison of the basic and non-basic series that there is some relation between the rates of retardation of production series and the degree of generality of their industrial reference. Of course, this relation is not disclosed very satisfactorily by a dichotomous classification, inasmuch as there are considerable differences in the degree of generality of the series in both the basic and non-basic groups. Though it is not feasible to attempt a more detailed classification of the series from the standpoint of their degree of generality or specificity, effective comparisons can readily be made in the case of commodities whose records of both production and industrial consumption are contained among the series analyzed. Since the consumption of a given raw material extends over a wide geographic area and is shared by a large number of industries, a consumption series has a wider (direct) industrial reference than a corresponding production series. Of the nine commodities [78] admitting of comparison—cotton, wool, flaxseed, copper, lead, zinc, gold, tobacco, and silver—only the last two show a higher degree of retardation in their consumption than in their production.[79] This difference accords with theoretical expectations. As the number of uses to which raw materials are put normally increases in a progressive national economy, the forces making for retardation tend to be checked, with the result that the rates of retardation of consumption series are generally only moderately high. But as the domestic branch of the production of a given commodity constitutes only a portion of the world output, the national industry may experience a relative decline in foreign demand, or, if it experiences checks from domestic resources, it may become more dependent on foreign supplies. Such circum-

[78] Also rails, but such a comparison has less meaning for this commodity.

[79] These comparisons are based on periods which are identical for the production and consumption of each commodity, but different for the several commodities. Special computations of rates of retardation were necessary for certain of the series. They are as follows for the periods indicated: copper (1883–1929), −2.2 per cent; zinc (1873–1929), −1.4 per cent; silver (1880–1929), −1.0 per cent; gold (1880–1929), −2.4 per cent; and raw tobacco (1880–1929), 0.2 per cent.

stances are very likely to arise in what was once a swiftly progressive branch of a world industry; and when they eventuate, the rate of retardation in domestic production will be 'rapid'.

The industries covered in our statistical survey are of varying degrees of maturity. The age of an industry has considerable bearing on its rate of retardation, but the relation between the two is not simple. Most of the 'new' industries are found among those having the highest rates of retardation, but so are many 'old' industries. Some 'old' industries in an advanced stage of decadence actually show acceleration, and so do a few 'new' industries. This lack of uniformity in the relation between the age of an industry and its rate of retardation can be explained in terms of the preceding theoretical analysis. New industries grow very rapidly at the start, but their early pace is not long maintained; for as the new industries advance, they are subjected to increasing pressure by the older industries and the industries which are newer still. However, not all 'new' industries evidence growth at a rapidly diminishing rate; for a revolutionary stimulus will occasionally impinge even on a relatively new industry, and if that industry be observed over a period including portions of the two epochs marked off by the revolutionary change, mild retardation or even acceleration is likely to be found. As for those 'old' industries which have already vanished or which seem to be approaching extinction, it is self-evident that their rates of retardation will be very high. On the other hand, those 'old' industries which linger on are likely to show abatement in their rates of decline; the very fact that they persist is indicative of a slackening in the pressure of progressive forces.

Perhaps the best, though not a really good, statistical index of the 'economic age' of an industry is its average rate of growth. As we have seen, various causes occasionally make for the coincidence of a rapid rate of growth and a low rate of retardation in an industry, or of a low rate of growth and rapid retardation. However, as a general rule, the industries which have grown most rapidly show the most rapid rates of retardation, and the industries which have grown least rapidly the lowest rates of retardation. The coefficients of correlation in Table 29, especially for the 'II' groups which are

Table 29
COEFFICIENTS OF CORRELATION BETWEEN AVERAGE RATES OF GROWTH AND AVERAGE RATES OF RETARDATION, FOR SEVERAL GROUPS OF PRODUCTION SERIES

Group	Coefficient of correlation
'All' series	
(I) 99 series	−.63
(II) 88 series	−.68
Basic series	
(I) 59 series	−.30
(II) 55 series	−.59
Nonagricultural series	
(I) 75 series	−.59
(II) 65 series	−.59
Basic nonagricultural series	
(I) 46 series	−.30
(II) 42 series	−.59

the most significant,[80] indicate that this relationship is fairly close. In reading the coefficients it must be remembered that a negative rate of 'retardation' denotes retardation proper,

[80] For the composition of the several groups of series for which coefficients of correlation are given in Table 29, see Appendix A, Table 46, columns e, f, g, and h. The 'I' groups are those described in the Appendix. The 'II' groups are statistically more significant than the 'I' groups. The 'II' groups are more 'homogeneous', as they exclude (according to the composition of the several

while a positive rate of 'retardation' denotes acceleration. The coefficients of correlation are negative and fairly high; this means that, on the average, industries with relatively high rates of growth have experienced relatively marked retardation, and industries with low rates of growth limited retardation. Rapid industrial growth has been attained, generally, at the cost of a rapid decline in the rate of growth; or to put it more accurately, the growth of industries has tended to be self-effacing to the extent of their growth.

IV. ON A LAW OF INDUSTRIAL GROWTH

Our study of the tendency of industries to grow at a declining rate has encompassed a considerable variety of industries observed at various stages in their life histories. Many of the industries are still growing vigorously, others have passed their apex, some are practically extinct, and at least one decadent industry has recently experienced rejuvenation. Having studied industries from the standpoint of their development during a fixed period, we have observed only a segment of the life history of each. May we not, however, combine our partial visions of the development of individual industries into a general view of the typical life history of an industry?

Following writers on biology and population, some economic statisticians have come in recent years to speak of a

---

groups) the following: (a) several series representing industries which have received a revolutionary stimulus to accelerated development—rubber imports, cigarettes, petroleum, sulphur, rice; (b) series whose 'coordinates' are so large that they are likely to exercise an excessive influence on the correlation coefficients—aluminum, Portland cement; (c) series which have a very defective statistical constitution from the standpoint of a study of the relation between growth and retardation—shares traded, postage stamps, locomotives, unmanufactured silk imports (see Appendix C, I–II). The coefficients for the groups from which these exclusions were made are summaries of rather compact 'scatters'. That the coefficients could not result from differential clustering of distinct industry groups is indicated by the various coefficients in Table 29; tests by the method of subdivision, more detailed than those recorded in the table, also pointed to the conclusion of statistical significance.

'law of growth' in industries and to give this 'law' mathematical expression in the form of 'growth curves'. These curves differ with the investigator, but they have one fundamental feature in common: they approach with increasing closeness a fixed maximum value—in mathematical terms, a horizontal line as an asymptote, and in market terms, a saturation point. The various 'growth curves' have some philosophic basis in postulating limits to industrial expansion; for the conception of indefinite growth of industries can neither be supported by analysis nor by experience. But 'growth curves', when applied to industries, are arbitrary in covering the period of advance alone; for many of the causes impinging on an industry are likely to be the same during the period of decadence as during the period of advance. In the course of the life history of an industry, forces making for advance always act in combination with forces making for decadence, their balance determining whether a rise or decline takes place. Once the forces making for decline continue to gain in relative strength, they will at some point come to equal and then surpass the forces making for advance; so that the rise will culminate in an apex and be succeeded by a decline. It is difficult, therefore, to find any sound rational basis for the notion that industries grow until they approximate some maximum size and then maintain a stationary position for an indefinite period. Nor is the notion at all supported by experience: the production records of our industries practically never evidence a plateau at the apex: once an industry has ceased to advance, it rarely remains at a stationary level for any length of time, but rather soon embarks on a career of decadence. It is possible, of course, to formulate a 'law of decline', give it expression in a 'senescence curve', splice this curve on to a 'growth curve' at the apex, and in this way achieve a complete description of an industry's development. But such

RETARDATION IN GROWTH

procedure is arbitrary, even unsound if it presupposes a break in the underlying causation, and it involves an inelegant mode of mathematical expression. Both analysis and history require that if a 'law of growth' of industries is to be formulated, it should be sufficiently general to subsume the periods of both advance and decline.

One of the most salient features of the long-range histories of industries is that their percentage rates of growth tend to decline. In this study, we have grasped the facts of industrial retardation and given them unity through the summarizations yielded by, what is in effect, a 'logarithmic' parabola.[81] When its second derivative is negative, this mathematical function will subsume both the rise and decline of given industries, and it may therefore be considered as the 'law of growth' which industries 'obey'. But this is true in so rough a sense that little is to be gained from the conception. If we had complete records of the life histories of many industries, we would almost certainly find that a 'logarithmic' parabola could describe accurately the entire development of very few industries, and that any other single mathematical curve would serve the task just as badly. The fact that several investigators have found that certain simple functions describe satisfactorily the growth of many industries is of little relevance; for these investigators have worked with mere segments of the histories of industries, and almost exclusively with progressive segments at that—all of which is natural enough, since the production of decadent industries is scantily recorded, and the industries which chiefly attract attention are still progressive.

We may restrict the formulation of a 'law of growth' to a mere statement of the principle of decline in the per-

[81] It may be noted that the 'normal curve of error' is obtained when we take antilogs of a parabola fitted to logarithms of production data and natural time units.

centage rate of growth in individual industries; but even this requires qualification. In the first place, the rule of retardation does not hold in the stage of late decadence of some industries. In the second place, there are fair grounds for believing, though our statistical records give us little assistance on the point, that the same is true of the stage of infancy of many industries. When an industry is still in a 'precommercial stage', its rudimentary technical problems being only partly solved and its financing inadequate, it is likely to oscillate between no production at all and only a nominal volume of output, and to show, on the whole, acceleration rather than retardation. Apparently, this has been the case in the beet-sugar, cottonseed-oil, and tin-plate industries. In the third place, the rule of retardation does not hold throughout for the secular trends of even established industries, though it does hold for their primary trends— which are movements of longer duration than secular trends. And in the fourth place, when as a result of a structural change, a progressive industry is invigorated or a senescent industry rejuvenated, the rule of retardation will hold for the period preceding and also for the period following the structural change, but it may not hold for a period overlapping the two.

Barring structural changes, the course of the life history of a typical industry may be divided into a number of 'stages'. But irrespective of the number of stages of industrial development that may be distinguished, or how they may be defined, given stages will be found to differ in duration and intensity from industry to industry, as will the relative durations of the several stages. Thus, the stage of industrial 'nascence' was long in the beet-sugar and cottonseed-oil industries, but short in the aluminum and rayon industries. The stage of industrial 'maturation' extended over several centuries in the lumbering industry, over several decades in the wire-nail industry, but only over several years in the miniature-golf industry. The stage of 'decadence' has been rather long in the whaling industry, but brief in the iron-rail industry. Nor are the stages of industrial decline often symmetrical with the stages of advance. So diverse are the patterns of the development of industries that only this rule of uniformity can be allowed: an industry tends to grow at a declining rate, its rise being eventually followed by a decline. And even this general statement must be read in the light of the various qualifications to the rule of retardation enunciated in the preceding paragraph, and in the light of the further qualification that progressive industries are occasionally terminated at what is historically their apex—as when they are proscribed by law.

But if the life history of an industry is considered as consisting of a rise and decline, there are substantial grounds for believing that the life histories of industries are becoming shorter. An increasing share of our production is assuming the form of 'luxuries', 'superfluities', and 'style goods'. The demand for such products is determined in large part by caprice, and does not have the stability which staples enjoy. Since our statistical survey is restricted to industries of long duration, it throws practically no light at all on the changing period of the life histories of industries; though it is possibly of some significance that industries engaged in the production of rather specific commodities show often the very highest rates of retardation. There is considerable room for serious inquiry into the changes in the period of the life histories of industries; but such a study will be handicapped by the paucity of data, and the technical difficulty of distinguishing commodities according to the degree of their specificity.

Chapter V

CYCLES IN THE GROWTH OF INDUSTRIES

THE tendency of individual industries to grow at a declining rate has been an outstanding expression of the progressiveness of the American economy. This tendency indicates that, taking a long view, a fairly regular and orderly transformation in the pattern of national production has accompanied the rapid growth in its volume. Nevertheless, the march of retardation has not been continuous in any of the industries covered in our survey.[1] The purpose of this chapter, therefore, is to search for principles of order in the undulatory movements that apparently are always found in the slopes of the secular trends of production and at times are so sharp as to be expressed in negative slopes. We have previously spoken of these undulatory movements as 'trend-cycles'.[2]

The earlier study of the decade-by-decade correlation between the rates of growth of industries has already foreshadowed that there may be a fair degree of similarity in the trend-cycles of our series.[3] It will now be seen that there is actually a considerable degree of concurrence in the trend-cycle movements of nonagricultural industries, despite numerous differences in their trend-cycle patterns and amplitudes; that this concurrence creates a strong presumption that a long-term rhythm has been pervasive in the American

[1] See pp. 107–8.
[2] See p. 48.
[3] See pp. 87–90.

CYCLES IN GROWTH

economy since the Civil War; that the trend-cycle rhythm of national industry has been accompanied by a similar cycle in the degree of divergence of production trends; and that each time the national economy has experienced an exceptionally rapid rate of advance, its progress has been checked by a business depression of great severity. These findings indicate implicitly that the pattern of national industry has undergone fairly regular transformation even when our view is restricted to periods of intermediate duration, and that the extent of shifts in the pattern of national industry has tended to vary with the rate of progress of the general economy.

I. MEASUREMENT OF TREND-CYCLES

The decade rates of growth of the individual series are the basic data of this study of trend-cycles. The preceding chapter has established that the decade rates generally have a definite drift and that the drift is downward in a preponderant number of the series. Since the degree of drift of the decade rates varies from series to series, it is best to eliminate the drift before the oscillations of the decade rates of the individual series are subjected to analysis. In order to eliminate the drift, it must first be measured: this has been effected by fitting an exponential curve to the decade rates of each series.[4] The drift of each series was then eliminated by expressing the decade rates of the series as plus or minus deviations from the ordinates of the exponential curve fitted to the decade rates. These plus or minus deviations trace out the major oscillations in the percentage rate of growth of production—a correction having been made for the general

[4] The equations of the exponential curves were yielded by the study in the last chapter of retardation in the growth of industries. Exponential curves generally yielded 'good fits'; in the few cases where they did not, experimentation showed that the use of other types of curves would not alter any conclusion of importance. Variation in the type of curve used to measure the drift of the decade rates would have 'improved' the results only slightly, while it might have cast on them a shadow of doubt.

drift in the percentage rate of growth. The plus or minus deviations of the decade rates are the technical form in which trend-cycles are considered in this chapter.

The exact meaning of the technique will be grasped most easily if the decade rates of a given series be regarded as quinquennial observations on the 'slope' of the secular trend [5] of that series, and if the corresponding ordinates of the exponential curve fitted to the decade rates of the series be regarded as quinquennial observations on the slope of the primary trend of the series. The meaning is less simple, but not less definite, if the decade rates of a given series be regarded as measures of the average slope over decade periods of the secular trend of that series, and if the corresponding ordinates of the exponential curve fitted to the decade rates of the series be regarded as measures of the average slope over decade periods of the primary trend of the series. On the basis of either interpretation, a positive deviation of a given decade rate of a given series from an exponential curve fitted to the decade rates of the series denotes that the secular trend advanced more rapidly at the given time than the primary trend, a negative deviation denotes that the secular trend advanced less rapidly than the primary trend, and a zero deviation denotes that the secular trend advanced at the same rate as the primary trend. If the slope of the secular trend of a series correspond throughout the period to the slope of the primary trend, trend-cycles are non-existent; but if the slope of the secular trend diverge from the slope of the primary trend, trend-cycles do exist.

It will be noticed that trend-cycles are not considered in this chapter in the same way as in other investigations of

---

[5] Concerning the distinction between secular and primary trends, see pp. 44–6. In the inquiry of Chapter IV, the primary trends are conceived of, in effect, as parabolas fitted to the logarithms of production data; this is practically implicit in the use of exponential curves fitted to decade rates (see Ch. IV, sec. I).

this subject.[6] Ordinarily, a peak in the trend-cycle curve of a series denotes a maximum positive deviation of the ordinate of secular trend from the ordinate of primary trend of the volume of production, and a trough a maximum negative deviation. In our inquiry a peak in a trend-cycle curve denotes a maximum positive deviation of the *slope* of the secular trend from the *slope* of the primary trend of the volume of production, and a trough a maximum negative deviation. While trend-cycles are ordinarily considered as long waves in the absolute volumes of production, they are considered in this study as long waves in the percentage changes in the volumes of production. The relation between the two can be expressed exactly in the case of a hypothetical series of trend-cycles of absolute production volumes which have a sine-curve movement: here the trend-cycles in the percentage change curve will lead the trend-cycles in the absolute volume curve by one quarter of a period (or cycle). We may consider this sort of relationship as holding only roughly in the case of our series, inasmuch as our trend-cycle curves are not sine curves and our trend-cycle observations relate to quinquennial dates.[7]

There is another point, in part methodological and in part terminological, which must be carefully noted in connection with our technique. Ordinarily, a 'cycle' is taken to mean a recurrence of plus and minus phases, the idea of recurrence being crucial in the customary conception. Except when the term 'cycle' is used in a restricted historical sense, the idea of recurrence involves the notion of continuity and the expectation that a given pattern of events will extend into the

---

[6] The most important studies are by Kondratieff, Kuznets, and Wardwell. See Kuznets, *Secular Movements*, cited above, Chs. III-IV; and Wardwell, *An Investigation of Economic Data for Major Cycles* (Philadelphia, 1927). Kondratieff's investigations are presented most conveniently in "Die Langen Wellen der Konjunktur," *Archiv für Sozialwissenschaft und Sozialpolitik*, December, 1926.

[7] See p. 40, note 12.

future. The idea of recurrence has a sound logical basis in only certain types of theory, such as that oscillations in the economy are caused by some oscillatory movement 'outside' of the economic system, or that the oscillations arise out of the internal conditions of economic life and are self-generating. The idea of recurrence will not have a firm rational support if oscillations are considered to be initiated by accidents; for, although accidents are likely to occur in the future as in the past, they may be more or less frequent, and for a considerable period may be self-neutralizing. Inasmuch as towards the close of this chapter the conjecture is ventured that an upward trend-cycle movement is likely to originate, among other ways, in accidental causes, the propriety of using the term 'trend-cycle' throughout the discussion may be called into question.

There is little to be gained from an attempt to fix the most appropriate denotation of such a common word as 'cycle'. However, it is doubtful if restrictive notions of type of causation ought to be allowed to enter into our conception of a 'cycle' at a time when the basic forms of economic movement are still but vaguely known. From a statistical standpoint, the essential nature of a 'cycle' consists in the existence of plus and minus phases in one or more processes (or series). What the statistician may have to say about such 'cycles' is always of some importance in the study of the economic history of specific industries. From the standpoint of general economic theory, such plus and minus phases are of little or no importance when they are uncorrelated; but they are of considerable importance when diffused and synchronous in high degree—that is to say, when they suggest the operation of common causes. Since the idea of recurrence implies not only the operation of common causes, but as well definite types of causal sequence, it is desirable, in the initial stage of fact-finding, to strip the concept of 'cycle' from this idea.

CYCLES IN GROWTH

This is not to deny the importance of the idea of recurrence, which must obviously be the basis of any rational forecasting, but merely to insist that the initial task in a theoretical inquiry into 'cycles' is to determine the degree of concurrence in the plus and minus fluctuations of a group of economic elements that are related a priori. The present study proceeds from the conception that a high degree of concurrence in such plus and minus fluctuations defines the existence of an economic 'cycle'.

II. A GENERAL TREND-CYCLE IN PRODUCTION

The data of the trend-cycles of the individual production series are presented in Appendix A, Table 47. If the reader glance at this table, he will note that the trend-cycles of the series differ very considerably in pattern and amplitude; so it cannot be presumed that a given set of causes has operated exclusively and uniformly through the trend-cycles of all branches of industry. The trend-cycles of the individual series may, however, be viewed as resultants of two sets of causes: those which have operated at a uniform rate through all the members of the production 'system', in the sense of tending to produce common effects in these members; and those which have operated at random on individual industries or groups of industries, in the sense of tending to produce different and random effects (the individual causes operating at random possibly including among them, however, any of those operating at a uniform rate). From this point of view, our problem becomes to extract a common trend-cycle, if there be such a thing, from the mass of observations on trend-cycles; to obtain, if we can, measures of the effects of the common set of causes which may pervade the ensemble of production trend-cycles.

If a set of common causes, variable in time, operate uniformly through the trend-cycles of individual industries, their effects will be registered in the movements of the averages of the trend-cycles, even though random factors operate simultaneously with the set of common causes. We may, then, approach our problem by studying the averages of the trend-cycle observations of the individual series at quinquennial dates. The medians of the trend-cycle observations of four groups of series ('all' series, basic series, nonagricultural series, and basic nonagricultural series) are plotted in Chart 4 and recorded in Table 30.[8] It will be noticed that the four

Table 30

MEDIANS OF TREND-CYCLE OBSERVATIONS AT CENTRAL DECADE YEARS, FOR SEVERAL GROUPS OF PRODUCTION SERIES

(Unit: one per cent)

Central decade year	Medians of trend-cycle observations			
	'All' series	Non-agricultural series	Basic series	Basic non-agricultural series
1875	0.3	0.0	0.1	−0.1
1880	1.0	1.4	0.9	1.5
1885	−0.4	−0.3	−0.5	−0.3
1890	−1.0	−1.4	−0.8	−1.1
1895	−0.6	−0.9	−0.9	−1.1
1900	1.2	1.5	1.2	1.5
1905	0.0	0.0	0.1	0.3
1910	−0.2	−0.2	−0.1	−0.2
1915	0.2	0.1	0.4	0.4
1920	−0.9	−1.0	−0.9	−1.0
1925	0.5	0.7	0.6	0.6

[8] Since not all of the series go back to 1870, the medians for the several groups of series are based on a variable number of series in the early years. The composition of the several groups, for the central decade year 1890 and all following central decade years, is that given in Appendix A, Table 46, columns *e*, *f*, *g*, and *h*, except that series 49 and 50 are omitted for the central decade years 1920 and 1925. The composition of the groups for the cen-

lines of medians definitely trace out oscillatory movements. However, the movements of the medians cannot safely be

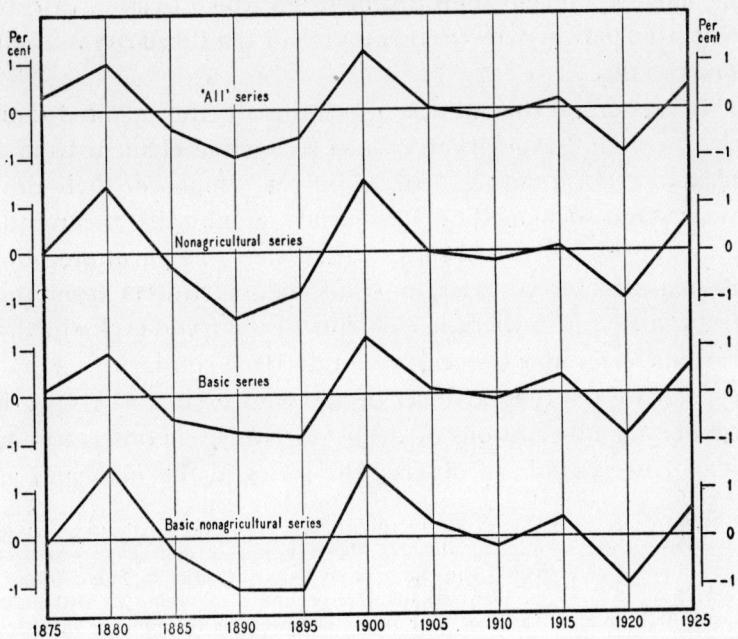

Chart 4

MEDIANS OF TREND-CYCLES OF SEVERAL GROUPS OF PRODUCTION SERIES

trusted to disclose the influence of a set of common causes operating through the production system; for our series cover

tral decade year 1875 is that given in columns *a, b, c,* and *d*. The composition for the central decade year 1880 differs from that for 1875 in including the following series in the several groups: 'all' series—73, 92, and 103; basic—73 and 92; nonagricultural—73, 92, and 103; basic nonagricultural—73 and 92. The composition for the central decade year 1885 differs from that for 1880 in including the following series in the several groups: 'all' series—17–20, 23, 35, 37–45, 74–82, 99, and 104; basic—18–20, 23, 36, 39, 43, 74, 78–80, 82–3, 99, and 104; nonagricultural—35, 37–45, 74–82, 99, and 104; basic nonagricultural—36, 39, 43, 74, 78–80, 82–3, 99, and 104.

only part of this system, and the averages may, therefore, reflect in considerable degree the accidental characteristics of our partial data. As presumptive evidence of a general trend-cycle in production, the similarity of the cyclical patterns of the several lines of medians is more significant than the oscillatory movements themselves. However, the fact that the medians relate to groups of series which overlap in considerable part may by itself account for the similarity in their movements.

It is essential that we use a technique better adapted than the method of averages to extract a common element from a mass of cyclical data which are only a 'sample' of their universe. One such method is to study graphically the trend-cycles of the individual series with a view to determining the degree of their covariation. This method suffers from the fact that the idiosyncratic elements in the trend-cycles of the various series may conceal any underlying similarities. However, if we resort to artifices of anonymity, such as arrays of trend-cycle observations or decils of trend-cycle observations, it will be possible to observe the series in the mass and at

---

Medians are used extensively in this chapter in averaging the trend-cycle observations of the individual series, because it was desirable to restrict the influence of extreme items—most often found in series of minor importance—on the averages. The medians were computed by taking an arithmetic mean of the middle three or four items, according as the number of series in the group was odd or even.

A few words are necessary about the manner in which the trend-cycle charts, especially those following for individual series, are to be interpreted. The quinquennial dates at the bottom of each chart are the central years of the decades to which the 'decade rates', adjusted for their drift, relate. It is natural to read the charts with reference to the areas on each side of the horizontal zero-line and also to the temporal location of the peaks and troughs. However, the latter method of reading is the more significant, for while a change in the type of curve fitted or in the length of period analyzed will almost always redistribute the plus and minus ordinates, the temporal location of the peaks and troughs will rarely be changed; the magnitude of the peaks and troughs may, of course, differ, but this is of secondary importance.

CYCLES IN GROWTH

the same time largely eliminate the idiosyncratic elements in the trend-cycle movements of the series. Accordingly, the trend-cycle observations for 1875, the first of our quinquennial dates, were ranked from the lowest minus to the highest plus value, and nine decil values were then located.[9] Decils were similarly determined for each of the ten following quinquennial dates. In all, then, eleven first decils were obtained, eleven second decils, and so on. Separate calculations of decils were made for each of the four groups of series, for which medians alone were given above. The decil values are recorded in Appendix A, Table 48, and are shown graphically in Charts 5 to 8.[10] The first decil curve in these charts simply joins the first decil values at the several quinquennial dates, and similarly with the other decil curves. A given decil curve may, of course, be based directly on as many individual series as there are quinquennial dates.[11]

[9] The first decil states the trend-cycle value which exceeds one-tenth and is exceeded by nine-tenths of the trend-cycle observations, the second decil states the trend-cycle value which exceeds two-tenths and is exceeded by eight-tenths of the observations, and so on. The exact method used in determining the decils was as follows: if a group consisted of, say, 75 series, the first decil was taken as the value of the 8.0 case, the second as the value of the 15.5 case, the third as the value of the 23.0 case, and so on. See S. Yang, "On Partition Values," *Journal of the American Statistical Association*, June, 1933.

[10] The composition of the several groups of series is stated on pp. 180–1, note 8, Section 1 of the basic nonagricultural series being there designated simply as the basic nonagricultural group. Section 2 is the same as Section 1, but its decils were computed, to use the example of note 9, by taking the values of the 7.5 case, 15.0 case, 22.5 case, and so on. This was done in order to reduce the influence of several 'misfitted' series on the decils (see p. 191, note, point 4). Section 3 differs from Section 2 in that it omits building permits, total cement, rail consumption, and flaxseed consumption, from the calculations of decils for the central decade year 1915 (see pp. 190–1, note 14, points 2 and 3). Section 4 differs from Section 3 in omitting for the entire period analyzed the following series: phosphate rock, silver, raw sugar consumption, building permits, coastal trade, postage stamps, tonnage entered and cleared. The propriety of originally including phosphate rock and silver in the basic nonagricultural group is questionable; as for the remaining five series, see Appendix C, III.

[11] The number of series contributing directly to a given decil curve may

The most important feature of the decil charts is the direction of the decil curves. If a set of common causes operating

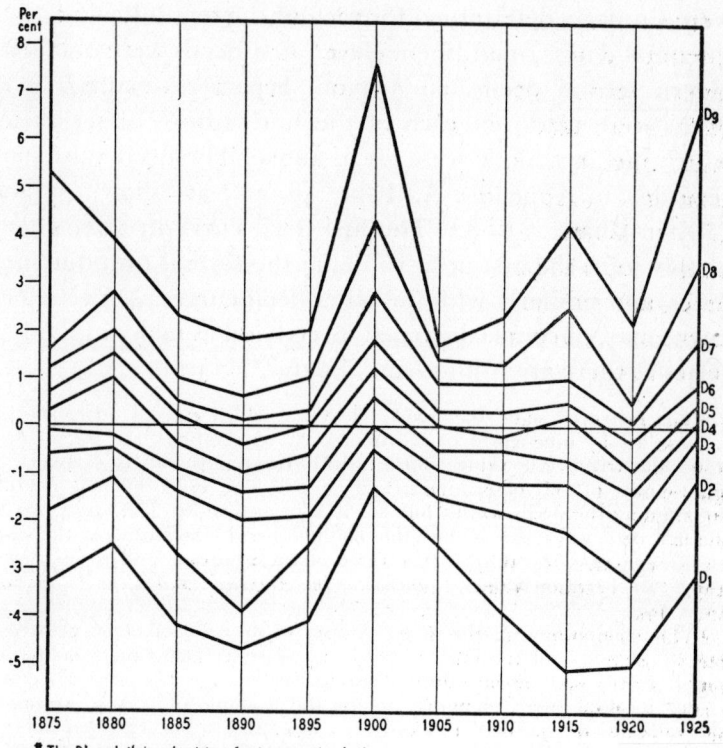

Chart 5

DECILS OF TREND-CYCLES OF 'ALL' SERIES*

* The D's and their subscripts refer to successive decils.

through a system of variables impart to it an upward fillip, the average level of the system will be raised, as will also the middle 20 per cent of the cases, taken as a unit, the middle 40 per cent, the middle 60 per cent, and so on. Thus, the

---

be even larger, since linear arithmetic interpolation was used in determining all of the decils except the fifth (median). See p. 182, note, for method of determining the medians.

fourth and sixth decils move upward between the central decade years 1875 and 1880 in Charts 6–8, but not in Chart

Chart 6

DECILS OF TREND-CYCLES OF NONAGRICULTURAL SERIES*

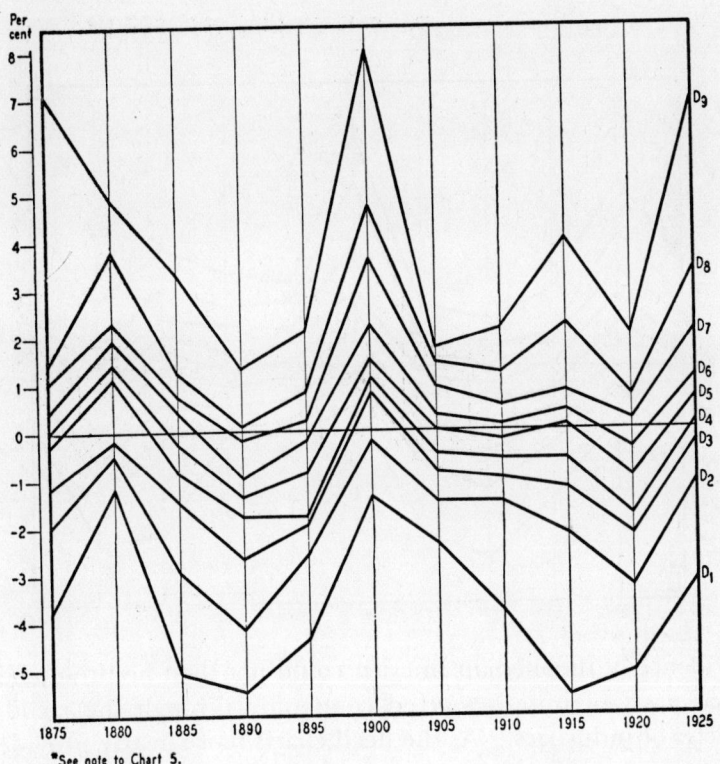

*See note to Chart 5.

5: this means that the middle 20 per cent of the trend-cycle observations, taken as a unit, show an upward movement in the first three charts, but not in the last. When all of the decils of a given group move in the same direction between successive time units, the evidence of the decil lines is in harmony with the evidence of the median line, and a shift in the whole system of trend-cycle observations is indicated.[12] But whenever there is a generally irregular or fan-like arrangement of decil lines between successive central decade years, the evidence of the decil charts is in conflict with the

Chart 7
DECILS OF TREND-CYCLES OF BASIC SERIES*

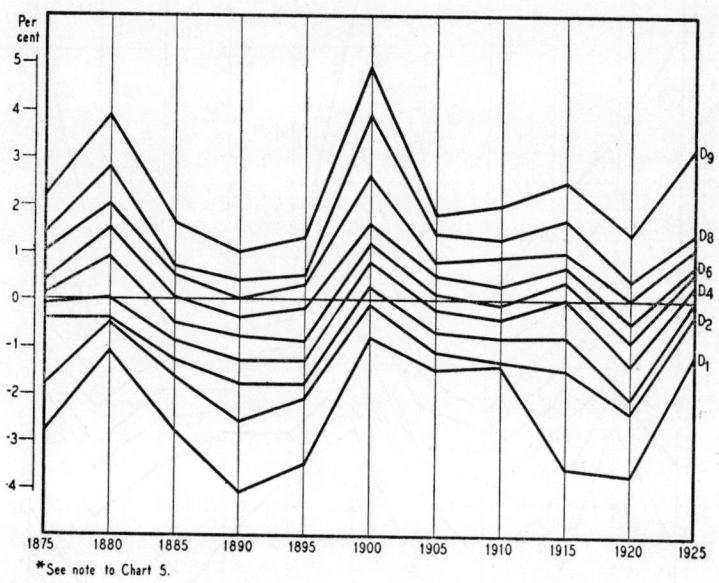

*See note to Chart 5.

evidence of the median lines: it could not then be presumed that a set of impulses acted commonly through the trend-cycles of industries.[13] As the decil charts more nearly provide

---

[12] This would be more strictly accurate, were the lowest and highest values plotted with the decils. But such extreme values, being often erratic, are of little consequence, and might only confuse the picture.

[13] An exception must be noted. One of the 'normal' concomitants of a change in the average level of the elements of a system may be a correlated (direct or inverse) change in the dispersion. If now the ratio of the change in the dispersion to the change in the average be very large, a fan-like arrangement of decil lines is possible. But the factor of dispersion can be 'controlled' by expressing the individual values in units of a dispersion measure and then proceeding to the decil analysis.

a composite picture of the movements of the entire system of trend-cycle observations, they reveal much more than the median lines.

The decil charts warrant careful study,—all the more so because the decil technique is a sensitive instrument when used on groups of the size here considered. It will be noticed that the degree of comovement in the direction of decil lines is rather high in all of the charts. But the 'parallelism' of decil lines is somewhat greater in the groups which exclude agricultural series than in those which include them, and in the groups which exclude non-basic series than in those which include them. The basic nonagricultural group, presented in four sections, is marked by greater regularity of decil lines than any other group. The sharp 'irregularity' in the first decil line between the central decade years 1875 and 1880, evidenced in Chart 8A, is purely technical and disappears in Chart 8B, which is based on a minor modification in technique. The persisting irregularity between the central decade years 1910 and 1915 virtually disappears in Chart 8C, as a consequence of dropping the few series relating to construction (an industry subject to special influences during this period) from the calculations of decils for the decade centered at 1915. Finally, almost perfect 'parallelism' emerges in Chart 8D, which excludes from the group analyzed seven rather dubious series, the reappearance of an erratic movement in the first decil line having no real significance. The set of decil charts plainly indicates that the basic nonagricultural group, which is the most homogeneous a priori is also the most homogeneous in fact; if the trend-cycles were of a random character, the basic nonagricultural group, containing fewer series than any other, would in all likelihood evidence the greatest irregularities in the movements of decil lines. Apparently, common impulses have operated through the members of the basic nonagricultural group.

Chart 8
DECILS OF TREND-CYCLES OF BASIC NONAGRICULTURAL SERIES*

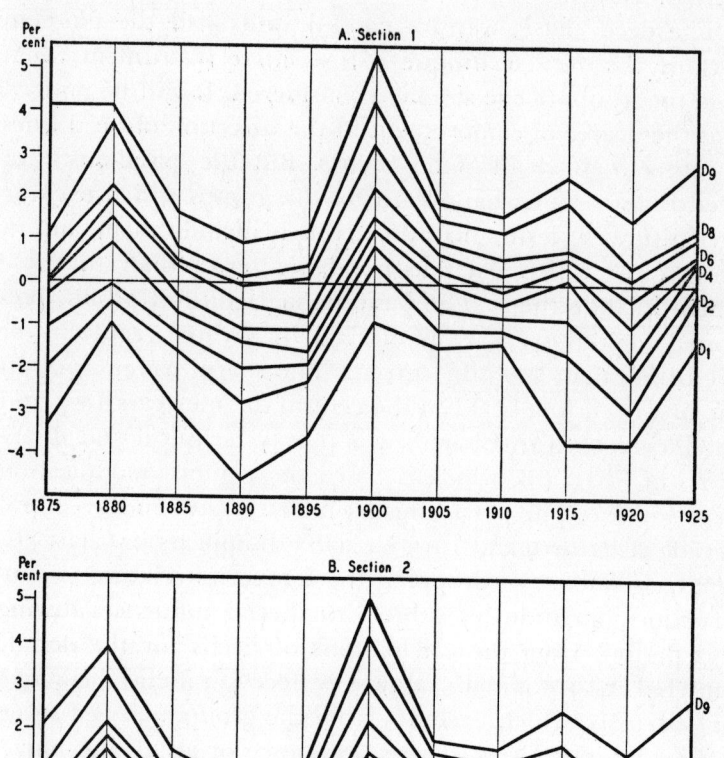

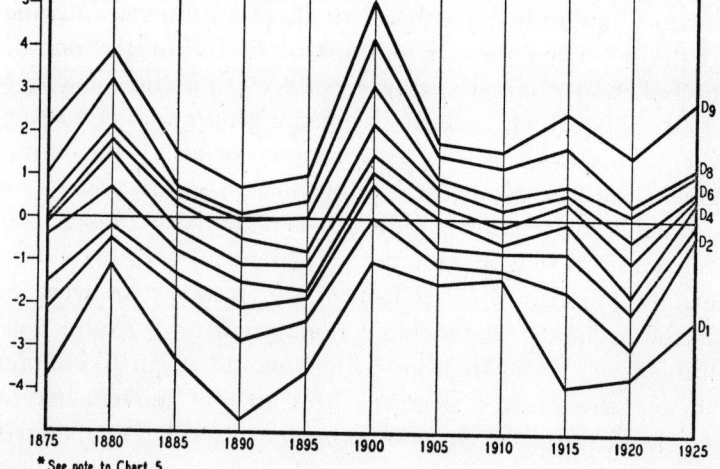

*See note to Chart 5.

Chart 8 (cont.)

DECILS OF TREND-CYCLES OF BASIC NONAGRICULTURAL SERIES*

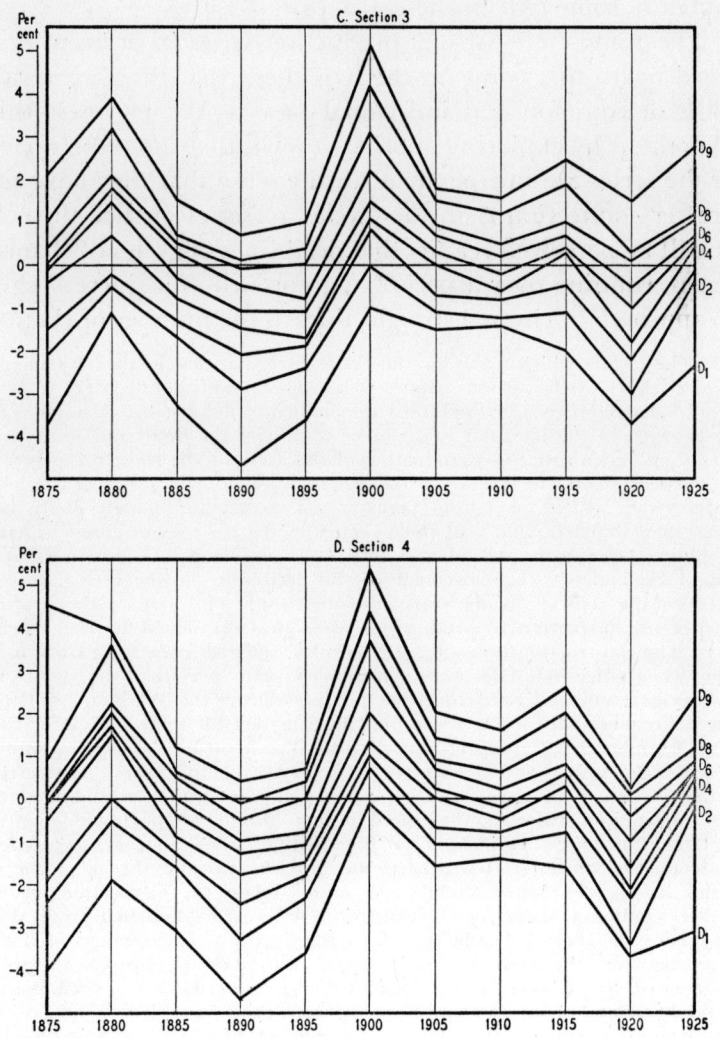

*See note to Chart 5.

The other groups are less homogeneous a priori, and also appear to be less homogeneous in fact.[14] Apparently, the influence of the commonly acting impulses has been obliterated in some part in these groups.

The trend-cycles of our production series have been analyzed up to this point on the hypothesis that they are resultants of common and individual factors. We may test this hypothesis by exploring another—to wit, that the trend-cycles of the series are independent, in the sense that they have no greater connection than the 'cycles' of series of dice throws. It will be perceived readily that decil lines of cycles of chance series, running over a period of time, will tend increasingly to approach horizontal straight lines as the number of chance

[14] The factors which make for the major 'irregularities' in the movements of decil lines of the various groups of series are easily located. (1) At the central decade years 1875 and 1880 the influence of agricultural series may be detected in the irregular behavior of certain of the decils in the groups including agriculture. An examination of the array of the trend-cycle values at the central decade year 1880 discloses that 8 of the 15 series in the 'all' series group (Chart 5) falling between the second and fourth decils are crops; and similarly, that 5 of the 13 series in the basic series group (Chart 7) falling beween the second and fifth decils are crops. (2) In all charts, except 8C and 8D, the movement of the decil lines is somewhat fan-like between the central decade years 1910 and 1915. This reflects the drastic change in the pattern of production, which was occasioned by the World War. The construction industry, in particular, suffered a severe setback at a time when other industries were expanding rapidly (see Chart 18); this was due to governmental restrictions on building during the War-years, and to the depressant influence of the capital loan market for some time after the War. Examining the group of nonagricultural series (Chart 6) at the central decade year 1915, we find that the 8 series having the lowest trend-cycle values include 7 series representing volume of construction or the production of building materials, that the lowest 11 include 9 'construction' series, and that the lowest 15 include 10 'construction' series. In the category of basic nonagricultural series (Charts 8A and 8B), we find that 4 of the 6 series having the lowest trend-cycle values relate to construction. It is rather significant that when construction series are eliminated from this group for the central decade year 1915, the degree of comovement of decil lines between the central decade years 1910 and 1915 is considerably augmented (see Chart 8C). (3) An obtrusive irregularity of the decil charts is the horizontal or upward movement between the central decade years 1915 and 1920 in the first decil curves of Charts 5, 6, 8A, and 8B. This is accounted for by the peculiar behavior of the construction industry (see Chart 18).

CYCLES IN GROWTH 191

series becomes larger and larger; for with a very large number of series, the cyclical observations at any one date will form a frequency distribution similar to that at any other date, and a given decil for any one date will therefore tend to be identical with the corresponding decil for any other date. If the number of chance series were no more than, say, a hundred, the tendency for decil lines to be horizontal would not operate as strongly; but in this case,—no less than in the case of a very much larger number of chance series,—although any kind of decil chart would be possible, the possibilities would have varying degrees of probability. The probability of the decil lines moving in the same direction between two time units is less than the probability of an irregular arrangement of decil lines. Even if we assume that the probability of the decil lines moving in the same direction between two time units is $\frac{1}{2}$, the probability of the decil lines moving in the same direction between successive time

---

Though the trend-cycle position of general industry was low during the decade centered at 1920, the lowest group of industries in that decade was still higher in most of the groups than the lowest group of industries, primarily associated with construction, during the decade centered at 1915 (compare Chart 8C). (4) Another irregularity in the detail of the decil charts is the downward or horizontal movement from the central decade year 1875 to 1880 in the ninth decil curves of Charts 5, 6, 8A, and 8D. This irregularity derives in large part from the sharp upward trend of several industries during the 'seventies, which is not taken account of adequately by the exponential curves fitted to the decade rates. The curves give poor fits in the early period of a few series—steel, antimonial lead, domestic lead, total lead, petroleum, and raisins (see Charts 15 and 17); and this is manifested in extremely high positive deviations at the central decade year 1875. The series which dominate the first decil at 1875 in Chart 8A are petroleum, domestic lead, and steel; the influence of these series disappears in Charts 8B and 8C as a result of a simple modification in the computation of decils (see p. 183, note 10); but the influence of these series reappears in Chart 8D, the total number of series having been reduced. (5) The minor irregularities between the central decade years 1890 and 1895 in Charts 7, 8A, 8B, and 8C are apparently due in some measure to several dubious series—those excluded from Chart 8D. To be sure, the dubious series are included in Charts 5 and 6 which are not marked by these irregularities; but these charts represent the largest groups we have analyzed, so that the influence of the dubious series is submerged.

units (the movement may be upward during some periods and downward during others) of a period consisting of eleven time units (the number of quinquennial dates covered) is only $\frac{1}{1024}$. 'Parallelism' in the direction of decil lines can arise under chance conditions, but the probability is so low that it may virtually be dismissed. In view of the high degree of 'parallelism' of the decil charts, it is very unlikely that the hypothesis of independence of trend-cycles is valid.

But there are two modified forms of this hypothesis which warrant some attention. First, suppose that common factors acted through the trend-cycles of one important section of the production 'system', but that the trend-cycles in the other sections were of a random character. In this case, considerable comovement of decil lines might be evidenced by a group of series whose members were drawn from these heterogeneous branches of industry. This hypothesis has already been tested in some part through our decil analysis of several groups of series. Strong indications have appeared that agricultural industries are subject to somewhat different trend-cycle influences than nonagricultural industries; and it is later shown that trend-cycles in agriculture are, in fact, quite erratic. There are portions, then, of the production system to which the apparently systematic factors making for trend-cycles do not extend.

The second modified form of the hypothesis of independent trend-cycles is more formal. Suppose that the production system consisted of a number of sections, each of which was subject to a set of common trend-cycle influences, but that the trend-cycles of any one section bore no relation to the trend-cycles of any other. If, now, one section had trend-cycles of exceptionally large magnitude, it would play a major rôle in determining the pattern of a decil chart comprising all of the sections, and a considerable 'parallelism' of

CYCLES IN GROWTH

decil lines might result. One way of checking this possibility is to observe separately the trend-cycle patterns of groups of series having trend-cycle amplitudes of varying degree. Accordingly, the series in the nonagricultural group were subdivided into three subgroups on the basis of the magnitude

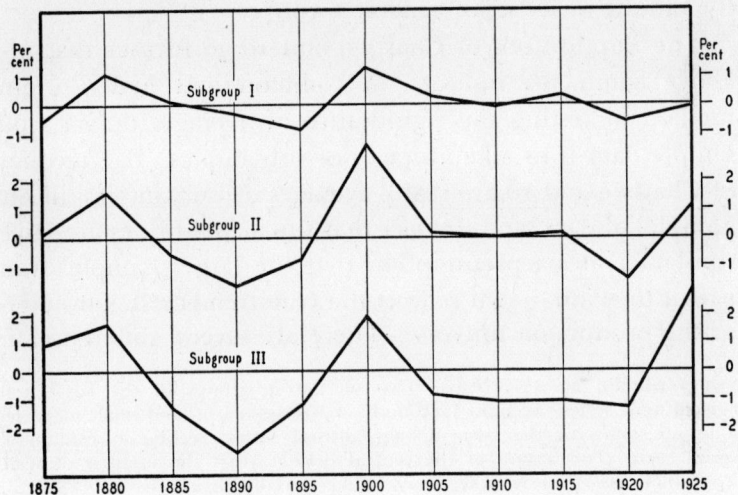

Chart 9

MEDIANS OF TREND-CYCLES OF SUBGROUPS OF NONAGRICULTURAL SERIES, VARYING IN THEIR AMPLITUDES.

of their trend-cycle amplitudes,[15] and the medians of the trend-cycle observations of the series falling in each subgroup were then determined. The same thing was done with the basic nonagricultural group. The medians of the trend-cycle observations of these subgroups are shown in Charts 9 and 10, and are recorded in Appendix A, Table 49.[16] Though

---

[15] Measures of trend-cycle amplitude are considered in section IV of this chapter.

[16] The groups containing agricultural series were not analyzed in the same way, because the trend-cycle movements of the agricultural series are distinctive; see pp. 207–15. The subgroups of the nonagricultural

the several lines of medians differ markedly in their specific contours, they bear a definite family resemblance, and also conform to the general trend-cycle pattern of the decil charts. Apparently, then, the same sort of trend-cycle rhythm as runs through the industries with small trend-cycle amplitudes runs through the industries with large trend-cycle amplitudes. Though our data support the preceding modified form of the hypothesis of randomness of trend-cycle movements, they do not support the present any more than the hypothesis in its strict general form.

The implications of Charts 9 and 10 go further than the above comments indicate. A common and highly useful method of testing the significance of averages drawn from sample data is to take averages of subsamples. The medians of Charts 9 and 10 are really averages of 'subsamples' of our 'sample' of data; and the fact that the median lines are fairly similar creates a presumption that the larger 'sample' from which they are drawn reflects the true trend-cycle movement of the production universe. There are several differences in

group contain 25 series each. Two of the subgroups of the basic nonagricultural series, Section 1, contain 15 series each, and one 16 series. The subgroups of the basic nonagricultural series, Section 4, contain 13 series each. (For certain of the central decade years the number of series is smaller; see p. 181, note. Concerning the distinction between Sections 1 and 4 of basic nonagricultural series, see p. 183, note 10.) The series composing the subgroups of the nonagricultural group are as follows. Subgroup I: 24, 33, 43, 47–8, 50, 52, 58, 64, 66, 69, 72, 77–9, 86–7, 89, 93, 95–7, 101–2, and 104. Subgroup II: 25, 27, 29, 32, 34, 39, 46, 49, 51, 53–4, 56–7, 63, 68, 70–1, 73–4, 80, 82, 85, 88, 90, and 99. Subgroup III: 28, 30–1, 35, 37–8, 40–2, 44–5, 59, 61–2, 65, 67, 75–6, 81, 84, 91–2, 94, 98, and 103. The series composing the subgroups of the basic nonagricultural group, Section 1, are as follows. Subgroup I: 24, 47–8, 50, 52, 58, 64, 79, 83, 86, 95, 97, 101–2, and 104. Subgroup II: 32–4, 39, 43, 49, 55–6, 66, 68, 73, 78, 82, 85, and 93. Subgroup III: 25, 27–9, 31, 36, 46, 59, 62, 71, 74, 80, 90–2, and 99. The series composing the subgroups of the basic nonagricultural group, Section 4, are as follows. Subgroup I: 24, 47–8 50, 52, 64, 66, 79, 83, 86, 97, 101, and 104. Subgroup II: 25, 34, 39, 43, 49, 55–6, 68, 73–4, 78, 82, and 85. Subgroup III: 27–9, 31, 36, 46, 59, 62, 71, 80, 90–1, and 99.

Chart 10

MEDIANS OF TREND-CYCLES OF SUBGROUPS OF BASIC NONAGRICULTURAL SERIES, VARYING IN THEIR AMPLITUDES

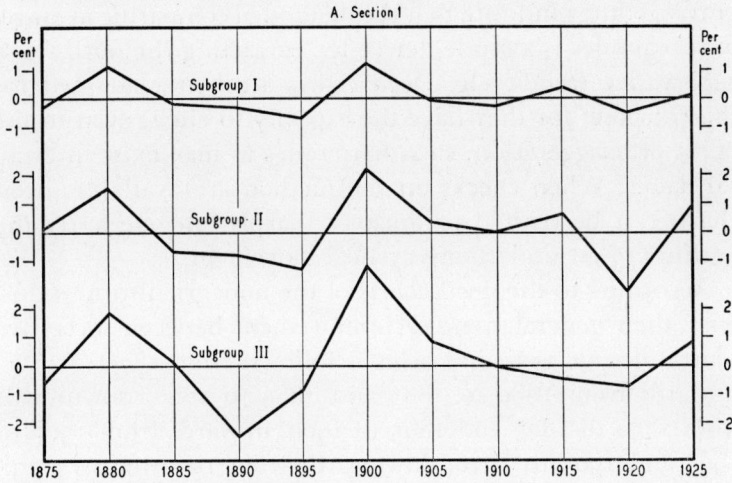

A. Section 1

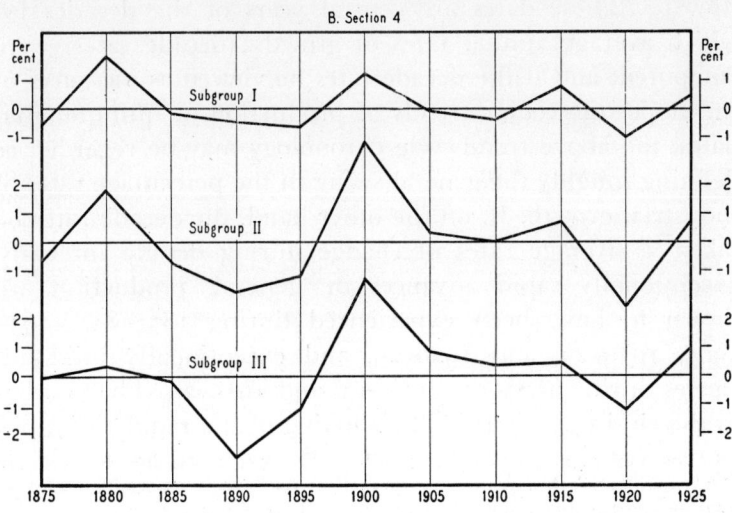

B. Section 4

the movements of the median lines; but that is to be expected in the case of small subsamples, since the chances of cancellation of erratic trend-cycle movements are seriously restricted. However, the differences are of some technical importance: they indicate that the method of comparing averages of subsamples is a crude device for extracting the outlines of a pervasive trend-cycle. Decil charts are better adapted for this purpose; for they have the capacity to elicit, even to the point of exaggeration, such harmonies as may exist in cyclical data.[17] When checks on the method are available, decil charts can be trusted to uncover sharply and elegantly the outlines of an underlying cyclical movement.

According to the decil charts of the nonagricultural industries, their general trend-cycle movement between successive central decade years has been as follows: from 1875 to 1880, upward; from 1880 to 1885 and 1885 to 1890, downward; from 1890 to 1895 and 1895 to 1900, upward; from 1900 to 1905 and 1905 to 1910, downward; from 1910 to 1915, upward; from 1915 to 1920, downward; and from 1920 to 1925, upward. These dates are central years of the decades for which average annual rates of growth (decade rates) were computed; and if the decade rates be viewed as measures of the slopes of secular trends of production at quinquennial dates, the above trend-cycle chronology may be regarded as defining roughly the general swing in the percentage rates of industrial growth. If, on the other hand, the decade rates be taken as average rates of change during decade intervals, exceptionally rapid advances in 'general' production are shown to have been experienced during 1875–85, 1895–1905, 1910–20, and 1920–29, and exceptionally mild advances during 1885–95, 1905–15, and 1915–25. The overlap in the closing periods is illuminating of the rapid variations

[17] The method may be used generally in trying to determine the existence of a common rhythm in a mass of cyclical data. It is especially useful in locating the turning points in a general cyclical movement.

Table 31
TYPES OF MOVEMENT OF TREND-CYCLES BETWEEN SUCCESSIVE CENTRAL DECADE YEARS, FOR SEVERAL GROUPS OF PRODUCTION SERIES

Type of movement	1875–1880	1880–1885	1885–1890	1890–1895	1895–1900	1900–1905	1905–1910	1910–1915	1915–1920	1920–1925
'All' series										
Upward	37	17	39	54	75	26	36	53	31	68
Downward	27	48	53	44	23	72	62	44	65	29
Horizontal	...	2	1	1	1	1	1	2	1	...
Total	64	67	93	99	99	99	99	99	97	97
Percentage excess of upward	15.6	–46.3	–15.1	10.1	52.5	–46.5	–26.3	9.1	–35.1	40.2
Nonagricultural series										
Upward	31	8	25	45	59	16	27	40	24	51
Downward	14	38	43	29	15	59	47	34	48	22
Horizontal	...	2	1	1	1	...	1	1	1	...
Total	45	48	69	75	75	75	75	75	73	73
Percentage excess of upward	37.8	–62.5	–26.1	21.3	58.7	–57.3	–26.7	8.0	–32.9	39.7
Basic series										
Upward	23	8	23	32	46	12	24	32	16	44
Downward	17	34	33	27	13	46	35	24	40	13
Horizontal	...	...	1	...	...	1	...	3	1	...
Total	40	42	57	59	59	59	59	59	57	57
Percentage excess of upward	15.0	–61.9	–17.5	8.5	55.9	–57.6	–18.6	13.6	–42.1	54.4
Basic nonagricultural series										
Upward	21	5	16	25	39	9	18	26	12	33
Downward	10	28	27	21	7	37	28	18	31	11
Horizontal	...	...	1	...	...	...	...	2	1	...
Total	31	33	44	46	46	46	46	46	44	44
Percentage excess of upward	35.5	–69.7	–25.0	8.7	69.6	–60.9	–21.7	17.4	–43.2	50.0

in the rate of general industrial growth; but it also indicates that our 'decade rates' fit the actual trend-cycle swing of the American economy less well after 1900 than before. The pattern of the trend-cycles of production here described will be frequently referred to in the following pages as the 'standard' trend-cycle pattern.

If the 'standard' trend-cycle movement from the central decade years 1875 to 1880 was upward and from 1880 to 1885 downward, and so on, it is worth asking to what extent the upward or downward movement of the individual series was general between successive central decade years. Such information will check and supplement the evidence already presented about a general trend-cycle rhythm in American industry. Table 31 furnishes the answer for each of the groups of series whose trend-cycles have been analyzed by the decil technique.[18] The entries in the table designated as 'percentage excess of upward' are the significant figures and were determined as follows: the number of series having a downward trend-cycle movement between one central decade year and the next was subtracted from the number of series having an upward trend-cycle movement, and this difference was expressed as a percentage of the total number of series. The theoretical range of the percentages is from —100 to +100; the percentages indicate by their signs the dominant type of direction of the ensemble of series, and by their magnitudes the degree of dominance. It will be noticed that the percentages confirm the earlier description of the contours of the 'standard' trend-cycle pattern, and that they also confirm the differences among the various groups of series which were noted in the course of the decil analysis of the trend-cycle homogeneity of the series.[19]

[18] For the composition of the groups, see pp. 180–1, note 8.
[19] Taking the 'percentage excess' figures and averaging them, without regard to signs, we get 29.7 per cent for the 'all' series group, 34.5 per cent for the basic group, 37.1 per cent for the nonagricultural group, and

Production indexes may be used in a final check of the conclusions reached on the basis of our production series.[20] It is to be expected that the trend-cycles of indexes of production of nonagricultural groups of industries will confirm the trend-cycle pattern of Charts 6 and 8; that the trend-cycles of the separate indexes for agriculture and for nonagricultural groups will corroborate the suggestion of the decil lines in Charts 5–8 that the trend-cycle movements of agricultural and nonagricultural industries are disparate; and that the trend-cycles of indexes of total production will corroborate the evidence of the median lines in Chart 4. But these expectations are somewhat stronger for unweighted

---

40.2 per cent for the basic nonagricultural group (these are unweighted arithmetic means). These figures indicate the average conformity of the direction of the trend-cycle movements of the individual series in each of the several groups to the direction of the standard trend-cycle.

Taking separate averages for the positive 'percentage excess' figures and for the negative 'percentage excess' figures, we get 25.5 and −33.9 per cent for the 'all' series group, 29.5 and −39.5 per cent for the basic group, 33.1 and −41.1 per cent for the nonagricultural group, and 36.2 and −44.1 per cent for the basic nonagricultural group. It will be noticed that the averages of both the positive and negative 'percentage excess' figures bear the same order in the several groups as the averages that disregard signs. It will be noticed further that the averages of negative figures are in each group larger than the averages of positive figures; the indications are, then, that there has been somewhat greater consistency of movement among the individual series during downward trend-cycle swings than during upward swings.

Some of the percentages recorded in Table 31 are quite low; this indicates that the degree of regularity in the direction of the trend-cycle movements of the individual series has been low in some cases. Table 31 enables us to enter a caveat to this effect, while the preceding techniques did not. But the percentages in this table may prove quite misleading when taken at their face value, because they do not take account of the degree of trend-cycle movement of the series. The changes in the trend-cycle values from one central decade year to the next of the conforming series (with respect to the standard trend-cycle pattern) are, on the whole, more decisive than those of the non-conforming series.

[20] Concerning the meaning of production indexes, see Ch. VI, sec. I. It need now be noted merely that, although production indexes are of restricted coverage, series of partial coverage often suffice to delineate the form of the trend-cycle pattern, even when they are strongly deficient from the standpoint of a study of primary trends.

than for weighted production indexes. A production index which is deliberately weighted might expose a trend-cycle pattern altogether different from that of a decil chart based on the same series, if the trend-cycles of leading industries characteristically moved at random while the trend-cycles of minor industries moved in concert. Such a possibility is as remote as certain others earlier posited; but only if weighted production indexes trace out a trend-cycle pattern differing from that of the decil charts can production indexes be expected to add new knowledge and reopen our inquiry.

The trend-cycles of several indexes of 'total' production are plotted in Chart 11, and the corresponding figures are given in Appendix A, Table 50.[21] The indexes in the upper portion of the chart are weighted in form, King's index being cruder than the others. The trend-cycles of the Day-Persons and Warren-Pearson indexes harmonize almost perfectly with the median lines of Chart 4. The trend-cycles of King's index show also the same general pattern as the median lines. Snyder's index shows a significant departure from our trend-cycle charts between the central decade years 1875 to 1880; but this is due to the disproportionately large weight assigned to crops in this index.[22] On the whole, then,

[21] Snyder's '49 series' and '87 series' indexes are given in his *Business Cycles*, cited above, p. 239; the data for recent years through 1928 have been furnished by Mr. Snyder. The figures of Snyder's '28 series' index, running from 1880 through 1919, have also been furnished by Mr. Snyder. These several indexes are described by Mr. Snyder as relating to 'general production'. For the figures of King's index, which covers 1880–1919, see his "Is Production Keeping Pace with Population?" (Bankers Statistics Corporation, *Weekly Service*, August 24, 1920); this index is described by Dr. King as relating to 'total production'. For the figures of Snyder's index of 'basic' production, see Warren and Pearson, *The Physical Volume of Production*, cited above, p. 64; this index is described by Mr. Snyder as relating to the production of 'leading basic commodities'. For the sources and the presumptive reference area of the remaining indexes of 'total' production, see pp. 262–4, note 11.

[22] The percentage 'contributions' of crops to the several indexes of

Chart 11
TREND-CYCLES OF INDEXES OF TOTAL PRODUCTION

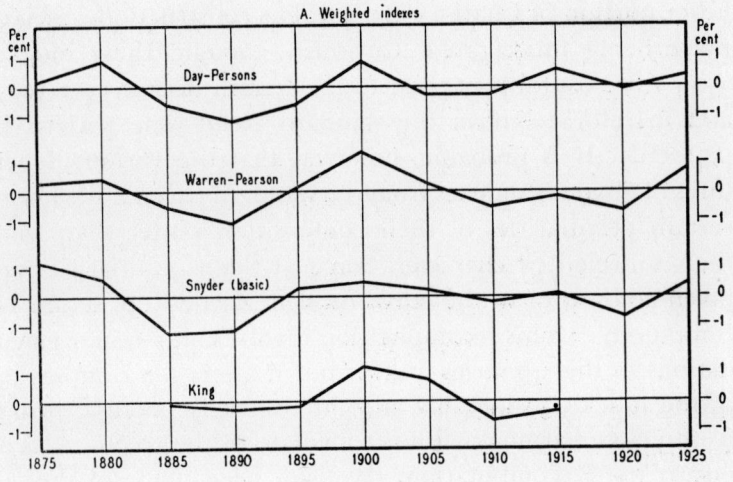

A. Weighted indexes

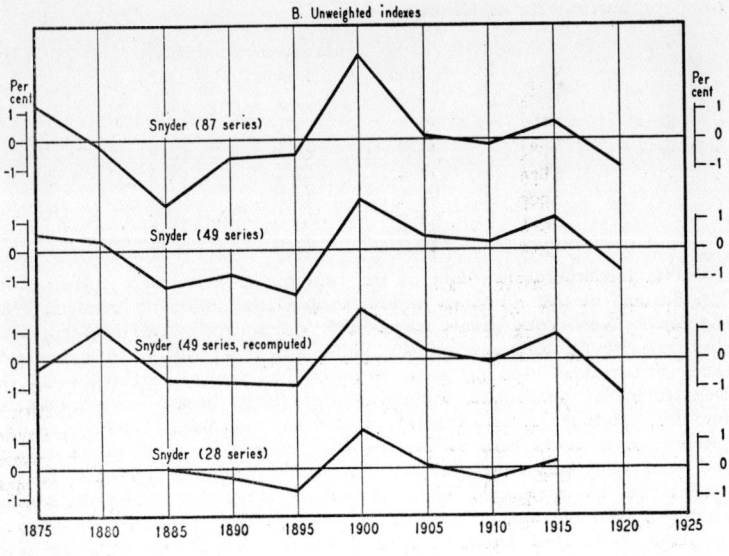

B. Unweighted indexes

202   PRODUCTION TRENDS

the several weighted indexes of 'total' production evidence trend-cycle movements which confirm the rhythm extracted from our individual production series. The indexes in the lower portion of Chart 11 are Snyder's constructions, each of them being unweighted. Curiously enough, these indexes show little conformity prior to the central decade year 1895, and therefore confirm the standard trend-cycle pattern in part only. It is probable, however, that the various departures of Snyder's indexes from the standard pattern arise from certain peculiarities of their composition rather than from their unweighted character. Some of these peculiarities are taken account of in the curve headed 'Snyder (49 series, recomputed)'.[23] This recomputation involves only minor emendations in the '49 series' index; but it alters the complexion of the index considerably and, interestingly enough, brings it into close harmony with the medians of the trend-cycles of our series. Recomputations have not been made of the '28

'total' production are as follows:

Year	Snyder	Warren-Pearson	Day-Persons
1869	89.9	72.2	55.8
1879	89.5	73.9	56.3
1889	81.8	62.9	47.6
1899	74.4	57.7	43.4
1909	62.3	49.9	36.8
1919	58.2	49.0	32.6
1929	50.0	39.0	25.2

[23] The recomputation (data of the component series were furnished by Mr. Snyder) of the '49 series' index involved the following changes. First, the series 'New York canals traffic' and 'quicksilver' were dropped, since they exercise an influence on the index altogether out of proportion to their importance (see p. 260). Second, the 'revised' estimates of the Department of Agriculture for eight crops (listed below) were substituted for the 'original' estimates which apparently had been used by Snyder. (Reference is made here to the revisions effected in 1918, which covered the years 1879 and 1889–1909; see *Yearbook of Agriculture*, 1918, p. 452.) This makes a considerable difference, as may be gathered from the average annual percentage rates of growth during 1890–1900 shown by the original estimates (stated in parentheses) and by the revised estimates for eight

CYCLES IN GROWTH

series' and '87 series' indexes,[24] since they are constructed on much the same plan as the '49 series' index.

The trend-cycles of the indexes of production of several major industrial groups are shown in Chart 12, and the corresponding figures are given in Appendix A, Table 50.[25] The five indexes in the upper portion of the chart relate to nonagricultural industries—three cover mining, one manufactures, and one 'industrial activity'. Each of these indexes

---

crops: rye (−1.7) 1.0; barley (−2.2) 2.7; hay (−0.8) 2.0; oats (2.6) 3.3; corn (2.8) 4.8; potatoes (1.6) 3.1; buckwheat (−1.1) 0.7; and wheat (1.9) 4.1. (The rates based on the revised estimates are in most instances different from those presented in Appendix A, Table 45. The reason is that the present rates refer to the exact calendar period 1890–1900, while the rates in the Appendix table are corrected for the cyclical factor. Further, the figure for wheat given here is based on estimates of the Department of Agriculture, while the figure in Table 45 is based on the estimates of the Food Research Institute.)

[24] A few words are pertinent with respect to a conspicuous oddity of Snyder's '87 series' index—its extreme trough at the central decade year 1885. This is easily explained: the index is an arithmetic mean of relatives on a 1910–14 base, is composed of 49 series in the decade of the 'seventies, and of an increasing number of series in later years. Beginning with the 'eighties, a fairly large number of series are included for industries which in the early years were small in size, but subsequently grew at a rapid rate: in 1880, coke, cement, salt, and roofing slate are incorporated for the first time; in 1885, asphalt, barytes, mica, gypsum, and fluorspar; in 1888, oleomargarine. Most of the newly incorporated series have very low relatives during the 1880's, and this tends to pull down the level of the index in these years—so much so, that the index registers an annual rate of decline of 0.1 per cent during the decade 1880–90. Another point of interest concerning the '87 series' index is that, unlike the '49 series' index, it does not show a trough in the decade centered at 1895; this is due to the fact that nonagricultural series play a much more important rôle in the '87 series' index than in the '49 series' index.

[25] Figures of the Cleveland Trust Company index of 'industrial activity' (presented graphically in the company's *Business Bulletin*, May 15, 1931) have been furnished by Mr. Bradford B. Smith, who states that the general scope of the index, though not its specific coverage, is similar to that of the Federal Reserve Board index of industrial production. Figures of Snyder's 'B' index of crops are given in Warren and Pearson, *The Physical Volume of Production*, cited above, p. 64; this index is described by Mr. Snyder as relating to the production of 'products of the soil (leading crops)'. For the sources and the presumptive reference area of the other indexes of major industrial groups, see pp. 262–4, note 11.

traces out a trend-cycle path very similar to that of the standard pattern. The five indexes in the lower portion of the chart relate to crop production: these indexes resemble one another closely, although Snyder's two indexes show individuality at a few points.[26] What is most significant is that the crop indexes evidence a trend-cycle swing of an altogether different cast than the decil charts or the several indexes of nonagricultural production. Chart 12 suggests more forcefully than the preceding analysis of different groups of series that agricultural commodities have not been subject to the same trend-cycle influences as nonagricultural commodities. In view of the peculiar trend-cycle path of the crop indexes, it is now quite clear why the decil charts of the groups including agricultural series are less regular than the decil charts of the groups excluding agricultural series.

Thus, several lines of evidence—averages of trend-cycles, decil charts, averages for subgroups, summaries of direction of trend-cycle movements, and production indexes—lead independently to the conclusion that there has been a general trend-cycle in the production of the nonagricultural industries of this country during the period since the Civil War.[27] The most powerful of the instruments which we have used in an attempt to uncover and test the validity of a general

[26] In the case of index 'A', this is probably due to the use of the 'original' crop estimates; see pp. 202-3, note 23. As for index 'B', it differs from the other indexes of 'crop' production in excluding hay; also, it includes wool production, and the production of artificial silk.

[27] Though the present investigation of production trends is restricted to the period since 1870, it seemed desirable to determine whether or not there was a general trend-cycle in production during the earlier years. Unfortunately, statistical data on production prior to 1870 are very meagre. And there are other and (in a sense) more fundamental difficulties: the farther back we go, the greater is the importance of agriculture, and the looser the links between nonagricultural industries. An analysis of the trend-cycles of the few (more or less) important series which go back of 1870 (lead, copper, zinc, pig iron, petroleum, rails, vessels, total coal, railway ton-miles, and cotton consumption) disclosed only a mild degree of trend-cycle consistency. The results of the study hardly warrant particularization.

Chart 12

TREND-CYCLES OF INDEXES OF PRODUCTION
OF SEVERAL MAJOR INDUSTRIAL GROUPS

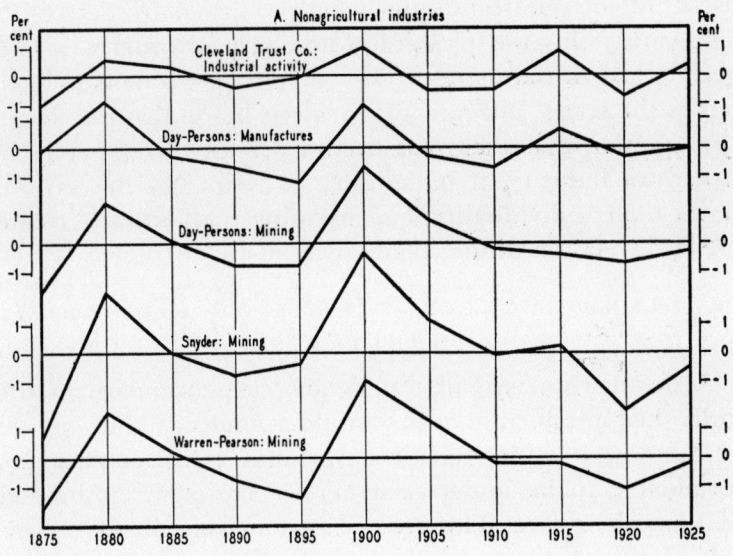

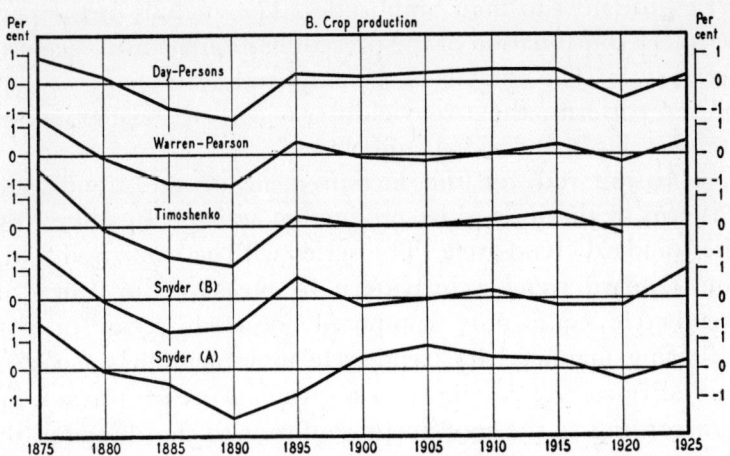

trend-cycle are the decil charts and averages for subgroups; but the other techniques have provided valuable checks, even though it be true that, if used exclusively, they could furnish only very inconclusive evidence concerning a general trend-cycle. All of our techniques have proceeded by devices of anonymity; this was practically necessary in order to avoid getting lost in the maze of idiosyncratic movements of various of the series. But now that analysis has built up a strong presumption that there has been a pervasive trend-cycle in American industry, it is desirable to restore to the various series their individuality, and examine their specific trend-cycles in relation to the standard trend-cycle pattern.

III. TREND-CYCLE PATTERNS OF INDIVIDUAL INDUSTRIES

A detailed analysis of the trend-cycle movements of the individual production series would round out the analysis and endow it with realistic flavor; but as this task is too formidable to be undertaken here, a cursory examination will have to suffice. The present section is devoted to a survey of the patterns of the trend-cycles of the individual series, the next to their amplitudes. The analysis of the patterns is a continuation of the preceding inquiry into a general trend-cycle. The analysis of the amplitudes supplements that of the patterns, the two yielding a general description of trend-cycles in individual industries.

A basing rod for the measurement of the trend-cycle patterns of the individual production series is furnished by the standard trend-cycle. The series will be compared with the standard trend-cycle pattern by means of an index of trend-cycle conformity computed for each series in the following manner: the trend-cycle movement between two successive central decade years is given a score of $+1$, -1, or 0, according as the movement conforms to the direction of the standard trend-cycle, is opposite to it, or is merely horizontal; the scores are then combined by taking the excess of pluses over minuses, and expressing the difference as a ratio to the total number of scores. The index of conformity may vary between the limits $+1$ and -1, the former denoting maximum direct conformity to the standard trend-cycle pattern, and the latter maximum inverse conformity. Though it is convenient to compare the series through their indexes of trend-cycle conformity, the comparisons may be very inexact for individual series taken by themselves; and it is therefore best to pay chief attention to the general level of the indexes in various industrial groups.[28]

1. Agricultural Industries

In inquiring about the existence of a pervasive trend-cycle in production, we encountered several indications that agricultural industries have not followed the characteristic pattern which seems to run through the trend-cycle movements of nonagricultural industries. The agricultural industries provide the outstanding group of exceptions to a really general trend-cycle movement in production. It is therefore desirable to examine the trend-cycles of the agricultural series apart from the nonagricultural.

A fairly definite story about trend-cycles in agricultural production is disclosed by Tables 32–34 and Chart 13. The chart shows clearly that the leading crops trace out trend-cycle patterns of strong individuality, and that few have more than a faint resemblance to the standard trend-cycle

[28] Several factors make for error in the indexes: the original data are not always accurate, the method of determining the decade rates lacks absolute nicety, the exponential curves fitted to the decade rates give poor fits in a few cases, and only the direction of the trend-cycle movement is considered in the measures of conformity. Also, the comparability of the indexes of conformity for the various series is impaired somewhat by the fact of their being based on such variable periods as the series cover. See Appendix C, III.

pattern. It will be seen from Table 32 that the average level of the indexes of trend-cycle conformity of the agricul-

Table 32
CONFORMITY OF TREND-CYCLES OF PRODUCTION SERIES TO STANDARD TREND-CYCLE: AGRICULTURE AND FISHERIES

Series	Period covered by series	Index of conformity
Cattle	1880–1929	.75
Hay	1870–1930	.70
Oats	1870–1930	.60
Rice	1870–1929	.60
Fish, total	1880–1929	.50
Flaxseed	1879–1929	.50
Hogs	1880–1929	.50
Tobacco, raw	1870–1929	.40
Beet sugar	1870–1929	.20
Cod and mackerel	1870–1929	.20
Whale	1870–1929	.20
Wool	1870–1929	.20
Barley	1870–1929	.00
Molasses and sirup	1870–1929	.00
Raisins	1872–1929	.00
Corn	1870–1929	−.10
Cane sugar	1870–1929	−.20
Cotton	1870–1929	−.20
Potatoes	1870–1929	−.20
Rye	1870–1929	−.20
Wheat	1870–1930	−.40
Sheep	1880–1929	−.50
Buckwheat	1870–1929	−.60

tural and fisheries series is quite low. Table 33 shows that the conformity of the crop series to the trend-cycle in total crop production [29] is no greater than their conformity to the

[29] The form of the trend-cycle pattern in total crop production was assumed to be that of the Day-Persons, Warren-Pearson, and Timoshenko crop indexes, which agree substantially in their trend-cycle movements, despite certain differences in their construction and coverage. The trend-

Chart 13

TREND-CYCLES OF PRODUCTION OF EIGHT LEADING CROPS

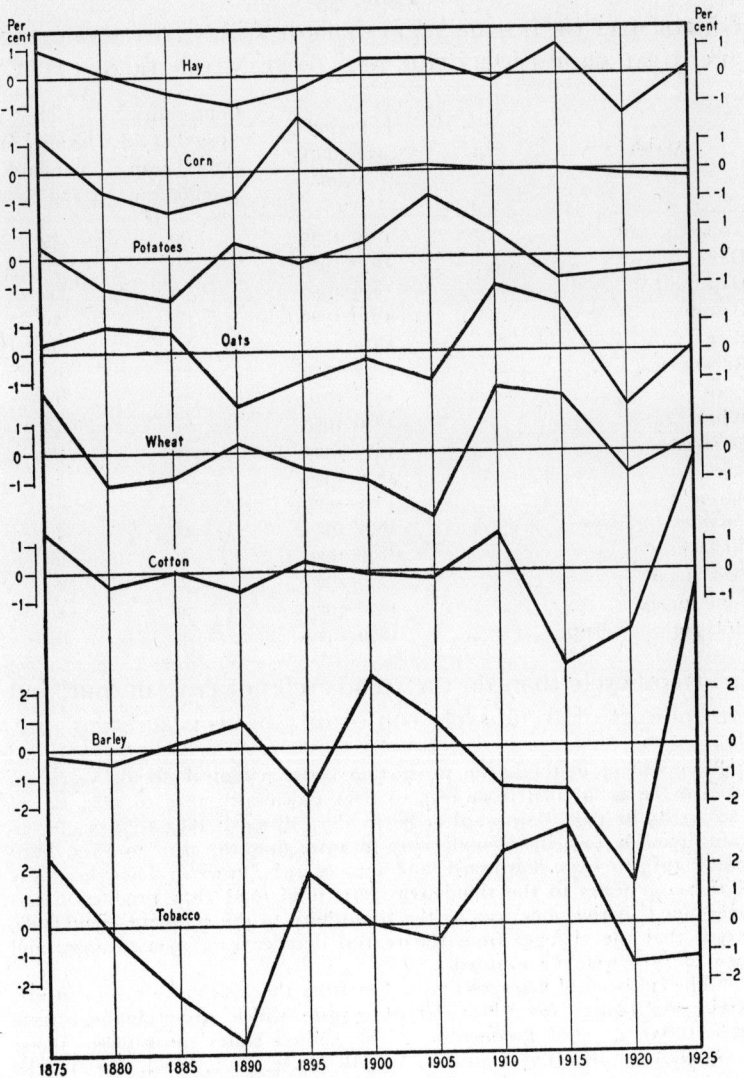

standard trend cycle. It might have been expected that trend-cycles in acreage [30] would conform more closely to the stand-

Table 33

CONFORMITY OF TREND-CYCLES OF CROP SERIES TO TREND-CYCLE IN TOTAL CROP PRODUCTION AND TO STANDARD TREND-CYCLE

Series	Period covered by series	Conformity to trend-cycle in total crop production	Conformity to standard trend-cycle
Tobacco, raw	1870–1929	1.00	.40
Hay	1870–1930	.50	.70
Oats	1870–1930	.50	.60
Cotton	1870–1929	.50	−.20
Rice	1870–1929	.25	.60
Raisins	1872–1929	.25	.00
Corn	1870–1929	.25	−.10
Wheat	1870–1930	.25	−.40
Flaxseed	1879–1929	.00	.50
Rye	1870–1929	.00	−.20
Barley	1870–1929	−.25	.00
Potatoes	1870–1929	−.25	−.20
Buckwheat	1870–1929	−.25	−.60
Beet sugar	1870–1929	−.50	.20
Cane sugar	1870–1929	−.50	−.20
Molasses and sirup	1870–1929	−.75	.00

ard trend-cycle than do the trend-cycles of crop output; but the indexes of trend-cycle conformity of crop acreages, pre-

cycle movement in total crop production between central decade years was taken to be as follows: from 1875 to 1880, downward; 1880 to 1885, downward; 1885 to 1890, downward; 1890 to 1895, upward; 1895 to 1900, downward; 1900 to 1905, horizontal; 1905 to 1910, upward; 1910 to 1915, horizontal; 1915 to 1920, downward; and 1920 to 1925, upward. The conformity of the crop series to the trend-cycle pattern of total crop production was determined in the same way as the conformity to the standard trend-cycle, except that the changes from the central decade years 1900 to 1905, and 1910 to 1915 were disregarded.

[30] The statistics of acreages were taken from the *Yearbook of Agriculture*, except the figures for wheat for 1870–1910, which were obtained from "Wheat Acreage and Production in the United States since 1866" (Food Research Institute, *Wheat Studies*, Vol. II, No. 7, June, 1926). Trend-cycles

sented in Table 34, have much the same general level as the indexes of trend-cycle conformity of the crop production

Table 34

CONFORMITY OF TREND-CYCLES OF ACREAGES AND PRODUCTION VOLUMES OF EIGHT LEADING CROPS TO STANDARD TREND-CYCLE

Crop	Period covered by series	Index of conformity	
		Acreage	Production
Hay	1870–1930	.40	.70
Barley	1870–1929	.20	.00
Cotton	1870–1929	.20	–.20
Potatoes	1870–1929	.20	–.20
Wheat	1870–1930	.20	–.40
Oats	1870–1930	.10	.60
Tobacco, raw	1870–1929	–.20	.40
Corn	1870–1929	–.20	–.10

series.[31] The randomness of trend-cycles in agricultural production cannot, then, be attributed simply to erratic trend-cycles in acre-yields.

---

of the acreage series were determined in the same way as the trend-cycles of the production series. Data of the trend-cycles of acreages are given in Appendix A, Table 51.

[31] As indexes of trend-cycle conformity are summaries for a rather long period, they may conceal correlated movements during shorter intervals. (1) Thus, indexes of the trend-cycle conformity of the agricultural production series to the standard trend-cycle obscure the fairly uniform downward movement of the series between the central decade years 1915 and 1920, and the fairly uniform upward movement of the series between 1920 and 1925. (2) Similarly, indexes of the trend-cycle conformity of the outputs of the various crops to the trend-cycle of total crop production obscure the close conformity between the central decade years 1875 and 1880, 1915 and 1920, and 1920 and 1925. (3) Once more, indexes of the trend-cycle conformity of crop acreages to the standard trend-cycle obscure the fairly general conformity between the central decade years 1880 and 1885, 1885 and 1890, and 1915 and 1920.

It would seem, then, that during certain periods of intermediate duration, general factors impinging on agriculture may have been more important than, and may have dominated over, the specific factors affecting the

The individual character of the trend-cycles in agriculture arises out of the basic conditions of agricultural production. The use of farm land is influenced in very large part by price movements: the trends in the acreages of crops tend to respond, though to a variable degree, to trends in prices which are normally divergent. The result is little harmony in the secular movements of the acreages of the various crops. The shifts in acreage are made possible by the considerable mobility of agricultural resources—land, equipment, and labor—from one product to another. Speaking broadly, agricultural commodities constitute a single industry—in any event, this is true of the various agricultural regions taken separately. Thus oats, barley, corn, and winter rye compete with spring wheat for acreage; oats and corn with winter wheat; corn, velvet beans, and cow peas with cotton; peanuts and cotton with tobacco; hay with various cash crops; and various crops with pasture. The competitive relations among the various agricultural products tend to make for discrepant trend-cycles in acreage, and therefore, in output.

The technical relations among agricultural products, unlike the competitive relations, conduce generally to similarity in trend-cycles; but this is not true of all technical relations and, in any case, the technical relations are in a sense less important than the competitive. Technical ties in the form of sequences (that is, rigid rotation systems) and complementary schemes of production (for example, hogs and corn) make for similar trend-cycles. But the influence of these technical ties is not diffusive, since they are restricted to distinct groups of crops and distinct areas. Nor are the technical relations among products absolutely rigid: they tend to

---

production of the individual crops. But this has definitely not been the case over a sizable period of economic history. We have spoken above of a trend-cycle in total crop production, but its meaning is merely statistical; there is no general (pervasive) trend-cycle in crop production.

CYCLES IN GROWTH

vary, as a matter of fact, with considerations of price advantage. Finally, certain technical relations among crops, especially those realized in response to the operation of the natural elements, tend to make for discrepant trend-cycles. Thus, buckwheat is very commonly resorted to when physical conditions for growing other crops are unfavorable; and a good deal of barley acreage serves to complement the fluctuations in other crops, especially when winter killing affects them. The technical relations in agriculture are not, therefore, of a sort to reduce materially the influence of the competitive relations which make for individual trend-cycles in production.

The trend-cycle movement of acre-yields is a contributory cause of individual trend-cycles in agricultural production, but it is apparently a minor cause only. Though natural factors dominate year-by-year changes in acre-yields, it may be expected that their effects will be self-cancelling over a period of ten years or longer, so that the secular trend of acre-yields will tend to bear primarily the impress of the human factor.[32] Chart 14 shows that there is generally an inverse relationship between the trend-cycles of the acreage and acre-yield of the leading crops.[33] This systematic feature of the trend-cycles of acre-yields suggests that agricultural industries have responded to economic stimuli chiefly through modifications in acreage. When for one reason or another

[32] To be sure, natural determinants of yields occasionally dominate over periods as long as a decade or even longer; for example, the influence of the boll weevil on cotton yields in recent years. It is only when natural factors dominate that trend-cycles in acre-yields are truly erratic.

[33] See pp. 210–1, note 30. The decade rates of acre-yields were obtained by dividing the decade rates for production by the corresponding decade rates for acreage, each expressed in ratio form—that is, as 1.054 and not 5.4 per cent, and so on (see F. C. Mills, *The Behavior of Prices*, National Bureau of Economic Research, 1927, pp. 71–2). The trend-cycles of the acre-yields of each crop were then determined in the same way as the trend-cycles of the production series. Data of the trend-cycles of the acre-yields are given in Appendix A, Table 51.

PRODUCTION TRENDS

Chart 14
TREND-CYCLES OF ACREAGES AND ACRE-YIELDS OF EIGHT LEADING CROPS

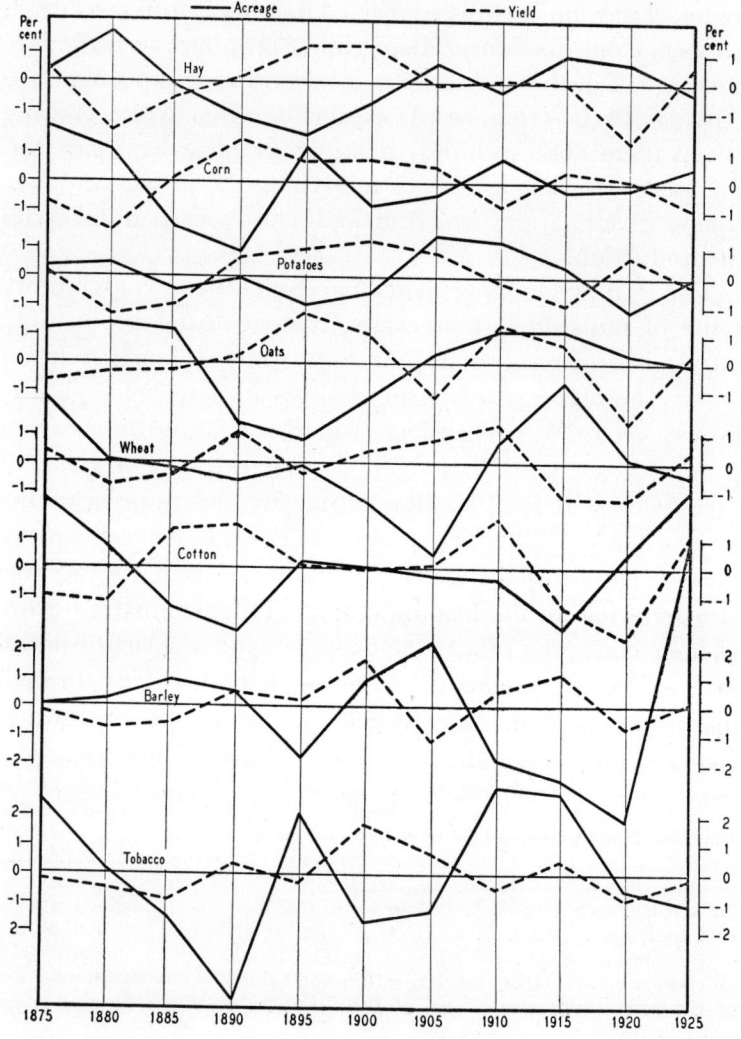

CYCLES IN GROWTH

acreage was expanded at a relatively rapid rate, crop culture was practiced less intensively (or else improvements proceeded at a relatively mild pace), and lands of inferior quality were brought under the plough; so, a rise in the trend-cycle of acreage generally meant a decline in the trend-cycle of yields. On the other hand, when the rate of expansion in acreage slackened, relatively more care was devoted to crop cultivation; and when the trend of acreage actually declined, it was on the whole the poorer lands which were withdrawn from use; so, a decline in the trend-cycle of acreage generally meant a rise in the trend-cycle of yields. It will be seen from Chart 14 that the inverse relationship between trend-cycles in acreage and yield is slightly higher for the early period than for recent decades. This may mean that the agricultural community has come of late to respond to considerations of price advantage by controlling yields in slightly greater degree than formerly; which would be but a natural consequence of the passing of the frontier and the diminution of virgin land.

2. Nonagricultural Industries

Except for agriculture, a general trend-cycle rhythm seems to have been pervasive in industrial production. The indexes of trend-cycle conformity of the nonagricultural series are distributed by industrial groups in Tables 35–37. For illustrative purposes, the trend-cycles of a number of nonagricultural series are presented graphically, for several groups of related series, in Charts 15 and 17–19. Chart 16 shows medians of trend-cycles of manufactures from agricultural and from mineral raw materials.

Most of the nonagricultural series have positive indexes of trend-cycle conformity, and the more important of the series are generally found among those having rather high

Table 35

CONFORMITY OF TREND-CYCLES OF PRODUCTION SERIES TO STANDARD TREND-CYCLE: MINING

Series	Period covered by series	Index of conformity
Iron ore	1880–1929	1.00
Natural gas	1882–1929	.75
Pyrites	1880–1929	.75
Bituminous coal	1870–1929	.60
Coal, total	1870–1929	.60
Copper	1870–1929	.60
Cement, total	1880–1929	.50
Fluorspar	1880–1929	.50
Salt	1880–1929	.50
Sulphur	1880–1929	.50
Anthracite coal	1870–1929	.40
Zinc	1870–1929	.40
Non-Portland cements	1880–1929	.25
Lead, domestic	1870–1929	.20
Mercury	1870–1929	.10
Gold	1870–1929	.00
Phosphate rock	1870–1929	.00
Portland cement	1880–1929	.00
Petroleum	1870–1929	−.20
Silver	1870–1929	−.20
Gypsum	1880–1929	−.25
Asphalt	1880–1929	−.50

indexes.[34] In the mineral group, the industrial metals and fuels are conspicuous by their generally high indexes of conformity. Among manufactures, the iron and steel series have the highest indexes; series of transportation equipment, textile products, tobacco products, and nonferrous industrial

[34] The arithmetic mean of the indexes of trend-cycle conformity of Section 1 of the basic nonagricultural series is .40; of Section 4 of the basic nonagricultural series, .49. (For the composition of these groups, see pp. 180–1, note 8, and p. 183, note 10.) The arithmetic mean of the non-basic nonagricultural series (this group consists of 31 series, these being the series above number 23, as listed on p. 163, note 77) is .34.

Chart 15
TREND-CYCLES OF PRODUCTION OF EIGHT LEADING MINERALS

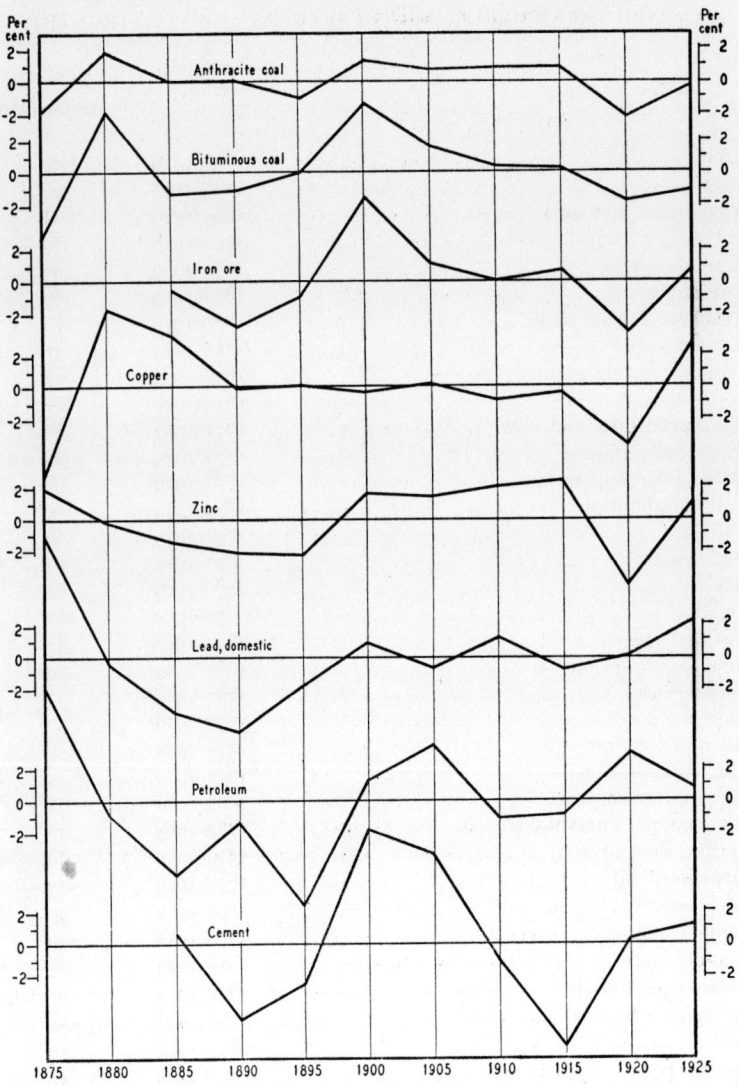

Table 36
CONFORMITY OF TREND-CYCLES OF PRODUCTION SERIES TO STANDARD TREND-CYCLE: MANUFACTURES AND CONSTRUCTION

Series	Period covered by series	Index of conformity
Cigars	1880–1929	1.00
Coke	1880–1929	1.00
Rolled iron and steel	1885–1929	1.00
Pig iron	1870–1929	.80
Superphosphate	1870–1929	.80
Tin imports	1870–1929	.80
Tin-plate consumption	1871–1929	.80
Canned corn	1885–1929	.71
Tobacco consumption	1880–1929	.62
Cocoa imports	1870–1929	.60
Cottonseed cake and meal	1872–1929	.60
Lead consumption	1870–1929	.60
Minor fiber imports	1870–1929	.60
Rail consumption	1870–1929	.60
Rails	1870–1929	.60
Sisal imports	1870–1929	.60
Steel	1870–1929	.60
Vessels	1870–1929	.60
Distilled spirits	1870–1918	.50
Gold consumption	1880–1929	.50
Locomotives	1880–1929	.50
Nails	1872–1929	.50
Silk imports, raw	1870–1929	.50
Zinc consumption	1873–1929	.44
Copper consumption	1883–1929	.43
Silk imports, unmanufactured	1883–1929	.43
Cotton consumption	1870–1929	.40
Cottonseed oil	1872–1929	.40
Jute imports	1870–1929	.40
Rubber imports	1870–1929	.40
Roofing slate	1879–1929	.37
Tobacco and snuff	1871–1929	.30
Fermented liquors	1870–1918	.25
Coffee imports	1870–1929	.20
Manila hemp imports	1870–1929	.20

Table 36 (cont.)
CONFORMITY OF TREND-CYCLES OF PRODUCTION SERIES TO STANDARD TREND-CYCLE: MANUFACTURES AND CONSTRUCTION

Series	Period covered by series	Index of conformity
Wool consumption	1870–1930	.20
Flaxseed consumption	1879–1929	.00
Flour	1880–1929	.00
Silver consumption	1880–1929	.00
Building permits	1874–1929	–.11
Aluminum	1883–1929	–.14
Canned tomatoes	1885–1929	–.14
White lead	1884–1929	–.14
Antimonial lead	1871–1929	–.20
Lead, total	1870–1929	–.20
Raw sugar consumption	1870–1930	–.20
Cigarettes	1880–1929	–.25

metals and their derivatives have, speaking generally, fairly high indexes; and manufactures from mineral materials have, on the average, somewhat higher indexes of conformity

Chart 16
MEDIANS OF TREND-CYCLES OF TWO GROUPS OF MANUFACTURES

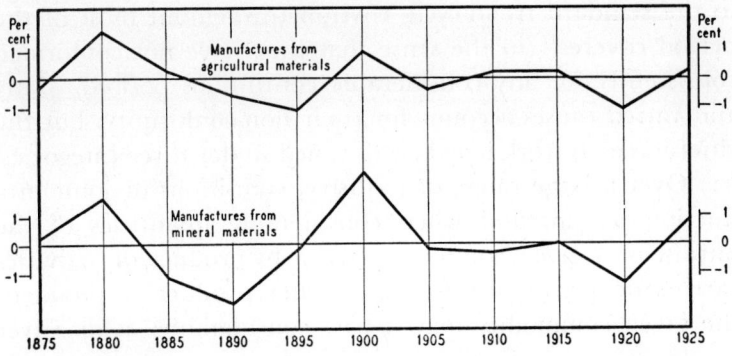

than manufactures from agricultural materials. The several railway series, shares traded, and deflated clearings have the highest indexes in the transportation and trade division. On the other hand, little direct conformity to the standard trend-cycle pattern is evidenced by the precious metals, many of the series relating to construction, a number of food products, and the series on foreign trade.

Table 37
CONFORMITY OF TREND-CYCLES OF PRODUCTION SERIES TO STANDARD TREND-CYCLE: TRANSPORTATION AND TRADE

Series	Period covered by series	Index of conformity
Railway freight	1882–1929	1.00
Shares traded	1875–1929	1.00
Deflated clearings	1870–1929	.80
Railway ton-miles	1870–1929	.80
Railway passenger-miles	1882–1929	.50
S. S. Marie canals traffic	1870–1929	.50
N. Y. canals traffic	1870–1929	.40
Postal money orders	1870–1929	.20
Postage stamps	1870–1929	.00
Agricultural exports	1870–1929	–.20
Coastal trade	1870–1929	–.20
Tonnage entered and cleared	1870–1929	–.20

Certain of the nonagricultural series have been insensitive to the standard trend-cycle rhythm throughout most of the period covered (in the sense that they have not conformed consistently for any considerable continuous period). Many and varied causes account for their non-conformity, but the chief forces at work may be subsumed under three categories. (1) Over a large range of industry, conditions of joint production obtain; and when considerable quantities of the output of a given commodity are a by-product of activities carried on principally for some other product or products, the given commodity may depart considerably, as do silver

Chart 17
TREND-CYCLES OF PRODUCTION OF IRON, STEEL, AND COKE

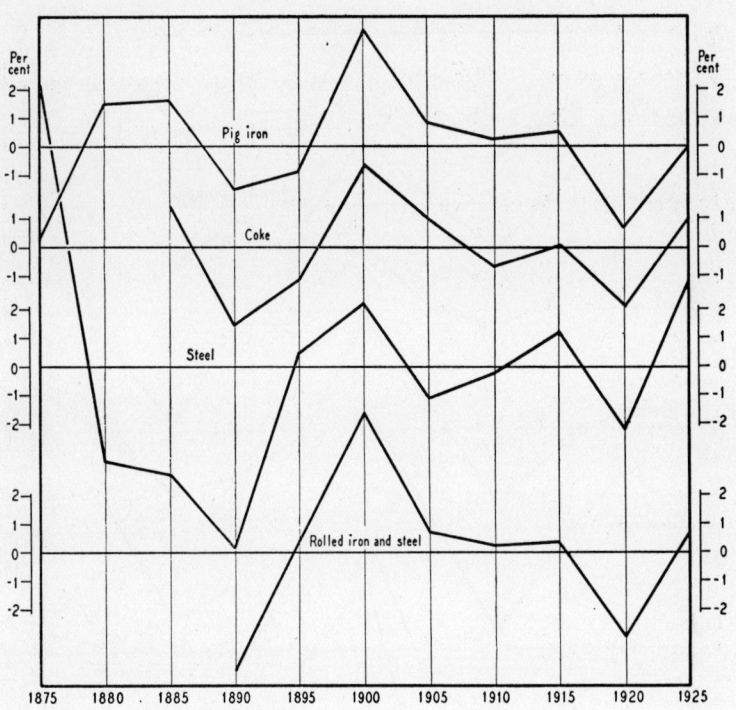

and lead,[35] from the general rhythm of the secular trends of industry. (2) Competitive relations among commodities are most important when the output of a number of commodities constitutes a composite supply for the satisfaction of a given want or limited range of wants: natural cement and

[35] For a time in the latter part of the nineteenth century, lead was in large part a by-product of silver mining. At present, the bulk of American silver production (in 1928, about 80 per cent) is a by-product of ores mined primarily for some other metal; see C. W. Merrill, *Economic Relations of Silver to Other Metals in Argentiferous Ores* (Bureau of Mines, Economic Paper 10).

Chart 18
TREND-CYCLES OF PRODUCTION SERIES RELATING TO CONSTRUCTION

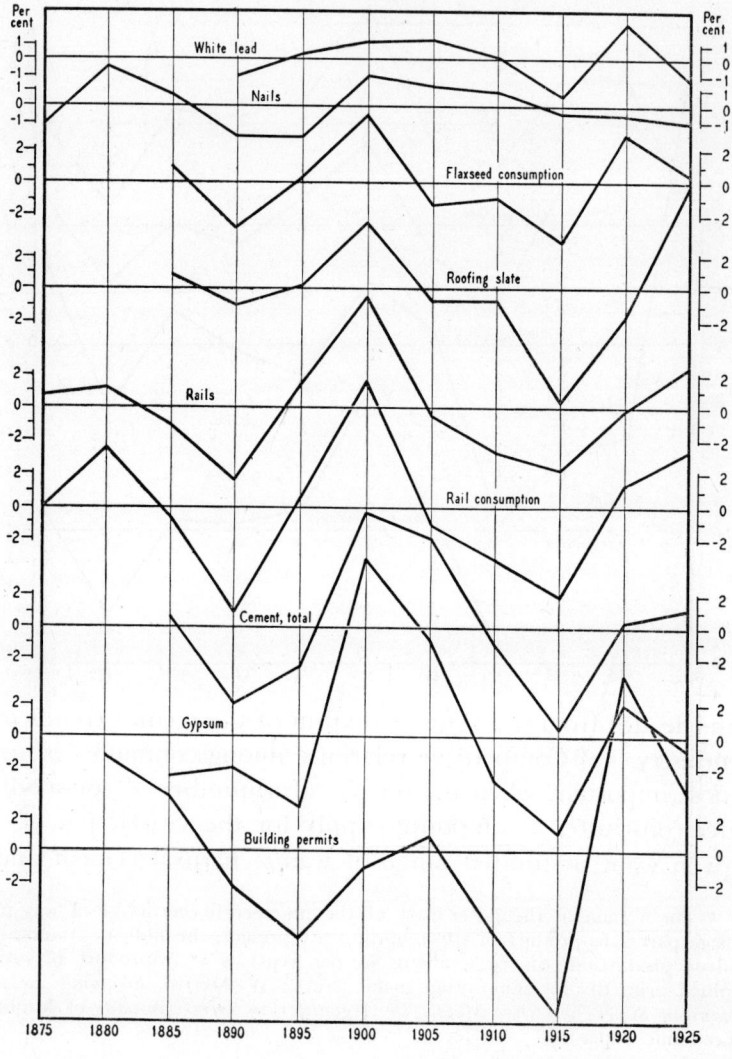

CYCLES IN GROWTH

Chart 19
TREND-CYCLES OF SEVERAL SERIES RELATING TO TRANSPORTATION AND TRADE

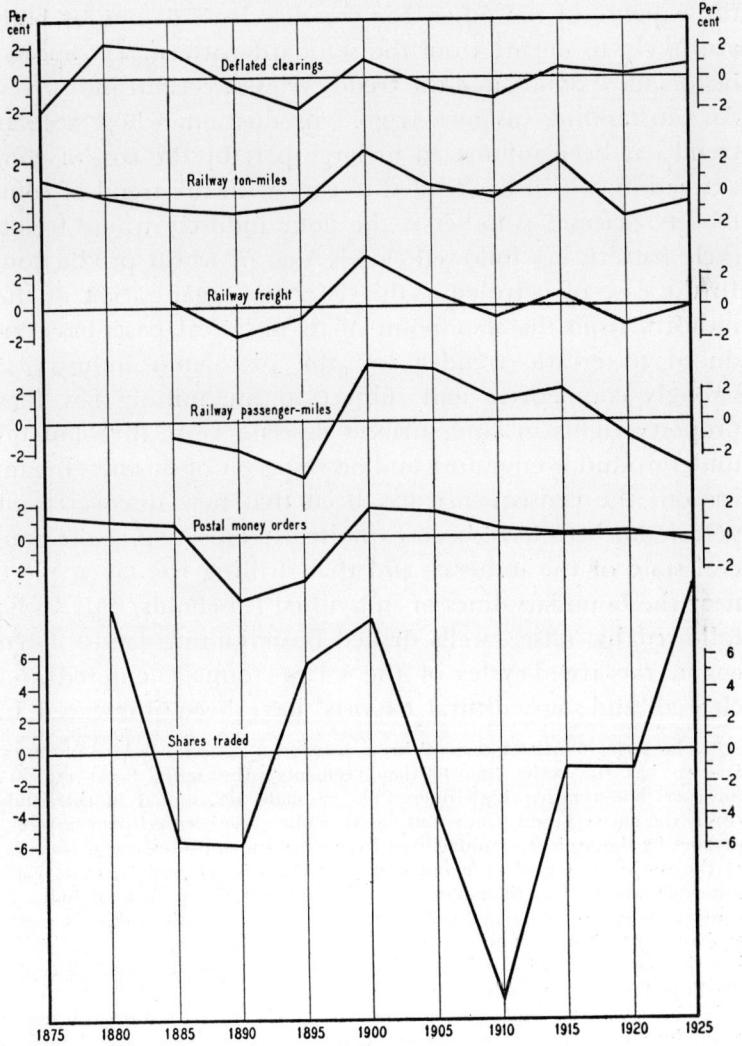

Portland cement, native asphalt and manufactured asphalt, white lead and zinc oxide, wool and other textiles, and so on, have been rivals in such a sense. Taken separately, such industries are 'incomplete'; and when one gains rapidly at the expense of the other, the trend-cycles [36] of one or both are likely to depart from the standard pattern. (3) Special factors have dominated the trend-cycles of certain industries. An outstanding instance is gold production, whose secular trend has been influenced in large part by the cost of gold extraction, which has tended to vary with the trend of commodity prices.[37] Another is the flour industry whose trend-cycle pattern has followed closely that of wheat production. In the case of petroleum, the defective organization of the industry from the standpoint of its technical basis has conduced to erratic trend-cycles: the petroleum industry is strongly competitive and subject to the mining law that property rights in land surfaces descend vertically,—but oil underground is migratory and no respecter of business organization; the consequence has been that new discoveries of petroleum beds have been exploited irrespective of the general state of the industry and that drilling has taken place near the boundary lines of individual leaseholds, only to be followed by 'offset' wells drilled on adjoining lands. Then again, the trend-cycles of the series 'tonnage entered and cleared' and 'agricultural exports' have been influenced in

[36] The series 'Portland cement' has a low index of trend-cycle conformity, and so has the series 'non-Portland cements'; the series 'total cement', however, has a rather high index. The 'asphalt' series used in this study covers the native product only, but native asphalt has been eclipsed in recent decades by the asphalt manufactured from domestic and Mexican petroleum; as the statistical record of manufactured asphalt is incomplete, exact computations are not worth making, but the indications are that an index of conformity of total asphalt production would be higher than that of native asphalt alone. Wool consumption has a low index of trend-cycle conformity; but the numerical indications are that an index of production of all textile products would show high conformity.

[37] The trend-cycles of gold production appear to have varied inversely with the trend of *actual* commodity prices.

considerable part by trend-cycles in the output of the domestic agriculture, which, as we have seen, bear little relation to the standard trend-cycle.

In addition to those nonagricultural series which have been insensitive to the standard trend-cycle during most of the period since 1870, there are some series which have been sensitive at one end of the period but not at the other, and for only this reason have low indexes of trend-cycle conformity. And although most of the series conform rather well to the standard pattern during the period taken as a whole, all but six of the series fail to conform during one or another portion of the period. All kinds of special factors account for the numerous departures of the series from the standard pattern during certain periods; but the most obtrusive are those associated with fundamental changes in the position of given industries in the economic system. Thus, the non-conformity of railway ton-miles to the standard pattern between the central decade years 1875 and 1880 is due partly to the relatively large importance of agricultural freight at that early time.[38] It is only in the last decade that the series of railway passenger-miles has conspicuously failed to conform to the standard trend-cycle; and its recent erratic behavior is doubtless traceable to the appreciable replacement of the railway by the automobile as an agency for the transport of passengers: the volume of railway passenger traffic reached an absolute peak in 1920 and by 1929 it had declined almost 35 per cent from its high point. Sulphur production shows perfect conformity to the standard trend-cycle since 1900;[39] prior to that date, it shows little conformity, but the industry was of negligible size before the turn of the century. Nail production shows perfect conform-

[38] See Appendix C, III.
[39] This is shown by calculations restricted to the period since 1900, but not by the trend-cycle data for sulphur given in Appendix A, Table 47. The latter, however, are of little significance; see p. 103, note 8.

ity during most of the period covered, but of late its movement has diverged from that of the standard pattern and also from that of the other series of 'construction' materials; this probably reflects the sharp curtailment in the use of wood for building and packing. Then again, the series of postal money orders shows fairly close conformity during the early decades; but in recent decades, probably as a result of the growing practice of keeping checking accounts, its movement has been insensitive to the general trend-cycle. Apart from those industries whose position in the economic system has undergone a fundamental change, the construction series provide the most conspicuous instances of non-conformity to the standard pattern during certain periods. Beginning with the central decade year 1910, the construction series (see Chart 18) have diverged more or less uniformly—a result in considerable part of the authoritarian restrictions on construction during the War period.

IV. TREND-CYCLE AMPLITUDES OF INDIVIDUAL INDUSTRIES

The measures of inconstancy in the rates of growth of individual industries have already suggested that the magnitude of the swings in trend-cycles is considerable and varies from series to series.[40] Now that the statistical analysis of the trend-cycle patterns has been concluded, we may strive for exact notions concerning their amplitudes. A measure of the trend-cycle amplitude of a series may be obtained by taking the standard deviation of its trend-cycle observations; the latter, it will be recalled, are deviations of the decade rates of a series from an exponential curve fitted to the rates. The standard deviation of the trend-cycle observations of a series states the degree of variation in the slope of the secular trend of the series with reference to the slope of a primary

[40] See Ch. III, sec. II.

CYCLES IN GROWTH

trend that is in effect a 'logarithmic' parabola.[41]

The measures of trend-cycle amplitude are summarized analytically [42] in Table 38 and are recorded by individual series in Table 39. The first table shows that agricultural series account largely for the lowest of the amplitudes, and mineral series for the highest; and that within each industrial division, non-basic series account mainly for the extremely high amplitudes. The average level of the amplitudes is relatively low in the division of agriculture and fisheries, and of transportation and trade; and relatively high in the division of mining, and of manufactures and construction. Chart 16 indicates that the trend-cycles of manufactures from agricultural materials are of smaller amplitude than of manufactures from mineral materials.[43] The most obtrusive in-

[41] See Ch. IV, sec. I, and this chapter, sec. I. The standard deviation of the decade rates of a series (see Ch. III, sec. II) measures the influence of two factors: the drift of the decade rates and the amplitude of the fluctuations of the decade rates about a line defining their general drift. The influence of the first factor is eliminated largely in the measure of trend-cycle amplitude. This has two consequences. First, the measures of trend-cycle amplitude are lower than the standard deviations of decade rates in all series except the following, in which the two are identical: 13, 21, 23, 31, 40, 74, 91, and 102. Second, the variation of the measures of trend-cycle amplitude is lower than that of the standard deviations of decade rates. The correlation between the two measures is high; the coefficient of correlation for the 'all' series group is .95 (the coefficient for this group becomes .91, when the five series having the largest values—series 2, 35, 44, 65, and 84—are dropped).

[42] For the composition of the 'all' series and basic series groups, see Appendix A, Table 46, columns e and f.

[43] The medians of the trend-cycle observations of the two groups are given in Appendix A, Table 52. The manufactures from agricultural materials include the following series: 46–51, 54, 58, 61, 66, 69–71, 74, 76–7, 79, 86, and 88–9; for the central decade years 1875, 1880, and 1885, series 60 is substituted for series 86. The manufactures from mineral materials include the following series: 52–3, 56–7, 62–4, 67–8, 72–3, 75, 78, 80–2, 84–5, 87, and 90. (For certain of the central decade years, not all of these series are included; see pp. 180–1, note 8.)

The amplitude of the medians of the trend-cycles of manufactures from agricultural materials is 0.8 per cent, of the medians of the trend-cycles of manufactures from mineral materials 1.3 per cent. As for the individual series, 8 manufactures from mineral materials have trend-cycle amplitudes

Table 38
FREQUENCY DISTRIBUTIONS OF MEASURES OF TREND-CYCLE AMPLITUDE, FOR 'ALL' SERIES AND BASIC SERIES, BY INDUSTRIAL GROUPS

Measure of trend-cycle amplitude (per cent)	Agriculture and fisheries	Mining	Manufactures and construction	Transportation and trade	All industries
		'All' series			
0.0 to 0.9	4	..	1	1	6
1.0 to 1.9	9	4	16	6	35
2.0 to 2.9	4	4	13	2	23
3.0 to 3.9	1	2	5	..	8
4.0 to 4.9	1	1	3	2	7
5.0 to 5.9	2	2	2	..	6
6.0 to 6.9	..	2	2	..	4
7.0 to 7.9	1	..	..	..	1
8.0 to 8.9	..	..	..	1	1
9.0 to 9.9	..	..	..	..	..
10.0 to 10.9	..	2	..	..	2
11.0 to 11.9	..	1	1	..	2
12.0 to 12.9	..	..	..	..	..
13.0 and over *	1	2	1	..	4
Total	23	20	44	12	99
		Basic series			
0.0 to 0.9	4	..	2	1	7
1.0 to 1.9	7	4	11	5	27
2.0 to 2.9	2	4	9	1	16
3.0 to 3.9	..	2	1	..	3
4.0 to 4.9	..	2	3	..	5
5.0 to 5.9	..	..	1	..	1
Total	13	12	27	7	59

* The items in this class are: agriculture and fisheries, 13.0 per cent; mining, 16.8 and 31.6 per cent; manufactures and construction, 16.7 per cent.

of 3.0 per cent or over, but only 2 manufactures from agricultural materials. On the other hand, 9 manufactures from agricultural materials have amplitudes of 1.5 per cent or less, but only 4 manufactures from mineral materials.

dustrial difference, then, is between agricultural products and their processed derivatives, on the one hand, and minerals and their derivatives, on the other; or what comes substantially to the same thing, between consumers' goods and producers' goods industries.[44]

These industrial differences in trend-cycle amplitude are traceable to four factors: type of technology and organization, type of demand, scope of industry, and its degree of maturity. The influence of the first factor can be detected in the difference between the trend-cycle amplitudes of the agricultural and mineral industries. In agriculture, the control over output is widely diffused, much of the output of each of the various products is an incidental result of activities carried on principally for other products, and managerial policy is such as to lead generally to an inverse movement in the trend-cycles of acreages and acre-yields.[45] Thus, those factors making for trend-cycles which arise in the technology and organization of agriculture operate through numerous channels, often work in different directions, and therefore are self-cancelling in considerable part; so that the trend-cycle amplitudes tend to be low. In contrast to agriculture, most mineral industries are characterized by fair concentration of control, and practically all of the output of most minerals results from activities carried on almost solely for those minerals. Therefore, those factors making for trend-

[44] Consumers' goods are viewed as products destined for human consumption, producers' goods as products which find final realization in industrial equipment. Of the 59 basic series (see Appendix A, Table 46, column f), 29 may be listed fairly unequivocally as consumers' goods series, and 14 as producers' goods series. The first group includes series 1, 5–6, 9–10, 13–5, 18–20, 23–4, 43, 46–50, 58, 66, 68, 71, 79–80, 82–3, 86, and 99; the second includes series 25, 27, 29, 34, 36, 39, 52, 56, 62, 73, 78, 85, 90, and 91. The median of the trend-cycle amplitudes of the consumers' goods series is 1.6 per cent, as is the arithmetic mean. The median of the amplitudes of the producers' goods series is 2.4 per cent, the arithmetic mean 2.6 per cent.

[45] See pp. 213–5.

Table 39
MEASURES OF TREND-CYCLE AMPLITUDE
(Unit: one per cent)

Series	Period covered by series	Trend-cycle amplitude
Agriculture and fisheries		
Beet sugar	1870–1929	13.0
Raisins	1872–1929	7.9
Flaxseed	1879–1929	5.0
Rice	1870–1929	5.0
Rye	1870–1929	4.1
Whale	1870–1929	3.7
Molasses and sirup	1870–1929	2.6
Barley	1870–1929	2.5
Cane sugar	1870–1929	2.5
Tobacco, raw	1870–1929	2.2
Cattle	1880–1929	1.8
Cotton	1870–1929	1.8
Cod and mackerel	1870–1929	1.7
Sheep	1880–1929	1.7
Wool	1870–1929	1.7
Wheat	1870–1930	1.4
Oats	1870–1930	1.3
Buckwheat	1870–1929	1.2
Potatoes	1870–1929	1.0
Corn	1870–1929	0.9
Hogs	1880–1929	0.9
Fish, total	1880–1929	0.8
Hay	1870–1930	0.8
Mining		
Sulphur	1880–1929	31.6
Asphalt	1880–1929	16.8
Non-Portland cements	1880–1929	11.5
Portland cement	1880–1929	10.5
Natural gas	1882–1929	10.3
Fluorspar	1880–1929	6.9
Mercury	1870–1929	6.6
Pyrites	1880–1929	5.3
Gypsum	1880–1929	5.2

Table 39 (cont.)
MEASURES OF TREND-CYCLE AMPLITUDE
(Unit: one per cent)

Series	Period covered by series	Trend-cycle amplitude
Mining (cont.)		
Gold	1870–1929	4.5
Cement, total	1880–1929	4.2
Petroleum	1870–1929	3.6
Lead, domestic	1870–1929	3.1
Copper	1870–1929	2.8
Bituminous coal	1870–1929	2.4
Iron ore	1880–1929	2.4
Zinc	1870–1929	2.1
Coal, total	1870–1929	2.0
Phosphate rock	1870–1929	1.9
Salt	1880–1929	1.7
Silver	1870–1929	1.6
Anthracite coal	1870–1929	1.2
Manufactures and construction		
Vessels	1870–1929	16.7
Aluminum	1883–1929	11.6
Cigarettes	1880–1929	6.4
Locomotives	1880–1929	6.3
Building permits	1874–1929	5.9
Antimonial lead	1871–1929	5.4
Rubber imports	1870–1929	4.9
Rail consumption	1870–1929	4.1
Steel	1870–1929	4.1
Sisal imports	1870–1929	3.7
Roofing slate	1879–1929	3.6
Gold consumption	1880–1929	3.2
Rails	1870–1929	3.1
Superphosphate	1870–1929	3.0
Canned corn	1885–1929	2.9
Lead, total	1870–1929	2.7
Cocoa imports	1870–1929	2.5
Cottonseed oil	1872–1929	2.5

Table 39 (cont.)
MEASURES OF TREND-CYCLE AMPLITUDE
(Unit: one per cent)

Series	Period covered by series	Trend-cycle amplitude
Manufactures and construction (cont.)		
Rolled iron and steel	1885–1929	2.5
Cottonseed cake and meal	1872–1929	2.4
Flaxseed consumption	1879–1929	2.4
Jute imports	1870–1929	2.3
Silver consumption	1880–1929	2.3
Distilled spirits	1870–1918	2.2
Copper consumption	1883–1929	2.1
Pig iron	1870–1929	2.0
Tin-plate consumption	1871–1929	2.0
Zinc consumption	1873–1929	1.9
Manila hemp imports	1870–1929	1.8
Silk imports, raw	1870–1929	1.8
Coke	1880–1929	1.7
Minor fiber imports	1870–1929	1.7
Wool consumption	1870–1930	1.6
Coffee imports	1870–1929	1.5
Nails	1872–1929	1.5
Cigars	1880–1929	1.4
Fermented liquors	1870–1918	1.4
White lead	1884–1929	1.4
Canned tomatoes	1885–1929	1.3
Tobacco and snuff	1871–1929	1.2
Cotton consumption	1870–1929	1.0
Lead consumption	1870–1929	1.0
Raw sugar consumption	1870–1930	1.0
Silk imports, unmanufactured	1883–1929	1.0
Tin imports	1870–1929	1.0
Tobacco consumption	1880–1929	0.9
Flour	1880–1929	0.5
Transportation and trade		
Shares traded	1875–1929	8.0
N. Y. canals traffic	1870–1929	4.6
S. S. Marie canals traffic	1870–1929	4.1

Table 39 (cont.)
MEASURES OF TREND-CYCLE AMPLITUDE
(Unit: one per cent)

Series	Period covered by series	Trend-cycle amplitude
Transportation and trade (cont.)		
Railway passenger-miles	1882–1929	2.5
Agricultural exports	1870–1929	2.1
Postal money orders	1870–1929	1.7
Coastal trade	1870–1929	1.6
Tonnage entered and cleared	1870–1929	1.6
Deflated clearings	1870–1929	1.4
Railway freight	1882–1929	1.4
Railway ton-miles	1870–1929	1.3
Postage stamps	1870–1929	0.9

cycles which arise in the technology and organization of mining are not self-cancelling to the same extent as in agriculture, and tend to make for large amplitudes. But the technological factors underlying mining resemble in some cases, most notably in the silver industry, those of agriculture: as the mining of the various ores containing silver is influenced by somewhat different causes, the trend-cycles in the various ores are partly self-cancelling, and silver production has consequently a low trend-cycle amplitude.

The powerful influence of type of demand on the trend-cycle amplitudes of industries is expressed in the lower amplitude of consumers' goods than of producers' goods industries, previously mentioned, and in the lower amplitude of industries producing consumers' staples than of luxury goods. Trends of consumption of consumers' staples are closely linked to the trend of population which is superlatively regular. Whatever secular changes take place in the per-capita consumption of staples tend to be gradual, in part, because trend-cycles of real earnings are of mild amplitude,[46] but primarily, because staples are deeply ingrained in the customs of the people. In the case of luxury products, however, demand factors tend to make for large trend-cycle amplitudes, in part, because such products are 'marginal' in consumers' outlays, and in part, because fashions in their use are often volatile. Finally, the demand for producers' goods, being derived from the demand for consumers' goods, ordinarily exaggerates the secular variations in that demand, and therefore tends to make for large trend-cycle amplitudes. Thus, a change from, say, an upward to a downward trend-cycle movement will tend to be accompanied by a sharp curtailment in capital extensions, since a diminished rate of growth in the production of consumers' goods means that the productive facilities extended earlier on the basis of the former higher rate of growth in production can amply provide for the moderately increasing demand for some years. Delays will also tend to take place in repairs and replacements, for the overextension of capital facilities makes shifts possible to idle equipment in good condition. These factors make for a very sharp downward trend-cycle movement in producers' goods industries, but they do not hold sway exclusively and are counteracted, though only in part, by other factors: only a limited number of enterprises provide capital facilities for their anticipated growth over a long period, new industries require instrumental equipment, and a period of general trend-cycle contraction is yet a period of trend-cycle expansion for a goodly number of industries.

The lower trend-cycle amplitude of basic than of non-basic series is traceable to differences in the scope and maturity of the industries in the two groups. The broader the industrial coverage of a series, the more potent are the influences mak-

[46] The trend-cycle amplitude of an index of real earnings (see p. 240, note 53) is 0.8 per cent for 1890–1926.

CYCLES IN GROWTH

ing for a low trend-cycle amplitude. For when the composite demand for a good is wide and diversified, the various components of that demand are likely to be subject to trend-cycle movements which are to some extent antithetical; the output of that good is therefore likely to have a small trend-cycle amplitude. On the other hand, the demand for a specialized commodity flows through a single channel or a limited number of channels; the output of that good is therefore likely to have a large trend-cycle amplitude. The influence of the industrial scope of a series on its trend-cycle amplitude is continuous and works within and across the groups of basic and non-basic series. Thus, the basic series of greatest industrial coverage or reference—such as deflated clearings, railway freight, railway ton-miles, and postage stamps—have exceptionally low trend-cycle amplitudes. Where aggregate series and their components are both included in our list of series, the aggregate series generally have the lower amplitudes.[47] In the simple industrial sequences represented by the production of a raw material and its industrial consumption, the consumption series have a wider industrial reference and generally have also the lower amplitudes.[48]

Finally, the trend-cycle amplitude of an industry tends to reflect its age or degree of maturity. The trend-cycles of 'mature' industries tend to be of mild amplitude: since the

---

[47] Coal is an exception, but this results from the very high direct correlation between the trend-cycles of anthracite and bituminous.

[48] Of nine such sequences among our series (see p. 166), all but two—copper and silver—conform to the rule stated; and it is of some significance that the ores of these two metals are generally combined with other ores. The present comparisons are based on periods which are identical for the production and consumption of each commodity, but different for the several commodities. Special computations of trend-cycle amplitudes were necessary for certain of the series. They are as follows for the periods indicated: copper (1883–1929), 1.6 per cent; zinc (1873–1929), 2.1 per cent; silver (1880–1929), 1.7 per cent; gold (1880–1929), 4.0 per cent; and raw tobacco (1880–1929), 2.1 per cent.

236   PRODUCTION TRENDS

absolute size of their output is large and the slopes of their primary trends are mild, even appreciable changes in the volume of production are likely to mean only small changes in their percentage rates of growth. On the other hand, the trend-cycles of 'new' and 'decadent' industries tend to be of large amplitude: since the absolute size of their output is small and the slopes of their primary trends are sharp, at least during the phases of infancy and late retrogression, even minor changes in the volume of production are likely to mean considerable changes in their percentage rates of growth. Since high average rates of growth or of decline equally imply considerable capacity for variation over time in the rates of growth, a rectilinear relationship cannot be expected to hold between the average rate of growth, previously accepted as a rough indicator of industrial maturity, and the trend-cycle amplitude of industries; but it may be expected to hold for the consistently progressive or retrogressive divisions of industry—or to use the terminology earlier employed, for series with measures of continuity of growth of $+1$ or -1.[49]

Table 40 indicates that our statistical records consist with these expectations.[50] The coefficients of correlation are negli-

[49] See pp. 74–6.
[50] The 5 series having the highest trend-cycle amplitudes and the 5 having the highest average rates of growth (for the full period covered) were omitted from the 'all' series group (see Appendix A, Table 46, column *e*); since 3 series had extreme values for both variables, only the following 7 series had to be dropped: 2, 16, 35, 41, 44, 65, and 84. The last 5 series were dropped also from the nonagricultural group (see Table 46, column *g*). For the composition of the basic and basic nonagricultural groups, see Table 46, columns *f* and *h*; of the basic consumers' goods and basic producers' goods groups, see p. 229, note 44. The group with measures of continuity of growth of 1.00 includes series 19, 29, 31, 36, 38, 43, 46–7, 52–3, 58–9, 62–4, 68, 73, 82–3, 85–6, 88, 90, 95–7, 101, and 104. The group with measures of continuity of growth from .50 to 1.00 includes series 1, 5–14, 18, 20, 23–5, 27, 32, 34, 37, 39, 42, 45, 48–50, 54, 56, 61, 66–7, 69–72, 74, 76–80, 87, 89, 93, 98–99, and 102. The group with measures of continuity of growth below .50 includes series 3–4, 15, 17, 21–2, 28, 30, 33, 40, 51, 57, 75, 81, 91–2, 94, 100, and 103. (In all, the last 3 groups include 94

gible for the 'all' series and nonagricultural groups, because the high positive correlation for the rapidly growing industries is cancelled by the negative correlation for decadent

Table 40

COEFFICIENTS OF CORRELATION BETWEEN AVERAGE RATES OF GROWTH AND TREND-CYCLE AMPLITUDES, FOR SEVERAL GROUPS OF PRODUCTION SERIES

Group	Number of series included	Coefficient of correlation
'All' series	92	.14
Nonagricultural series	70	.07
Basic series	59	.39
Basic nonagricultural series	46	.29
Basic consumers' goods series	29	.48
Basic producers' goods series	14	.31
Series with measures of continuity of growth of 1.00	28	.72
Series with measures of continuity of growth from .50 to 1.00	47	.66
Series with measures of continuity of growth below .50	19	.09

industries and the absence of correlation for industries in the twilight zone of progress. On the other hand, the coefficients are fairly high for the basic and basic nonagricultural groups, because none of the industries in these groups show an average rate of decline and a smaller number are in the twilight zone of progress, so that only a part of the correlation for the progressive group is cancelled.[51] But the most illuminating

---

series, which is two more than is contained in the 'all' series group with extremes dropped. Series 36 and 83, which were dropped earlier because of their duplicative character—see p. 52, note—are retained in the group with measures of continuity of 1.00 because they do not involve there any duplication.)

[51] The coefficients for basic consumers' goods and basic producers' goods

coefficients are for the several groups of series of varying degrees of progressiveness as indicated by measures of continuity of growth: the correlation is seen to decline with the continuity of growth of the series. In the progressive division of industry, then, the industries having grown relatively at the highest rates tend to be the same as those having relatively the highest trend-cycle amplitudes; and the industries having grown at the lowest rates tend to be the same as those having the lowest trend-cycle amplitudes.[52]

---

are of the same order of magnitude as the coefficient for the entire basic group; this indicates that the correlation in the basic group does not reflect merely the lower (average) rate of growth and lower trend-cycle amplitude of consumers' goods than of producers' goods series.

[52] The correlation study indicates emphatically that the average rate of growth, taken algebraically, does not bear a linear relationship to trend-cycle amplitude. Yet, if the average rate of growth—which may be viewed as an index of the potential capacity for variation in the characteristic represented by a series having positive values throughout—is replaced by a generalized and more significant index of capacity for variation, a consistently linear relationship does emerge between trend-cycle amplitude and such a modified measure. A general index of capacity for variation may be readily secured by observing a few elementary points. It is accepted in Statistics that the average value of a series is an index of the capacity of the series to vary; otherwise, there is no sense in taking an average as the denominator of the coefficient of relative variability. Yet, an average can logically serve, as an index of capacity for variation, only in the case of a series with positive values. When all items are negative, a negative capacity for variation would be indicated, which is nonsense. When positive and negative items balance exactly, that is, when their arithmetic mean is zero, we have the paradox of a series having no capacity for variation showing nevertheless infinite relative variation. These considerations point to the necessity of redefining just what it is which measures the capacity of a series to vary.

The characteristic of potential variability can be determined statistically from only the direct behavior of a series—that is, if there is no a priori knowledge of the causes making for its variability. Every individual departure of a series from zero constitutes an observation on the capacity of the series to vary. Therefore, an average deviation or a standard deviation measured from zero expresses synthetically the degree of potential variation. An average deviation from zero is simply the arithmetic mean of the series when all items are positive; this means that the average deviation from zero is a general measure of potential capacity for variation, containing the arithmetic mean as a special case when all items are positive. But the standard deviation from zero is a preferable measure of capacity

V. THE EXPLANATION OF TREND-CYCLES

An attempt has already been made in section III to explain the individual character of the trend-cycles in agriculture, and also the various departures of nonagricultural series from the standard trend-cycle pattern. We must now direct our attention to the causes of the similarities among the series— that is, the trend-cycle rhythm proper. Presumably, the trend-cycles of production tend to run a similar course in the various industries because of their technical and commercial interdependence. The interconnection of economic processes

---

for variation; for it bears a definite mathematical relation to the standard deviation taken from the mean and to the standard deviation taken from a line of trend: the latter two cannot be greater than the former. (One implication is that the coefficient of relative variability can be expressed as the ratio of a standard deviation measured from the mean to a standard deviation measured from zero.)

It is to be expected that a coefficient of correlation between this index of capacity for variation and trend-cycle amplitude will be higher than that between the average rate of growth and trend-cycle amplitude. In fact, the correlation for the 'all' series group (see note 50) now becomes .69, while it was formerly only .14. Similarly, the correlation for the basic series group is raised from .39 to .61. The high relationship between indexes of trend-cycle amplitude and indexes of capacity for variation means simply that the potential capacity of the rate of growth of an industry to vary is actually realized in a fairly consistent degree by the ensemble of series. Of itself, this is not very important; but it provides indirectly a useful standard for the segregation of series that have realized to an exceptionally large or small (relative) extent the potential capacity for variation in the rates of their development. Such a standard may be taken to be defined by the zone traced out by the 'standard error' measured on each side of the line of regression of trend-cycle amplitude on the index of capacity for variation. The series of the basic group lying above this zone are gold, gold consumption, rail consumption, building permits, and rubber imports: these are series whose actual trend-cycle amplitude is 'abnormally' large in relation to their potential capacity for variation. The series lying below the zone are cottonseed oil, phosphate rock, tin imports, unmanufactured silk imports, postage stamps, and railway ton-miles: these are series whose actual trend-cycle amplitude is 'abnormally' small in relation to their potential capacity for variation. Only this conclusion is warranted: when the capacity for variation in the rate of industrial growth is considered, the construction series have exceptionally large trend-cycle amplitudes, while the series of broadest industrial reference have exceptionally small trend-cycle amplitudes.

in turn suggests that the standard trend-cycle cannot be confined to the sphere of physical production alone, that it must pervade as well all other major elements in the economy. A brief study of series relating to economic processes other than production—nonagricultural prices, 'all-commodity' prices, real earnings, money in circulation, gold stocks, business failures, and patents issued—shows (see Chart 20) that such series do in fact run a trend-cycle course similar to that of the standard trend-cycle.[53] There is some evidence, then, that the

[53] The indexes of trend-cycle conformity of the series are as follows: nonagricultural prices 1.00, 'all-commodity' prices 1.00, real earnings .60, money in circulation .60, gold stocks .80, business failures (inverted) .80, patents issued .80.

The trend-cycles of these non-production series were determined in the same way as the trend-cycles of the production series, except that, in the case of the price indexes, the deviations of the decade rates were taken from natural straight lines. (This minor technical departure was resorted to, because there is no sense in considering the primary trend of prices as a 'logarithmic' parabola. The results obtained do not differ perceptibly from those yielded by an exponential curve fitted to the decade rates.) The trend-cycles of the price indexes are not given beyond the central decade year 1910, since decade rates for the later period of violent price movements would be fictive. However, if trend-cycles of the price indexes were computed for the later years, they would continue to conform to the standard trend-cycle. The failure of the wage series to cover the full period since 1870 is due to absence of data.

For the figures corresponding to Chart 20, see Appendix A, Table 53. The curve in Chart 20, headed 'standard trend-cycle' is a graph of the arithmetic means of the nine decil curves of the basic nonagricultural group (Section 4, see Chart 8D and Table 48). The other curves in Chart 20 are based on the following data: (1) Nonagricultural wholesale prices: 1870–90, index by Bureau of Agricultural Economics, derived from the Aldrich report indexes, the foods group being excluded; since 1890, an index furnished by Professor Mills (this index is an unweighted geometric of relatives of nonagricultural prices, manufactured derivatives of farm products not being included). (2) 'All-commodity' wholesale prices: 1870–89, the Aldrich report index; beginning with 1890, index of the Bureau of Labor Statistics. (The Warren-Pearson index of wholesale commodity prices—see New York State College of Agriculture, *Farm Economics*, September, 1931, pp. 1586–7—gives much the same results for the period 1870–90 as the notorious Aldrich index.) (3) Real earnings: this is an index of real earnings (not real wages) of employees "attached to the manufacturing, transportation, and coal-mining industries." See P. H. Douglas, *Real Wages in the United States, 1890–1926* (Pollak Foundation for Economic Research, 1930), p. 468. (4) Money in circulation: this series covers money in circula-

CYCLES IN GROWTH

Chart 20
TREND-CYCLES OF PROCESSES OTHER THAN PRODUCTION COMPARED WITH STANDARD TREND-CYCLE

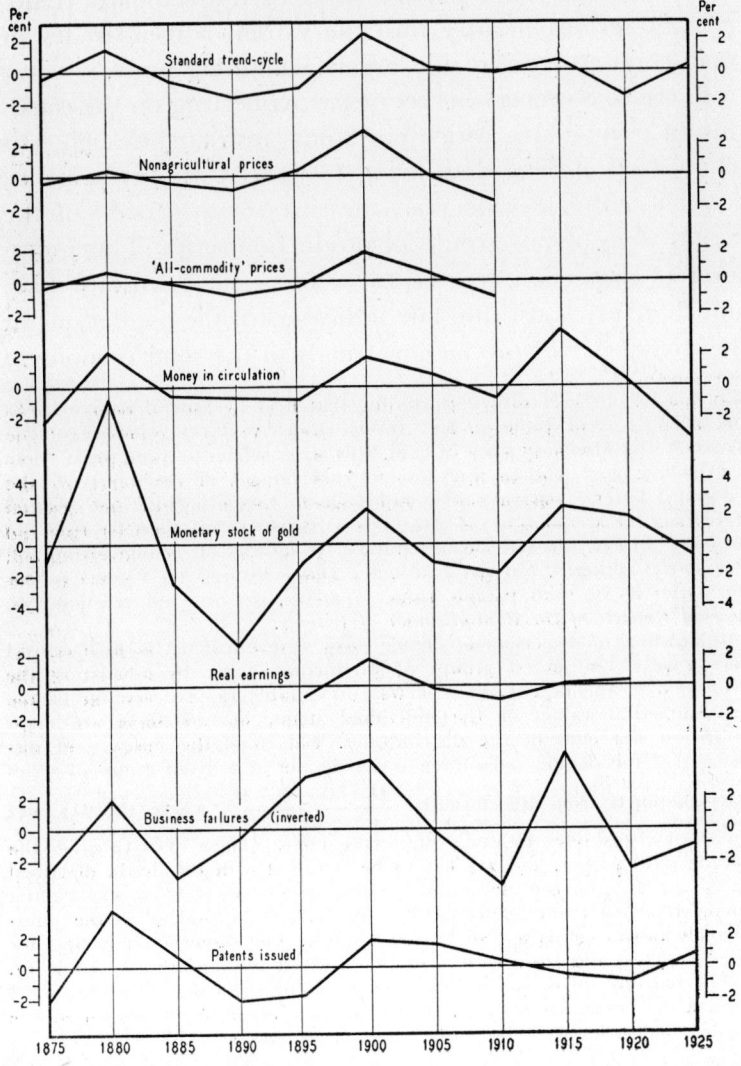

impress of the standard trend-cycle is diffused generally through the economic system; though only a thorough statistical study of processes other than production could establish satisfactorily the pervasiveness of the standard trend-cycle. A serious inquiry into the causes of trend-cycles in production must await this larger fact-finding study.

There is, however, one set of factors bearing on the causation of trend-cycles, which our study, restricted though it is to production data, does bring to light. Chart 21 presents, at each central decade year, measures of dispersion of the decade rates of two groups of production series. These measures of dispersion are 'adjusted' for their downward bias, and therefore constitute fair indicators of the oscillations in the divergence of production trends in the total economy.[54]

---

tion outside of the Treasury (including that held by Federal reserve banks and agents), as of June 30. See *Annual Reports of the Secretary of the Treasury*. (5) Monetary stock of gold: this series relates to June 30; it "does not include gold bullion and foreign coin outside of the vaults of the Treasury, Federal reserve banks, and Federal reserve agents." See *Annual Reports of the Secretary of the Treasury*, particularly the report for 1928. (6) Business failures: this series covers number of failures of manufacturing and commercial concerns, but not banks. See *Dun's Review*. (7) Patents issued: this series is for total patents issued (patents, designs, and reissues). See *Annual Reports of the Commissioner of Patents*.

[54] Measures of dispersion of decade rates were calculated at each central decade year, for several groups of production series. In calculating the dispersion of the decade rates, it was undesirable to take account of the full numerical values of the individual items, because these are often erratic at the ends of the distributions. Therefore, the measure of dispersion of the decade rates for a given decade in a given group of series was computed from the formula: $\frac{D_7 + D_8 - D_2 - D_3}{2}$, where the D's and their subscripts refer to deciles of decade rates. (These decils are for the decade rates proper, and are not to be confused with the decils, described on pp. 182–3, of the deviations of the decade rates from exponential curves fitted to them.) This measure is virtually equivalent to the interquartile range, but is apt to be more stable. The dispersion measures for the 'all' series and basic series groups are given in Appendix A, Table 54.

The measures of dispersion for each group of series showed a downward drift with the march of time, suggesting that the rates of growth of the various industries were becoming increasingly similar. This is contrary to

It will be noticed that the cyclical movements of the dispersion measures trace out patterns very similar to that of the standard trend-cycle. This correspondence means that when the trends of production have on the whole moved steeply upward, the degree of divergence of production trends has

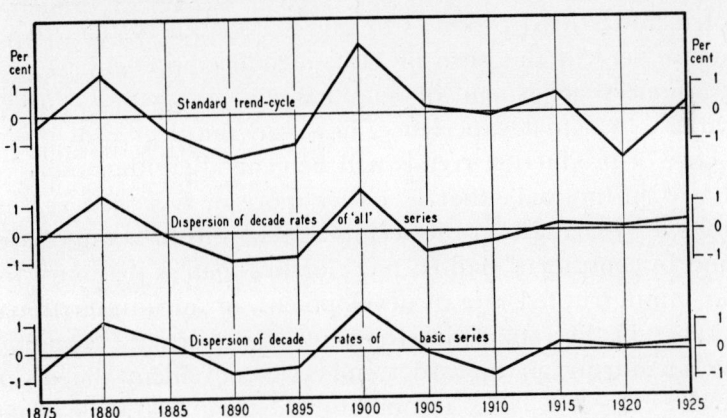

Chart 21
CYCLES OF DISPERSION OF DECADE RATES OF PRODUCTION SERIES COMPARED WITH STANDARD TREND-CYCLE

also been high; and that when the trends of production have on the whole moved only moderately upward, the degree of divergence of production trends has also been only moderate. In fine, the degree of divergence of production trends has varied with the degree of progressiveness of the economy.

---

expectations, for technical progress and rising standards of living work incessantly in the direction of increasing the divergence of production trends. The downward drift is a bias which originates in the fact that the forces making for retardation in industrial growth tend to act most potently in the more rapidly growing industries, so that the rates of growth of a virtually fixed list of individual industries tend to become increasingly similar as the length of period covered increases. It was necessary to adjust the measures of dispersion for their bias; this was done by expressing the decade-by-decade dispersion measures of a given group as plus or minus deviations from a straight line fitted to the dispersion measures by the method of least squares. These deviations constitute the cycles of dispersion: they are

The divergence of production trends over periods of some ten years has a different meaning than over periods of a half-century or longer: the latter indicates the extent of the actual transformation in the pattern of national production, the former indicates partly a real (lasting) transformation in the pattern of production and partly a disruption of the 'normal' relationships among industries. A certain degree of trend divergence is a necessary condition of smooth development in a progressive economy; for, in such an economy, the ratio of manufactured products to raw materials will tend to increase, as will the ratio of instrumental equipment to final consumers' goods, and of 'comforts' and 'luxuries' to 'necessaries'. In actual experience, however, the degree of divergence of production trends will be generally either more or less than 'normal'; that is, either more or less than is warranted by changes in the technical relations of commodities and in consumers' habits; more or less than is necessary for an uninterrupted rate of development, or an uninterrupted change in the rate of development, in the general economy. When during an upward trend-cycle movement the divergence exceeds what is 'normal' for the time, a strain will develop in the economic system; this is likely to lead to a general

---

plotted in Chart 21 for the 'all' series and basic series groups (for the exact decade-by-decade composition of these groups, see pp. 180–1, note 8); the figures corresponding to the chart are given in Table 54.

Cycles of dispersion measures determined for identical lists of series of the above two categories (see groups a, b, e, and f, in Table 46) showed practically the same type of fluctuation as the groups in Chart 21. On the other hand, cycles of dispersion measures for nonagricultural groups of series (see groups c, d, g, and h, in Table 46, and the nonagricultural groups noted on pp. 180–1, note 8) departed considerably from the standard trend-cycle. This fact is important: in the first place, it renders suspect the easy interpretation that the similarity of the cycles in the dispersion measures (plotted in Chart 21) to the standard trend-cycle emanates from the mere circumstance that dispersions are apt to be closely correlated with averages; in the second place, it lends support to the a priori expectation that, if divergence of production trends is a causal factor in trend-cycle movements, it must be the divergence of the trends of all industries rather than of nonagricultural industries alone.

crisis and to a curtailment in the rate of development of the system. The unique correspondence, then, between relatively sharp divergence of production trends and an upward trend-cycle movement in industry suggests that one of the factors serving to terminate an upward trend-cycle movement is a partial loss of industrial balance that develops during the upward movement.

When the divergence of production trends falls below what is 'normal' for the time, it might of itself indicate either increasing strain in the system or increasing approach to industrial relationships 'normal' for that time. But when the divergence of production trends falls to a 'subnormal' level during a downward trend-cycle movement, it is practically certain to be symptomatic of increasing readjustment; for the 'subnormal' degree of divergence will then derive mainly from the sharp curtailment in the rates of development of those industries which had grown at a disproportionately rapid rate during the upward trend-cycle movement. Although the divergence of production trends is invariably lower during a downward than during an upward trend-cycle movement, it may yet, for all that we know, remain above 'normal' for some time. This may express either a very rapid readjustment of industrial trends or an increasing strain in the industrial system, depending on the particular relative positions of the individual trends; but if the latter be the condition, it cannot continue indefinitely, and with the passage of years, a realignment of industrial rates of growth favorable to the inception of a 'new era' is virtually bound to emerge. The unique correspondence, then, between relatively mild divergence of production trends and a downward trend-cycle movement suggests that a restoration of industrial balance develops during the downward movement, which creates conditions favorable to (or permissive of) the initiation of a new upward movement.

This is the sum of light which our data throw definitely on the causation of trend-cycles in production. The correspondence between the trend-cycles of several non-production series and the standard trend-cycle (Chart 20) suggests, of course, other hypotheses, such as that trend-cycles in monetary supply and in prices generate the trend-cycle in production, or that trend-cycles in technical progress (the series 'patents issued' probably serves well enough as an index of technical progress, in decade comparisons) generate trend-cycles in production. However, statistical correlations cannot lend to such theories any sort of real support; for the correlations might also be plausibly interpreted as indicating that trend-cycles in production generate trend-cycles in prices and in technical progress. Furthermore, any linear theory of trend-cycles in production is likely to be faulty: the connections between economic processes are seldom of the nature of mechanical sequences, and, if it be true that the standard trend-cycle is diffused through the entire economic system, it is unlikely that there is an independent rhythm in some one part of the system, which causes a rhythm in the entire economy. In analyzing the relation between variations in the degree of divergence of production trends and trend-cycles in production, we have called attention to but one factor in the causation of trend-cycles in production; but it is worth noting that this factor implies an organic relation among industrial trends, and does not presuppose any linear chain of causation.

We may reasonably expect that when the study of trend-cycles is extended to economic processes other than production, it will become possible to describe with some exactness the mechanism of the trend-cycle process. To go any further now than we already have would be to excogitate hypotheses unlikely to carry conviction to any discerning inquirer. Nevertheless, one partial hypothesis—as yet an intuitive conjecture and no more—may be ventured. The partial hypothesis is that accidental forces play a large rôle in trend-cycle movements. In formal terms, an upward trend-cycle movement is likely to be initiated, provided industrial relationships are favorable, by a single accidental cause operating in the same direction over a number of years (such as a continuing increase in the quantity of gold or a persisting shortage in construction), or by numerous independent accidents cumulating in the same direction over a number of years; and a downward trend-cycle movement is likely to be prolonged by random factors. In the light of what has previously been stated, this partial hypothesis implies that there might be a plateau of some duration between one trend-cycle and the next. These closing observations are, it is necessary to insist, entirely unsupported; the main, if not the sole, contribution of this chapter lies in the problem which it poses.

VI. RELATION OF TREND-CYCLES TO BUSINESS DEPRESSIONS

'Business cycles' are closer to direct experience than trend-cycles; that is the primary reason why business cycles are so generally recognized, while trend-cycles have not as yet won, and rightly so in view of their restricted study, common acceptation. But it appears that business cycles are short-term waves in national economic life which are superimposed on the long-term waves that we have designated as trend-cycles.[55] These two types of cyclical movement are not independent of each other. The preceding study of the relation between trend-cycles and divergence of production trends

[55] As the study of economic fluctuations progresses, our cyclical terminology will have to be altered. 'Trend-cycles' and 'business cycles' are equally cycles in *business*; so are 'seasonal cycles' in economic activities, for they tend to synchronize roughly within such broad industrial groups as manufacturing and distribution (see S. Kuznets, *Seasonal Variations in Industry and Trade*, National Bureau of Economic Research, 1933, Ch. IX).

enables us to trace tentatively one important connection between them.

We have seen that a sharp divergence of production trends develops during an upward trend-cycle movement, and have argued that the disparity in production trends sows the seeds of a reversal in the trend-cycle movement. Although the process of reversal cannot as yet be described, one symptom of the process of reversal may be suggested. Is it not likely that, once an upward trend-cycle movement has continued for some time, the strain and loss of industrial balance will culminate in a general economic crisis serving to terminate the upward movement? In one form or another, this hypothesis is a very old one. It has frequently been argued that the severity of a business depression is correlated with the intensity of the period of expansion preceding it, though reference is generally had to the preceding upward phase of the business cycle rather than to secular movements. Another common theory is that the degree of severity of a business depression is associated with the divergence in the rates of advance in production during the preceding period; though here again, reference is generally had to the divergence of cyclical rather than secular rates of expansion. The hypothesis relating business depressions to trend-cycles cannot be attacked very confidently with the statistical tools of the present study, for these were forged mainly with a view to other purposes. Still, the decade rates furnish an instructive tentative approach to the problem.

The first peak in the standard trend-cycle and in the cycle of divergence in production trends comes in the decade 1875–85. In April 1882, a severe business depression set in, which lasted through May 1885. The depression occurred towards the end of the decade during which the standard trend-cycle and the cycle in the dispersion of the decade rates reached a peak. But the rates of production growth and their dispersion would not differ very much for a period of some eight to ten years immediately antedating the depression. This is to be expected from the fact that the cyclical factor was corrected for in the computation of the decade rates; and the expectation is confirmed by the charts of the individual production series. The statistical record in the present case is therefore roughly consistent with the hypothesis that the severity of business depressions is connected with the magnitude of the preceding secular advance in general production and the divergence in the rates of secular advance of individual industries.

The second peak in the standard trend-cycle of production and in the cycle of divergence in production trends comes in the decade 1895–1905. This decade experienced extraordinarily rapid and almost uninterrupted growth. The annual charts for the more important nonagricultural series show virtually a continuous rise from 1896 to 1907. The setbacks in 1900 and 1903–04 are almost imperceptible in annual production data, and are of a quite different order of magnitude from the decline during the depression of 1907–08. Though this depression was of rather brief duration, running over some thirteen months from June 1907 through June 1908, it was of very considerable depth. Again, the statistical record confirms the hypothesis that a severe depression tends to follow a period during which the secular trends of production move sharply upward while the divergence in the rates of expansion is exceptionally large. It may reasonably be stated, and with even greater assurance for the present than for the previous case, that a plausible change in the time location or duration of the period for which rates of industrial growth might be studied in relation to the crisis of 1907–08 could not alter to any appreciable extent the general results.

The next peak in the standard trend-cycle comes in the

decade 1910–20. The peak for this period is not quite so significant as for other periods, since a considerable number of individual industries, especially those connected with construction, registered troughs. A more important characteristic of this period is the considerable diversity in the rates of industrial expansion—a natural consequence of the shifts in the economy from a peace to a war basis. The dispersion of the rates of production growth was probably greater than Chart 21 suggests. For the present purpose it suffices to state that the statistical evidence again satisfies our hypothesis; for this decade terminated with a crisis of extraordinary severity, the downturn lasting from February 1920 to September 1921.

The following and final peak in the standard trend-cycle and in the cycle of the dispersion in the rates of secular expansion comes in 1920–29. This is not an anomaly, as the trend-cycle observations relate to overlapping decades. Though we cannot be certain that a peak actually occurs in 1920–29, the statistics of production since 1925 suggest strongly that the level of the standard trend-cycle for the central decade year 1930 will compare unfavorably with that for the central decade year 1925. The peak of the cycle in divergence of production trends is not very impressive for the last decade; but the statistical series analyzed, being virtually fixed in number, have a smaller area of direct production reference for this period than for any other, and it is therefore likely that they are least representative for this period. It is a matter of common knowledge that differences in rates of industrial growth were very considerable during the last decade. Some industries of large magnitude, such as automobiles, rayon, radios, and electrical household devices, grew at excitingly rapid rates; other industries, such as men's clothing, sole leather, boots and shoes, certain knit goods, and certain lumber manufactures, experienced little growth or actual decline; but none of these are included among the

CYCLES IN GROWTH

statistical records we have analyzed. It is highly probable, then, that the divergence of production trends during 1920–29 was much greater in fact than our long-term series suggest. This decade of rapid advance in production and curious contrasts in rates of expansion came to a close with what is, if the rough statistical indicators available are to be trusted, the severest depression in the history of the nation. Beginning in July 1929, the contraction in business has continued relentlessly; and although since April of this year (1933) the curve of business has shown signs of vigorous revival, it is not certain that the trough of the depression has been reached even yet. Apparently, our hypothesis is borne out also by the experience of the last decade.

There are only two severe depressions since 1870 which have not been reviewed, those of 1873–79 and 1893–94. The first does not admit of a test of our hypothesis, since this study does not go back far enough. As for the depression of 1893–94, it was preceded neither by a trend-cycle expansion nor by very marked divergence of production trends. Not every severe depression, then, has an upward trend-cycle movement as an antecedent. Many other factors may conduce to this result; the severity of the depression of 1893–94 being traceable to the intense uncertainty of the business community, both here and abroad, concerning the stability of our monetary system. We may therefore conclude from our analysis of American experience since 1870: first, that periods of sharp advance in the trend of general production, which are characterized invariably by considerable divergence in production trends, have been followed invariably by severe business depressions; second, that most of the business depressions of marked severity have been preceded by a sharp advance in the trend of general production and considerable divergence in the trends of individual industries.

We must, however, recognize fully the tentative nature of

this conclusion. The analysis is based on a limited range of historical experience; the hypothesis should therefore be checked by data for earlier years, and what is even more important, by data for recent decades of other highly industrialized countries. Moreover, the statistical instruments which we have used in attempting to verify the hypothesis are extremely crude. The dating of cyclical depressions should determine the periods to be analyzed, rather than the reverse which has been our procedure. The proper length of the periods for which rates of growth in production are to be studied is a nice question; but it cannot be handled adequately by an arbitrary and non-experimental method. And for more recent decades much fuller materials are available than we have used, our list of series having been determined by their availability over a rather long period. Nevertheless, the consilience of such statistical records as we have examined and of theoretical expectations is sufficiently close to warrant more attention to the relation between production trends and business depressions than has been possible in the present work.

Chapter VI

THE GROWTH OF TOTAL PRODUCTION

OUR national industry has experienced a continual transformation in its pattern since the Civil War. Yet, the change in pattern has been marked by a fair degree of order and regularity: individual industries have grown at widely unequal rates, but their rates of advance have generally declined with their age; retardation in the growth of individual industries has not been continuous, but the fluctuations in the rates of industrial growth have been synchronous in considerable degree; periods of exceptionally rapid advance and rapid change in the pattern of production have been terminated by general crises, but the sequence itself has been regular. The vast changes in the pattern of production have accompanied and in very large part have expressed the same forces as the astonishing increase in the size of total production.

The preceding chapters contain considerable information bearing on the size of total production, but that information lacks compactness. It remains in this final chapter to consider systematically the quantitative increase in the physical volume of total production. In an age dominated by the idea of material progress, this is the most important question that economic history can consider. Our present concern will be with the rate of advance of the secular trend of total production, especially with the degree of regularity of that advance. While the preceding analysis of the elements of order in the

254   PRODUCTION TRENDS

secular changes in the pattern of production resolved itself into a study of the common characteristics of the production trends of individual industries, the present analysis of elements of order in the secular trend of total production will constitute a study of the elements of regularity in the single trend of total production.

I. MEASUREMENT OF TOTAL PRODUCTION

Measurements of changes in the physical volume of total production have only recently been attempted; but a fair number of indexes of production are already available, some of them going far back into the past. These long-range indexes are the data for our immediate inquiry. Before putting the indexes to specific use, it is necessary, however, to understand their logical basis and to grasp their shortcomings firmly.[1]

The 'production' of any industry is measured by the valuable utilities which the industry adds to the materials and supplies that it works up, that is, by the 'net value product' of the industry. Correspondingly, the total production of an economy is given by the sum of the net value products of its industries. But the individual goods to which valuable utilities have been added have a physical side; and, just as in the case of individual goods we obtain measurements of such of their distinguishable physical characteristics as are of economic interest, so in the case of the ensemble of goods we may seek a measure or index of the physical quantity of the ensemble. The available measurements of the physical volume of production of individual goods are expressed in

[1] This section is in some ways a continuation of section I of Chapter I. In the present section, the consideration of defects in production indexes is confined to indexes of the total movement of production, running over a long period. The same defects characterize also indexes of total movement running over a short period, and indexes of 'cycles' in production—irrespective of the length of period they may cover; but other considerations are more important in such indexes.

TOTAL PRODUCTION 255

divers physical units, since statistical agencies ordinarily follow the usages of commerce. In practice, therefore, the problem of devising a measure of changes in the physical volume of total production is a problem in making the right combination of the divers measurements for the individual goods.

Some makeshift is obviously necessary, and the most plausible is to proceed on the assumption that the 'net value product' per unit of output is constant over time for all individual goods. These constants may be obtained from the statistical records of any single year or series of years, and they will vary, of course, from good to good. We may, now, for each year considered, multiply the datum of the physical volume of production of each good by its respective 'net value product' constant, and summate these products for all goods. We will obtain in this way an annual series of dollar sums, which we may regard as an index series of changes in the physical volume of total production.

It is difficult, however, to state in words the exact meaning of these measurements. Unlike measurements of the physical volume of production of individual goods, our indexes of the physical volume of total production no longer express the number of units of some one physical attribute; they state, at best, something hypothetical—viz., what total production (in the sense of economic theory) would have been in each of a series of successive years, if the net value product per unit of output of the actually experienced 'physical' production of each good had remained constant throughout the period. But this statement requires elaboration. When we reduce the net value products of individual goods to constants and allow their physical volumes of production to vary, we obtain, in a sense, measurements of total production corrected for changes in net value products; but this is not equivalent to saying that the net value products do not enter into the indexes of the physical volume of production, for our 'net value product' constants are restricted to some one year (or series of years), and if we changed the year (or series of years) we would obtain a different set of constants and therefore a different set of index numbers.[2] All that we can be certain of, then, is that our dollar sum for the year (or series of years) yielding the constants is an accurate measure of the total production (in the sense of economic theory) for that year (or series of years taken as a unit), and that our dollar sums for all other years (in case a series of years yield the constants, also for the individual years of the series) measure neither the total production nor the purely physical aspect of total production. It follows that any so-called index series of the physical volume of production in a changing economic system is inherently ambiguous, quite apart from the limitations of the data on which it must in practice be based; and that the ambiguity is apt to increase with the length of the period covered by the index.[3]

Economic statisticians construct and make extensive use of production indexes, in spite of the fact that their meaning is nebulous in large part and must always remain so in our changing economy. The reason is, perhaps, that economists are most frequently concerned with the utilities which the economic system creates; and, since value measurements reflect the volatility of prices, they seek measurements of production which will be free from the price factor, and which may, therefore, bear a closer correspondence to the volume of created utilities than do the value measurements.[4] So im-

[2] Moreover, in the case of an economy which is continually gaining in new products, it is impossible to obtain a set of 'net value product' constants relating to the same period for all goods. And, as a matter of fact, the procedure of taking weights as of a fixed date or period is not obvious, except as a piece of arithmetic or verbal convenience.

[3] For a fuller discussion, see the writer's "The Measurement of the Physical Volume of Production," *Quarterly Journal of Economics*, February, 1930.

[4] See, however, pp. 8–9, note 2. A theoretical alternative to the procedure described of constructing a measure of changes in the physical volume of total production is to calculate the man-hours of labor expended on 'pro-

portant are the questions which production indexes could answer, were they free from ambiguity, that investigators have ignored the ambiguity and have set about deliberately "to do as logically as possible the illogical." [5] The effectiveness of their labors has been restricted by the quantitative and qualitative shortcomings of the data which are readily available. Next to ambiguity, the principal defect of production indexes is the inadequacy of their composition.

There is an effective statistical method of indicating the nature of the bias that, as a result of the inadequacies of the available data, is likely to be found in a production index covering a long period. In the course of this investigation, a detailed study was made of the decade-by-decade frequency distributions of the decade rates of the eight fixed groups of production series listed in Appendix A, Table 46, with a view (among other purposes) to testing the representativeness of these series for the purpose of constructing an index of the physical volume of total production. The distributions showed, first, a rapid secular shift to ever lower positions on the scale of growth, second, a secular decline in their dispersions, third, a secular decline in their 'positive' skewness—the later distributions generally showing 'negative' skewness. For a rapidly progressive national economy, however, one would expect to find generally increasing dispersion and persistently high positive skewness in frequency distributions of decade rates, and only moderate decline, if any, in the rate of growth of total production. If our series constituted a representative sample of the production universe, the distri-

---

duced' goods; this is the only physical attribute of 'produced' goods, which admits of their general commensuration (see p. 50, note 1). But this method of measuring the physical volume of production is shunned because it is deemed to understate the volume of utilities created in a progressive industrial economy.

[5] F. G. Perry and A. G. Silverman, "A New Index of the Physical Volume of Canadian Business," *Journal of the American Statistical Association*, June, 1929, p. 127.

butions of their decade rates could not depart so widely from reasonable expectations. The nature of the departures indicates that these series are likely to understate the growth in the 'actual' volume of total production.

A critical examination of the statistical composition of a 'typical' long-term index of the physical volume of total production will lead to the same conclusion.[6] Ordinarily, the index covers material goods only, and though it occasionally includes transportation and trade, it never covers 'services' in the narrow sense of that term; the census of occupations suggests, however, that the latter have grown more rapidly than the production of material goods. The index is based on a fixed, or virtually fixed, list of production series; this is equivalent to saying that the index becomes progressively anachronistic,[7] for the new industries which are not covered are generally in the vanguard of industrial advance. It includes a goodly number of industrial consumption series and, occasionally, some equipment series; but our growing technology has made generally for more effective conversion of raw materials into finished products and for more effective utilization of equipment. It does not, ordinarily, take account of 'secondary' production; but such production has been growing at a more rapid rate than 'primary' production. It gives inadequate representation to such by-products as constitute additions to the production of old commodities, although such by-products are of increasing importance. And

[6] Qualifications would have to be made if the following description were applied to any specific index. It is not feasible to enter here on a comparison of the various indexes.

[7] Statistical data bearing on this point will be found in *A Graphic Analysis of the Census of Manufactures, 1849 to 1919* (National Industrial Conference Board, 1923), pp. 171–3; F. C. Mills, *Economic Tendencies in the United States* (National Bureau of Economic Research, 1932), pp. 39–43, 198–201, 307–10; A. R. Eckler, cited above, p. 86. Some statistical data bearing on the other points are given in Ch. IV, sec. III, 2–3. Concerning the growth bias of individual production series, see pp. 25–7, and Appendix C, I.

TOTAL PRODUCTION

it makes no allowance for variations in quality, while improvements in quality have been, as a matter of fact, almost universal in raw materials, and also very extensive in manufactures—as in steel, rayon, automobiles, agricultural machinery, radios, and electric appliances. All of these inadequacies of the data entering into a 'typical' production index tend to make for a downward growth bias. Other inadequacies work in the opposite direction. The index never includes industries which vanished at some point, and ordinarily does not include decadent industries which have lingered on. Also, the index ordinarily includes a few series with an upward growth bias arising out of some peculiarity in their statistical constitution. These factors making for an upward growth bias are obviously less important than those making for a downward bias; the statistical constitution of a 'typical' index is, therefore, such as to tend to understate the physical volume of total production.

The third defect of long-range production indexes derives from the type of formula employed in combining the different goods into an index number series. The various commodities and services cannot be aggregated directly since they are expressed in different units and are of unequal industrial importance. But they may be aggregated once weights are assigned which serve to commensurate, and express the importance of, the various outputs. The mathematical formula which describes this kind of arithmetic operation is the 'weighted aggregate'. This formula alone is logically adequate; for an index of production is conceptually an aggregate of the outputs of different goods, and not some sort of an average of their movements. Most of the existing long-range indexes of production are formally defective, since they are not weighted aggregates. They need not, however, be any worse in practice on this account; for the quality of the data and weights is generally more important than the arithmetic method of their combination. Yet, there is one formula which must render suspect any production index embodying it—that is, the unweighted arithmetic mean of fixed base relatives. Snyder's index of 49 series with 1910–14 as base is of this type and will serve as an example. If this index were a reliable indicator of the trend of total production, it might be expected that the omission of one or two minor series would not alter its complexion appreciably. But, as a matter of fact, when quicksilver production and New York canals traffic are excluded from the index, its level in the period 1870–80 is reduced by something like 20 per cent, its level in later years but prior to the base period is reduced by a declining percentage, and its level in years subsequent to the base period is raised.[8] The explanation is that prior to the base period the relatives of progressive series could vary only from zero to 100, while the relatives of retrogressive series, the two excluded being of this type, could vary freely between 100 and any higher figure; and that subsequent to the base period, the restrictions on the movements of the relatives of progressive and retrogressive series are reversed.

The defects in long-range production indexes are not peculiar to them alone, but they are probably more serious than in the more familiar long-range indexes of prices. Since monetary factors exercise an influence on all prices, acting as a common brake on their movements, an average of a reasonably large number of commodities is likely to disclose fairly accurately the influence of the common monetary factors. But there is no single dominant force acting pervasively on the production trends of industries; their movements are

[8] It should be noted that Mr. Snyder has recently replaced this index by a long-term weighted index (see pp. 200–1); and that he has recently constructed, for the period since 1919, an exceptionally elaborate and, in every way, improved index. Few statisticians have been as courageous as he in pioneering efforts, as critical of their own work, and as willing to place at the disposal of others the results of their researches.

TOTAL PRODUCTION

therefore more heterogeneous, the problem of sampling for an index number is more baffling, and the problem of combining individual elements into index form more exacting. The differential homogeneity of price and production trends bears strongly on the technique of weighting. When price data are available for only a few commodities falling in a group, it may perhaps be assumed with some plausibility that the prices of unrepresented commodities have moved sympathetically with those included, but not so in the case of production data, especially when the groups embrace competing commodities. This is but another way of indicating how intricate is the problem of sampling for a long-range production index.[9]

[9] The series analyzed in this study are more numerous and some of them are, perhaps, also of better quality than those entering into the various long-term production indexes. Nevertheless, the series fall so far short of satisfactory standards of quantity and quality that a new index derived from them would in all likelihood merely add to a growing list of defective indexes. A substantial improvement over any of the existing indexes might possibly be effected if a painstaking study were made of the various discontinuous quantity series scattered through census reports and trade journals, of the extensive data on the pecuniary volume of production contained in the census reports, and of the economic histories of individual industries recorded in countless periodicals and monographs. In this way, many of the gaps in the continuous record of physical output might be filled. With unstinted experimentation, the various data might then be welded together into an index number series inspiring more confidence as an indicator of the trend of the physical volume of total production than any index now available; but any index of production, no matter how ably constructed, can be even roughly true for periods of only intermediate duration, say, no more than twenty years, in a rapidly changing economy such as ours—so that a long index series will best be presented on a shifting base, if misinterpretation is to be minimized. One of the most important questions which would have to be analyzed in the course of a study aiming at improved measurements of changes in total physical production is the degree to which the available data are representative of total production. A partial answer to this question might be obtained by using some such method as we have used to test the representativeness of our series for the purpose of constructing a production index, the method being just as applicable to a variable as to a fixed number of series, though the method yields only a negative test: we can be reasonably certain that a sample is poor when distributions of rates of growth fail to conform to such a priori expectations as we have set forth, but we cannot be at all

II. AVERAGE RATE OF INDUSTRIAL GROWTH

Strict logic is a stern master, and if one respected it, one would never construct or use any production index.[10] Nevertheless, such questions as: How much better off are we now than formerly? How rapid has been our rate of material advance? Has there been any decline in the rate of increase of total physical production? press insistently and cannot be dismissed. If we proceed with caution, something may possibly be learned from such materials as we have. We shall consider in this section the long-term average rate of industrial growth of the nation, and in the next section the changes in the rate of growth. The evidence of indexes of certain major industrial groups will serve to introduce and give content to the evidence of the indexes of total physical production.

The most pertinent data bearing on the average rate of industrial growth since 1870 are summarized in Table 41.[11]

---

certain that the sample is satisfactory when the distributions conform to the expectations. A comprehensive study of the kind suggested is a statistical enterprise outside the practical scope of this investigation.

[10] But the same strict logic would forbid also the use of most individual production series, since practically every series is, in miniature, an 'index', and a 'bad' index at that, of physical volume: when commodities are not of uniform quality, which is the case generally, physical volume series—such as bushels of wheat produced, number of locomotives, tons of bituminous coal—may be described as index numbers of the unweighted aggregate type (see Ch. I, sec. I). Yet, it is ironic that economic history and statistics can never report satisfactorily how much the total goods production, in a non-pecuniary sense, of any one time or place exceeds or is exceeded by that of another time or place.

[11] For method of computing the average rates of growth, see pp. 50-1. In the case of population, lumber, and Snyder's index of trade, these several series being discontinuous, the method is the same except that the decade rates do not refer to overlapping periods. In the case of population, the datum used for 1870 is the figure corrected by the Census Bureau for the undercount in that year.

The several indexes referred to as the Day-Persons indexes were constructed by E. E. Day, W. M. Persons, and others. See W. M. Persons, *Forecasting Business Cycles* (John Wiley, 1931), Ch. XI, and the references there

Table 41
RATES OF GROWTH SHOWN BY POPULATION AND INDEXES OF PRODUCTION

Index	Period covered by index	Average annual rate of growth (per cent)
POPULATION	1870–1930	1.9
CROPS		
Day-Persons	1870–1930	2.3
Snyder	1870–1930	2.2
Timoshenko	1870–1927	2.4
Warren-Pearson	1870–1930	2.5
FISHERIES		
Fish, total	1880–1929	0.9
FORESTRY		
Lumber	1869–1929	1.8
MINING		
Day-Persons	1870–1930	5.7
Snyder	1870–1930	5.7
Warren-Pearson	1870–1930	5.7
MANUFACTURES		
Day-Persons	1870–1930	4.3
CONSTRUCTION		
Building permits	1874–1929	4.2
TRADE		
Deflated clearings	1870–1929	5.2
Railway freight	1882–1929	4.3
Snyder	1870–1930	4.7
TOTAL PRODUCTION		
Day-Persons	1870–1930	3.7
Warren-Pearson	1870–1930	3.8

cited. The composite of the separate indexes of crops, minerals, and manufactures is described by Dr. Persons as an index of 'total production'. The several indexes referred to as the Warren-Pearson indexes are given in

The table states the average rate of growth in population, in the physical production of several major groups of industries (as indicated by the best of the available indexes, a few of the series earlier analyzed being now used as 'indexes'), and in total physical production (as indicated by the best of the available indexes). The most obtrusive fact disclosed by the table is that population has grown at a lower rate than the production of any of the industrial divisions except the fisheries and forestry. The considerable excess in the rate of growth of the indexes of the physical volume of total production over the rate of growth of population means that there has been a considerable increase in per-capita production.

The progress of agriculture is recorded by several indexes which are restricted to crops and do not include animal husbandry. The indexes of crop production agree rather well: they indicate an average rate of advance of something like 2.3 per cent per annum. There is considerable evidence, however, that the rate of growth of agriculture has been more rapid. The indications are that the production of truck crops, fruits and vegetables, dairy products, and poultry products has expanded, at least in recent years, at a more rapid rate than other agricultural commodities; but these several groups are either not represented at all, or else inade-

---

Warren and Pearson, *The Physical Volume of Production*, cited above, pp. 8–10. The indexes here used are those designated by the authors as 'total crop production', 'all minerals and water power', and 'total basic production, variable group weights, weighted by value plus value added by manufacture'; they are referred to in this work as indexes of crops, mining, and total production, respectively. Snyder's index of crop production (index 'A' in Chart 12B) is given in his *Business Cycles*, cited above, p. 237; figures for recent years have been furnished by Mr. Snyder. Timoshenko's index of crop production is given in his *Rôle of Agricultural Fluctuations in the Business Cycle* (Michigan Business Studies, Vol. II, No. 9), pp. 70–1. The figures of Snyder's index of mineral production are given in Warren and Pearson, cited above, p. 64; this index is described by Mr. Snyder as an index relating to the production of 'minerals and metals'. The remaining 'indexes' in Table 41 are series earlier used; for data and sources, see Appendix A, Table 44, and Appendix B.

quately, in the long-range indexes of crop production.¹² The Warren-Pearson index is unique in that it does include a considerable number of truck crops and fruits; and this is reflected in its having a somewhat steeper trend than the other long-range crop indexes. It is significant that a rather comprehensive index of agricultural production, constructed by the Department of Agriculture for the period since 1919, shows a higher rate of growth during 1919–30 than any of the long-term crop indexes.¹³

[12] The annual percentage rates of increase of the components of the index of the 'volume of net agricultural production', constructed by the Department of Agriculture for the period since 1919 (*Yearbook of Agriculture*, 1931, p. 974), are as follows for the period 1919–30: grains, –1.5; fruits and vegetables, 2.2; truck crops, 5.9; meat animals, 0.9; dairy products, 4.0; poultry products, 3.0; cotton and cottonseed, 3.6. (See note 13.) It seems that, at least since the turn of the century, the output of animal products has increased at an average rate more rapid than that of the output of crops. Certain preliminary indexes, made available to the writer by Dr. Baker of the Department of Agriculture, show an average annual rate of increase during 1897–1930 of 1.6 per cent in the production of 'animal products', but only 1.3 per cent in 'plant foodstuffs' and 1.0 per cent in 'industrial crops'. If the production of all animal products has actually increased more than the production of all crops, that is probably due largely to the rapid growth in milk production; for, 'total' meat and lard production (according to data in *Statistics of Meat Production*, cited above) experienced an annual rate of increase of 1.2 per cent during 1900–30, which is about the same as that shown by the indexes of crop production during 1900–30 (the Day-Persons index of crops, 1.1 per cent; Snyder's index, 1.2 per cent; the Warren-Pearson index, 1.2 per cent).

[13] For the period 1919–30, the index of the Department of Agriculture (see note 12) shows an annual rate of increase of 1.8 per cent; but the several crop indexes show very much lower annual rates of advance: the Day-Persons index 0.1 per cent, Snyder's index 0.1 per cent, and the Warren-Pearson index 0.6 per cent. (These several indexes, including that of the Department of Agriculture, are based on unrevised data of crop production; that is to say, they do not take account of the revisions for the period 1919–28, which are reported for major crops in the *Yearbooks of Agriculture* of 1932 and 1933. The revisions for minor crops are as yet uncompleted; but it now seems reasonably certain that if the several indexes were to be recomputed on the basis of the fully revised data, all of them would show a somewhat lower rate of increase, and the discrepancy between the index of the Department of Agriculture and the other indexes would be greater than it now is.) Mr. Snyder is fully aware of the limitations of his index of crops. In a communication to the writer, he makes the interesting comment

The rate of growth of the mining industry has been considerably greater than that of agriculture. The three indexes of mining agree in showing an annual rate of growth of 5.7 per cent during the period 1870–1930 taken as a whole; but the averages conceal the higher rate of advance of the Day-Persons and Snyder indexes prior to about 1900 and the higher rate of advance of the Warren-Pearson index subsequent to that date. The Day-Persons index probably gives a somewhat better indication of the growth of mining than do the others.[14] To be sure, this index falls short of a comprehensive coverage of mining: it does not include the production of sulphur, phosphate rock, gypsum, fluorspar, asphalt, and several other minerals of secondary importance, which have had, for the period since 1870 taken as a whole, an upward trend more rapid than that of the index; but it also does not include the production of mercury, whose trend has been downward, or of salt and several other minerals of secondary importance, whose trend has been upward though at a rate less rapid than that of the index. Taking the Bureau of Mines estimates of the 'value of mineral products' as a base for comparison, the component series of the Day-Persons index account for as much as 80 per cent or more of total

---

that when he took all the crop data available, the index for 1930 showed a slight advance over 1929, while his index of principal crops (the one used in Table 41) showed a considerable decline.

[14] The Day-Persons index has a greater coverage than Snyder's index, but a smaller coverage than the Warren-Pearson index. The larger coverage of the latter index arises mainly from its inclusion of secondary production of metals, natural-gas gasoline, electricity from water power, and water power other than electric, along with the minerals. The Day-Persons index comes closest to being strictly an index of mining, but even this index prior to 1909 is not confined to mineral series: the encroachment of the Warren-Pearson index on other areas has just been stated; in Snyder's list are found steel (in addition to pig iron) and aluminum (see p. 11, note 5); the Day-Persons list includes coke prior to 1909 (also, pig iron, though this is replaced by iron ore in 1909). It must be repeated, however, (see p. 264, note) that the Warren-Pearson and Snyder indexes, discussed in this chapter as indexes of 'mining', are described by their authors as indexes respectively of 'all minerals and water power' and 'minerals and metals'.

mineral production during most of the period considered.[15] The relative coverage of the index tended to decline for some time, but the inclusion of additional series in 1909 and in subsequent years raised the coverage. The slight decline in the coverage prior to 1909 suggests that the index probably understates somewhat the progress of the mining industry. However, since the coverage of the index has been very large throughout, the understatement, if there be any, is probably small.

Turning to manufactures, we encounter an industry whose 'physical' growth defies anything but the roughest measurement, so great is its variety of products and so changeable their form. The Day-Persons index, the only continuous index of manufactures covering the period since 1870, shows a rate of advance of 4.3 per cent per annum; but there are cogent reasons for regarding this as an understatement of the growth actually experienced. The previous analysis of the factors making for a downward growth bias in a 'typical' index of the physical volume of total production applies with almost full force to the Day-Persons index of manufactures. Moreover, if manufacture is defined, as is customary, to cover factory production alone, then, the index does not reflect even moderately the transfer of elaborative activities from the home and farm to the factory; for its coverage is restricted in large part to the initial stages of fabrication. For recent decades, some statistical evidence can be added to this general statement. Professor Mills' index of manufactures based on from 35 to 62 industries shows an annual rate of increase of 3.9 per cent during 1899–1929, while his index based on an adjustment for the incomplete and variable coverage of the first index shows a rate of increase of 4.2 per

[15] The coverage is 83 per cent for 1880, 83 per cent for 1890, 80 per cent for 1900, and 76 per cent for 1908. After this date, new commodities are included: the coverage rises to 83 per cent for 1910, 89 per cent for 1920, and 85 per cent for 1929.

cent. The Day-Persons index, however, shows a rate of increase of only 3.8 per cent for the same period.[16]

With all their imperfections, the indexes of production of the three great divisions of commodity production, just reviewed, probably suffice to indicate the lower limits of the average year-by-year progress. There is little that can be said concerning the other industrial divisions. The series of total fish catch should record with fair accuracy the progress of the fisheries industry, and the discontinuous series of lumber production the progress of the forestry industry. Some indication of the progress of the construction industry, viewing it as distinct from manufactures, is given by the series of building permits; but the statistical basis of this series is so slender that an average calculated from it can have only slight significance. The progress of trade may be guessed at through the indications given by Snyder's index of trade, the series of deflated clearings, and the series of railway freight. In the case of transportation and the host of service industries, numerical definiteness concerning the average rate of progress is almost out of the question.

All in all, this survey of group indexes indicates, more concretely perhaps than the analysis of the preceding section, how slender is the quantitative basis of indexes of the physical volume of total production; but it also reinforces the previous observation that production indexes (ignoring their intrinsic ambiguity, which, indeed, we must do if we are to use them at all) are likely to have a downward growth bias— all the more so, paradoxically enough, if they are ably con-

[16] See F. C. Mills, *Economic Tendencies*, cited above, pp. 42, 200, and 309. The indexes given by Mills were spliced to form a continuous series on a common base. For the purpose of the present comparison, the Day-Persons and Mills indexes were confined to census years. The average annual rates of growth of the several indexes were determined in each case by fitting a 'least squares' line to the logarithms of the indexes, the figures of the index series being weighted by 5 for the census years through 1919 and by 2 for the census years thereafter.

structed. The Day-Persons and the Warren-Pearson indexes are the only long-range indexes of the physical volume of 'total' production meriting our attention; even though the former is confined to crops, mining, and manufactures; while the latter covers basic production only, the branches of raw material production being covered more thoroughly than in the Day-Persons index, but manufactures being excluded except insofar as they round out the record of 'raw' production and furnish weights for the raw material components of the index. The Day-Persons index shows an average annual rate of growth of 3.7 per cent during 1870–1930, and the Warren-Pearson index a rate of 3.8 per cent; these figures compare with an average annual rate of growth in population of 1.9 per cent. But the indexes probably understate the average rate of advance in the physical volume of total production, even if production be considered in the narrow sense of transformation. The increase of total physical production has almost certainly been greater—quite possibly, a good deal greater.

The moving factors in the rapid increase of total physical production have been technical knowledge, abundance of natural resources, and the industrial intelligence of the population. These factors are interrelated and the efficacy of each has been increased by the progressive improvement in the state of national well-being. If the ambition, sturdiness, and enterprise of the American population have tended to promote rapid industrial advance, it is well to remember that the abundance of natural resources has been important in causing such qualities to be bred in the population and in attracting the more venturesome from foreign lands. The economic significance of our generous store of natural resources has been extended by advances in science and technology. Their progress in turn has been stimulated by the richness of the natural resources awaiting exploitation, the eagerness of an enterprising people to exploit them, and the improving state of general well-being. And the fundamental forces making for industrial advance have worked themselves out cumulatively through the stimulation coming from some of their effects, such as a population growing in numbers and improving in industrial quality, increasing use of machinery and mechanical power, increasing size of industrial units, and improving technique of industrial and business management.

When we adopt an historical view, we can take considerable satisfaction in the pace at which we have travelled: for the enrichment of the material side of our national life has proceeded at a rather rapid rate. But when we take a normative view, and compare the production of today with the consumption that would be required by even modest standards of comfort and decent living, our quantity of production appears seriously inadequate.[17] It is undoubtedly true that a decrease in the inequality of incomes would go some distance towards improving the welfare of the masses, even if production did not rise above the level of the past decade; and it is probable that a modified system of distribution would result in a more efficient use of our existing productive resources, that it would increase the material product of industry and therefore the general level of real incomes. However, for some time to come, increase in the physical volume of production through improvements in industrial technique will continue to be the road along which the greatest advances in the material improvement of mankind are to be won.

III. CHANGE IN THE RATE OF INDUSTRIAL GROWTH

The average rates of industrial growth, indicated by the

[17] Some pertinent data are presented in P. H. Douglas' *Wages and the Family* (University of Chicago Press, 1925), Chs. I–II.

ensemble of indexes reviewed in the preceding section, testify to the remarkable progress of the American economy during the period investigated; but these averages conceal the variability in the rates of secular advance of both the group and total indexes. Actually, the indications are that while the rate of secular advance in the physical volume of total production has been more nearly uniform than the rates of advance of the generality of individual industries, it has still been decidedly inconstant. Several measures of the inconstancy in the rates of advance of the various continuous production indexes are presented in Table 42;[18] but these measures may reflect chiefly the inconstancy in the rates of increase of the indexes, rather than of the underlying quantities which the indexes purport to measure. Better evidence of inconstancy is afforded by the analysis of Chapter V; for, the considerable synchronism in the undulatory movements of the production trends of numerous individual industries means that the rate of advance in the trend of total physical production has, in all likelihood, also been variable. The instability of the rates of advance of the major industrial groups and of total production, as indicated by various index numbers, is depicted in Charts 11 and 12.

Though the evidence is fairly conclusive that the rate of advance in the secular trend of total physical production in the United States has been variable, it is practically impossible to ascertain from such data as are now available whether or not that variability has expressed itself in the form of a persistent drift over time. Several investigators have, indeed, attempted to demonstrate on the basis of certain production indexes that the rate of material progress has been abating during the past half-century or longer. Attempts have also

[18] Concerning the computation of the measure of continuity of growth, range of decade rates, and standard deviation of decade rates, see p. 74; the measure of continuity of retardation, p. 103; and the measure of trend-cycle amplitude, p. 226.

Table 42
MEASURES OF INCONSTANCY OF GROWTH, FOR INDEXES OF PRODUCTION

Index	Period covered by index	Measure of continuity of growth	Measure of continuity of retardation	Range of decade rates	Standard deviation of decade rates	Measure of trend-cycle amplitude
				(Unit: one per cent)		
CROPS						
Day–Persons ..	1870–1930	1.00	–.60	5.2	1.4	0.6
Snyder	1870–1930	1.00	–.30	5.7	1.5	0.8
Timoshenko ...	1870–1927	1.00	–.78	6.0	1.6	0.9
Warren–Pearson	1870–1930	1.00	–.60	5.2	1.4	0.6
FISHERIES						
Fish, total	1880–1929	.67	.50	2.9	0.8	0.8
MINING						
Day–Persons ..	1870–1930	1.00	–.60	6.5	2.0	1.2
Snyder	1870–1930	1.00	–.40	8.0	2.3	1.7
Warren–Pearson	1870–1930	1.00	–.40	4.4	1.4	1.3
MANUFACTURES						
Day–Persons ..	1870–1930	1.00	–.30	3.6	1.2	0.8
CONSTRUCTION						
Building permits	1874–1929	.40	–.33	20.8	6.0	5.9
TRADE						
Deflated clearings	1870–1929	1.00	–.20	4.7	1.5	1.4
Railway freight	1882–1929	1.00	.00	7.3	2.4	1.4
TOTAL PRODUCTION						
Day–Persons ..	1870–1930	1.00	.00	3.4	1.1	0.6
Warren–Pearson	1870–1930	1.00	–.30	4.0	1.2	0.7

TOTAL PRODUCTION

been made to demonstrate on the basis of other production indexes that the trend of total physical production has increased at a constant percentage rate, and this notion has gained wide currency. It is only natural that students concerned with the question of drift in the rate of increase in the physical volume of total production should employ to the full whatever apparatus they command. But production indexes are very crude instruments and must be used cautiously if fictive results are to be avoided.

Our study in Chapter IV of retardation in the growth of individual industries does not, despite its rather extensive industrial coverage, offer any clue to the problem of whether or not the physical volume of our total production has been growing at a declining rate. The pervasiveness of retardation in individual industries does not mean that the rate of progress of total physical production has been slackening; it reflects simply the vigorous growth of the economy, retardation in individual industries being a consequence of the pressure of progressive forces. Even if the stream of aggregate production consisted of a fixed number of industrial components, declining percentage rates of growth in all of the individual industries would still be mathematically consistent with an increase in the percentage rate of growth of aggregate production. Certainly, therefore, the aggregate production of an economy experiencing continual accessions of new industries may, if the new industries be of sufficient scope and their inception properly timed, be growing at a constant or increasing rate, even though both old and new industries experience retardation throughout their history.

The technique which has been used to determine the extent of retardation in the individual production series may be carried over to the production indexes.[19] Table 43 gives average rates of retardation of the indexes whose average

[19] See Ch. IV, sec. I, and p. 105, note 10.

Table 43
RATES OF RETARDATION SHOWN BY POPULATION AND INDEXES OF PRODUCTION

Index	Period covered by index	Average rate of retardation (per cent per decade)
POPULATION	1870–1930	–0.2
CROPS		
Day-Persons	1870–1930	–0.8
Snyder	1870–1930	–0.8
Timoshenko	1870–1927	–0.9
Warren-Pearson	1870–1930	–0.8
FISHERIES		
Fish, total	1880–1929	–0.1
FORESTRY		
Lumber	1869–1929	–0.9
MINING		
Day-Persons	1870–1930	–1.0
Snyder	1870–1930	–0.9
Warren-Pearson	1870–1930	–0.3
MANUFACTURES		
Day-Persons	1870–1930	–0.5
CONSTRUCTION		
Building permits	1874–1929	–0.9
TRADE		
Deflated clearings	1870–1929	–0.3
Railway freight	1882–1929	–1.4
Snyder	1870–1930	–0.8
TOTAL PRODUCTION		
Day-Persons	1870–1930	–0.5
Warren-Pearson	1870–1930	–0.6

rates of advance were presented in a preceding table. All indexes, those for the various industrial groups as well as those for total production, show retardation. However, the evidence of the indexes must be appraised in the light of what we know concerning their constitution. Some aid may also be obtained, though not very much, from our study of retardation in individual industries.

It is possible to speak with moderate assurance of the several major divisions of the raw materials category. Forestry has certainly grown at a declining rate, its apex having been reached about a quarter of a century ago. It is, also, virtually certain that the mining industry has experienced retardation. It has already been brought out that the Day-Persons index covers a very considerable portion of total mineral production, and that its relative area of inclusion has been fairly constant over the period. These facts coupled with the rather sharp rate of retardation of the index imply almost necessarily that the physical volume of total mineral production has grown at a declining rate. The fairly moderate rate of retardation of the Warren-Pearson index of mineral production in no sense affects this conclusion, for the coverage of this index extends beyond mining. As for crop production, the several indexes of crops (with the possible exception of the Warren-Pearson index) account for a declining percentage of all crop production; but, even as late as 1929, Snyder's index accounted for 72 per cent of the farm value of all crops,[20] and the Day-Persons and Warren-Pearson indexes for a somewhat higher percentage. These facts coupled with the fairly high rates of retardation of the crop indexes make it highly probable that the physical volume of total crop production has increased at a declining percentage rate. The case of animal husbandry is more uncertain, as is the case of total agricultural production. Total meat and lard production, as estimated by the Department of Agri-

[20] This estimate is based on figures of farm value of crop production, given in *Crops and Markets*, September, 1931, p. 402.

culture for the period since 1900, shows very slight retardation for this period; while Dr. Baker's preliminary index of 'animal products', which includes milk and other items in addition to meats, does not show any retardation at all for the period which it covers, 1897 to date. However, these two series show only mild annual rates of advance,[21] 1.2 and 1.6 per cent respectively; and, if the general numerical indications of our series of wool production, hog slaughter, cattle slaughter, and sheep slaughter are at all reliable, it seems likely that the rate of increase of animal products was higher during the closing quarter of the past century, so that the rate of increase has tended, on the average, to decline. If it be true that crop production and animal products have grown at declining percentage rates, then, it is probably true that the physical volume of total agricultural production has also grown at a declining rate; for, when one of two components of an aggregate is consistently the more important (in this case crops) and the declining rates of growth of the two are fairly similar, it is virtually certain that the aggregate will also grow at a declining percentage rate. There are reasonable grounds, then, for believing that each of the several major divisions of raw material production, with the possible exception of the fisheries, has experienced, on the average, abatement in its rate of growth since 1870.

Greater doubts must attach to any generalization one might make for other major divisions of industry. The Day-Persons index of manufactures shows a retardation of −0.5 per cent per decade; but the coverage of this index is all too meagre to warrant the generalization that there has been a downward drift in the rate of growth of the aggregate of manufactures. Mills' 'census' index of manufactures has a more extensive coverage for the period which it covers; but it covers too short a period, especially in view of its

[21] See p. 265, note 12.

discontinuity, to give a reliable indication of change in the rate of growth of the physical volume of manufactures.[22] While it is fairly probable that the Day-Persons index exaggerates the retardation which has taken place in the aggregate of manufactures, there is no way of telling whether or not there has actually been any retardation at all. In the case of other major industrial divisions, our statistical materials are even more imperfect. The indexes of construction and trade do not serve to reveal satisfactorily even those rates of growth which may be accepted as statements of the lower limits of actual progress; they are all too insensitive, therefore, to reveal whether or not there has been any retardation. As for transportation, the rapid growth of certain new transport media—such as the telephone, wireless, automobile, airplane, and pipeline—precludes any extrapolation of the characteristics of the trend of the railway industry, for which alone index numbers are available,[23] to the aggregate volume of transportation. When we pass to other major divisions of industry, we enter what is even more a statistical 'no man's land'.

It should be evident from this survey of industrial groups that only indefinite conclusions are possible concerning the drift in the rate of growth of the physical volume of total production in this country since the Civil War. But it is worth noting that even if we were equipped with exact measurements of the drift in the rates of growth of the various industrial groups, we could not pass at once from such data to a generalization concerning total physical production; for the rate of retardation of an aggregate may differ even in sign from the rates of retardation of each of its components—especially when the components grow at

[22] See pp. 267–8, and p. 117, note 16.
[23] An index of railway transportation for 1890–1919 is presented by Stewart, in his "An Index Number of Production," *American Economic Review*, March, 1921.

widely unequal rates, which is true of the various industrial groups.[24] So, if we wish to discover what the drift in the rate of growth of total physical production has been, we must turn to the most reliable measurements we have of changes in the physical volume of total production. The two indexes of total production given in Table 43 show rates of retardation of –0.5 and –0.6 per cent per decade.

It is impossible to state a priori whether or not the various factors listed in the first section of this chapter as tending to cause a downward growth bias in a 'typical' index of total physical production tend also to exaggerate the retardation of the Day-Persons and Warren-Pearson indexes;[25] but some statistical evidence may be cited which suggests that these indexes do overstate the retardation, while practically no evidence can be cited to the contrary. The Warren-Pearson index of 'all minerals and water power' differs from the Day-Persons index of 'minerals' chiefly in taking greater account of relatively new industries and in including secondary production of metals;[26] and this difference in composition is expressed in a very much lower rate of retardation in the Warren-Pearson index of 'all minerals and water power'. Two of Snyder's indexes of total production, known respectively as the '49 series' and '87 series' indexes,[27] though not

[24] The Day-Persons index of total production and Snyder's '49 series' index of total production throw some statistical light on this mathematical point. Table 43 shows that while the Day-Persons indexes of crops, mining, and manufactures have rates of retardation of –0.8, –1.0, and –0.5 per cent per decade, respectively, the Day-Persons index of total production has a rate of retardation of only –0.5 per cent (however, if carried out to an additional place, the rate of retardation of the index of manufactures is –0.48 per cent, and of total production –0.54 per cent). Snyder's '49 series' index (see p. 200, note 21) affords a more striking instance: while most of its component series evidence fairly marked retardation, the index proper has a retardation of only –0.1 per cent.

[25] See pp. 99–100, note 4.

[26] Electricity from water power, aluminum, natural-gas gasoline, and secondary metals have a combined weight of 26.4 per cent in the Warren-Pearson index; see p. 266, note 14.

[27] See p. 200, note 21, and p. 260.

covered in Table 43, are also of interest in the present connection. While the '49 series' index, which is based on a fixed list of series, shows retardation, the '87 series' index, which is based on a variable and increasing number of series, shows acceleration.[28] Such statistical knowledge as we have suggests, therefore, that since the Day-Persons and Warren-Pearson indexes of total production take insufficient account of new industries, they probably overstate the degree of retardation in the physical volume of total production.

Our evidence is slender, however, and all that it permits is this indefinite conclusion: if there has been any decline in the rate of growth in the total physical production of this country, its extent has probably been slight, and it is even mildly probable that the rate of growth may have been increasing somewhat. This indefinite conclusion is unsatisfactory, but it is as much as the exiguous statistical basis warrants: to profess definiteness would be to ignore or to misread such data as we have. The available evidence simply does not admit of an exact answer to the primary scientific question of this chapter—viz., whether there has been any striking regularity in the secular trend of the physical volume of total production.

However, our conclusion concerning the drift in the rate of growth of total physical production should be read in the light of further data. First, we know definitely that population has grown at a declining percentage rate; it follows, therefore, that if total physical production has experienced retardation, the production per capita has experienced retardation at a lower rate, and that if the rate of retardation of total physical production has been less than that of population, the production per capita has been growing at an increasing percentage rate. Second, if we assume that the

[28] The '49 series' index shows a retardation of −0.1 per cent, the '87 series' index an acceleration of 0.2 per cent. See p. 203, note 24.

percentage rates of retardation shown by the Day-Persons or the Warren-Pearson indexes of total physical production are substantially accurate, it is still true that each of these indexes, and for that matter, all other similar indexes, show an increase, on the average, in the absolute year-by-year increments to the national production aggregate. It goes without saying that the drift in the percentage rate of increase of total physical production per capita is of greater social significance than the drift in the percentage rate of increase of total physical production as such; and though the drift in relative increments to the aggregate of physical production is probably of somewhat greater social significance than the drift in the absolute increments, the latter must not be ignored. Thus, while it may be true that the percentage rate of growth in our total physical production has been declining, that does not mean necessarily that our 'economic welfare'—even if we should view the physical volume of production as the sole factor in economic welfare—has been growing at a 'declining rate'.

These arithmetic considerations are very pertinent on the assumption that the percentage rate of increase in the physical volume of total production has been declining somewhat; though this is, and probably will remain for the period investigated, an assumption whose implications are worth considering, but an assumption and no more. Irrespective of what the exact facts may be, our data suffice to show that there has not been any marked drift in the rate of growth of total physical production during the period since the Civil War; this is of considerable importance, for, as the period advanced, natural factors making for industrial progress became less important and human factors more important.[29] Our data also suffice to show that, while the secular trend of

[29] See E. Durand, *American Industry and Commerce* (Ginn and Company, 1930), Chs. I–V.

the physical volume of total production has escaped but a portion of the undulations in the secular trends of individual industries, the primary trend of the physical volume of total production has definitely escaped the sharp retardation in the primary trends of most individual industries.

Appendix A
SUPPORTING STATISTICAL DATA

Table 44
CONTINUOUS PRODUCTION SERIES: 1870–1929

(This table gives figures for the series listed in Table 1. For sources and descriptive notes, see Appendix B, 1.)

Year	(1) Barley Million bushels	(2) Beet sugar Thousand short tons	(3) Buckwheat Million bushels	(4) Cane sugar Thousand short tons	(5) Corn Million bushels	(6) Cotton Thousand bales	(7) Hay Million short tons	(8) Molasses and sirup Million gallons	(9) Oats Million bushels	(10) Potatoes Million bushels
1870	26.3	.45	9.8	89	1,094	4,025	24.5	10.9	247	115
1871	26.7	.45	8.3	78	992	2,757	22.2	10.7	256	120
1872	26.8	.56	8.1	67	1,093	3,651	23.8	9.5	272	114
1873	32.0	.78	7.8	54	932	3,874	25.1	8.7	270	106
1874	32.6	.11	8.0	71	850	3,528	25.1	12.2	240	106
1875	36.9	.11	10.1	86	1,321	4,303	27.9	12.3	354	167
1876	38.7	.11	9.7	100	1,284	4,118	30.9	12.9	321	125
1877	35.6	.11	10.2	80	1,343	4,494	31.6	15.2	406	170
1878	42.2	.22	12.2	125	1,388	4,745	39.6	14.2	414	124
1879	48.7	1.34	17.5	89	1,823	5,466	39.9	13.4	451	182
1880	45.2	.56	14.6	143	1,717	6,357	31.9	17.0	418	168
1881	41.2	.56	9.5	86	1,195	5,136	35.1	12.0	416	109
1882	49.0	.56	11.0	159	1,617	6,833	38.1	19.0	488	171
1883	50.1	.60	7.7	151	1,551	5,522	46.9	18.4	571	208
1884	61.2	1.07	11.1	113	1,796	5,477	48.5	14.7	584	191
1885	58.4	.67	12.6	151	1,936	6,369	44.7	21.5	629	175
1886	59.4	.90	11.9	96	1,665	6,315	41.8	12.4	624	168
1887	56.8	.29	10.8	188	1,456	6,885	41.5	26.6	660	134
1888	63.9	2.1	12.0	172	1,988	6,924	46.6	18.5	702	202
1889	78.2	2.5	12.1	151	1,999	7,473	49.2	22.4	802	201
1890	73.0	3.9	12.7	249	1,460	8,562	49.1	29.2	573	150
1891	96.6	6.0	13.0	185	2,056	8,941	48.8	20.6	840	256
1892	92.0	13.5	12.6	249	1,714	6,658	49.2	21.5	695	165
1893	83.7	22.6	12.9	305	1,708	7,433	55.6	26.9	676	195
1894	78.1	22.5	13.7	365	1,340	10,026	50.5	37.6	716	184

APPENDIX A

1895	114.7	32.7	16.7	272	2,311	7,147	41.8	27.2	886	317
1896	99.4	42.0	15.8	322	2,503	8,516	54.4	27.7	780	272
1897	103.3	45.2	17.3	354	2,145	10,985	58.9	29.3	791	191
1898	99.9	36.4	14.0	284	2,261	11,435	66.8	30.3	843	219
1899	116.6	81.7	13.0	161	2,455	9,460	57.4	21.8	926	260
1900	96.0	86.1	11.8	312	2,505	10,267	53.2	37.6	914	248
1901	121.8	184.6	15.7	364	1,614	9,676	55.8	31.4	778	199
1902	149.4	218.4	15.3	373	2,619	10,827	65.3	37.3	1,053	294
1903	146.9	240.6	15.2	278	2,347	10,046	68.2	25.2	869	262
1904	162.1	242.1	16.3	415	2,529	13,680	69.2	41.9	1,009	352
1905	170.1	312.9	15.8	391	2,749	10,805	73.0	27.7	1,090	279
1906	192.3	483.6	15.7	272	2,898	13,595	66.3	21.2	1,036	332
1907	170.0	463.6	14.9	394	2,512	11,875	72.3	27.3	805	323
1908	184.9	425.9	16.5	414	2,545	13,587	78.4	38.5	851	302
1909	188.0	512.5	18.0	332	2,572	10,315	74.4	41.6	1,068	395
1910	173.8	510.2	17.6	355	2,886	12,006	69.4	51.6	1,186	349
1911	160.2	599.5	17.5	361	2,531	16,250	54.9	26.1	922	293
1912	223.8	692.6	19.2	163	3,125	14,313	72.7	46.3	1,418	421
1913	178.2	733.4	13.8	301	2,447	14,795	64.1	38.0	1,122	332
1914	195.0	722.1	16.9	247	2,673	16,992	70.1	31.1	1,141	410
1915	228.9	874.2	15.1	139	2,995	12,123	85.9	27.3	1,549	360
1916	182.3	820.7	11.7	311	2,567	12,781	91.2	79.5	1,252	287
1917	211.8	765.2	16.0	246	3,065	12,428	83.3	56.3	1,593	442
1918	256.2	760.9	16.9	284	2,503	12,970	76.7	64.4	1,538	412
1919	131.1	726.5	12.3	122	2,649	12,029	76.6	51.2	1,106	299
1920	171.5	1,089.0	11.9	176	3,049	13,880	76.2	55.8	1,446	371
1921	130.7	1,020.5	11.8	328	2,912	8,351	71.0	66.6	1,045	327
1922	153.8	675.0	11.8	296	2,689	10,370	80.8	64.3	1,148	420
1923	159.0	881.0	11.7	165	2,860	10,808	75.3	51.1	1,227	368
1924	165.8	1,090.0	12.5	88	2,305	14,488	80.1	29.7	1,423	386
1925	192.7	913.0	12.5	139	2,853	17,219	67.2	38.2	1,410	299
1926	163.7	897.0	11.1	47	2,575	19,135	67.5	28.8	1,142	323
1927	241.0	1,093.0	12.8	71	2,678	13,972	83.6	27.5	1,093	370
1928	331.1	1,061.0	10.1	132	2,715	15,760	72.6	33.9	1,318	427
1929	280.2	1,018.0	8.7	200	2,535	16,066	76.1	39.0	1,118	329

PRODUCTION TRENDS

Table 44 (cont.)

Year	(11) Rice Million bushels	(12) Rye Million bushels	(13) Tobacco, raw Million pounds	(14) Wheat Million bushels	(15) Wool Million pounds	(16) Raisins Thousand short tons	(17) Flaxseed Million bushels	(18) Cattle Thousands	(19) Hogs Thousands	(20) Sheep Thousands
1870	2.0	15.5	251	330	162					
1871	1.4	15.4	263	315	160					
1872	1.9	14.9	342	336	150	.06				
1873	2.2	15.1	373	368	158	.06				
1874	2.4	15.0	178	382	170	.09				
1875	3.0	17.7	379	368	181	.11				
1876	3.1	20.4	381	365	192	.19				
1877	2.8	21.2	460	509	200	.32				
1878	2.9	25.8	393	504	208	.48				
1879	4.0	25.2	507	549	211	.65	7.2			
1880	4.0	24.5	446	535	232	.75	9.0	2,137	16,353	3,516
1881	3.7	20.7	450	418	240	.90	7.5	2,107	15,056	3,968
1882	3.6	30.0	513	554	272	1.1	7.5	2,145	13,158	4,490
1883	4.0	28.1	452	469	290	1.4	6.5	2,404	13,938	4,695
1884	3.9	28.6	542	571	300	1.7	8.5	2,389	14,089	4,808
1885	5.4	21.8	563	432	308	5.0	13.0	2,527	16,671	4,634
1886	5.6	24.5	533	555	302	7.0	10.0	2,660	17,428	4,685
1887	4.1	20.7	386	559	285	8.0	10.5	2,946	15,976	4,993
1888	4.5	28.4	566	516	269	9.6	9.0	3,519	15,609	5,147
1889	4.6	28.4	458	618	265	9.9	10.2	4,015	18,179	5,239
1890	4.9	26.4	519	516	276	19.0	8.5	4,748	23,557	5,423
1891	5.6	32.8	552	787	285	26.0	19.0	4,687	21,999	5,741
1892	8.6	29.3	495	681	294	28.5	11.1	5,206	20,519	6,038
1893	4.4	28.6	483	539	349	42.5	10.0	5,190	16,368	7,125
1894	4.0	29.6	407	634	325	51.5	7.5	5,190	21,270	8,109
1895	6.1	31.1	492	669	294	45.5	15.0	4,809	21,203	8,765
1896	3.5	28.9	403	613	272	34.0	17.4	4,939	22,228	8,478

APPENDIX A

Year									
1897	4.2	33.4	611	685	259	47.0	12.5	5,053	26,065	8,417
1898	4.9	32.9	699	832	267	40.5	16.4	5,045	30,324	8,458
1899	9.0	30.3	802	682	272	36.0	20.0	5,748	28,697	8,858
1900	9.1	30.8	814	639	289	47.0	17.6	5,801	29,294	8,940
1901	14.0	31.1	819	829	303	37.0	25.3	6,312	31,129	9,996
1902	11.5	35.3	822	738	316	54.0	29.3	6,465	26,375	10,519
1903	20.2	32.0	816	681	287	60.0	27.3	6,755	26,971	10,508
1904	21.1	31.8	660	581	292	40.0	28.4	6,702	30,072	10,046
1905	13.6	35.2	633	727	295	45.0	28.5	7,259	31,855	10,026
1906	17.9	36.6	682	760	299	50.0	25.6	7,541	31,610	10,385
1907	18.7	35.5	698	637	298	75.0	25.9	7,633	32,885	10,252
1908	21.9	35.8	718	654	311	65.0	25.8	7,279	38,643	10,305
1909	20.6	35.4	1,055	713	328	70.0	19.7	7,714	31,395	11,343
1910	24.5	34.9	1,103	660	321	62.5	12.7	7,808	26,014	11,408
1911	22.9	33.1	905	621	319	65.0	19.4	7,619	34,133	14,020
1912	25.1	35.7	963	730	304	95.0	28.1	7,253	33,053	14,979
1913	25.7	41.4	954	763	296	66.0	17.9	6,978	34,199	14,406
1914	23.6	42.8	1,035	891	290	91.0	13.7	6,757	32,532	14,229
1915	28.9	54.0	1,062	1,026	286	128.0	14.0	7,153	38,381	12,212
1916	40.9	48.9	1,153	636	288	132.0	14.3	8,310	43,084	11,941
1917	34.7	62.9	1,249	637	282	163.0	9.2	10,350	33,910	9,345
1918	38.6	91.0	1,439	921	299	167.0	13.4	11,829	41,214	10,320
1919	42.0	75.3	1,444	952	298	182.5	6.8	10,091	41,812	12,691
1920	52.1	62.3	1,509	843	294	177.0	10.9	8,609	38,019	10,982
1921	37.6	61.1	1,005	819	290	145.0	8.1	7,608	38,982	13,005
1922	41.4	104.7	1,254	847	270	237.0	10.5	8,678	43,114	10,929
1923	33.7	53.9	1,518	760	272	290.0	16.6	9,163	53,334	11,529
1924	32.2	57.7	1,245	840	281	170.0	31.2	9,593	52,873	11,991
1925	33.2	40.5	1,376	669	300	200.0	22.3	9,853	43,043	12,001
1926	42.5	32.9	1,289	834	318	285.0	18.5	10,180	40,636	12,961
1927	44.8	51.8	1,211	875	340	300.0	25.2	9,520	43,633	12,883
1928	43.4	37.6	1,373	926	366	268.0	19.1	8,467	49,795	13,488
1929	40.6	34.9	1,537	813	382	224.5	15.9	8,324	48,445	14,023

Table 44 (cont.)

Year	(21) Cod and mackerel Thousand gross tons	(22) Whale Thousand gross tons	(23) Fish, total Million pounds	(24) Anthracite coal Million short tons	(25) Bituminous coal Million short tons	(26) Coal, total Million short tons	(27) Copper Million pounds	(28) Gold Thousand fine ounces	(29) Lead, domestic Thousand short tons	(30) Mercury Thousand flasks
1870	91.5	68.0		15.7	17.4	33.0	28	2,419	17.8	30.7
1871	92.9	61.5		19.3	27.5	46.9	29	2,104	20.0	32.3
1872	97.5	51.6		24.2	27.2	51.5	28	1,741	25.7	32.3
1873	109.5	44.8		26.2	31.4	57.6	35	1,741	41.9	28.2
1874	78.3	39.1		24.8	27.8	52.6	39	1,620	51.2	28.3
1875	80.2	38.2		22.5	29.9	52.3	40	1,619	58.6	51.3
1876	87.8	39.1		22.8	30.5	53.3	43	1,932	62.9	74.2
1877	91.1	40.6		25.7	34.8	60.5	47	2,269	80.4	81.0
1878	86.4	39.7		21.7	36.2	57.9	48	2,477	89.1	65.2
1879	79.9	40.0		30.2	37.9	68.1	52	1,882	90.8	75.2
1880	77.5	38.4	1,615	28.6	42.8	71.5	60	1,741	95.7	61.1
1881	76.1	38.6	1,568	31.9	54.0	85.9	72	1,679	114.5	62.1
1882	77.9	32.8	1,521	35.1	68.4	103.6	91	1,572	129.8	53.8
1883	95.0	32.4	1,475	38.5	77.3	115.7	116	1,451	140.3	47.7
1884	82.9	27.2	1,428	37.2	83.0	120.2	145	1,490	136.3	32.5
1885	82.6	25.2	1,385	38.3	72.8	111.2	166	1,538	126.2	32.7
1886	80.7	23.1	1,337	39.0	74.6	113.7	158	1,687	127.2	30.6
1887	79.5	26.2	1,290	42.1	88.6	130.7	181	1,603	141.6	34.5
1888	76.0	24.5	1,436	46.6	102.0	148.7	226	1,604	147.4	33.9
1889	74.5	22.0	1,598	45.5	95.7	141.2	227	1,595	151.8	27.0
1890	68.4	18.6	1,676	46.5	111.3	157.8	260	1,589	139.7	23.4
1891	68.9	17.2	1,616	50.7	117.9	168.6	284	1,605	174.5	23.4
1892	69.5	17.1	1,595	52.5	126.9	179.3	345	1,597	168.3	28.5
1893	70.6	16.6	1,574	54.0	128.4	182.4	329	1,739	159.0	30.8
1894	71.6	16.5	1,562	51.9	118.8	170.7	354	1,911	153.9	31.0
1895	69.1	15.8	1,549	58.0	135.1	193.1	381	2,255	159.6	36.8
1896	68.6	15.1	1,547	54.3	137.6	192.0	460	2,568	179.7	31.4

APPENDIX A

Year										
1897	66.6	12.7	1,545	52.6	147.6	200.2	494	2,775	198.5	27.2
1898	52.3	11.5	1,613	53.4	166.6	220.0	527	3,118	202.2	31.7
1899	50.7	11.0	1,744	60.4	193.3	253.7	569	3,437	202.1	31.1
1900	51.6	9.9	1,833	57.4	212.3	269.7	606	3,830	260.9	28.9
1901	52.4	9.5	1,921	67.5	225.8	293.3	602	3,805	258.6	30.3
1902	56.6	9.3	1,951	41.4	260.2	301.6	660	3,870	267.3	35.0
1903	57.5	9.5	1,924	74.6	282.7	357.4	698	3,560	280.6	36.3
1904	57.6	10.1	1,920	73.2	278.7	351.8	813	3,892	297.6	35.3
1905	60.3	10.8	1,887	77.7	315.1	392.7	889	4,266	307.5	30.5
1906	61.4	11.0	1,889	71.3	342.9	414.2	918	4,565	336.2	26.1
1907	57.0	9.7	1,891	85.6	394.8	480.4	869	4,375	352.4	21.6
1908	53.5	9.7	1,893	83.3	332.6	415.8	943	4,574	311.7	19.8
1909	50.2	9.0	1,927	81.1	379.7	460.8	1,093	4,822	352.8	21.1
1910	47.3	9.3	1,961	84.5	417.1	501.6	1,080	4,657	375.4	20.6
1911	45.8	9.2	1,995	90.5	405.9	496.4	1,097	4,687	392.0	21.3
1912	45.0	8.9	2,029	84.4	450.1	534.5	1,243	4,521	392.5	25.1
1913	41.8	8.6	2,063	91.5	478.4	570.0	1,224	4,300	411.9	20.2
1914	34.2	9.9	2,135	90.8	422.7	513.5	1,150	4,573	512.8	16.5
1915	31.5	8.8	2,187	89.0	442.6	531.6	1,388	4,888	507.0	21.0
1916	33.4	6.7	2,193	87.6	502.5	590.1	1,928	4,479	552.2	29.9
1917	32.1	5.6	2,226	99.6	551.8	651.4	1,886	4,051	548.4	36.2
1918	38.3	4.5	2,263	98.8	579.4	678.2	1,909	3,321	539.9	32.9
1919	36.1	4.3	2,243	88.1	465.9	554.0	1,286	2,919	424.4	21.4
1920	37.7	3.9	2,215	89.6	568.7	658.3	1,209	2,476	476.8	13.4
1921	37.3	4.3	2,160	90.5	415.9	506.4	506	2,422	398.2	6.3
1922	35.7	4.1	2,053	54.7	422.3	477.0	950	2,363	468.7	6.4
1923	34.9	3.7	2,076	93.3	564.6	657.9	1,435	2,503	543.8	7.9
1924	32.3	3.2	2,076	87.9	483.7	571.6	1,634	2,529	566.4	10.1
1925	35.0	3.5	2,197	61.8	520.1	581.9	1,675	2,412	654.9	9.2
1926	37.5	2.7	2,131	84.4	573.4	657.8	1,740	2,335	680.7	7.6
1927	37.6	7.9	2,325	80.1	517.8	597.9	1,684	2,197	668.3	11.3
1928	36.5	6.8	2,384	75.3	500.7	576.1	1,826	2,233	626.2	18.1
1929	38.9	6.9	2,916	73.8	535.0	608.8	2,003	2,208	672.5	24.0

Table 44 (cont.)

Year	(31) Petroleum Million barrels	(32) Phosphate rock Thousand long tons	(33) Silver Million fine ounces	(34) Zinc Thousand short tons	(35) Asphalt Thousand short tons	(36) Cement, total Thousand barrels	(37) Fluor-spar Thousand short tons	(38) Gypsum Thousand short tons	(39) Iron ore Million long tons	(40) Non-Portland cements Thousand barrels
1870	5.3	65	12.4	5.4						
1871	5.2	74	17.8	6.9						
1872	6.3	59	22.2	7.8						
1873	9.9	79	27.7	9.6						
1874	10.9	109	28.9	13.1						
1875	8.8	123	24.5	16.7						
1876	9.1	132	30.0	17.0						
1877	13.3	163	30.8	15.6						
1878	15.4	210	35.0	19.6						
1879	19.9	199	31.6	21.3						
1880	26.3	211	30.3	25.1	.44	2,073	4.0	90	7.1	2,031
1881	27.7	267	33.3	30.3	2.0	2,500	4.0	85	7.1	2,440
1882	30.3	332	36.2	33.8	3.0	3,250	4.0	100	8.7	3,165
1883	23.4	378	35.7	36.9	3.0	4,190	4.0	90	8.8	4,100
1884	24.2	432	37.7	38.5	3.0	4,000	4.0	90	7.7	3,900
1885	21.9	395	39.9	40.7	3.0	4,150	5.0	90	7.6	4,000
1886	28.1	431	39.7	42.6	3.5	4,500	5.0	95	10.0	4,350
1887	28.3	481	41.7	50.3	4.0	6,943	5.0	95	11.3	6,693
1888	27.6	452	45.8	55.9	50.5	6,503	6.0	110	12.1	6,253
1889	35.2	546	50.1	58.9	51.8	6,832	9.5	268	14.5	6,532
1890	45.8	510	54.5	63.7	41.0	7,777	8.2	183	16.0	7,441
1891	54.3	588	58.3	80.9	45.1	8,223	10.0	208	14.6	7,768
1892	50.5	682	63.5	87.3	87.7	8,759	12.2	256	16.3	8,211
1893	48.4	941	60.0	78.8	47.8	8,002	12.4	254	11.6	7,412
1894	49.3	997	49.5	75.3	60.6	8,362	7.5	239	11.9	7,563
1895	52.9	1,039	55.7	89.7	68.2	8,731	4.0	266	16.0	7,741

APPENDIX A

Year										
1896	61.0	931	58.8	81.5	80.5	9,526	6.5	224	16.0	7,983
1897	60.5	1,039	53.9	100.0	75.9	11,038	5.1	289	17.5	8,360
1898	55.4	1,309	54.4	115.4	76.3	12,344	7.7	292	19.4	8,652
1899	57.1	1,516	54.8	129.1	75.1	15,855	15.9	486	24.7	10,203
1900	63.6	1,491	57.6	123.9	54.4	17,231	18.4	594	27.6	8,749
1901	69.4	1,484	55.2	140.8	63.1	20,069	19.6	634	28.9	7,358
1902	88.8	1,490	55.5	156.9	84.6	25,754	48.0	816	35.6	8,523
1903	100.5	1,582	54.3	159.2	55.1	29,899	42.5	1,042	35.0	7,556
1904	117.1	1,874	57.7	186.7	64.2	31,675	36.5	941	27.6	5,169
1905	134.7	1,947	56.1	203.8	62.9	40,102	57.4	1,043	42.5	4,855
1906	126.5	2,081	56.5	224.8	73.1	51,000	40.8	1,541	47.7	4,537
1907	166.1	2,265	56.5	249.9	85.9	52,230	49.5	1,752	51.7	3,445
1908	178.5	2,386	52.4	210.4	78.6	52,911	38.8	1,722	36.0	1,838
1909	183.2	2,338	54.7	255.8	99.1	66,690	50.7	2,253	51.3	1,698
1910	209.6	2,655	57.1	269.2	98.9	77,785	69.4	2,379	57.0	1,235
1911	220.4	3,053	60.4	286.5	87.1	79,548	87.0	2,324	43.9	1,019
1912	222.9	2,973	63.8	338.8	95.2	83,351	116.5	2,501	55.2	913
1913	248.4	3,111	66.8	346.7	92.6	92,949	115.6	2,600	62.0	852
1914	265.8	2,734	72.5	353.0	79.9	89,950	95.1	2,476	41.4	820
1915	281.1	1,836	75.0	489.5	75.8	86,708	136.9	2,448	55.5	794
1916	300.8	1,982	74.4	668.3	98.5	92,363	155.7	2,758	75.2	842
1917	335.3	2,584	71.7	669.6	81.6	93,454	218.8	2,696	75.3	639
1918	355.9	2,491	67.8	517.9	60.0	71,515	263.8	2,057	69.7	433
1919	378.4	2,272	56.7	465.7	88.3	81,307	188.3	2,420	61.0	529
1920	442.9	4,104	55.4	463.4	198.5	100,791	186.8	3,129	67.6	767
1921	472.2	2,064	53.1	200.5	296.4	99,381	35.0	2,891	29.5	539
1922	557.5	2,418	56.2	354.3	327.8	115,679	141.6	3,780	47.1	889
1923	732.4	3,007	73.3	510.4	400.2	138,732	121.2	4,753	69.4	1,272
1924	713.9	2,868	65.4	517.3	562.4	150,777	125.0	5,043	54.3	1,418
1925	763.7	3,482	66.2	572.9	584.8	163,388	113.7	5,678	61.9	1,729
1926	770.9	3,210	62.7	618.4	715.2	166,635	128.7	5,635	67.6	2,105
1927	901.1	3,171	60.4	592.5	839.0	175,330	112.5	5,347	61.7	2,124
1928	901.5	3,501	58.5	602.6	807.9	178,509	140.5	5,102	62.2	2,210
1929	1,007.3	3,761	61.3	625.4	804.0	173,856	146.4	5,016	73.0	2,209

Table 44 (cont.)

Year	(41) Portland cement Thousand barrels	(42) Pyrites Thousand long tons	(43) Salt Million barrels	(44) Sulphur Thousand long tons	(45) Natural gas Billion cubic feet	(46) Cocoa imports Million pounds	(47) Coffee imports Million pounds	(48) Cotton consumption Thousand bales	(49) Distilled spirits Million tax gallons	(50) Fermented liquors Million barrels
1870						3.6	272	1,027	72.6	6.6
1871						2.8	308	1,147	57.0	7.7
1872						1.5	289	1,116	69.4	8.7
1873						3.7	292	1,213	71.2	9.6
1874						3.7	283	1,098	69.6	9.6
1875						4.0	360	1,256	62.7	9.5
1876						4.4	267	1,314	58.6	9.9
1877						4.1	349	1,459	61.4	9.9
1878						4.6	325	1,457	57.3	9.8
1879						5.9	438	1,501	72.9	10.2
1880	42	2.0	6.0			5.9	396	1,866	91.4	11.1
1881	60	10.0	6.2	.54		8.4	426	1,849	119.5	13.3
1882	85	12.0	6.4	.54	3.4	7.5	484	2,038	107.3	14.3
1883	90	25.0	6.2	.54	7.7	9.0	488	1,814	75.3	17.0
1884	100	35.0	6.5	.89	24	9.6	494	1,687	76.5	17.8
1885	150	49.0	7.0	.45	76	8.6	534	2,095	76.4	19.0
1886	150	55.0	7.7	.64	157	11.0	521	2,050	81.8	19.2
1887	250	52.0	8.0	2.23	241	11.9	423	2,205	79.4	20.7
1888	250	54.3	8.1	2.68	343	15.6	507	2,309	71.7	23.1
1889	300	93.7	8.0	.00	250	14.4	534	2,518	91.1	24.7
1890	335	99.9	8.9	.00	239	18.7	481	2,604	111.1	25.1
1891	455	106.5	10.0	1.07	183	18.0	574	2,847	117.8	27.6
1892	547	109.8	11.7	2.40	159	23.4	601	2,416	118.4	30.5
1893	591	75.8	11.9	1.07	149	19.3	535	2,300	131.0	31.9
1894	799	105.9	13.0	.45	144	19.6	601	2,984	92.2	34.6
1895	990	99.5	13.7	1.6	137	28.9	634	2,500	81.9	33.4

APPENDIX A

1896	1,543	115.5	13.9	4.7	140	26.1	621	2,841	90.0	35.9
1897	2,678	143.2	16.0	2.0	149	25.5	787	3,472	64.3	34.5
1898	3,692	193.4	17.6	1.1	173	26.9	781	3,672	83.7	37.5
1899	5,652	174.7	19.7	4.3	223	35.8	852	3,687	100.2	36.7
1900	8,482	204.6	20.9	3.1	237	42.1	741	3,604	109.2	39.5
1901	12,711	234.8	20.6	6.9	264	49.2	1,028	4,080	128.6	40.6
1902	17,231	200.4	23.8	5.0	281	53.8	901	4,187	132.8	44.6
1903	22,343	225.7	19.0	25.0	298	60.2	940	3,981	148.2	46.7
1904	26,506	207.1	22.0	85.0	310	70.9	1,074	4,523	139.5	48.3
1905	35,247	253.0	26.0	220.0	351	77.7	859	4,877	153.3	49.5
1906	46,463	261.4	28.2	295.1	389	83.7	844	4,974	150.1	54.7
1907	48,785	247.4	29.7	188.9	407	82.7	930	4,493	174.7	58.6
1908	51,073	222.6	28.8	364.4	402	94.0	926	5,199	133.9	58.8
1909	64,991	247.1	30.1	274.0	481	117.7	1,126	4,759	199.9	56.3
1910	76,550	241.6	30.3	247.1	509	110.9	797	4,713	163.9	59.5
1911	78,529	301.5	31.2	205.1	513	130.0	796	5,400	183.4	63.3
1912	82,438	350.9	33.3	787.7	562	146.7	938	5,867	187.6	62.2
1913	92,097	341.3	34.4	491.1	582	149.0	845	5,943	193.6	65.3
1914	88,230	336.7	34.8	417.7	592	164.0	975	6,087	181.9	66.2
1915	85,915	394.1	38.2	520.6	629	187.7	1,137	7,327	140.7	59.8
1916	91,521	439.1	45.4	649.7	753	232.3	1,132	7,721	253.3	58.6
1917	92,814	482.7	49.8	1,134.4	795	377.2	1,218	7,555	286.1	60.8
1918	71,082	464.5	51.7	1,353.5	721	345.8	1,014	6,289	178.8	50.3
1919	80,778	420.6	49.2	1,190.6	746	348.8	1,256	6,808	100.8	27.7
1920	100,023	310.8	48.9	1,255.2	798	314.9	1,248	5,478	101.3	9.2
1921	98,842	157.1	35.6	1,879.1	662	274.3	1,304	6,560	87.9	9.2
1922	114,790	169.0	48.5	1,830.9	763	331.5	1,220	7,350	82.2	6.3
1923	137,460	181.6	50.9	2,036.1	1,007	401.1	1,388	6,225	124.6	5.3
1924	149,358	160.1	48.6	1,220.6	1,142	364.7	1,395	6,878	137.5	4.9
1925	161,659	170.1	52.8	1,409.3	1,189	365.2	1,269	7,307	167.5	5.1
1926	164,530	166.6	52.7	1,890.0	1,313	414.2	1,482	8,178	203.8	4.9
1927	173,207	215.8	54.1	2,111.6	1,445	413.6	1,419	7,829	185.5	4.4
1928	176,299	182.0	57.7	1,981.9	1,568	359.7	1,447	8,215	170.5	4.2
1929	170,646	164.4	61.0	2,362.4	1,918	494.0	1,475	7,197	203.3	3.9

Table 44 (cont.)

Year	(51) Jute imports Thousand long tons	(52) Lead consumption Thousand short tons	(53) Lead, total Thousand short tons	(54) Manila hemp imports Thousand long tons	(55) Minor fiber imports Thousand long tons	(56) Pig iron Thousand long tons	(57) Rails Thousand long tons	(58) Raw sugar consumption Million pounds	(59) Rubber imports Million pounds	(60) Silk imports, raw Million pounds
1870	17.1	60.8	17.8	16.9	36.7	1,665	554	1,284	7.5	.73
1871	23.3	70.7	20.0	19.3	45.2	1,707	693	1,445	11.2	1.26
1872	27.1	75.2	25.7	19.4	49.2	2,549	893	1,653	12.5	1.23
1873	60.4	88.1	41.9	21.0	85.5	2,561	795	1,679	13.2	.82
1874	35.4	82.5	51.2	19.5	59.2	2,401	651	1,791	14.6	.81
1875	38.1	78.0	58.6	19.1	62.4	2,024	708	1,928	9.7	1.3
1876	51.2	74.3	62.9	19.0	76.2	1,869	785	1,650	10.4	1.2
1877	46.1	89.2	80.4	16.6	69.4	2,067	683	1,851	14.5	1.0
1878	29.7	94.4	89.1	16.1	53.7	2,301	788	1,690	11.8	1.6
1879	58.3	93.4	90.8	19.5	87.9	2,742	994	2,075	16.8	2.3
1880	77.0	101.2	95.7	22.1	111.9	3,835	1,305	1,998	18.0	2.6
1881	59.2	119.2	114.5	27.1	101.2	4,144	1,647	2,222	18.4	2.6
1882	61.9	135.9	129.8	30.9	111.6	4,623	1,508	2,156	23.7	3.1
1883	74.8	146.0	140.3	26.4	119.9	4,596	1,215	2,455	21.8	3.3
1884	77.3	141.4	136.3	13.1	116.0	4,098	1,022	3,050	23.1	3.4
1885	93.2	132.3	126.2	25.3	150.2	4,045	977	2,938	25.1	3.9
1886	94.8	144.4	132.2	19.7	147.4	5,683	1,601	2,983	30.8	4.8
1887	90.4	149.1	156.6	23.4	147.1	6,417	2,140	3,314	30.7	4.8
1888	88.8	153.2	176.0	37.0	158.5	6,490	1,404	3,050	33.9	5.4
1889	95.9	158.8	178.4	35.1	166.1	7,604	1,522	3,101	31.8	5.8
1890	100.8	151.7	157.8	29.0	158.2	9,203	1,885	3,215	33.9	4.6
1891	128.2	180.2	198.4	46.6	223.9	8,280	1,307	3,976	35.7	7.1
1892	60.0	181.8	208.2	44.0	158.6	9,157	1,552	3,922	36.5	7.8
1893	88.3	166.0	224.3	52.2	187.4	7,125	1,136	4,256	37.8	4.4
1894	57.8	192.4	213.6	35.6	140.7	6,657	1,022	4,907	33.7	7.8
1895	105.8	241.0	235.8	43.5	192.8	9,446	1,306	4,286	39.4	9.1

APPENDIX A

1896	84.2	213.9	257.5	47.6	182.4	8,623	1,122	4,439	30.8	4.9
1897	83.2	219.2	282.2	53.5	204.3	9,653	1,648	5,523	39.1	10.0
1898	113.6	227.5	302.1	46.3	230.3	11,774	1,981	3,885	41.3	8.4
1899	87.6	226.3	298.0	49.5	203.1	13,621	2,273	4,542	51.6	11.7
1900	93.1	269.3	367.8	41.0	209.3	13,789	2,386	4,336	45.5	8.1
1901	100.3	271.9	371.0	50.0	228.7	15,878	2,875	5,422	51.4	12.2
1902	141.4	332.5	367.9	59.7	286.2	17,821	2,948	4,659	47.6	13.6
1903	70.0	300.2	368.9	66.3	237.6	18,009	2,992	5,959	52.0	11.5
1904	96.8	319.5	393.5	53.1	249.7	16,497	2,285	5,233	58.4	16.4
1905	104.2	347.0	388.3	69.9	274.6	22,992	3,376	5,613	60.5	15.4
1906	104.3	376.3	404.7	47.2	247.4	25,307	3,978	5,912	64.2	16.7
1907	108.3	390.9	413.4	57.3	258.7	25,781	3,634	6,157	64.5	15.6
1908	118.4	318.6	396.6	47.1	267.6	15,936	1,921	5,701	72.6	18.6
1909	139.3	368.7	446.9	84.5	316.5	25,795	3,024	6,527	89.1	22.1
1910	59.9	379.3	470.3	67.7	226.2	27,304	3,636	6,388	84.0	21.5
1911	70.1	385.3	487.0	61.0	238.1	23,650	2,823	6,288	77.2	20.7
1912	112.8	388.1	480.9	78.3	341.8	29,727	3,328	6,762	112.6	24.7
1913	124.4	419.5	462.5	51.4	323.9	30,966	3,503	6,912	117.7	27.8
1914	83.4	452.5	542.1	49.7	332.2	23,332	1,945	7,400	137.2	25.5
1915	107.5	419.6	550.1	60.1	337.3	29,916	2,204	7,750	216.8	30.8
1916	116.2	460.7	571.1	74.5	398.8	39,435	2,855	7,859	260.9	32.0
1917	87.0	515.5	610.8	90.7	313.8	38,621	2,944	8,086	396.7	36.0
1918	69.8	543.0	640.2	77.7	290.4	39,055	2,541	7,133	319.8	32.3
1919	60.7	434.1	482.2	66.5	260.8	31,015	2,204	8,317	530.8	44.3
1920	92.5	538.0	529.7	65.0	320.4	36,926	2,604	9,822	557.2	29.3
1921	61.7	444.9	448.6	31.0	198.2	16,688	2,179	8,961	402.5	44.9
1922	76.8	492.7	532.7	73.9	220.7	27,220	2,172	11,219	663.6	50.1
1923	82.4	573.5	618.3	103.0	275.0	40,361	2,905	11,198	672.8	49.1
1924	65.9	602.9	690.5	76.2	235.7	31,406	2,433	9,753	711.8	50.5
1925	63.7	655.7	767.0	58.7	240.4	36,701	2,785	11,330	855.2	63.1
1926	68.3	717.7	798.9	63.3	235.2	39,373	3,218	12,034	886.3	65.6
1927	92.0	663.0	796.5	50.1	230.5	36,566	2,806	11,411	892.5	72.7
1928	89.0	657.6	781.1	45.5	244.4	38,156	2,647	11,077	906.1	74.4
1929	87.5	692.8	774.6	69.0	261.8	42,614	2,722	12,445	1,181.2	85.9

296 PRODUCTION TRENDS

Table 44 (cont.)

Year	(61) Sisal imports Thousand long tons	(62) Steel Thousand long tons	(63) Super-phosphate Thousand short tons	(64) Tin imports Million pounds	(65) Vessels Thousand gross tons	(66) Wool consumption Million pounds	(67) Antimonial lead Thousand short tons	(68) Tin-plate consumption Thousand long tons	(69) Tobacco and snuff Million pounds	(70) Cottonseed cake and meal Thousand short tons
1870	2.7	69	103	10.2	277	214		83	106	18
1871	2.7	73	76	13.6	273	245	.03	86	107	18
1872	2.7	143	58	12.3	209	262	.16	97	116	26
1873	4.0	199	124	10.9	359	210	.60	80	119	30
1874	4.3	216	136	12.6	433	218	.85	91	129	43
1875	5.2	390	121	10.9	298	230	1.0	90	120	34
1876	6.1	533	125	10.9	204	229	1.1	112	127	53
1877	6.7	570	135	13.5	177	247	1.5	108	119	64
1878	7.9	732	201	13.0	236	238	1.9	154	131	82
1879	10.1	935	177	22.6	193	278	1.9	158	146	64
1880	12.9	1,247	320	29.0	157	340	2.1	183	172	103
1881	14.9	1,588	474	17.6	280	292	2.6	214	159	137
1882	18.8	1,737	528	23.5	282	339	3.1	221	194	138
1883	18.7	1,674	578	28.0	265	364	3.7	216	172	174
1884	25.7	1,551	571	25.1	226	367	3.6	229	207	202
1885	31.7	1,712	563	23.5	159	403	3.2	258	210	243
1886	32.9	2,563	573	29.4	95	423	3.4	284	226	288
1887	33.3	3,339	578	29.0	150	385	4.1	298	209	278
1888	32.8	2,899	676	34.2	218	374	4.5	331	246	306
1889	35.1	3,386	837	35.0	231	389	4.6	329	253	358
1890	28.3	4,277	606	33.8	294	382	3.9	329	271	374
1891	49.1	3,904	787	41.0	369	421	4.0	287	274	368
1892	54.6	4,928	649	46.8	200	458	5.0	308	251	501
1893	46.9	4,020	885	39.9	212	453	5.0	289	269	587
1894	47.3	4,412	863	39.1	131	437	5.4	333	274	
1895	43.5	6,115	900	53.9	112	535	6.1			

APPENDIX A

1896	50.6	5,282	893	44.3	227	417	7.5	280	261	502
1897	67.6	7,157	972	54.3	232	613	8.9	340	297	570
1898	70.3	8,933	1,511	62.0	180	362	8.5	394	275	785
1899	65.9	10,640	1,427	70.2	300	361	6.3	420	295	823
1900	75.2	10,188	1,868	68.9	394	425	9.9	440	301	884
1901	78.3	13,474	1,720	72.5	483	424	10.7	476	314	845
1902	85.0	14,947	1,524	84.0	469	489	9.2	419	348	1,125
1903	101.3	14,535	1,717	82.0	436	457	9.6	527	351	1,165
1904	99.8	13,860	2,151	82.0	379	476	11.0	524	354	1,156
1905	100.6	20,024	1,955	88.0	330	538	11.0	551	368	1,360
1906	95.9	23,398	2,197	99.2	419	491	10.5	622	391	1,272
1907	93.2	23,363	2,330	81.3	471	483	9.9	562	388	1,563
1908	102.0	14,023	2,222	82.0	614	447	13.6	584	408	1,043
1909	92.7	23,955	2,419	94.4	238	639	12.9	665	431	1,492
1910	98.5	26,095	2,876	103.7	342	492	14.1	777	447	1,326
1911	106.9	23,676	3,301	104.7	291	471	14.1	737	424	1,792
1912	150.7	31,251	3,255	114.7	233	540	13.6	883	435	2,151
1913	148.2	31,301	3,146	101.8	346	444	16.7	787	444	1,999
1914	199.1	23,513	3,172	93.3	316	540	16.7	887	441	2,220
1915	169.7	32,151	2,776	114.4	225	678	23.2	904	442	2,648
1916	208.1	42,774	3,020	141.6	325	725	24.0	1,009	466	1,923
1917	136.0	45,061	4,230	155.2	664	695	18.7	1,279	483	2,225
1918	142.9	44,462	4,161	162.5	1,301	745	18.6	1,215	497	2,068
1919	133.6	34,671	3,274	113.4	3,327	729	13.9	947	424	2,170
1920	162.8	42,133	5,351	159.3	3,881	527	12.5	1,220	413	1,817
1921	105.5	19,784	2,363	74.2	2,265	603	10.1	687	387	1,786
1922	70.1	35,603	2,960	150.6	661	632	8.1	1,214	420	1,355
1923	89.6	44,944	3,720	167.0	336	637	14.2	1,392	413	1,487
1924	93.6	37,932	3,664	144.6	224	516	20.8	1,259	414	1,518
1925	118.1	45,394	4,659	170.0	200	629	19.7	1,497	414	2,126
1926	103.6	48,294	4,367	169.1	225	604	22.5	1,534	411	2,597
1927	88.3	44,935	3,847	154.7	245	593	24.3	1,436	396	2,840
1928	109.8	51,544	4,592	171.4	257	602	33.1	1,590	386	2,093
1929	105.3	56,433	4,598	191.1	129	657	25.7	1,710	381	2,282

298 PRODUCTION TRENDS

Table 44 (cont.)

Year	(71) Cotton-seed oil Million pounds	(72) Nails Thousand kegs	(73) Zinc consumption Thousand short tons	(74) Flaxseed consumption Million bushels	(75) Roofing slate Thousand squares	(76) Cigarettes Millions	(77) Cigars Millions	(78) Coke Million short tons	(79) Flour Million barrels	(80) Gold consumption Thousand fine ounces
1870										
1871										
1872	16	4,065								
1873	16	4,025	16.3							
1874	22	4,912	14.8							
1875	25	4,727	20.5							
1876	37	4,158	18.7							
1877	30	4,829	18.1							
1878	45	4,396	18.9							
1879	54	5,011	21.2	8.7	368					
1880	71	5,371	28.6	9.9	457	533	2,510	3.3	62.8	489
1881	55	5,794	32.0	8.1	454	595	2,806	4.1	66.1	511
1882	88	6,147	44.4	8.1	501	599	3,118	4.8	65.4	509
1883	118	7,763	46.6	9.3	506	844	3,232	5.5	70.1	747
1884	119	7,581	41.9	11.0	481	920	3,373	4.9	71.4	701
1885	150	6,697	43.3	14.0	537	1,080	3,294	5.1	74.3	572
1886	174	8,761	44.9	10.4	537	1,607	3,462	6.8	73.3	703
1887	208	8,159	54.9	12.0	573	1,865	3,662	7.6	78.1	716
1888	247	7,994	57.9	12.3	662	2,212	3,668	8.5	80.0	799
1889	238	8,246	60.0	12.6	836	2,413	3,787	10.3	78.9	808
1890	262	8,777	67.1	9.9	*	2,505	4,229	11.5	83.5	854
1891	307	9,117	78.5	15.7	893	3,137	4,422	10.4	84.1	952
1892	321	9,227	78.0	9.4	953	3,282	4,675	12.0	89.1	935
1893	315	8,145	72.8	8.5	622	3,661	4,341	9.5	92.0	747
1894	429	8,107	72.4	11.7	738	3,621	4,164	9.2	93.7	612
1895	503	7,971	87.7	15.6	730	4,238	4,099	13.3	93.6	746
1896	430	6,336	70.1	12.8	673	4,967	4,048	11.8	94.4	648

APPENDIX A

Year									
1897	488	11,104	88.8	12.4	1,001	4,927	4,136	13.3	95.9	671
1898	630	8,991	108.2	13.7	916	4,843	4,459	16.0	98.2	753
1899	706	9,522	124.6	17.3	1,101	4,367	4,910	19.7	102.9	960
1900	700	8,807	99.4	16.4	1,194	3,870	5,566	20.5	104.9	1,071
1901	725	11,346	141.7	21.9	1,304	3,503	6,139	21.8	107.0	1,155
1902	890	12,616	152.7	25.2	1,435	3,647	6,232	25.4	108.0	1,339
1903	922	11,068	154.4	26.6	1,378	3,959	6,806	25.3	111.8	1,406
1904	914	13,210	180.9	23.6	1,234	4,170	6,640	23.7	110.0	1,386
1905	1,004	12,212	200.4	22.4	1,241	4,477	6,748	32.2	102.9	1,606
1906	943	12,676	220.8	19.2	1,215	5,502	7,148	36.4	109.0	1,893
1907	1,153	12,840	227.0	21.5	1,278	6,345	7,302	40.8	111.7	1,970
1908	773	11,619	214.2	25.4	1,333	6,833	6,489	26.0	111.0	1,523
1909	1,101	15,124	270.7	24.7	1,134	7,880	6,668	39.3	108.0	1,820
1910	982	13,710	245.9	24.7	1,261	9,782	6,810	41.7	108.0	2,021
1911	1,260	14,405	280.1	26.4	1,125	11,700	7,049	35.6	109.9	1,975
1912	1,512	15,638	340.3	32.7	1,197	14,239	7,044	44.0	111.3	2,127
1913	1,393	14,402	295.4	26.2	1,114	16,530	7,572	46.3	112.6	2,219
1914	1,450	13,902	300.0	24.1	1,020	17,944	7,174	34.6	114.2	1,748
1915	1,719	15,358	364.9	28.4	968	18,945	6,599	41.6	119.2	1,748
1916	1,253	17,912	459.3	26.3	836	26,203	7,042	54.5	118.7	2,421
1917	1,408	17,502	413.6	22.1	704	36,323	7,560	55.6	115.8	2,439
1918	1,312	12,699	423.8	21.7	380	47,528	7,054	56.5	115.4	2,565
1919	1,325	13,489	324.0	31.5	454	53,865	7,072	44.2	122.5	3,683
1920	1,211	17,294	323.0	27.6	396	48,091	8,097	51.3	130.4	3,856
1921	1,309	12,428	203.6	30.6	348	52,770	6,726	25.3	97.2	2,344
1922	930	15,863	373.1	38.4	479	56,413	6,722	37.1	113.8	2,739
1923	1,003	18,502	446.5	37.0	508	67,239	6,950	57.0	114.7	3,236
1924	980	15,843	448.3	45.8	469	73,256	6,598	44.3	118.7	3,134
1925	1,404	16,190	500.1	42.5	495	82,712	6,463	51.3	117.5	2,962
1926	1,617	15,531	557.0	42.7	466	92,523	6,499	56.9	116.2	3,047
1927	1,888	15,092	516.4	43.2	469	100,260	6,519	51.1	122.0	2,749
1928	1,477	14,854	578.1	42.9	483	109,131	6,373	52.8	120.6	2,737
1929	1,604	13,635	568.5	36.7	462	122,882	6,519	59.9	123.6	2,753

300 PRODUCTION TRENDS

Table 44 (cont.)

Year	(81) Locomotives Number	(82) Silver consumption Million fine ounces	(83) Tobacco consumption Million pounds	(84) Aluminum Thousand pounds	(85) Copper consumption Million pounds	(86) Silk imports, unmanufactured Million pounds	(87) White lead Thousand short tons	(88) Canned corn Thousand cases	(89) Canned tomatoes Thousand cases	(90) Rolled iron and steel Thousand long tons
1870										
1871										
1872										
1873										
1874										
1875										
1876										
1877										
1878										
1879										
1880	1,405	2.8	215							
1881	1,977	2.8	244							
1882	2,282	5.2	238							
1883	2,067	4.4	276		37	4.4	65			3,101
1884	1,149	4.3	251	.08	43	4.2	60	1,062	1,384	4,377
1885	800	4.1	283	.15	52	5.4	60	1,675	2,297	5,236
1886	1,436	3.9	288	.28	91	6.6	70	2,276	2,765	4,617
1887	2,044	4.2	299	3	142	6.1	84	3,437	3,269	5,237
1888	2,180	6.3	281	18	119	6.7	80	1,726	2,942	6,023
1889	1,860	6.8	319	19	182	7.2				
1890	2,300	7.1	325	47	193	6.2	78	1,523	3,093	5,391
1891	2,165	7.4	348	61	213	8.3	78	2,837	3,316	6,166
1892	2,012	7.2	355	150	265	8.9	74	3,417	3,223	4,976
1893	2,011	7.5	330	260	158	5.4	72	4,184	4,298	4,642
1894	695	8.4	339	334	189	8.9	76	3,278	6,427	

APPENDIX A

Year										
1895	1,101	9.5	344	920	266	10.4	91	2,992	4,035	6,190
1896	1,175	7.9	330	1,300	229	6.1	89	2,539	3,424	5,516
1897	1,251	8.7	363	4,000	274	12.0	96	2,787	3,964	7,002
1898	1,875	9.2	352	5,200	274	9.9	96	4,315	5,654	8,513
1899	2,475	12.1	369	6,500	392	13.4	110	6,366	7,174	10,294
1900	3,153	13.2	381	7,150	357	9.5	98	6,486	5,498	9,487
1901	3,384	14.1	398	7,150	383	13.5	101	5,028	4,234	12,349
1902	4,070	19.3	428	7,300	552	15.5	115	4,191	9,262	13,944
1903	5,152	20.0	468	7,500	526	14.4	114	4,861	10,155	13,208
1904	3,441	20.5	476	7,700	482	20.6	123	11,163	8,517	12,013
1905	5,491	23.7	487	11,350	581	19.4	137	13,019	5,575	16,840
1906	6,952	21.9	513	14,350	677	18.5	132	9,137	8,631	19,588
1907	7,362	24.4	517	26,000	488	17.5	127	6,654	12,918	19,865
1908	2,342	23.9	510	13,000	480	19.8	133	6,779	11,479	11,828
1909	2,887	27.9	530	15,000	689	24.6	148	5,787	10,984	19,645
1910	4,755	24.8	551	34,000	732	25.1	145	10,063	9,235	21,621
1911	3,530	32.0	565	37,000	682	25.9	133	14,301	9,749	19,039
1912	4,915	29.9	579	40,000	776	29.5	147	13,109	14,022	24,657
1913	5,332	31.0	593	46,000	812	34.0	143	7,283	14,206	24,791
1914	2,235	29.3	589	58,000	702	30.6	159	9,789	15,222	18,370
1915	2,085	30.0	565	99,000	1,137	37.0	156	10,124	8,469	24,393
1916	4,075	32.1	612	110,200	1,479	40.4	129	9,130	13,142	32,380
1917	5,446	27.0	660	143,300	1,395	43.0	115	10,803	15,076	33,068
1918	6,475	36.3	692	143,300	1,662	48.2	103	11,722	15,882	31,156
1919	3,272	32.7	648	128,000	914	55.0	139	13,550	10,810	25,102
1920	3,672	28.0	640	138,000	1,054	38.8	146	15,040	11,368	32,348
1921	1,823	35.9	612	54,000	611	51.8	170	8,843	4,017	14,774
1922	1,534	37.9	647	74,000	897	57.8	195	11,419	11,538	26,452
1923	3,785	36.8	689	129,000	1,300	61.5	163	14,106	14,672	33,277
1924	2,036	33.6	694	150,000	1,355	59.6	187	12,131	12,519	28,086
1925	1,285	39.8	718	140,000	1,401	76.0	164	24,320	19,770	33,387
1926	1,770	39.4	737	145,000	1,570	76.9	150	19,069	9,455	35,496
1927	1,176	38.6	744	160,000	1,423	85.0	158	10,347	13,137	32,879
1928	747	35.5	755	210,000	1,609	87.2	154	14,497	8,539	37,663
1929	1,161	42.4	797	225,000	1,779	96.8	147	17,487	14,145	41,069

Table 44 (cont.)

Year	(91) Rail consumption Thousand long tons	(92) Building permits Year 1913=100	(93) Coastal trade Thousand gross tons	(94) N.Y. canals traffic Thousand short tons	(95) Postage stamps Million dollars	(96) Postal money orders Millions	(97) Railway ton-miles Billion short ton-miles	(98) S.S. Marie canals traffic Thousand short tons	(99) Railway passenger-miles Millions	(100) Agricultural exports Average 1909-13 = 100
1870	910		2,638	6,174	16.6	1.7	13.0	540		34
1871	1,198		2,765	6,468	17.7	2.2	14.8	586		32
1872	1,367		2,930	6,673	19.0	2.6	17.0	746		40
1873	1,026		3,163	6,365	20.3	3.4	19.8	888		47
1874	747	24.5	3,293	5,805	23.4	4.5	20.5	655		40
1875	724	24.0	3,220	4,860	24.5	5.1	20.8	833		46
1876	782	21.7	2,599	4,172	26.9	5.1	23.1	1,074		50
1877	676	19.4	2,540	4,956	25.8	5.0	23.2	913		62
1878	780	20.3	2,497	5,171	27.4	5.7	28.3	937		72
1879	1,030	*	2,598	5,362	28.1	6.5	34.6	1,051		79
1880	1,564	27.9	2,638	6,458	31.5	7.5	38.4	1,322		85
1881	1,991	39.1	2,646	5,179	34.8	8.0	42.6	1,568		60
1882	1,705	42.6	2,796	5,467	39.7	8.8	43.0	2,030	7,688	68
1883	1,247	48.3	2,838	5,664	43.0	9.3	44.1	2,267	8,541	62
1884	1,019	48.8	2,884	5,009	40.7	12.0	44.7	2,875	8,779	66
1885	971	56.6	2,895	4,732	40.1	13.2	49.2	3,257	9,134	65
1886	1,639	63.2	2,939	5,294	41.4	14.4	52.8	4,528	9,660	71
1887	2,277	66.8	3,011	5,554	45.7	16.2	61.6	5,495	10,570	66
1888	1,460	60.2	3,172	4,943	49.5	17.4	65.4	6,411	11,191	70
1889	1,519	78.5	3,211	5,370	53.0	17.8	68.7	7,516	11,965	85
1890	1,869	92.1	3,409	5,246	57.7	18.4	76.2	9,041	11,848	85
1891	1,296	87.2	3,610	4,563	62.6	19.2	81.1	8,889	12,844	103
1892	1,544	95.0	3,701	4,282	67.4	20.1	88.2	11,214	13,363	81
1893	1,119	67.2	3,855	4,332	72.4	22.1	93.6	10,797	14,229	89
1894	1,009	65.3	3,696	3,883	70.2	23.0	80.3	13,196	14,289	96

APPENDIX A

Year										
1895	1,292	91.7	3,729	3,500	73.5	22.9	85.2	15,063	12,188	85
1896	1,057	76.1	3,790	3,715	78.4	24.9	95.3	16,239	13,049	108
1897	1,500	85.9	3,897	3,618	79.0	26.1	95.1	18,983	12,257	136
1898	1,680	72.8	3,960	3,360	85.0	28.8	114.1	21,235	13,380	131
1899	1,997	90.8	3,965	3,686	87.3	30.0	123.7	25,256	14,591	122
1900	2,026	58.7	4,287	3,346	94.0	33.2	141.6	25,643	16,038	124
1901	2,558	95.9	4,583	3,421	102.0	36.8	147.1	28,403	17,354	113
1902	2,944	85.3	4,859	3,275	112.2	41.8	157.3	35,961	19,690	110
1903	3,057	82.2	5,141	3,615	123.5	47.9	173.2	34,674	20,916	96
1904	1,906	97.8	5,335	3,139	131.9	52.6	174.5	31,546	21,923	108
1905	3,098	133.4	5,442	3,227	140.5	55.9	186.5	44,271	23,800	112
1906	3,655	128.9	5,674	3,541	154.0	61.5	215.9	51,751	25,167	121
1907	3,298	111.1	6,011	3,408	168.5	65.7	236.6	58,217	27,719	107
1908	1,726	102.5	6,372	3,052	176.4	68.6	218.4	41,391	29,083	104
1909	2,726	139.1	6,451	3,117	188.4	72.5	218.8	57,895	29,109	78
1910	3,291	115.1	6,669	3,073	206.5	81.4	255.0	62,363	32,338	92
1911	2,405	114.2	6,720	3,097	218.7	86.0	253.8	53,477	33,202	114
1912	2,885	120.9	6,737	2,606	227.0	89.0	264.1	72,473	33,132	110
1913	3,053	100.0	6,817	2,602	245.8	95.3	301.7	79,718	34,673	106
1914	1,793	98.1	6,818	2,081	265.1	108.6	288.6	55,370	35,357	138
1915	1,891	114.4	6,486	1,858	263.6	108.1	277.1	71,290	32,475	118
1916	2,340	116.5	6,245	1,625	286.4	124.6	343.5	91,888	34,309	118
1917	2,441	54.6	6,393	1,297	304.6	136.1	398.3	89,814	40,100	101
1918	2,096	25.1	6,282	1,159	363.6	124.3	408.8	85,680	43,212	145
1919	1,568	84.4	6,201	1,239	403.4	134.4	367.2	68,236	46,838	134
1920	2,055	68.0	6,358	1,421	392.5	150.3	413.7	79,282	47,370	127
1921	1,879	123.8	7,163	1,270	418.0	145.7	309.5	48,259	37,706	137
1922	1,921	192.4	7,703	1,873	438.3	155.0	342.2	66,067	35,811	112
1923	2,667	210.7	9,177	2,006	480.8	174.3	416.3	91,380	38,294	104
1924	2,268	221.6	8,911	2,032	515.7	191.3	391.9	72,037	36,368	126
1925	2,670	263.1	9,216	2,344	546.9	200.0	417.4	81,875	36,167	106
1926	3,085	257.0	9,552	2,369	600.4	196.7	447.4	85,679	35,673	136
1927	2,644	231.4	9,433	2,582	622.0	198.0	432.0	83,354	33,798	112
1928	2,471	229.4	9,706	3,090	632.2	200.1	436.1	86,993	31,718	117
1929	2,582	203.1	9,526	2,876	639.1	203.3	450.2	92,622	31,165	97

304 PRODUCTION TRENDS

Table 44 (cont.)

Year	(101) Deflated clearings Year 1913=100	(102) Tonnage entered and cleared Million net tons	(103) Shares traded Millions	(104) Railway freight Million short tons	Year	(101) Deflated clearings Year 1913=100	(102) Tonnage entered and cleared Million net tons	(103) Shares traded Millions	(104) Railway freight Million short tons
1870	9.6	18.3		*	1900	56.3	56.4	138	1,082
1871	11.1	19.9			1901	63.2	59.6	266	1,089
1872	11.5	21.5			1902	65.2	61.1	188	1,200
1873	12.2	23.5			1903	66.9	62.4	161	1,304
1874	11.8	26.3			1904	67.1	60.0	187	1,310
1875	12.5	23.6	54		1905	74.7	62.1	263	1,428
1876	12.4	25.2	40		1906	80.7	67.9	284	1,631
1877	12.1	26.9	50		1907	81.9	72.6	195	1,796
1878	11.9	29.3	40		1908	76.8	76.8	197	1,533
1879	15.8	32.3	73		1909	87.2	77.3	214	1,557
1880	18.4	36.1	98		1910	90.7	79.9	164	1,850
1881	22.0	36.8	115		1911	94.0	85.1	127	1,782
1882	21.3	35.4	116	360	1912	97.4	92.6	131	1,845
1883	22.6	32.9	97	400	1913	100.0	101.8	83	2,058
1884	22.2	30.3	96	399	1914	96.1	106.6	48	2,002
1885	23.0	30.8	93	437	1915	99.8	93.6	173	1,829
1886	27.3	30.5	101	482	1916	116.3	104.0	233	2,256
1887	30.4	31.6	85	552	1917	124.0	102.5	185	2,453
1888	31.3	31.1	65	591	1918	130.3	91.5	143	2,477
1889	34.9	32.3	72	619	1919	142.5	92.9	313	2,185
1890	39.9	36.3	71	637	1920	146.1	108.5	224	2,428
1891	39.6	36.5	69	676	1921	137.5	138.1	171	1,809
1892	44.2	42.2	86	707	1922	147.4	122.9	261	1,975
1893	40.6	39.4	81	745	1923	159.4	133.5	237	2,503
1894	39.5	40.3	49	638	1924	160.4	135.5	282	2,331
1895	43.1	39.0	67	697	1925	176.3	138.9	452	2,464
1896	41.9	42.4	55	754	1926	183.6	139.7	449	2,627
1897	44.0	47.5	77	729	1927	192.7	159.5	577	2,510
1898	42.6	51.3	113	864	1928	203.1	152.5	921	2,504
1899	57.5	52.4	176	944	1929	216.5	166.0	1,125	2,584

* No figure available.

Table 45
DECADE RATES OF PRODUCTION SERIES*

(Average annual rates of growth during decades indicated by their central years, expressed in units of one per cent.)

Series No.	Series	1875	1880	1885	1890	1895	1900	1905	1910	1915	1920	1925
					Agriculture							
1	Barley	5.8	5.1	5.4	5.7	2.7	6.5	4.4	1.7	1.2	-2.5	7.6
2	Beet sugar	3.4	15.0	23.5	50.0	28.2	27.0	14.2	8.1	4.3	2.0	0.7
3	Buckwheat	4.1	0.6	1.8	2.9	1.4	0.0	1.8	0.4	-3.1	-2.4	-2.0
4	Cane sugar	5.8	4.1	5.5	10.0	2.7	1.5	0.5	-5.2	-2.3	-4.7	-7.1
5	Corn	5.3	2.9	1.7	1.7	4.0	1.6	1.2	0.6	0.1	-0.6	-1.2
6	Cotton	6.0	3.7	3.8	2.7	3.3	2.5	2.0	3.1	-1.9	-1.2	4.4
7	Hay	5.6	4.1	2.9	2.0	2.0	2.6	2.1	0.8	1.5	-1.4	-0.3
8	Molasses and sirup	4.9	4.2	4.9	6.0	2.4	1.8	2.6	1.3	5.1	-4.0	-7.1
9	Oats	6.2	6.2	5.4	2.1	2.4	2.5	1.2	3.9	2.6	-1.5	-0.1
10	Potatoes	4.5	2.6	1.8	3.4	2.3	2.6	3.8	2.2	0.1	-0.1	-0.3
11	Rice	6.7	5.5	2.9	1.3	1.0	18.8	5.8	5.2	7.7	-0.3	0.9
12	Rye	5.6	3.4	0.3	2.8	1.1	1.1	0.9	3.6	10.9	0.1	-8.0
13	Tobacco, raw	6.1	3.2	0.8	-1.0	4.7	2.7	1.9	4.8	5.3	0.4	0.4
14	Wheat	5.2	1.6	1.5	2.4	1.2	0.5	-1.1	3.1	2.5	-0.5	0.4
15	Wool	4.7	5.9	0.7	0.7	-0.3	0.6	0.9	-0.9	-0.9	0.0	2.4
16	Raisins	40.2	34.0	36.0	26.5	2.9	2.7	5.4	6.5	10.7	5.7	4.7
17	Flaxseed			3.9	3.3	5.7	7.1	-0.4	-5.2	-7.5	5.3	7.6
18	Cattle			8.2	7.3	1.3	4.1	2.7	-0.3	2.8	0.4	0.7
19	Hogs			3.3	2.6	4.2	2.8	1.5	0.5	2.9	2.6	1.6
20	Sheep			3.4	6.6	4.8	2.4	1.2	3.6	-1.7	1.1	1.5
					Fisheries							
21	Cod and mackerel	-1.9	0.0	-1.4	-2.2	-2.8	-1.5	-0.6	-5.7	-3.3	0.7	0.2
22	Whale	-5.4	-4.5	-6.3	-5.4	-5.9	-4.5	-0.5	-1.7	-7.4	-9.9	5.3
23	Fish, total			0.0	1.1	1.2	2.5	0.1	1.2	1.3	-0.4	1.0

306   PRODUCTION TRENDS

Table 45 (cont.)

Series No.	Series	1875	1880	1885	1890	1895	1900	1905	1910	1915	1920	1925
					Mining							
24	Anthracite coal	4.0	6.9	4.4	3.7	1.8	3.5	2.2	1.6	0.9	-2.8	-1.5
25	Bituminous coal	5.4	12.5	6.5	5.8	6.1	9.6	6.1	4.0	3.0	0.1	0.0
26	Coal, total	5.1	10.4	6.0	5.3	4.9	8.2	5.7	3.6	2.7	-0.2	-0.3
27	Copper	7.8	17.2	14.2	9.7	8.7	7.1	6.5	4.3	3.6	-0.9	4.4
28	Gold	-0.9	-2.7	-0.2	3.4	10.4	5.2	3.0	0.3	-4.6	-8.0	-1.3
29	Lead, domestic	17.3	8.3	4.5	2.4	4.5	6.3	3.9	5.0	2.1	2.2	3.6
30	Mercury	10.0	-8.7	-9.0	-0.1	1.3	0.5	-4.7	-2.8	1.4	-14.7	5.1
31	Petroleum	17.2	9.0	5.0	8.1	2.7	10.3	12.2	7.5	7.5	11.2	8.6
32	Phosphate rock	15.5	14.2	8.7	10.2	10.0	6.7	6.5	3.9	-0.8	3.4	3.4
33	Silver	5.2	3.3	5.4	4.1	-0.4	0.0	-0.2	2.8	0.6	-1.4	0.5
34	Zinc	14.2	11.0	8.8	7.2	6.2	9.0	7.8	7.5	7.0	-0.6	3.8
35	Asphalt	...	...	56.2	18.0	2.6	-2.4	4.0	1.3	-2.3	28.3	14.7
36	Cement, total	...	...	12.7	6.6	8.1	17.0	14.7	7.2	1.0	7.1	7.3
37	Fluorspar	...	...	9.7	4.5	6.9	23.0	7.2	12.7	10.5	-5.4	-0.5
38	Gypsum	...	...	7.8	8.2	5.2	20.3	14.7	5.2	1.4	9.0	5.5
39	Iron ore	...	...	8.5	5.1	5.9	11.2	5.9	3.8	3.5	-1.5	1.4
40	Non-Portland cements	...	...	12.5	5.2	2.2	-3.5	-15.6	-19.0	-6.3	8.8	16.5
41	Portland cement	...	...	21.7	21.2	45.0	37.7	20.2	7.9	1.1	7.6	7.2
42	Pyrites	...	...	25.0	8.1	8.4	6.9	2.3	5.0	4.1	-10.3	2.0
43	Salt	...	...	4.0	7.3	8.2	6.0	4.7	3.0	6.3	1.2	2.8
44	Sulphur	...	...	1.6	8.0	14.7	110.0	25.5	9.9	16.7	8.1	4.3
45	Natural gas	...	...	36.5	-4.3	0.9	10.1	7.5	5.9	5.0	5.6	10.5
					Manufactures							
46	Cocoa imports	9.0	9.9	10.5	9.4	7.4	12.7	10.0	9.2	11.5	3.2	3.5
47	Coffee imports	3.9	5.8	1.8	2.3	5.1	3.6	0.4	0.3	4.0	2.2	1.9
48	Cotton consumption	5.4	4.8	4.1	3.2	4.2	4.6	2.7	4.5	2.3	0.0	2.9
49	Distilled spirits	1.5	3.4	0.9	2.9	-0.8	7.8	2.8	2.4	4.8	...	...

APPENDIX A 307

50	Fermented liquors	5.3	8.4	6.9	5.8	2.6	4.3	4.6	1.7	-0.1	...	...
51	Jute imports	7.0	7.5	5.3	-1.2	-0.1	0.8	0.4	-0.4	-1.6	-4.4	1.3
52	Lead consumption	4.2	6.4	2.7	4.3	4.4	5.3	2.9	2.4	2.9	3.7	4.1
53	Lead, total	17.3	8.3	4.5	6.0	6.7	5.2	2.5	3.3	2.1	3.0	4.0
54	Manila hemp imports	0.4	2.1	3.5	6.8	2.0	3.3	2.5	1.2	2.1	0.3	-1.3
55	Minor fiber imports	7.3	8.1	5.4	2.1	2.3	3.4	1.7	3.2	1.3	-4.5	-0.6
56	Pig iron	5.3	9.4	8.8	5.1	5.1	9.4	5.5	4.3	4.0	-0.1	2.1
57	Rails	5.6	5.5	2.7	-1.3	4.3	9.3	1.3	-1.5	-3.1	4.3	2.4
58	Raw sugar consumption	3.6	5.4	4.7	4.8	1.7	2.5	2.7	2.9	3.2	12.0	2.0
59	Rubber imports	4.1	10.0	7.0	2.9	3.2	5.2	5.9	12.5	23.2	7.9
60	Silk imports, raw	11.0	13.2	8.7	5.9	6.0	7.5	7.0	6.8	6.5	7.2	8.7
61	Sisal imports	18.5	20.0	8.2	5.7	6.4	6.1	3.1	7.7	3.8	-7.3	-2.6
62	Steel	30.0	14.7	12.2	7.7	12.7	12.5	7.3	6.4	6.0	0.9	4.4
63	Superphosphate	12.0	17.5	4.7	4.5	9.3	8.6	5.4	4.2	3.9	1.5	3.0
64	Tin imports	7.6	8.1	6.0	5.8	6.8	6.3	3.0	2.3	4.6	1.7	2.5
65	Vessels	-4.1	-3.7	1.4	0.2	1.4	9.0	-2.3	-4.4	39.7	-2.5	-37.1
66	Wool consumption	2.9	6.2	2.2	2.4	0.1	0.3	1.6	2.0	3.3	-2.2	0.2
67	Antimonial lead	24.5	12.2	5.2	4.8	8.3	4.1	3.5	6.6	1.3	-4.5	10.0
68	Tin-plate consumption	8.2	11.2	7.4	1.7	3.5	6.2	5.2	5.5	5.1	3.5	4.2
69	Tobacco and snuff	3.3	5.5	5.0	3.0	1.3	3.6	3.3	1.7	0.6	-1.5	-0.6
70	Cottonseed cake and meal	19.5	19.0	15.2	11.2	10.5	9.6	4.8	7.0	1.8	-4.3	3.2
71	Cottonseed oil	19.2	19.0	15.2	11.2	10.2	8.0	2.7	5.5	0.3	-3.8	3.6
72	Nails	3.0	6.3	4.1	1.0	0.6	4.1	3.1	2.3	0.5	0.0	-0.9
73	Zinc consumption	...	11.2	7.1	5.9	5.1	9.8	7.6	6.0	3.3	2.8	5.8
74	Flaxseed consumption	...	...	3.9	0.2	3.4	7.4	1.9	2.4	-0.2	6.6	4.2
75	Roofing slate	...	...	6.5	3.1	2.9	5.6	-0.8	-2.2	-9.9	-5.9	1.0
76	Cigarettes	...	...	20.0	11.5	3.5	-0.6	11.5	16.5	19.8	11.2	10.7
77	Cigars	...	...	4.0	2.2	2.6	6.0	1.1	0.2	0.2	-0.7	-1.3
78	Coke	...	...	11.5	6.2	6.6	9.4	6.4	3.5	3.2	-0.1	1.9
79	Flour	...	...	2.7	2.8	2.1	1.5	0.2	0.7	1.1	-0.2	0.6
80	Gold consumption	...	...	5.4	1.5	0.7	10.3	5.1	2.5	6.3	2.4	-1.5
81	Locomotives	...	...	0.8	0.9	1.2	17.3	1.2	-4.3	1.2	-6.6	-11.9
82	Silver consumption	...	...	7.1	7.4	5.6	12.0	5.1	3.6	1.2	2.3	1.5
83	Tobacco consumption	...	...	3.5	2.3	1.1	4.2	3.3	1.8	1.7	1.5	2.8
84	Aluminum	...	...	...	66.0	52.0	15.7	9.6	24.0	18.0	1.5	8.0

Table 45 (cont.)

Series No.	Series	1875	1880	1885	1890	1895	1900	1905	1910	1915	1920	1925
					Manufactures (cont.)							
85	Copper consumption ...	...	...	...	8.2	6.6	10.3	4.8	5.4	7.4	0.4	4.7
86	Silk imports, unmanufactured	...	...	...	...	...	...	...	...	...	...	...
87	White lead	...	...	...	4.3	5.5	8.5	6.7	7.5	7.7	6.6	7.9
88	Canned corn	...	...	...	2.5	3.4	3.7	3.3	1.7	-1.2	2.8	-1.4
89	Canned tomatoes	...	...	...	6.5	7.2	12.7	3.6	0.6	2.0	3.2	3.2
90	Rolled iron and steel ..	...	...	...	7.9	4.3	7.1	5.3	4.0	2.1	1.2	-1.8
					2.3	6.4	10.5	5.9	5.0	4.6	0.9	4.2
					Construction							
91	Rail consumption	2.0	5.7	1.2	-4.9	2.3	9.5	0.3	-2.0	-4.4	2.6	4.6
92	Building permits	...	12.0	9.0	2.9	-0.7	3.3	4.9	-1.6	-7.1	13.7	5.7
					Transportation							
93	Coastal trade	-0.5	1.0	2.3	3.1	1.8	4.2	4.1	1.4	-0.9	4.3	3.8
94	N. Y. canals traffic	-1.6	0.8	-1.3	-3.2	-3.9	-1.1	-1.0	-4.5	-10.1	4.1	9.4
95	Postage stamps	6.0	5.9	5.4	6.1	4.2	7.2	8.0	6.7	7.2	7.2	5.9
96	Postal money orders ...	12.5	11.5	10.5	5.2	5.7	9.7	8.7	7.1	6.0	5.5	4.3
97	Railway ton-miles	10.7	8.8	7.2	6.2	5.9	8.6	5.7	4.1	5.8	1.5	1.7
98	S. S. Marie canals traffic	6.3	16.5	20.5	13.7	12.5	11.0	7.3	5.6	3.4	-0.4	1.8
99	Railway passenger-miles.	...	...	5.5	4.0	1.4	7.8	6.8	4.1	4.0	0.3	-2.5
					Trade							
100	Agricultural exports ...	9.7	1.8	3.1	3.6	3.7	0.5	-2.0	1.1	2.7	-0.4	-1.4
101	Deflated clearings	4.1	8.2	7.5	5.0	3.5	6.3	4.3	3.5	5.1	4.5	4.9
102	Tonnage entered and cleared	5.6	2.3	-0.2	3.6	4.4	4.7	3.7	4.9	2.0	4.2	3.2
103	Shares traded	...	8.8	-4.6	-3.8	8.9	12.7	1.4	-9.1	6.8	7.9	21.2
104	Railway freight ./.....	...	...	7.6	4.6	4.9	8.1	5.1	2.9	3.5	0.8	1.2

* This table is confined to the series listed in Table 1. Concerning 'decade rates', see Ch. II, sec. II.

Table 46
COMPOSITION OF SEVERAL GROUPS OF SERIES ANALYZED
(The series checked (x) are those included.)

Series No.	Series	1870–1929				1885–1929			
		(a) 'All' series (64 series)	(b) Basic series (40 series)	(c) Nonagricultural series (45 series)	(d) Basic nonagricultural series (31 series)	(e) 'All' series (99 series)	(f) Basic series (59 series)	(g) Nonagricultural series (75 series)	(h) Basic nonagricultural series (46 series)
1	Barley	x	x	.	.	x	x	.	.
2	Beet sugar	x	.	.	.	x	.	.	.
3	Buckwheat	x	.	.	.	x	.	.	.
4	Cane sugar	x	.	.	.	x	.	.	.
5	Corn	x	x	.	.	x	x	.	.
6	Cotton	x	x	.	.	x	x	.	.
7	Hay	x	.	.	.	x	.	.	.
8	Molasses and sirup	x	x	.	.	x	x	.	.
9	Oats	x	x	.	.	x	x	.	.
10	Potatoes	x	.	.	.	x	.	.	.
11	Rice	x	.	.	.	x	x	.	.
12	Rye	x	x	.	.	x	x	.	.
13	Tobacco, raw	x	x	.	.	x	.	.	.
14	Wheat	x	.	.	.	x	x	.	.
15	Wool	x	.	.	.	x	x	.	.
16	Raisins	x	.	.	.	x	.	.	.
17	Flaxseed	.	.	.	.	x	.	.	.
18	Cattle	.	.	.	.	x	x	.	.
19	Hogs	.	.	.	.	x	x	.	.
20	Sheep	.	.	.	.	x	.	.	.
21	Cod and mackerel	x	.	.	.	x	.	.	.

Table 46 (cont.)

Series No.	Series	1870-1929 (a) 'All' series (64 series)	1870-1929 (b) Basic series (40 series)	1870-1929 (c) Nonagricultural series (45 series)	1870-1929 (d) Basic nonagricultural series (31 series)	1885-1929 (e) 'All' series (99 series)	1885-1929 (f) Basic series (59 series)	1885-1929 (g) Nonagricultural series (75 series)	1885-1929 (h) Basic nonagricultural series (46 series)
22	Whale	x				x			
23	Fish, total						x		
24	Anthracite coal	x	x	x	x	x	x	x	x
25	Bituminous coal	x	x	x	x	x	x	x	x
26	Coal, total								
27	Copper	x	x	x	x	x	x	x	x
28	Gold	x	x	x	x	x	x	x	x
29	Lead, domestic	x	x	x	x	x	x	x	x
30	Mercury	x		x		x		x	
31	Petroleum	x	x	x	x	x	x	x	x
32	Phosphate rock	x	x	x	x	x	x	x	x
33	Silver	x		x	x	x	x	x	x
34	Zinc	x	x		x	x	x	x	x
35	Asphalt	x	x						
36	Cement, total					x	x	x	x
37	Fluorspar					x		x	
38	Gypsum					x		x	
39	Iron ore					x	x	x	x
40	Non-Portland cements					x		x	
41	Portland cement					x		x	
42	Pyrites					x	x	x	x
43	Salt					x		x	
44	Sulphur					x		x	
45	Natural gas					x		x	

APPENDIX A   311

46	Cocoa imports
47	Coffee imports
48	Cotton consumption
49	Distilled spirits
50	Fermented liquors
51	Jute imports
52	Lead consumption
53	Lead, total
54	Manila hemp imports
55	Minor fiber imports
56	Pig iron
57	Rails
58	Raw sugar consumption
59	Rubber imports
60	Silk imports, raw
61	Sisal imports
62	Steel
63	Superphosphate
64	Tin imports
65	Vessels
66	Wool consumption
67	Antimonial lead
68	Tin-plate consumption
69	Tobacco and snuff
70	Cottonseed cake and meal
71	Cottonseed oil
72	Nails
73	Zinc consumption
74	Flaxseed consumption
75	Roofing slate
76	Cigarettes
77	Cigars
78	Coke
79	Flour
80	Gold consumption

Table 46 (cont.)

Series No.	Series	1870–1929				1885–1929			
		(a) 'All' series	(b) Basic series	(c) Nonagricultural series	(d) Basic nonagricultural series	(e) 'All' series	(f) Basic series	(g) Nonagricultural series	(h) Basic nonagricultural series
		(64 series)	(40 series)	(45 series)	(31 series)	(99 series)	(59 series)	(75 series)	(46 series)
81	Locomotives					×		×	
82	Silver consumption					×	×	×	×
83	Tobacco consumption								
84	Aluminum	×				×	×	×	×
85	Copper consumption	×				×		×	
86	Silk imports, unmanufactured	×				×	×	×	×
87	White lead	×				×	×	×	×
88	Canned corn	×	×	×	×	×	×	×	×
89	Canned tomatoes	×	×	×	×	×	×	×	×
90	Rolled iron and steel	×	×	×	×	×	×	×	×
91	Rail consumption	×	×	×	×	×	×	×	×
92	Building permits	×		×		×	×	×	×
93	Coastal trade	×	×	×	×	×	×	×	×
94	N. Y. canals traffic	×	×	×	×	×	×	×	×
95	Postage stamps	×	×	×		×	×	×	×
96	Postal money orders	×	×	×	×	×	×	×	×
97	Railway ton-miles	×	×	×	×	×	×	×	×
98	S. S. Marie canals traffic ..	×		×		×	×	×	×
99	Railway passenger-miles ..					×	×	×	×
100	Agricultural exports	×	×			×	×	×	×
101	Deflated clearings	×	×	×	×	×	×	×	×
102	Tonnage entered and cleared	×	×	×	×	×	×	×	×
103	Shares traded					×		×	
104	Railway freight					×	×	×	×

Table 47
TREND-CYCLES OF PRODUCTION SERIES*
(Unit: one per cent)

Series No.	Series	1875	1880	1885	1890	1895	1900	1905	1910	1915	1920	1925
					Agriculture							
1	Barley	-0.2	-0.5	0.2	0.9	-1.7	2.5	0.9	-1.4	-1.5	-4.8	5.7
2	Beet sugar	-22.7	-9.0	1.6	30.1	10.3	11.1	0.3	-3.9	-5.9	-6.3	-5.8
3	Buckwheat	0.6	-2.3	-0.5	1.2	0.3	-0.5	1.9	1.1	-1.8	-0.5	0.5
4	Cane sugar	-2.3	-2.6	0.3	6.3	0.4	0.6	1.0	-3.3	0.9	-0.1	-1.2
5	Corn	1.2	-0.7	-1.4	-0.9	1.9	0.0	0.1	0.0	0.0	-0.2	-0.3
6	Cotton	1.4	-0.5	0.0	-0.7	0.3	-0.1	-0.2	1.3	-3.3	-2.1	3.9
7	Hay	1.0	0.1	-0.6	-1.0	-0.5	0.6	0.6	-0.2	1.0	-1.4	0.2
8	Molasses and sirup	-1.7	-1.5	0.2	2.2	-0.5	-0.2	1.5	1.1	5.8	-2.4	-4.6
9	Oats	0.3	0.9	0.7	-1.9	-1.0	-0.3	-1.0	2.3	1.6	-1.9	0.1
10	Potatoes	0.4	-1.1	-1.5	0.5	-0.2	0.5	2.1	0.9	-0.8	-0.6	-0.4
11	Rice	0.6	-0.4	-2.8	-4.2	-4.3	13.8	1.0	0.6	3.3	-4.5	-3.1
12	Rye	1.6	-0.2	-2.9	0.0	-1.4	-0.9	-0.7	2.4	10.1	-0.3	-8.0
13	Tobacco, raw	2.4	-0.3	-2.5	-4.1	1.8	0.0	-0.6	2.5	3.3	-1.4	-1.2
14	Wheat	2.1	-1.1	-0.9	0.3	-0.6	-1.0	-2.3	2.2	1.9	-0.8	0.4
15	Wool	1.4	3.0	-1.8	-1.4	-2.0	-0.6	0.1	-1.3	-0.9	0.4	3.2
16	Raisins	5.1	3.1	9.2	3.6	-16.2	-12.7	-6.4	-1.8	5.7	4.0	6.1
17	Flaxseed	...	...	0.5	0.2	2.9	4.6	-2.6	-7.1	-9.1	4.0	6.6
18	Cattle	...	...	1.9	1.8	-3.4	0.3	-0.3	-2.5	1.4	-0.2	0.9
19	Hogs	...	...	0.0	-0.5	1.3	0.2	-0.9	-1.7	0.9	0.8	0.0
20	Sheep	...	...	-1.6	2.2	1.0	-0.7	-1.3	1.7	-3.0	0.4	1.4
					Fisheries							
21	Cod and mackerel	-0.2	1.7	0.3	-0.5	-1.1	0.2	1.1	-4.0	-1.6	2.4	1.9
22	Whale	0.7	1.2	-1.0	-0.4	-1.3	-0.3	3.3	1.7	-4.3	-7.2	7.6
23	Fish, total	...	...	-0.9	0.2	0.3	1.6	-0.8	0.3	0.4	-1.3	0.1

314 PRODUCTION TRENDS

Table 47 (cont.)

Series No.	Series	1875	1880	1885	1890	1895	1900	1905	1910	1915	1920	1925
					Mining							
24	Anthracite coal	-1.9	1.8	0.0	0.0	-1.1	1.3	0.7	0.8	0.8	-2.2	-0.2
25	Bituminous coal	-4.2	3.8	-1.4	-1.2	-0.1	4.3	1.6	0.3	0.2	-1.9	-1.2
26	Coal, total	-3.3	2.8	-0.9	-0.8	-0.5	3.6	1.8	0.4	0.2	-2.0	-1.4
27	Copper	-5.7	4.9	3.2	-0.1	0.1	-0.3	0.2	-0.8	-0.4	-3.7	2.7
28	Gold	-3.8	-5.1	-2.1	2.0	9.5	4.8	3.1	0.9	-3.5	-6.4	0.8
29	Lead, domestic	7.6	-0.5	-3.5	-4.7	-1.8	0.9	-0.7	1.2	-0.8	0.1	2.3
30	Mercury	10.5	-7.9	-7.9	1.3	3.0	2.5	-2.4	-0.2	4.3	-11.6	8.5
31	Petroleum	7.1	-0.9	-4.7	-1.4	-6.5	1.3	3.4	-1.1	-0.9	3.0	0.7
32	Phosphate rock	1.0	1.2	-2.9	0.1	1.3	-0.6	0.5	-0.7	-4.1	1.5	2.8
33	Silver	0.8	-0.5	2.1	1.3	-2.7	-1.8	-1.5	2.0	0.3	-1.2	1.2
34	Zinc	1.9	-0.3	-1.5	-2.1	-2.2	1.6	1.4	2.0	2.4	-4.2	1.1
35	Asphalt			33.2	-2.5	-15.4	-18.0	-9.2	-9.6	-10.9	21.9	10.5
36	Cement, total			0.6	-4.8	-2.5	7.2	5.6	-1.1	-6.5	0.3	1.2
37	Fluorspar			-2.7	-6.7	-3.1	14.2	-0.4	6.3	5.2	-9.5	-3.5
38	Gypsum			-3.0	-2.0	-4.5	11.2	6.1	-2.8	-6.1	2.0	-0.9
39	Iron ore			-0.6	-2.9	-1.0	5.3	1.1	0.0	0.7	-3.2	0.7
40	Non-Portland cements			12.0	4.8	1.9	-3.7	-15.7	-19.0	-6.2	9.0	16.8
41	Portland cement			-12.2	-8.6	19.1	15.6	1.7	-7.0	-10.4	-0.5	2.3
42	Pyrites			8.5	-5.5	-2.5	-1.2	-3.2	2.1	3.7	-8.3	6.4
43	Salt			-2.9	0.9	2.3	0.7	-0.1	-1.3	2.5	-2.1	0.0
44	Sulphur			-26.4	-18.5	-10.5	86.5	3.5	-10.7	-2.5	-9.6	-12.0
45	Natural gas			23.1	-16.5	-10.1	0.3	-1.1	-1.5	-1.2	0.5	6.6
					Manufactures							
46	Cocoa imports	-1.9	-0.6	0.4	-0.2	-1.8	4.0	1.7	1.3	4.0	-3.8	-3.1
47	Coffee imports	0.0	2.1	-1.7	-1.0	2.1	0.8	-2.2	-2.1	1.8	0.2	0.1

APPENDIX A

48	Cotton consumption	0.3	0.0	-0.3	-0.9	0.4	1.1	-0.5	1.6	-0.3	-2.3	0.9
49	Distilled spirits	-0.1	1.5	-1.3	0.4	-3.7	4.6	-0.7	-1.4	0.7	...	...
50	Fermented liquors	-2.4	1.5	0.9	0.6	-1.8	0.8	1.9	-0.2	-1.2	...	...
51	Jute imports	1.1	2.5	-1.3	-4.3	-2.3	-0.5	0.0	0.1	-0.2	-2.1	4.5
52	Lead consumption	-0.3	2.0	-1.5	0.2	0.4	1.4	-0.9	-1.3	-0.7	0.2	0.7
53	Lead, total	6.8	-1.2	-4.1	-1.6	0.1	-0.5	-2.2	-0.5	-0.8	1.0	3.0
54	Manila hemp imports	-3.2	-1.2	0.5	4.1	-0.4	1.2	0.7	-0.3	0.9	-0.6	-1.9
55	Minor fiber imports	-0.1	1.7	-0.1	-2.4	-1.3	0.7	0.0	2.4	1.4	-3.5	1.2
56	Pig iron	-3.2	1.5	1.6	-1.5	-0.9	4.1	0.8	0.2	0.5	-2.9	-0.1
57	Rails	0.7	1.2	-1.1	-4.6	1.5	7.0	-0.5	-2.8	-3.9	-0.2	2.6
58	Raw sugar consumption	-0.9	1.1	0.6	1.0	-1.9	-0.9	-0.5	-0.1	0.4	1.7	-0.4
59	Rubber imports	-0.2	4.9	1.1	-3.9	-4.4	-3.3	-3.5	2.3	12.1	0.0	-5.0
60	Silk imports, raw	1.3	3.9	-0.3	-2.8	-2.4	-0.5	-0.7	-0.6	-0.6	0.4	2.3
61	Sisal imports	1.3	5.1	-4.4	-4.7	-1.8	0.0	-0.9	5.7	3.8	-5.3	1.3
62	Steel	10.0	-3.3	-3.8	-6.4	0.5	2.2	-1.1	-0.2	1.2	-2.2	3.0
63	Superphosphate	-0.2	6.4	-5.3	-4.4	1.5	1.9	-0.3	-0.4	0.3	-1.1	1.5
64	Tin imports	-0.5	0.6	-0.9	-0.4	1.2	1.3	-1.3	-1.4	1.5	-0.8	0.6
65	Vessels	-6.4	-5.5	0.1	-0.6	1.1	9.2	-1.6	-3.2	41.4	-0.3	-34.4
66	Wool consumption	-0.9	2.8	-0.7	-0.1	-2.0	-1.4	0.3	1.1	2.8	-2.3	0.5
67	Antimonial lead	10.6	-0.3	-5.8	-4.8	0.1	-2.7	-1.9	2.5	-1.5	-5.9	9.9
68	Tin-plate consumption	0.5	3.9	0.5	-4.7	-2.5	0.6	0.0	0.7	0.8	-0.4	0.7
69	Tobacco and snuff	-1.6	1.2	1.2	-0.3	-1.5	1.3	1.5	0.4	-0.2	-1.8	-0.4
70	Cottonseed cake and meal	0.1	1.8	0.2	-1.6	-0.2	0.9	-1.9	2.3	-0.9	-5.1	4.3
71	Cottonseed oil	-0.1	2.0	0.5	-1.2	0.0	-0.1	-3.2	1.6	-1.5	-3.6	5.7
72	Nails	-1.2	2.5	0.7	-2.0	-2.0	1.9	1.3	0.9	-0.5	-0.6	-1.1
73	Zinc consumption	...	2.3	-1.2	-1.9	-2.1	3.1	1.4	0.3	-1.8	-1.8	1.7
74	Flaxseed consumption	...	...	1.0	-2.8	0.3	4.2	-1.4	-1.0	-3.7	3.0	0.5
75	Roofing slate	...	...	0.8	-1.1	0.1	4.2	-0.8	-0.8	-7.1	-1.8	6.4
76	Cigarettes	...	...	9.3	0.6	-7.6	-11.9	-0.1	4.7	7.8	-1.0	-1.8
77	Cigars	...	...	-0.4	-1.5	-0.4	3.7	-0.5	-0.7	0.0	-0.2	-0.1
78	Coke	...	...	1.4	-2.7	-1.1	2.9	1.0	-0.7	0.1	-2.1	1.1
79	Flour	...	...	0.2	0.6	0.2	-0.1	-1.1	-0.3	0.4	-0.6	0.5
80	Gold consumption	...	...	0.5	-3.1	-3.6	6.4	1.5	-0.8	3.3	-0.3	-3.9

PRODUCTION TRENDS

Table 47 (cont.)

Series No.	Series	1875	1880	1885	1890	1895	1900	1905	1910	1915	1920	1925
				Manufactures (cont.)								
81	Locomotives	...	...	-5.6	-3.9	-1.9	15.8	1.3	-2.6	4.4	-1.8	-5.6
82	Silver consumption	...	...	-1.8	-0.5	-1.4	6.0	0.0	-0.5	-2.0	0.0	0.1
83	Tobacco consumption	...	...	0.6	-0.5	-1.6	1.6	0.8	-0.6	-2.6	-0.7	0.7
84	Aluminum	...	...	...	13.5	8.5	-19.3	-17.4	4.6	5.6	-4.2	8.6
85	Copper consumption	...	...	...	-0.4	-1.2	3.2	-1.5	-0.2	2.5	-3.7	1.3
86	Silk imports, unmanufactured	...	...	...	...	...	...	...	...	...	...	...
87	White lead	...	...	...	-1.4	-0.5	2.1	0.0	0.5	0.4	-1.0	-0.1
88	Canned corn	...	...	...	-1.1	0.3	1.1	1.2	0.1	-2.3	2.2	-1.5
89	Canned tomatoes	...	...	...	-1.7	0.0	6.4	-1.7	-3.8	-1.5	0.7	1.6
90	Rolled iron and steel	...	...	...	-0.2	-2.6	1.5	1.0	0.9	0.2	0.5	-1.3
					-4.1	0.4	4.9	0.7	0.2	0.3	-3.0	-0.7
				Construction								
91	Rail consumption	0.0	3.8	-0.6	-6.6	0.7	8.0	-1.1	-3.3	-5.6	1.5	3.6
92	Building permits	...	5.9	3.3	-2.3	-5.5	-1.1	0.9	-5.2	-10.3	10.9	3.4
				Transportation								
93	Coastal trade	-1.7	-0.4	0.7	1.3	-0.2	2.0	1.7	-1.2	-3.7	1.2	0.5
94	N. Y. canals traffic	1.5	3.5	1.0	-1.3	-2.4	0.0	-0.3	-4.2	-10.2	3.6	8.5
95	Postage stamps	0.2	0.0	-0.6	0.0	-2.0	0.9	1.5	0.1	0.5	0.4	-1.0
96	Postal money orders	1.4	1.0	0.7	-4.0	-2.8	1.8	1.5	0.5	0.1	0.2	-0.4
97	Railway ton-miles	0.9	-0.2	-1.0	-1.3	-0.8	2.6	0.4	-0.4	2.0	-1.6	-0.7
98	S. S. Marie canals traffic	-10.4	1.5	7.0	1.8	2.2	2.2	0.0	-0.2	-1.0	-3.3	0.3
99	Railway passenger-miles	...	...	-0.9	-1.7	-3.5	3.6	3.3	1.3	2.0	-1.0	-3.1

APPENDIX A

				Trade						
100	Agricultural exports ...	4.1	-3.1	-1.1	0.2	1.0	-1.5	-3.3	0.5	2.8	0.4	0.1
101	Deflated clearings	-2.1	2.2	1.7	-0.6	-1.9	1.1	-0.7	-1.3	0.6	0.2	0.8
102	Tonnage entered and cleared	-2.1	-1.2	-3.7	0.1	0.9	1.2	0.2	1.4	-1.5	0.7	-0.3
103	Shares traded	...	8.9	-5.6	-5.9	5.6	8.3	-4.1	-15.8	-1.1	-1.2	10.9
104	Railway freight	...	...	0.4	-1.9	-0.8	3.1	0.8	-0.7	0.7	-1.3	-0.2

* For method of computation, see Ch. V, sec. I.

Table 48
DECILS OF TREND-CYCLES OF SEVERAL GROUPS OF PRODUCTION SERIES*
(Unit: one per cent)

Decil	1875	1880	1885	1890	1895	1900	1905	1910	1915	1920	1925
					'All' series						
1	-3.3	-2.5	-4.2	-4.7	-4.1	-1.3	-2.5	-3.9	-5.1	-5.0	-3.1
2	-1.8	-1.1	-2.7	-3.9	-2.5	-0.5	-1.5	-1.8	-2.2	-3.2	-1.1
3	-0.6	-0.5	-1.4	-2.0	-1.9	0.0	-0.9	-1.2	-1.2	-2.1	-0.2
4	-0.1	-0.2	-0.9	-1.4	-1.3	0.6	-0.5	-0.5	-0.7	-1.4	0.1
5	0.3	1.0	-0.4	-1.0	-0.6	1.2	0.3	-0.2	0.2	-0.9	0.5
6	0.7	1.5	0.2	-0.4	0.0	1.8	0.3	0.3	0.5	-0.3	0.9
7	1.2	2.0	0.5	0.1	0.3	2.8	0.9	0.9	1.0	0.1	1.8
8	1.6	2.8	1.0	0.6	1.0	4.3	1.4	1.3	2.5	0.5	3.4
9	5.3	3.9	2.3	1.8	2.0	7.6	1.7	2.3	4.2	2.2	6.6
					Nonagricultural series						
1	-3.8	-1.2	-5.1	-5.5	-4.4	-1.4	-2.4	-3.8	-5.6	-5.1	-3.1
2	-2.0	-0.5	-3.0	-4.2	-2.6	-0.2	-1.5	-1.5	-2.2	-3.3	-1.0
3	-1.2	-0.2	-1.5	-2.7	-2.0	0.8	-0.9	-1.0	-1.2	-2.2	-0.2
4	-0.3	1.1	-0.9	-1.8	-1.8	1.1	-0.5	-0.6	-0.6	-1.8	0.2
5	0.0	1.4	-0.3	-1.4	-0.9	1.5	0.0	-0.2	0.1	-1.0	0.7
6	0.4	1.9	0.4	-1.0	-0.2	2.2	0.3	0.1	0.4	-0.4	1.1
7	1.0	2.3	0.7	-0.2	0.2	3.6	0.9	0.5	0.8	0.2	2.1
8	1.4	3.8	1.2	0.1	0.8	4.7	1.4	1.2	2.2	0.7	3.4
9	7.1	4.9	3.3	1.3	2.1	8.0	1.7	2.1	4.0	2.0	7.0
					Basic series						
1	-2.8	-1.1	-2.8	-4.1	-3.5	-0.8	-1.5	-1.4	-3.6	-3.7	-1.2
2	-1.8	-0.5	-1.6	-2.6	-2.1	-0.1	-1.1	-1.3	-1.5	-2.4	-0.3

APPENDIX A

3	−0.4	−0.4	−1.3	−1.8	−1.8	0.3	−0.7	−0.8	−0.8	−2.1	0.0
4	−0.1	0.0	−0.9	−1.3	−1.3	0.8	−0.2	−0.4	0.0	−1.4	0.3
5	0.1	0.9	−0.5	−0.8	−0.9	1.2	0.1	−0.1	0.4	−0.9	0.6
6	0.4	1.5	0.0	−0.4	−0.2	1.6	0.5	0.3	0.7	−0.5	0.7
7	1.0	2.0	0.5	0.0	0.3	2.6	0.8	0.9	1.0	0.0	1.1
8	1.4	2.8	0.7	0.4	0.5	3.9	1.4	1.3	1.7	0.4	1.4
9	2.2	3.9	1.6	1.0	1.3	4.9	1.8	2.0	2.5	1.4	3.2

Basic nonagricultural series (Section 1)

1	−3.4	−1.0	−3.0	−4.6	−3.6	−0.9	−1.5	−1.4	−3.7	−3.7	−1.4
2	−2.0	−0.5	−1.6	−2.8	−2.3	0.4	−1.1	−1.1	−1.6	−3.0	−0.3
3	−1.1	−0.1	−1.2	−2.0	−1.9	0.8	−0.6	−0.8	−0.8	−2.2	0.0
4	−0.3	0.9	−0.7	−1.4	−1.6	1.2	0.0	−0.5	0.1	−1.8	0.5
5	−0.1	1.5	−0.3	−1.1	−1.1	1.5	0.3	−0.2	0.4	−1.0	0.6
6	0.0	1.9	0.4	−0.5	−0.8	2.2	0.7	0.2	0.6	−0.4	0.7
7	0.6	2.2	0.5	−0.1	0.1	3.2	1.0	0.6	0.8	0.1	1.1
8	1.1	3.7	0.8	0.1	0.4	4.2	1.5	1.2	1.9	0.4	1.3
9	4.1	4.1	1.6	0.9	1.2	5.3	1.9	1.6	2.5	1.5	2.8

Basic nonagricultural series (Section 2)

1	−3.7	−1.1	−3.3	−4.7	−3.6	−1.0	−1.5	−1.4	−3.9	−3.7	−2.3
2	−2.1	−0.5	−1.7	−2.9	−2.4	0.0	−1.1	−1.2	−1.7	−3.0	−0.3
3	−1.5	−0.2	−1.3	−2.1	−1.9	0.8	−0.7	−0.8	−0.8	−2.2	−0.1
4	−0.4	0.7	−0.8	−1.5	−1.7	1.1	0.0	−0.6	−0.1	−1.8	0.5
5	−0.1	1.5	−0.3	−1.1	−1.1	1.5	0.3	−0.2	0.4	−1.0	0.6
6	0.0	1.8	0.3	−0.5	−0.8	2.2	0.7	0.2	0.6	−0.5	0.7
7	0.4	2.1	0.5	−0.1	0.0	3.1	0.9	0.5	0.8	0.1	1.1
8	1.0	3.2	0.7	0.1	0.4	4.2	1.5	1.2	1.7	0.3	1.2
9	2.1	3.9	1.5	0.7	1.0	5.1	1.8	1.6	2.5	1.5	2.8

Table 48 (cont.)

Basic nonagricultural series (Section 4)

Decil	1875	1880	1885	1890	1895	1900	1905	1910	1915	1920	1925
1	−4.0	−1.9	−3.1	−4.7	−3.6	−0.1	−1.6	−1.4	−1.6	−3.7	−3.1
2	−2.4	−0.5	−1.6	−3.3	−2.3	0.7	−1.1	−1.1	−0.8	−3.4	−0.2
3	−1.9	0.0	−1.3	−2.5	−1.8	1.0	−0.7	−0.8	−0.3	−2.3	0.0
4	−0.5	1.5	−0.9	−1.8	−1.5	1.3	0.0	−0.5	0.3	−2.1	0.5
5	−0.1	1.7	−0.4	−1.3	−1.1	2.0	0.2	−0.2	0.6	−1.6	0.7
6	−0.1	2.0	0.0	−1.0	−0.8	3.0	0.7	0.2	0.8	−1.0	0.7
7	0.1	2.2	0.5	−0.5	0.0	3.7	0.9	0.6	1.4	−0.4	0.9
8	0.9	3.6	0.6	−0.1	0.4	4.4	1.4	1.1	2.0	0.1	1.2
9	4.5	3.9	1.2	0.4	0.7	5.4	2.0	1.6	2.6	0.2	2.4

* This table corresponds to Charts 5–8. Section 3 of the basic nonagricultural series is identical with Section 2 except for the central decade year 1915; the successive decils for this date are −2.0, −1.1, −0.5, 0.3, 0.4, 0.7, 1.0, 1.9, and 2.5.

APPENDIX A

Table 49
MEDIANS OF TREND-CYCLES OF SUBGROUPS OF NONAGRICULTURAL SERIES*
(Unit: one per cent)

Subgroup	1875	1880	1885	1890	1895	1900	1905	1910	1915	1920	1925
					Nonagricultural series						
I	-0.6	1.1	0.1	-0.3	-0.9	1.3	0.3	-0.1	0.3	-0.6	-0.1
II	0.1	1.6	-0.6	-1.7	-0.8	3.3	0.1	0.0	0.1	-1.5	1.1
III	0.9	1.6	-1.3	-2.9	-1.2	1.9	-0.9	-1.1	-1.1	-1.3	2.9
				Basic nonagricultural series (Section 1)							
I	-0.3	1.1	-0.2	-0.3	-0.7	1.2	-0.1	-0.3	0.4	-0.5	0.1
II	0.1	1.5	-0.7	-0.8	-1.3	2.2	0.3	0.0	0.6	-2.1	0.9
III	-0.6	1.8	0.1	-2.5	-0.9	3.5	0.8	-0.1	-0.5	-0.8	0.8
				Basic nonagricultural series (Section 4)							
I	-0.6	1.8	-0.2	-0.5	-0.7	1.2	-0.1	-0.4	0.8	-1.0	0.4
II	-0.7	1.8	-0.8	-1.8	-1.2	3.5	0.3	0.0	0.7	-2.3	0.7
III	-0.1	0.3	-0.2	-2.9	-1.2	3.3	0.8	0.3	0.4	-1.2	0.9

* This table corresponds to Charts 9-10.

Table 50
TREND-CYCLES OF INDEXES OF PRODUCTION*
(Unit: one per cent)

Index	1875	1880	1885	1890	1895	1900	1905	1910	1915	1920	1925
'Total' production											
Day-Persons	0.2	0.9	-0.6	-1.2	-0.6	0.9	-0.3	-0.3	0.6	-0.1	0.4
King	...	...	-0.1	-0.3	-0.2	1.2	0.7	-0.7	-0.4	...	...
Snyder (basic)	1.2	0.6	-1.3	-1.2	0.3	0.5	0.2	-0.2	0.1	-0.7	0.5
Snyder (87 series)	1.2	-0.2	-2.3	-0.6	-0.5	3.0	0.1	-0.2	0.6	-1.0	...
Snyder (49 series)	0.6	0.3	-1.3	-0.9	-1.6	1.7	0.4	0.2	1.1	-0.8	...
Snyder (49 series, recomputed)	-0.3	1.1	-0.7	-0.8	-0.9	1.7	0.3	-0.1	0.9	-1.2	...
Snyder (28 series)	...	...	0.0	-0.3	-0.8	1.3	0.1	-0.4	0.2	...	...
Warren-Pearson	0.3	0.4	-0.6	-1.1	0.1	1.3	0.2	-0.6	-0.2	-0.7	0.8
Production of major industrial groups											
Cleveland Trust Co.: Industrial activity	-1.0	0.6	0.3	-0.4	-0.1	1.0	-0.5	-0.5	0.9	-0.7	0.4
Day-Persons: Manufactures	-0.1	1.6	-0.3	-0.7	-1.2	1.5	-0.3	-0.7	0.6	-0.3	-0.1
Day-Persons: Mining	-1.8	1.4	0.1	-0.8	-0.8	2.7	0.8	-0.2	-0.4	-0.7	-0.3
Snyder: Mining	-3.0	2.1	0.0	-0.8	-0.4	3.5	1.1	-0.1	0.2	-2.0	-0.5
Warren-Pearson: Mining	-1.8	1.6	0.2	-0.8	-1.4	2.7	1.3	-0.2	-0.2	-1.1	-0.2
Day-Persons: Crops	0.9	0.2	-0.9	-1.3	0.3	0.2	0.3	0.4	0.4	-0.6	0.2
Snyder: Crops (A)	1.6	-0.1	-0.5	-1.7	-0.9	0.4	0.8	0.4	0.3	-0.4	0.3
Snyder: Crops (B)	1.6	-0.1	-1.2	-1.1	0.7	-0.3	-0.1	0.2	-0.3	-0.3	1.0
Timoshenko: Crops	2.0	-0.1	-1.1	-1.4	0.3	0.0	0.0	0.2	0.4	-0.3	...
Warren-Pearson: Crops	1.3	-0.1	-1.0	-1.1	0.4	-0.1	-0.2	0.0	0.3	-0.3	0.4

* This table corresponds to Charts 11-12.

Table 51
TREND-CYCLES OF ACREAGES AND ACRE-YIELDS OF EIGHT LEADING CROPS*
(Unit: one per cent)

Crop	1875	1880	1885	1890	1895	1900	1905	1910	1915	1920	1925
Acreage											
Barley	0.0	0.2	0.9	0.5	-1.8	0.9	2.2	-1.9	-2.6	-4.0	5.6
Corn	1.9	1.1	-1.6	-2.4	1.2	-0.8	-0.4	0.9	-0.3	-0.2	0.6
Cotton	2.4	0.7	-1.4	-2.2	0.2	0.0	-0.3	-0.4	-2.1	0.4	2.7
Hay	0.4	1.8	-0.1	-1.2	-1.8	-0.7	0.7	-0.3	1.0	0.7	-0.4
Oats	1.1	1.3	1.1	-2.1	-2.7	-1.3	0.3	1.1	1.1	0.3	-0.1
Potatoes	0.3	0.4	-0.5	-0.1	-1.0	-0.6	1.4	1.2	0.3	-1.2	0.0
Tobacco, raw	2.6	0.2	-1.6	-4.4	2.1	-1.7	-1.3	3.0	2.8	-0.6	-1.1
Wheat	2.3	0.1	-0.2	-0.6	-0.1	-1.4	-3.2	0.7	2.8	0.1	-0.5
Acre-yield											
Barley	-0.2	-0.7	-0.6	0.5	0.2	1.6	-1.2	0.5	1.1	-0.8	0.1
Corn	-0.7	-1.7	0.2	1.5	0.7	0.8	0.6	-0.8	0.4	0.1	-0.9
Cotton	-1.0	-1.2	1.3	1.5	0.1	-0.1	0.1	1.7	-1.2	-2.5	1.1
Hay	0.5	-1.7	-0.5	0.2	1.3	1.3	-0.1	0.1	0.0	-2.1	0.6
Oats	-0.7	-0.4	-0.3	0.2	1.7	1.0	-1.2	1.3	0.6	-2.1	0.3
Potatoes	0.1	-1.4	-1.0	0.6	0.9	1.2	0.8	-0.2	-1.0	0.7	-0.3
Tobacco, raw	-0.2	-0.5	-0.9	0.3	-0.3	1.7	0.7	-0.5	0.4	-0.9	-0.2
Wheat	0.4	-0.8	-0.4	1.1	-0.4	0.4	0.8	1.3	-1.2	-1.3	0.4

* This table corresponds to Chart 14.

Table 52
MEDIANS OF TREND-CYCLES OF TWO GROUPS OF MANUFACTURES*
(Unit: one per cent)

Group	1875	1880	1885	1890	1895	1900	1905	1910	1915	1920	1925
Manufactures from agricultural materials	-0.3	1.7	0.3	-0.6	-1.1	1.0	-0.4	0.2	0.2	-1.1	0.2
Manufactures from mineral materials	0.2	1.6	-1.2	-2.1	-0.2	2.5	-0.2	-0.3	0.0	-1.4	0.9

* This table corresponds to Chart 16.

Table 53
STANDARD TREND-CYCLE AND TREND-CYCLES OF SEVERAL NON-PRODUCTION SERIES*
(Unit: one per cent)

Series	1875	1880	1885	1890	1895	1900	1905	1910	1915	1920	1925
Standard trend-cycle	-0.4	1.4	-0.6	-1.6	-1.1	2.4	0.2	-0.1	0.6	-1.6	0.3
Nonagricultural prices	-0.4	0.3	-0.4	-0.9	0.3	2.8	0.0	-1.7	...	...	...
'All-commodity' prices	-0.4	0.6	-0.1	-0.9	-0.4	1.8	0.4	-1.1	...	...	...
Real earnings	...	...	...	...	-0.7	1.6	-0.3	-1.0	0.0	0.2	...
Money in circulation	-2.3	2.2	-0.6	-0.7	-0.8	1.8	0.7	-0.8	3.5	0.4	-3.3
Monetary stock of gold	-1.1	9.1	-2.5	-6.5	-1.2	2.2	-1.2	-1.9	2.3	1.6	-0.8
Business failures (inverted)	-2.7	1.8	-3.1	-0.6	3.2	4.3	-0.3	-3.6	4.7	-2.6	-1.1
Patents issued	-2.3	3.6	0.6	-2.2	-1.8	1.6	1.3	0.3	-0.6	-1.0	0.7

* This table corresponds to Chart 20.

APPENDIX A

Table 54
MEASURES OF DISPERSION, AND CYCLES IN DISPERSION, OF DECADE RATES*
(Unit: one per cent)

Group	1875	1880	1885	1890	1895	1900	1905	1910	1915	1920	1925
			Dispersion measures								
'All' series	5.9	7.3	5.7	4.6	4.5	6.6	4.4	4.5	4.9	4.6	4.6
Basic series	4.3	6.0	5.0	3.7	3.8	5.7	3.9	2.9	3.9	3.6	3.5
			Cycles of dispersion measures								
'All' series	−0.2	1.3	−0.1	−1.0	−0.9	1.4	−0.7	−0.4	0.2	0.1	0.3
Basic series	−0.7	1.1	0.3	−0.8	−0.6	1.5	−0.1	−0.9	0.2	0.1	0.2

* The lower part of this table corresponds to Chart 21.

Appendix B

SOURCES OF PRODUCTION DATA

The issuing authority for several of the more familiar statistical handbooks is not stated, or else not stated fully, in the descriptive notes that follow on various of the individual series. The *Yearbook of Agriculture*, published under slightly varying titles, is issued by the Department of Agriculture. *Merchant Marine Statistics* is a publication of the Bureau of Navigation. The *Annual Report on the Statistics of Railways in the United States* (referred to below as *Statistics of Railways*) is a publication of the Interstate Commerce Commission. *Mineral Resources of the United States* (referred to below as *Mineral Resources*) was published by the Geological Survey through 1923, but has been published by the Bureau of Mines since then. The *Statistical Abstract of the United States* (referred to below as the *Statistical Abstract*) is now published by the Bureau of Foreign and Domestic Commerce, but was published by the Bureau of Statistics of the Department of Commerce and Labor from 1903 to 1911, and by the Bureau of Statistics of the Treasury Department in earlier years. The *Annual Statistical Report* on the iron and steel trade, now published by the American Iron and Steel Institute, was published prior to 1912 by the American Iron and Steel Association.

I. CONTINUOUS SERIES

The series covered in this section of the Appendix are those listed in Table 1 and tabulated in Table 44. Where page references are not given, the data are scattered through successive issues of the indicated source. Unless otherwise stated, the data refer to calendar years.

The following general statement will hold for the sources of all the series on net imports, except when otherwise stated below. These series are based on publications of the Bureau of Statistics of the Treasury Department, for the period January 1869 to June 1903; of the Bureau of Statistics of the Department of Commerce and Labor, for the period July 1903 to June 1912; and of the Bureau of Foreign and Domestic Commerce, for the period since July 1912. The titles of the publications are as follows: *Monthly Report of the Chief of Bureau of Statistics*, January 1869 to June 1875; *Summary Statement of Imports and Exports*, July 1875 to December 1894; *Finance, Commerce and Navigation*, January to December 1895; *Monthly Summary of*

APPENDIX B

Finance and Commerce, January 1896 to June 1898; *Monthly Summary of Commerce and Finance,* July 1898 to June 1914; *Monthly Summary of Foreign Commerce,* July 1914 on.

1. Barley

    SOURCE: *Yearbook of Agriculture,* 1927, pp. 799–800; *ibid.,* 1932, p. 630.

    COMMENTS: Production. The figures used (including those for census years) are estimates of the Crop Reporting Board of the Department of Agriculture.

2. Beet sugar

    SOURCE: *Yearbook of Agriculture,* 1923, p. 845; *ibid.,* 1932, p. 676.

    COMMENTS: Production, chiefly refined. Figures are for years beginning July 1. See *Yearbook,* 1923, p. 845, note.

3. Buckwheat

    SOURCE: *Yearbook of Agriculture,* 1927, pp. 825–6; *ibid.,* 1932, p. 654.

    COMMENTS: Production. See (1).

4. Cane sugar

    SOURCE: *Yearbook of Agriculture,* 1923, p. 845; *ibid.,* 1932, p. 676.

    COMMENTS: Production (chiefly raw) of Louisiana and other states. Figures are for years beginning July 1. See *Yearbook,* 1923, p. 845, note.

5. Corn

    SOURCE: *Yearbook of Agriculture,* 1927, pp. 774–5; *ibid.,* 1933, p. 431.

    COMMENTS: Production. The figures relate to the grain equivalent on entire acreage. See (1).

6. Cotton

    SOURCE: *Cotton Production and Distribution, 1928–29* (Bureau of the Census, Bulletin 166), pp. 57–8; Bulletin 167, p. 9.

    COMMENTS: Production or commercial crop, including linters. Figures are expressed in units of 500-pound bales (gross weight). See Bulletin 166, p. 57.

7. Hay

    SOURCE: *Yearbook of Agriculture,* 1927, p. 927; *ibid.,* 1933, p. 575.

    COMMENTS: Production, tame. See (1).

8. Molasses and sirup

   SOURCE: *Statistical Abstract,* 1904, p. 354; *ibid.,* volumes through 1917; *Yearbook of Agriculture,* volumes for 1919–32.

   COMMENTS: Production of Louisiana cane molasses and United States sugar-cane sirup. Figures are estimates of Crop Reporting Board, for 1918–30.

9. Oats

   SOURCE: *Yearbook of Agriculture,* 1927, pp. 788–9; *ibid.,* 1932, p. 620.

   COMMENTS: Production. See (1).

10. Potatoes

    SOURCE: *Yearbook of Agriculture,* 1927, p. 881; *ibid.,* 1932, p. 728.

    COMMENTS: Production, excluding sweet potatoes. See (1).

11. Rice

    SOURCE: *Rice Crop of the United States, 1792–1911* (Department of Agriculture, Bureau of Statistics, Circular No. 34), pp. 9–10; *Yearbook of Agriculture,* 1927, p. 819; *ibid.,* 1932, p. 648.

    COMMENTS: Production or marketed production, rough. Estimates of Crop Reporting Board since 1904. Concerning earlier data, see Circular No. 34, pp. 3–4.

12. Rye

    SOURCE: *Yearbook of Agriculture,* 1927, pp. 764–5; *ibid.,* 1932, p. 599.

    COMMENTS: Production. See (1).

13. Tobacco, raw

    SOURCE: *Yearbook of Agriculture,* 1927, pp. 969–70; *ibid.,* 1933, p. 497.

    COMMENTS: Production. See (1).

14. Wheat

    SOURCE: "Wheat Acreage and Production in the United States since 1866" (Food Research Institute, *Wheat Studies,* Vol. II, No. 7), pp. 260–1; *Yearbook of Agriculture,* 1933, pp. 403–4.

    COMMENTS: Production. The figures since 1910 (including those for census years) are estimates of the Crop Reporting Board. The figures for earlier years are estimates of the Food Research Institute; see *Wheat Studies,* Vol. II, No. 7.

APPENDIX B   329

15. Wool

SOURCE: *Yearbook of Agriculture*, 1923, pp. 1001–2; *ibid.*, 1932, p. 811.

COMMENTS: Production, shorn and pulled. See *Yearbook*, 1923, p. 1002, note to Table 546; and *ibid.*, 1932, p. 811, note to Table 365.

16. Raisins

SOURCE: California Cooperative Crop Reporting Service, *California Crop Report*, 1928, p. 40. The figure for 1929 was furnished by the California Cooperative Crop Reporting Service.

COMMENTS: California production. The series includes production from raisin varieties of grapes, plus dried grapes from wine or table varieties. See *Crop Report*, 1928, pp. 39–40.

17. Flaxseed

SOURCE: *Statistical Abstract*, 1904, p. 391; *Yearbook of Agriculture*, 1927, p. 809; *ibid.*, 1933, p. 456.

COMMENTS: Production or commercial crop. The figures since 1902 (including those for census years) are estimates of production, by the Crop Reporting Board. The figures for earlier years, except for census years, are estimates of the commercial crop, by the Department of Agriculture.

18. Cattle

SOURCE: *Yearbook of Agriculture*, 1933, p. 596. Figures for 1880–1906 were furnished by Mr. C. L. Harlan, Livestock Statistician in the Department of Agriculture, prior to their publication.

COMMENTS: Number of animals slaughtered under federal inspection, since 1907. Estimated equivalent of federal slaughter, for earlier years. See Appendix C, I.

19. Hogs

SOURCE: *Yearbook of Agriculture*, 1933, p. 605. See (18).

COMMENTS: See (18).

20. Sheep

SOURCE: *Yearbook of Agriculture*, 1933, p. 616. See (18).

COMMENTS: See (18).

21. Cod and mackerel

SOURCE: *Merchant Marine Statistics*, 1930, pp. 26–7.

COMMENTS: Figures represent the gross tonnage of vessels licensed for the cod and mackerel fisheries and outstanding (i.e. then in existence) on June 30 of year given. "A gross ton is the capacity of the spaces within the frames or ceiling of the hull of a vessel and of the closed-in spaces above deck available for cargo, stores, passengers, or crew, with certain exemptions, expressed in tons of 100 cubic feet." See Appendix C, I and III; and *Merchant Marine Statistics*, 1930, p. 25, note 1.

22. Whale

    SOURCE: See (21).

    COMMENTS: Tonnage of vessels licensed for whaling. See (21); and Appendix C, I and III.

23. Fish, total

    SOURCE: Figures were obtained from the Department of Commerce, Bureau of Fisheries.

    COMMENTS: Yield of all the fisheries, in pounds. The data are estimates based on intermittent statistical canvasses by regions. See Appendix C, III.

24. Anthracite coal

    SOURCE: *Mineral Resources*, 1918, Part II, pp. 710–1; *ibid.*, 1929, Part II, p. 701.

    COMMENTS: Pennsylvania production. See *Mineral Resources*, 1929, Part II, pp. 690–3.

25. Bituminous coal

    SOURCE: See (24).

    COMMENTS: Production, including lignite. See (24).

26. Coal, total

    SOURCE: See (24).

    COMMENTS: Total of anthracite and bituminous. See (24) and (25).

27. Copper

    SOURCE: *Mineral Resources*, 1929, Part I, p. 535.

    COMMENTS: Smelter production from domestic ores. The series does not include secondary copper. See Appendix C, I; *Mineral Resources*, 1929, Part I, pp. 535–6; and *Summarized Data of Copper Production* (Bureau of Mines, Economic Paper 1), Table 26.

APPENDIX B

28. Gold

SOURCE: *Annual Report of the Director of the Mint*, 1910, p. 99; *ibid.*, 1919, p. 65; *ibid.*, 1930, p. 38.

COMMENTS: Production of United States, including dependencies. See *Annual Report*, 1930, pp. 27, 38; and *Mineral Resources*, 1929, Part I, pp. 884-5.

29. Lead, domestic

SOURCE: *Summarized Data of Lead Production* (Bureau of Mines, Economic Paper 5), p. 13, for 1870-85; *ibid.*, p. 14, figures headed 'from domestic ores and base bullion', for 1886-1927; *Mineral Resources*, 1929, Part I, p. 234, for 1928-29.

COMMENTS: Production of pig lead, from domestic ores and base bullion. The series does not include secondary lead, pigments made directly from ore, and primary lead accounted for in antimonial lead. See Appendix C, I.

30. Mercury

SOURCE: *Mineral Resources*, 1919, Part I, p. 152; *ibid.*, 1928, Part I, p. 264; *ibid.*, 1929, Part I, p. A62.

COMMENTS: Production. Data have been converted to a uniform 75-pound flask basis. It is assumed that the 1904 figure (see *Mineral Resources*, 1919, Part I, p. 152) is expressed in 75-pound flasks.

31. Petroleum

SOURCE: *Mineral Resources*, 1929, Part II, p. 470.

COMMENTS: Production, crude. Data are expressed in barrels of 42 U. S. gallons. See *Mineral Resources*, 1918, Part II, p. 971.

32. Phosphate rock

SOURCE: *Mineral Resources*, 1892, p. 782; *ibid.*, 1915, Part I, p. 31a; *ibid.*, 1915, Part II, p. 228; *ibid.*, 1925, Part II, p. 148; *ibid.*, 1929, Part II, p. 342.

COMMENTS: Marketed production (tonnage sold or used by producers). For the period 1870-80, South Carolina production represents total national production. The figures for the period 1870-85 are for years ending May 31. See *Mineral Resources*, 1915, Part II, pp. 228-9.

33. Silver

SOURCE: See (28).

COMMENTS: See (28).

PRODUCTION TRENDS

34. Zinc

    SOURCE: *Summarized Data of Zinc Production* (Bureau of Mines, Economic Paper 2), p. 19; *Mineral Resources*, 1929, Part I, p. 675.

    COMMENTS: Smelter production from domestic and foreign ores. The series does not include secondary zinc, zinc dust, and zinc produced in the forms of oxide and sulphide. See Appendix C, I; Economic Paper 2, pp. 1–2, and Table 15; and *Mineral Resources*, 1929, Part I, pp. 677–8.

35. Asphalt

    SOURCE: *Mineral Resources*, 1915, Part I, p. 31a; *ibid.*, 1918, Part II, p. 452; *ibid.*, 1926, Part II, p. 52; *ibid.*, 1929, Part II, p. 524.

    COMMENTS: Production (sold at mines) of native asphalt and related bitumens. See *Mineral Resources*, 1915, Part II, pp. 135–7.

36. Cement, total

    SOURCE: *Mineral Resources*, 1924, Part II, pp. 358–9; *ibid.*, 1929, Part II, p. 391.

    COMMENTS: Total of Portland and non-Portland cements. See (40) and (41); and Appendix C, I.

37. Fluorspar

    SOURCE: *Mineral Resources*, 1925, Part II, pp. 13–4; *ibid.*, 1929, Part II, p. 5.

    COMMENTS: Production, mined or shipped. See *Mineral Resources*, 1918, Part II, p. 320; and *ibid.*, 1925, Part II, pp. 9–14.

38. Gypsum

    SOURCE: *Mineral Resources*, 1915, Part II, p. 151; *ibid.*, 1924, Part II, p. 232; *ibid.*, 1929, Part II, p. 106.

    COMMENTS: Production, crude.

39. Iron ore

    SOURCE: *Mineral Resources*, 1915, Part I, p. 286; *ibid.*, 1929, Part I, p. 9.

    COMMENTS: Production, total for all classes. See *Mineral Resources*, 1915, Part I, pp. 285–6; and *ibid.*, 1929, Part I, p. 6.

40. Non-Portland cements

    SOURCE: See (36).

APPENDIX B

COMMENTS: Includes natural, puzzolan, and masonry cements. The figures are for production to 1911, shipments 1912–24, production 1925–29. The unit 'barrel' is inconstant: see *Mineral Resources*, 1915, Part II, p. 190. See *ibid.*, pp. 192–3.

41. Portland cement
    SOURCE: See (36).

    COMMENTS: Production. The unit 'barrel' is equivalent to 360 pounds net. See *Mineral Resources*, 1915, Part II, pp. 192–3.

42. Pyrites
    SOURCE: *Mineral Resources*, 1901, p. 838; *ibid.*, 1902, pp. 935, 939; *ibid.*, 1903, p. 1074; *ibid.*, 1915, Part I, pp. 31a–43a; *ibid.*, 1925, Part II, p. 390; *ibid.*, 1929, Part II, p. 188.

    COMMENTS: Production, exclusive of by-product pyrites. Figures for 1901–03 were obtained directly or indirectly from data in sources cited. See *Mineral Resources*, 1929, Part II, p. 188.

43. Salt
    SOURCE: *Mineral Resources*, 1915, Part I, pp. 31a–52a; *ibid.*, 1925, Part II, p. 93; *ibid.*, 1929, Part II, p. 147.

    COMMENTS: Production (sold or used by producers). Includes manufactured salt, salt in brine, and rock salt. The unit 'barrel' is equivalent to 280 pounds. See *Mineral Resources*, 1915, Part II, p. 266.

44. Sulphur
    SOURCE: *Mineral Resources*, 1902, p. 935; *ibid.*, 1915, Part I, pp. 31a–43a; *ibid.*, 1924, Part II, p. 2; *ibid.*, 1929, Part II, p. 176. Figures for 1902 and 1903 were furnished by the Bureau of Mines.

    COMMENTS: Production. The figures for 1902 and 1903 are based on the books of the sulphur companies, to which the government was given access in 1917.

45. Natural gas
    SOURCE: *Mineral Resources*, 1929, Part II, p. 322, for 1906–29. The figures for earlier years were obtained from Mr. F. G. Tryon, who has prepared them in connection with a study, sponsored by the Brookings Institution, of the energy supply of the country.

    COMMENTS: Produced and delivered to consumers. Data prior to 1906 are described by Mr. Tryon as estimates calculated "from contemporary estimates of the quantity of coal displaced by gas or of the value of the gas sold."

46. Cocoa imports

SOURCE: Figures for 1870–71 were furnished by the Bureau of Foreign and Domestic Commerce. Concerning the later figures, see the introductory notes to this Appendix, sec. I.

COMMENTS: Net imports (general imports minus foreign exports) of crude cocoa.

47. Coffee imports

SOURCE: See the introductory notes to this Appendix, sec. I.

COMMENTS: Net imports (general imports minus foreign exports).

48. Cotton consumption

SOURCE: *Cotton Production and Distribution, 1928–29* (Bureau of the Census, Bulletin 166), pp. 57–8; Bulletin 167, pp. 9, 31, 57.

COMMENTS: Consumption of cotton and linters. The figures are expressed in units of 500-pound bales (gross weight), and relate to the 12 months during which the crop of the specified year was chiefly marketed. See Bulletin 166, p. 57.

49. Distilled spirits

SOURCE: *Annual Report of the Commissioner of Internal Revenue*, 1901, pp. 428–9; Bureau of Prohibition, *Statistics Concerning Intoxicating Liquors*, 1930, p. 3.

COMMENTS: Production, total for all classes. The figures are for years ending June 30. See Appendix C, II.

50. Fermented liquors

SOURCE: *Annual Report of the Commissioner of Internal Revenue*, 1880, p. lxxxix; *ibid.*, 1901, pp. 440–3; Bureau of Prohibition, *Statistics Concerning Intoxicating Liquors*, 1930, p. 52.

COMMENTS: Production, total. The unit 'barrel' contains 31 gallons. Figures are for years ending June 30. See *Intoxicating Liquors*, p. 52.

51. Jute imports

SOURCE: Figures for 1870–90 were furnished by the Bureau of Foreign and Domestic Commerce. Concerning the later figures, see the introductory notes to this Appendix, sec. I.

COMMENTS: The figures for 1891–1929 are for net imports (general imports minus foreign exports) of jute and jute butts. The figures for 1870–90 are for imports entered for consumption during years

APPENDIX B

ending June 30. For 1870–83, small quantities of sunn hemp are included.

52. Lead consumption

   SOURCE: W. R. Ingalls, *Lead and Zinc in the United States* (Hill Publishing Co., 1908), p. 205, for 1870–93; *Mineral Resources*, for later years.

   COMMENTS: Prior to 1894, the figures ignore stocks completely. For later years, producers' stocks are taken into account, but not completely, while consumers' stocks are ignored. Secondary lead is excluded. See Ingalls, p. 204; *Mineral Resources*, 1907, Part I, pp. 655–6; *ibid.*, 1914, Part I, pp. 820–1; and *ibid.*, 1929, Part I, p. 259.

53. Lead, total

   SOURCE: See (29), for 1870–85 and 1928–29; *Summarized Data of Lead Production* (Bureau of Mines, Economic Paper 5), p. 14, for 1886–1927.

   COMMENTS: Production of pig lead, from both domestic and foreign ores and base bullion. See (29).

54. Manila hemp imports

   SOURCE: See (51).

   COMMENTS: The figures for 1891–1929 are for net imports (general imports minus foreign exports) of Manila hemp. The figures for 1870–90 are for imports entered for consumption, include India hemp, and refer to years ending June 30.

55. Minor fiber imports

   SOURCE: See (51).

   COMMENTS: Total net imports of jute, Manila hemp, and sisal. See (51), (54), and (61).

56. Pig iron

   SOURCE: American Iron and Steel Institute, *Annual Statistical Report*, 1929, pp. 10–1.

   COMMENTS: Production, including ferro-alloys. See *Statistical Report*, 1929, p. 3.

57. Rails

   SOURCE: American Iron and Steel Institute, *Annual Statistical Report* (Supplement), 1894, p. 15; *ibid.*, 1914, p. 47; *ibid.*, 1929, p. 44.

COMMENTS: Total production of iron and steel rails. Rerolled rails, and 'girder' and 'high T' rails, are included.

58. Raw sugar consumption

SOURCE: *Yearbook of Agriculture*, 1923, pp. 845–6; *ibid.*, 1932, pp. 676, 680.

COMMENTS: Production of cane sugar plus 'imports' from foreign countries and from insular possessions. Figures are for years ending June 30. See (4); Appendix C, III; *Yearbook*, 1923, notes to Table 360; and *ibid.*, 1932, notes to Table 157.

59. Rubber imports

SOURCE: See the introductory notes to this Appendix, sec. I.

COMMENTS: Net imports (general imports minus foreign exports) of India rubber. Imports of rubber scrap are excluded. For some years gums other than India rubber are included. See *Marketing of Crude Rubber* (Department of Commerce, Trade Promotion Series, No. 55), p. 176.

60. Silk imports, raw

SOURCE: See the introductory notes to this Appendix, sec. I.

COMMENTS: Net imports (general imports minus foreign exports) of raw silk. Waste, cocoons, silk worms, and eggs of silk worms are excluded. See (86).

61. Sisal imports

SOURCE: See (51).

COMMENTS: The figures for 1891–1929 are for net imports (general imports minus foreign exports). The figures for 1870–90 are for imports entered for consumption during years ending June 30.

62. Steel

SOURCE: American Iron and Steel Institute, *Annual Statistical Report* (Supplement), 1894, p. 10; *ibid.*, 1929, p. 25.

COMMENTS: Production of ingots and castings.

63. Superphosphate

SOURCE: K. D. Jacob and W. A. Shelton, "Development of Production of Superphosphate in the United States," *Proceedings of the National Fertilizer Association*, 1929–30, pp. 146–8.

COMMENTS: Production, estimates. For the period 1870–85 figures are for years ending May 31. See *Proceedings*, 1929–30, pp. 145–55.

APPENDIX B

64. Tin imports
   SOURCE: Concerning the figures on imports, see the introductory notes to this Appendix, sec. I. The figures on smelter production are from *Mineral Resources*, 1925, Part I, p. 67.

   COMMENTS: The figures for 1870–1915 are for net imports (general imports minus foreign exports) of metallic tin. The figures for 1916–24 are for general imports of metallic tin, plus domestic smelter output of tin, minus foreign and domestic exports of metallic tin. The figures for 1925–29 are for general imports of metallic tin, plus tin content of imported ore, minus foreign and domestic exports of metallic tin.

65. Vessels
   SOURCE: *Merchant Marine Statistics*, 1930, pp. 35–7.

   COMMENTS: Gross tonnage of vessels built in the United States and documented during the years given. The figures are for years ending June 30. See (21).

66. Wool consumption
   SOURCE: *Yearbook of Agriculture*, 1923, pp. 1001–2; *ibid.*, 1932, p. 811.

   COMMENTS: Apparent consumption of all wool, stocks not taken into account. See (15).

67. Antimonial lead
   SOURCE: *Mineral Resources*, 1914, Part I, p. 806; *ibid.*, 1919, Part I, p. 318; *ibid.*, 1929, Part I, p. 238.

   COMMENTS: Production from domestic and foreign ore. See *Mineral Resources*, 1919, Part I, p. 318.

68. Tin-plate consumption
   SOURCE: American Iron and Steel Institute, *Annual Statistical Report*, 1911, pp. 91, 96; *ibid.*, 1918, p. 54; *ibid.*, 1929, p. 59.

   COMMENTS: The series includes both tin-plate and terne-plate. For 1871–99, figures are for production plus imports; for later years, production plus imports minus exports. See *Statistical Report*, 1911, p. 91.

69. Tobacco and snuff
   SOURCE: *Annual Reports of the Commissioner of Internal Revenue*.

   COMMENTS: Total production, manufactured. For 1871–79, figures are for years ending June 30.

70. Cottonseed cake and meal

SOURCE: *Yearbook of Agriculture*, 1902, p. 815; *Cotton Production and Distribution, 1929-30* (Bureau of the Census, Bulletin 167), pp. 72-3.

COMMENTS: Production. Figures are for years ending July 31. See Bulletin 167, pp. 62, 72.

71. Cottonseed oil

SOURCE: See (70).

COMMENTS: Production, crude. See (70).

72. Nails

SOURCE: American Iron and Steel Institute, *Annual Statistical Report*, 1896, p. 73; *ibid.*, 1914, p. 64; *ibid.*, 1929, p. 61.

COMMENTS: Production, wire nails and cut nails. Figures for wire nails begin in 1886. Unit 'keg' includes 100 pounds. See *Statistical Report*, 1929, p. 61.

73. Zinc consumption

SOURCE: W. R. Ingalls, *Lead and Zinc in the United States* (Hill Publishing Co., 1908), p. 337, for 1873-94; *Mineral Resources*, for later years.

COMMENTS: Prior to 1895, the figures ignore stocks completely. In later years, smelter stocks are taken into account, but not consumers' stocks. Secondary zinc is excluded. See Ingalls, pp. 337-8; *Mineral Resources*, 1929, Part I, p. 721; and *ibid.*, 1914, Part I, pp. 908-9.

74. Flaxseed consumption

SOURCE: See (17), for production. For net imports, see *Statistical Abstract*, 1904, p. 391; *Yearbook of Agriculture*, 1927, p. 809. Figures on net imports for 1927-29 were obtained from the Department of Agriculture.

COMMENTS: Production plus net imports. Net imports include linseed oil in terms of seed. Figures are for years beginning July 1. See (17); Appendix C, II; and *Yearbook*, 1927, p. 809.

75. Roofing slate

SOURCE: *Mineral Resources*, 1913, Part II, p. 74; *ibid.*, 1915, Part II, p. 19; *ibid.*, 1918, Part II, p. 267; *ibid.*, 1922, Part II, p. 167; *ibid.*, 1929, Part II, p. 165.

COMMENTS: Sold by producers. Unit 'square' means 100 square feet. No figure is recorded for 1890 (see, however, *Mineral Resources*,

APPENDIX B

1891, p. 472). See *Slate Deposits and Slate Industry in the United States* (U. S. Geological Survey, Bulletin No. 275), pp. 125–6; and *Mineral Resources*, 1929, Part II, pp. 165–6.

76. Cigarettes

SOURCE: See (69).

COMMENTS: Production, number. Includes all 'cigarettes', and 'cigars' weighing not more than 3 pounds per 1000.

77. Cigars

SOURCE: See (69).

COMMENTS: Production, number. Excludes 'cigars' weighing not more than 3 pounds per 1000.

78. Coke

SOURCE: *Mineral Resources*, 1929, Part II, p. 582.

COMMENTS: Production, beehive and by-product. See *Mineral Resources*, 1929, Part II, p. 578.

79. Flour

SOURCE: "Statistics of American Wheat Milling and Flour Disposition since 1879" (Food Research Institute, *Wheat Studies*, Vol. IV, No. 2), p. 101; *ibid.*, Vol. IX, No. 3, p. 130.

COMMENTS: Production of wheat flour. Unit 'barrel' is equivalent to 196 pounds. Figures are for crop years ending June. See *Wheat Studies*, Vol. IV, No. 2.

80. Gold consumption

SOURCE: *Annual Report of the Director of the Mint*. 1919, p. 67; *ibid.*, 1930, p. 39.

COMMENTS: Gold (old and new) furnished for use in manufactures and the arts. Figures have been converted from dollars to fine ounces troy (1 fine ounce = \$20.6718). See *Annual Report*, 1929, pp. 116–36.

81. Locomotives

SOURCE: *Railroad Gazette*, Jan. 6, 1888, p. 10; *ibid.*, Jan. 3, 1890, p. 8; *ibid.*, Jan. 4, 1895, p. 8; *ibid.*, Dec. 25, 1896, p. 898; *Railway Age*, Jan. 3, 1931, p. 84.

COMMENTS: Production, number. From 1905 on, Canadian output is included. Prior to 1912, locomotives built in railroad repair shops are excluded. See Appendix C, I.

82. Silver consumption

SOURCE: *Annual Report of the Director of the Mint*, 1919, p. 68; *ibid.*, 1930, p. 40.

COMMENTS: Silver (old and new) furnished for use in manufactures and the arts.

83. Tobacco consumption

SOURCE: Figures for 1919–29, *Annual Report of the Commissioner of Internal Revenue*, 1929, p. 140; *ibid.*, 1930, p. 156. Figures for 1880–1918 were furnished by the Commissioner of Internal Revenue.

COMMENTS: Unstemmed equivalent of all kinds of tobacco used in the manufacture of cigars, cigarettes, and tobacco and snuff.

84. Aluminum

SOURCE: *Mineral Resources*, 1914, Part I, p. 191, for 1883–1903; American Metal Market, *Metal Statistics*, 1931, p. 439, for 1904–09; *Hearings on the Aluminum Company of America before the Committee on the Judiciary* (United States Senate, 69th Congress, First Session), p. 140, for 1910–14; *Metal Statistics*, 1931, p. 439, for 1915–18; *Hearings*, p. 140, for 1919–23; *Mineral Resources*, 1929, Part I, p. 493, for 1924–29.

COMMENTS: Production. Secondary aluminum is excluded. Estimates for many years. See *Metal Statistics*, 1931, p. 439; and *Hearings*, p. 140.

85. Copper consumption

SOURCE: *Mineral Industry* (ed. by R. P. Rothwell), Vols. II–IX, for 1883–99; *Mineral Resources*, for later years.

COMMENTS: Refiners' stocks are taken into account, but not consumers' stocks. Secondary copper is excluded. See *Mineral Resources*, 1919, pp. 600–1; and *ibid.*, 1929, Part I, p. 579.

86. Silk imports, unmanufactured

SOURCE: See the introductory notes to this Appendix, sec. I.

COMMENTS: Net imports (general imports minus foreign exports) of all types of unmanufactured silk. Spun silk is not included. See (60); and Appendix C, II.

87. White lead

SOURCE: *Mineral Resources*, 1904, p. 1115; *ibid.*, later volumes.

COMMENTS: Production ('dry' plus 'in oil'). See *Mineral Resources*, 1929, Part I, p. 508.

APPENDIX B

88. Canned corn
    SOURCE: *Vegetable Statistics* (Department of Agriculture, Statistical Bulletin No. 22), p. 67; *Yearbook of Agriculture*, 1932, p. 711.

    COMMENTS: Production. Unit 'case' consists of 24 No. 2 cans. See *Vegetable Statistics*, p. 67; and *Yearbook*, 1932, p. 711.

89. Canned tomatoes
    SOURCE: *Vegetable Statistics* (Department of Agriculture, Statistical Bulletin No. 22), p. 67; *Yearbook of Agriculture*, 1932, p. 740.

    COMMENTS: Production. Unit 'case' consists of 24 No. 3 cans. See *Vegetable Statistics*, p. 67; and *Yearbook*, 1932, p. 740.

90. Rolled iron and steel
    SOURCE: American Iron and Steel Institute, *Annual Statistical Report*, 1929, pp. 37–8, for 1887–1929. For 1885–86, estimates were furnished by Mr. Howard H. Cook, Secretary of the American Iron and Steel Institute.

    COMMENTS: Tonnage of all rolled products of iron and steel.

91. Rail consumption
    SOURCE: See (57).

    COMMENTS: Production plus imports minus exports, since 1874. Production plus imports, for prior years.

92. Building permits
    SOURCE: C. Snyder, *Business Cycles and Business Measurements* (Macmillan, 1927), p. 275, for 1882–1925. Figures for other years were furnished by Mr. Snyder.

    COMMENTS: Index of building permits in 1 to 7 cities (7 since 1895), the figures of building permits being deflated by an index of changes in costs of construction. No figure for 1879. See Appendix C, III; and Federal Reserve Bank of New York, *Monthly Review*, January 1, 1925, pp. 6–7.

93. Coastal trade
    SOURCE: See (21).

    COMMENTS: Gross tonnage of vessels licensed for domestic commerce and outstanding on June 30. See (21); and Appendix C, II–III.

PRODUCTION TRENDS

94. N. Y. canals traffic

SOURCE: State of New York Department of Public Works, *Annual Report of the Superintendent*, 1930, pp. 34–6.

COMMENTS: Tonnage moved on all canals. See *Annual Report*, 1922, p. 7; and *ibid.*, 1930, p. 28.

95. Postage stamps

SOURCE: *Annual Reports of the Postmaster General.*

COMMENTS: Revenue derived from sale of postage stamps, postal cards, stamped envelopes; and from first-, second-, third-, and fourth-class mail matter dispatched under permit without stamps. Does not include 'second-class postage paid in money' (which covers postage paid at pound rates on copies of publications entered as second-class matter). Figures are for years ending June 30. See Appendix C, II–III; and Post Office Department, *Postage Rates, 1789–1930*.

96. Postal money orders

SOURCE: *Annual Report of the Postmaster General*, 1930, p. 149.

COMMENTS: Number of money orders issued. Domestic money orders, plus international money orders (data for latter lacking for 1870–71), plus postal notes (issued from Sept. 3, 1883 to July 1, 1894: see *Annual Report*, 1893, p. 77; and *ibid.*, 1895, p. 138). Figures are for years ending June 30.

97. Railway ton-miles

SOURCE: C. Snyder, *Business Cycles and Business Measurements* (Macmillan, 1927), p. 238, for years through 1882. *Poor's Manual of Railroads*, 1895, p. xvi, for 1883–89. For later years, *Statistics of Railways*, 1926, p. ci; and *ibid.*, 1929, p. lxxxiii.

COMMENTS: Revenue tons carried one mile. Figures for 1883–1916 are for years ending June 30. Concerning Snyder's estimates, see his *Business Cycles*, p. 39; and Appendix C, III. Concerning the figures of Interstate Commerce Commission, see *Statistics of Railways*, 1926, p. xcviii.

98. S. S. Marie canals traffic

SOURCE: *Statistical Report of Lake Commerce Passing Through Canals at Sault Ste. Marie*, 1929, p. 19.

COMMENTS: Tonnage of total freight moved. See *Statistical Report*, pp. 1–2. On the average, less than 10 per cent of the tonnage is Canadian in origin; see *ibid.*, p. 11.

APPENDIX B 343

99. Railway passenger-miles

SOURCE: *Poor's Manual of Railroads*, 1893, p. vi, for 1882–89. For later years, *Statistics of Railways*, 1926, p. ci; and *ibid.*, 1929, p. lxxxiii.

COMMENTS: Passengers carried one mile. Figures for 1882–1916 are for years ending June 30. Concerning the figures of the Interstate Commerce Commission, see *Statistics of Railways*, 1926, p. xcviii.

100. Agricultural exports

SOURCE: Department of Agriculture, *Foreign Crops and Markets*, Dec. 14, 1925, pp. 903–4; *ibid.*, Oct. 13, 1930, p. 522.

COMMENTS: An index of the physical volume of total agricultural exports, the base period being the 5 years ending June 30, 1914. The figures are for years beginning July 1. See *Foreign Crops and Markets*, December 14, 1925, pp. 900–4.

101. Deflated clearings

SOURCE: These data were obtained from Mr. C. Snyder.

COMMENTS: Monthly averages of bank clearings outside New York City (bank debits in 140 cities outside New York, from 1919 to date), adjusted by an index of the general price level. These figures have been converted to percentages of the 1913 datum. See Appendix C, III.

102. Tonnage entered and cleared

SOURCE: *Merchant Marine Statistics*, 1930, pp. 79–80.

COMMENTS: Net registered tonnage of American and foreign vessels entered and cleared in the foreign trade of the United States. The tons "represent net tons of 100 cubic feet internal carrying capacity, after deducting space for crew and engines." See Appendix C, I–III.

103. Shares traded

SOURCE: National Monetary Commission, *Statistics for the United States*, Vol. 21, p. 9, for 1875–99; New York Stock Exchange, *Year Book*, 1929–30, p. 144, for later years.

COMMENTS: Number of shares of stock traded. See Appendix C, II; *Year Book*, 1929–30, p. 144; and J. E. Meeker, *Measuring the Stock Market* (pamphlet by New York Stock Exchange), sec. III.

104. Railway freight

SOURCE: *Poor's Manual of Railroads*, 1891, p. xiii, for 1882–89. For later years, *Statistics of Railways*, 1926, p. ci; and *ibid.*, 1929, p. lxxxiii.

COMMENTS: Total revenue tons. The figures include duplications of tonnage, since a shipment moving over the lines of several railroads is reported by each carrier participating in the shipment; see Appendix C, I. Figures for 1882–1916 are for years ending June 30. Concerning the figures of the Interstate Commerce Commission, see *Statistics of Railways*, 1926, p. xcviii.

II. DISCONTINUOUS SERIES

The discontinuous series are those marked with an asterisk in Tables 22, 24, and 25. The raw data for this group of series are not presented in this monograph.

Most of the data for the discontinuous series were obtained from reports of the Bureau of the Census. Unless otherwise stated, the data relate to 'production'. The following notes state the sources of the data in only those instances where the data have not been obtained from census reports. Also, the descriptive notes are limited to series having outstanding peculiarities.

Boards paper	The figures were furnished by the Forest Service of the Department of Agriculture.
Boots and shoes	Does not include rubber boots and shoes.
Broad silks	Includes broad silks (pure and mixed), velvets, plushes, upholstery, and tapestry. The unit is the linear yard through 1919, and the square yard beginning with 1921. (In the latter year the total expressed in linear yards is almost exactly the same as that in square yards.)
Broom corn	*Yearbook of Agriculture,* for data beginning with 1915.
Burning oils	Includes fuel oils and illuminating oils.
Butter	Includes both farm and factory output.
Common brick	The figures for 1895 through 1918, except for census years, are from *Mineral Resources*.
Condensed and evaporated milk	Includes butter-milk.
Cotton, woven goods	Does not include fabrics of less than 12 inches in width, beginning with 1899.
Face brick	The figures for 1889, 1899, and 1904 were combined with those for 'fancy or ornamental' brick. The figures for 1913 and 1915–18 are from *Mineral Resources*. See Appendix C, II.

APPENDIX B 345

Fertilizers	The figure for 1869 was obtained from *Proceedings of the National Fertilizer Association*, 1929–30, p. 145.
Fine paper	See 'boards paper'.
Gloves and mittens, knit	Includes the output of the knit-goods industry only (that is, the output of manufacturers engaged in knitting gloves and mittens, but not the output of those who manufacture gloves and mittens from purchased knit fabrics).
Hay loaders	See Appendix C, II.
Hops	*Hop Crop of the United States, 1790–1911* (Department of Agriculture, Bureau of Statistics, Circular 35), for data through 1910; *Yearbook of Agriculture*, for data since 1911.
Hosiery	Does not include infants', athletic, and golf hose.
Light petroleum distillates	Includes gasoline, naphtha, benzine, tops, other light products of distillation, and, beginning with 1914, natural-gas gasoline. The figures on natural-gas gasoline are from *Mineral Resources*.
Lumber	Figures include the production of custom mills, but are restricted to sawed lumber. The data were obtained from *A National Plan for American Forestry* (72d Congress, Senate Document No. 12), pp. 247–8.
Lumber consumption	See 'lumber'.
Maple sugar	Includes also the sugar content of maple sirup. *Yearbook of Agriculture*, for data beginning with 1917.
Newsprint and book paper	See 'boards paper'.
Snyder's index of trade	This index for quinquennial dates is an arithmetic mean of 3 to 4 of the middle link relatives of a varying number of series. Figures were furnished by Mr. Snyder. For a brief description, see *Proceedings of the Academy of Political Science*, January, 1930, pp. 21–2.

Structural shapes	American Iron and Steel Institute, *Annual Statistical Report*, for data beginning with 1892.
Sulphuric acid	The figures are in terms of 50° Baumé strength; the figure for 1879 being an estimate based on the total tonnage of sulphuric acid in 1879, 1889, and 1899, and the tonnage reduced to uniform strength (50°) in 1889 and 1899.
Sweet potatoes	*Yearbook of Agriculture*, for data beginning with 1899.
Wood pulp	*American Forests and Forest Products* (Department of Agriculture, Statistical Bulletin No. 21), for years through 1926.
Wrapping paper	See 'boards paper'.
Zinc oxide	*Mineral Resources.*

Appendix C

NOTES ON MEASURES FOR PRODUCTION SERIES

The following notes bear on the defects of various production series, from the standpoint of certain of the analyses to which they are subjected in this study. The notes supplement the text sections indicated below.

I. AVERAGE RATES OF GROWTH

(Chapter III, section I, 1)

It is possible to present quantitative evidence of the inexactness of the average rates of advance shown by certain of the production series. In some cases the evidence indicates definitely the existence of a growth bias.

Cattle, Hogs, and *Sheep.* The series 'cattle' and 'sheep' have an upward growth bias arising from the increasing tendency to bring these animals to slaughter at a younger age, which has meant a declining average weight per animal. During 1907–29, the number of federally inspected cattle slaughtered increased at an annual rate of 1.2 per cent, while the dressed weight of the slaughter increased at a rate of only 0.9 per cent; the number of federally inspected sheep slaughtered increased at a rate of 0.4 per cent, but the mutton and lamb yield of the slaughter increased at a rate of 0.0 per cent. On the other hand, while the number of federally inspected hogs slaughtered increased at a rate of 2.1 per cent, the pork and lard yield increased at a rate of 2.7 per cent. The several series of animals slaughtered have an upward growth bias arising also from the increasing relative importance of federally inspected slaughter. During 1907–29, the dressed yield of the federal slaughter of cattle increased at a rate of 0.9 per cent, but total slaughter at 0.1 per cent; the dressed yield of the federal slaughter of hogs increased at a rate of 2.7 per cent, but the total slaughter at 2.2 per cent. However, there is no discrepancy in the case of sheep during this period. The above calculations are based on data of the Department of Agriculture, given in *Statistics of Meat Production, Consumption and Foreign Trade of the United States, 1900–1930* (mimeographed).

Cod and mackerel. The series 'cod and mackerel', which runs in terms of the vessel tonnage documented for these fisheries, undoubtedly overstates their decline. Fairly complete data on the catch of the American mackerel fleet are available continuously by years, beginning with 1905; see *Fishery Industries of the United States, 1929* (Bureau of Fisheries, Document No. 1095), p. 856. Also, continuous annual data for the period 1893-1926 are available for the eastern cod catch which has been dominant in the cod industry; see O. E. Sette, *Statistics of the Catch of Cod Off the East Coast of North America to 1926* (Bureau of Fisheries, Document No. 1034), pp. 743-4. A composite of the above two series shows an average annual rate of decline of 0.1 per cent for 1905-26, while the series 'cod and mackerel' shows a rate of decline of 2.9 per cent. The discrepancy cannot, however, be so large for the earlier years; for, though the mackerel catch has been on the increase over the past twenty years, the current catch is still low in comparison with the early 'eighties. (See O. E. Sette, *Outlook for the Mackerel Fishery in 1931*, Bureau of Fisheries, Circular No. 4, p. 4.) The eastern cod series shows a rate of decline of 1.6 per cent for 1893-1926, and the series 'cod and mackerel' a rate of decline of 2.3 per cent.

Whale. This series, which runs in terms of the vessel tonnage documented for the whalery, may be compared with data on whalebone production (an important product of whaling during much of the period considered); see *Whalebone: Its Production and Distribution* (Bureau of Fisheries, Document No. 626), p. 7. During 1870-1906, whalebone production shows a decline at an annual rate of 2.7 per cent, and the 'whale' series at a rate of 5.3 per cent.

Copper, Zinc, and *Lead, domestic.* These series relate to some metallurgical stage, not to mine output. Official estimates of mine output are available since 1907 only; see Bureau of Mines, *Mineral Resources.* In the period 1907-29, the mine output of copper increased at an annual rate of 2.3 per cent, zinc at 4.1 per cent, and lead at 2.6 per cent. For the same period, the series 'copper' shows a rate of increase of 2.5 per cent, 'zinc' 3.7 per cent, and 'lead, domestic' 3.0 per cent.

Cement, total. The rate of growth of total cement production is understated somewhat by the series 'cement, total', which is expressed in barrel units. Since the poundage per barrel is greater for Portland than for other cements, and the proportion of Portland to other cements rose sharply during the 'eighties and 'nineties, the series 'cement, total' overstates the output in the early years relative to that of later years. Thoroughly consistent totals of cement output are unattainable: first, because of the inconstant weight of barrels of cement other than Portland; second, in recent years natural and puzzolan cements have not been distinguished in the statistical reports, so that it is impossible even to assign average weights to the different cements for purposes of estimation. If we reduce the cement figures for early years

APPENDIX C 349

to a poundage basis (by taking a barrel of Portland cement as equivalent to 380 pounds, natural cement 265 pounds, and puzzolan cement 330 pounds), we find that the annual rate of increase of total cement production was 11.0 per cent during 1890–1900 and 20.5 per cent during 1895–1905, while our series shows rates of 8.7 per cent and 17.0 per cent, respectively. These rates apply to the indicated calendar periods, and are not the same as our 'decade rates' (see Ch. II, sec. II, 2).

Locomotives. This series has a sharp downward growth bias (see, however, Appendix B, I), since it is expressed in terms of the number of units of output, taking no account of their quality. Some indication of the trend in quality is afforded by data, available back to 1903, on the average tractive effort of the steam locomotives of Class I railways; see the *Annual Reports on the Statistics of Railways in the United States,* by the Interstate Commerce Commission. During 1903–29 the average tractive effort of locomotives increased at an average annual rate of 2.7 per cent, while the number of locomotives manufactured declined at a rate of 4.6 per cent.

Tonnage entered and cleared. The evidence concerning the physical volume of foreign trade, yielded by this series, may be checked against other indicators. For the period 1879–1916, quantity indexes of exports and imports have been constructed by T. J. Kreps; see his "Import and Export Prices in the United States and the Terms of International Trade, 1880–1914," *Quarterly Journal of Economics,* August, 1926. His 'median' and 'aggregative' indexes show average annual rates of increase of 3.1 and 2.5 per cent respectively during 1879–1916 in the case of exports, and 4.0 and 3.6 per cent in the case of imports. In the same period, 'tonnage entered and cleared' increased at a rate of 3.8 per cent. For more recent years a check is available in the indexes of physical volume of exports and imports, published in the *Commerce Yearbook.* According to the indexes with 1923–25 as base, exports increased at a rate of 3.0 and imports at 4.7 per cent during 1919–29. An index of physical volume of foreign trade may be constructed by allocating weights to the indexes of exports and imports proportionate to the aggregate value of exports and imports during 1919–29; such an index shows a rate of increase of 3.7 per cent during 1919–29. In the same period, 'tonnage entered and cleared' increased at a rate of 4.4 per cent.

Railway freight. This series relates to 'total revenue tons', and may be checked for the period since 1899 by data on 'revenue tons originated', which are free from duplications. (See *Statistics of Railways.*) During 1899–1929 both series show average rates of increase of 2.8 per cent.

II. AVERAGE RATES OF RETARDATION
(Chapter IV, section II)

Although accelerative series do not have a monopoly on statistical defects, they seem, as a group, to be more heavily weighted with defects than the others. In any case, those accelerative series whose accuracy is doubtful or whose form is ambiguous are noted here specifically. But it is rarely possible to state definitely whether the defects in the data are of a kind to induce acceleration (see pp. 99-100, note 4).

Distilled spirits. This series probably covers more fully the production of late than of early years: 'whiskey frauds' tended to decline, and this may account partly for the acceleration noted.

Flaxseed consumption. The figures for flaxseed consumption are not altogether satisfactory, especially for years prior to 1902, since the figures of flaxseed production are estimates based to a considerable extent on data of receipts at primary markets (it should be noted, however, that flaxseed production does show retardation).

Silk imports, unmanufactured. Since this series does not include spun silk, it is defective as an indicator of the quantity of silk worked up by the silk industry. Very small quantities of spun silk were imported during the early and late decades of the period covered, but rather considerable quantities during the middle decades. When spun silk is added to unmanufactured silk, the aggregate does not show any acceleration. (It may appear from Table 24 that the two series of silk imports—the series of raw silk imports is the less inclusive—give inconsistent results, but this is not the case when they are compared for the same period: raw silk imports also show a slight acceleration for the period 1883-1929.)

Coastal trade. This series does not refer directly to the physical volume of traffic; it simply measures the tonnage capacity of ships documented for the coastal traffic.

Postage stamps. The significance of this series is vitiated to some extent by changes in postal rates. Concerning the adequacy of 'postage stamps' as a measure of one branch of the communications industry, see this Appendix, sec. III. ('Postage stamps' is indubitably a poorer indicator of the progress of general trade than 'deflated clearings' or 'Snyder's index of trade'—see p. 11, note 5.)

Tonnage entered and cleared. This series measures the tonnage capacity of ships entered and cleared in the foreign trade; it therefore represents incompletely and very indirectly the physical volume of foreign trade. It must also be borne in mind that the series 'tonnage entered and cleared', being symptomatic of the total volume of foreign trade, has a very general industrial reference, and is more comparable in economic dimension with the

APPENDIX C

volume of production of groups of industries than with the production of 'individual' industries. Of course, the same thing holds for the indicators of 'general trade'—deflated clearings, postage stamps, and so on. See Ch. VI, sec. III.

Shares traded. This series has a strong upward growth bias arising mainly from the increasing tendency towards 'split-ups' (using the term broadly to include stock dividends not paid out of accumulated earnings) of shares. Moreover, its measure of retardation is influenced to an excessive degree by the stock-market experience of the latter half of the last decade, as may be seen from the fact that for the period 1875–1925, the series shows an acceleration of only 0.4 per cent.

Face brick. As for the production of face brick, the census figures used for the years 1889, 1899, and 1904 may be inaccurate. The figures for these years were obtained by adding the production of 'fancy or ornamental brick' to the production of 'face brick', the reason being that "the best grade of 'face' or 'front' brick appears to have been classified as 'fancy or ornamental' brick" in these years (the quotation is a statement from the Census Bureau). However, so far as the observed acceleration is concerned, the tremendous expansion of production during the past decade is more important than any inaccuracies in early data (see pp. 155–6).

Hay loaders. The data on the production of hay loaders in some of the early years appear inaccurate (see *Twelfth Census of the United States*, Vol. X, pp. 351–2). Even if the data are accurate, the annual fluctuations in output are so large as to reduce very considerably the significance of a measure of retardation based on discontinuous data. Then again, the data show very marked retardation for the period since 1889.

III. TREND-CYCLE PATTERNS
(Chapter V, section III)

The defects in the production series bear unequally on the measurements of trend-cycles. The existence of a bias in growth, in retardation, or in both, is likely to exercise little influence on the trend-cycle pattern of a series. But when a series measures production indirectly, its trend-cycle pattern may depart considerably from that of the production volumes which it is taken to represent. When a series is spliced, its trend-cycle pattern may depart from that of the process represented, during the period centering about the date of the splicing. In all cases, other things being equal, the smaller the amplitude of the trend-cycles of a series, the larger are the errors in its trend-cycle pattern likely to be. Statistical defects in the data may, of course, influence the conformity of the series to the standard trend-cycle pattern for better or worse; but certain of the defects which are likely to influence the trend-cycle patterns of the series for the worse are sufficiently obtrusive to be noted specifically.

Cod and mackerel, and *Whale.* These two series relate to the volume of equipment available at yearly dates for use in certain 'fisheries'. The indirectness of the series, and the relatively low trend-cycle amplitude of the first, cast doubt on the fitness of these series to trace out accurately the trend-cycle patterns of the outputs of the respective 'fisheries'.

Fish, total. This series is based on very extensive interpolations, which serve to dampen the trend-cycle amplitude and may also distort the trend-cycle pattern. The actual trend-cycle amplitude of the series is low, and this casts further doubt on the reliability of its trend-cycle pattern.

Raw sugar consumption. This is a calculated series; and it has a very low trend-cycle amplitude. The data are 'defective' to the extent that the domestically produced cane sugar and imported sugar are not 'raw'; and to the extent that there is lack of synchronism between domestic production and imports, on the one hand, and sugar refining, on the other. In view of the low trend-cycle amplitude of the series, these errors may be sufficiently large to produce a discrepancy to some extent between the trend-cycle pattern of this series and that of sugar refining (other than that of domestic beet sugar).

Building permits. It will be seen from Chart 18 that the trend-cycles of 'building permits' differ at several points from the general movement of other series relating to construction. This is prima facie evidence that the series is inexact, which is not surprising in view of its varying and very limited coverage.

Coastal trade. This series expresses the volume of equipment available at yearly dates for use in one branch of transportation. The indirectness of the series, considering its relatively low trend-cycle amplitude, may make its trend-cycle pattern unrepresentative to some extent of that of coastal water transportation.

Postage stamps. This series reflects abrupt changes in postal rates and in the activities of the postal service. (See, however, C. J. Bullock and others, "Postal Revenues and the Business Cycle," *Review of Economic Statistics*, May, 1931, pp. 47–51.) Considering the low trend-cycle amplitude of the series, the changes in postal rates cast doubt on the capacity of the series to trace out accurately the trend-cycle pattern in the volume of postal service; and considering further the abrupt accessions of new postal func-

APPENDIX C

tions, on the capacity of the series to trace out accurately the trend-cycle pattern in the volume of 'communications' through letters, printed matter, and parcels.

Railway ton-miles. The non-conformity of 'railway ton-miles' (Chart 19) between the central decade years 1875 and 1880 may be due, in part, to inaccuracies of data, which are estimates for years prior to 1883. See, however, p. 225; the conformity, for the corresponding period, of rail production and rail consumption (Chart 18) should also be noted, but it is difficult to evaluate its significance.

Deflated clearings. It is reasonable to expect that 'deflated clearings' (Chart 19) should conform perfectly to the standard trend-cycle pattern. Except for the movement between the central decade years 1890 and 1895, this series does conform very closely to the standard pattern. There are some grounds for believing that 'deflated clearings' represent the physical volume of trade somewhat less satisfactorily in early than in recent decades: (1) checks have come to be of increasing importance in the making of payments, (2) the figures on clearings in early years may be distorted to some extent by the continual addition of new clearing centers, as data for them become available, (3) the price deflator is probably more accurate for recent decades.

Tonnage entered and cleared. This series expresses in units of capacity the actual use of vessels engaged in foreign trade. The indirectness of the series and its relatively low trend-cycle amplitude combine to cast doubt on the adequacy of its representation of the trend-cycle pattern of the volume of foreign trade.

INDEX

Academy of Political Science, *Proceedings*, 345
Acceleration, 101 (see also Retardation)
A Graphic Analysis of the Census of Manufactures, 1849 to 1919, 258
Agricultural exports, 13, 61, 73, 117, 150, 220, 224, 233, 302-3, 308, 312, 317, 343
Agriculture, Department of, 21, 23, 149, 203, 265, 327, 329, 338, 344
Agriculture, Yearbook of, 64, 80, 147, 149, 202, 210, 265, 326, 327, 328, 329, 336, 337, 338, 341, 344, 345, 346
Aluminum, 11, 12, 21, 56, 59, 71, 106, 112, 113, 132, 169, 172, 219, 231, 300-1, 307, 312, 316, 340
American Forests and Forest Products, 346
American Iron and Steel Institute, *Annual Reports*, 147, 159, 326, 335, 336, 337, 338, 341, 346
A National Plan for American Forestry, 345
Asphalt, 12, 57, 70, 76, 112, 216, 224, 230, 290-1, 306, 310, 314, 332
Avram, M. H., 134

Baker, O. E., 50, 124, 129, 265, 276
Barley
  acreage of, 211, 214, 323
  acre-yield of, 214, 323

  production of, 12, 55, 64, 70, 84, 111, 149, 203, 208, 209, 210, 211, 230, 284-5, 305, 309, 313, 327
Beans, dry, edible, 111, 118-9
Bias
  in divergence of trends, 242-4
  in growth, 25-7, 99-100, 237-9, 347-9
  in retardation, 99-100, 278-9, 349-51
Boots and shoes, 114, 344
Brick
  common, 114, 344
  face, 115, 116, 154, 155, 344, 350
Brissenden, P. F., 136
Brunsman, H. G., 43
Buckwheat, 12, 55, 70, 111, 203, 208, 210, 230, 284-5, 305, 309, 313, 327
Building permits, 13, 17, 23, 59, 71, 85, 112, 114, 183, 219, 222, 231, 239, 263, 268, 272, 274, 302-3, 308, 312, 316, 341, 351
Bullock, C. J., 351
Business cycles, 33-4, 177-9, 247-52
Butler, F. S., 142
Butter, 111, 344

California Crop Report, 329
Canals traffic
  New York, 13, 61, 73, 117, 118-9, 159-60, 220, 232, 302-3, 308, 312, 316, 342
  Sault St. Marie, 13, 61, 73, 117, 220, 232, 302-3, 308, 312, 316, 342

INDEX

Cattle, 12, 14, 23, 27, 55, 58, 70, 85, 111, 208, 230, 276, 286-7, 305, 309, 313, 329, 347
Cement
    non-Portland, 12, 56, 57, 60, 64, 70, 103, 112, 159, 160, 216, 224, 230, 290-1, 306, 310, 314, 332-3, 348
    Portland, 7, 12, 16, 56, 57, 59, 64, 70, 110, 112, 142, 169, 216, 224, 230, 292-3, 306, 310, 314, 333, 348
    total, 12, 15, 57, 59, 71, 84, 112, 183, 216, 217, 222, 224, 231, 290-1, 306, 310, 314, 332, 348-9
Census, Bureau of the, 11, 344, 350
Census of Manufactures, 18, 132
Chapin, F. S., 96
Chemical and Metallurgical Engineering, 126
Cigarettes, 12, 15, 36, 56, 58, 64, 71, 115, 116, 118-9, 154, 155, 169, 219, 231, 298-9, 307, 311, 315, 339
Cigars, 12, 15, 58, 72, 114, 218, 232, 298-9, 307, 311, 315, 339
Cincinnati Price Current, 147
Clark, V. S., 60
Clearings, deflated, 13, 23, 61, 73, 84, 117, 220, 223, 233, 235, 263, 268, 272, 274, 304, 308, 312, 317, 343, 350, 353
Cleveland Trust Company, index of industrial activity, 201, 203, 322
Coal
    anthracite, 12, 57, 64, 71, 85, 112, 137, 138, 216, 217, 231, 235, 288-9, 306, 310, 314, 330
    bituminous, 12, 57, 71, 83, 84, 112, 216, 217, 231, 235, 288-9, 306, 310, 314, 330
    total, 12, 15, 52, 57, 64, 71, 102, 112, 119, 130-1, 147, 148, 204, 216, 231, 235, 288-9, 306, 310, 314, 330
Cocoa, imports of, 12, 14, 58, 65, 72, 84, 114, 218, 231, 292-3, 306, 311, 314, 334
Cod and mackerel, 12, 14, 26, 55, 70, 110, 111, 118-9, 159, 208, 230, 288-9, 305, 309, 313, 329-30, 347-8, 351
Coffee, imports of, 12, 58, 72, 85, 114, 218, 232, 292-3, 306, 311, 314, 334
Coke, 12, 27, 59, 72, 83, 84, 113, 130, 218, 221, 232, 298-9, 307, 311, 315, 339
Cole, A. H., 157
Coleman, M., 136
Commerce Yearbook, 349
Commissioner of Internal Revenue, *Annual Reports*, 159, 334, 337, 340
Commissioner of Patents, *Annual Reports*, 242
Cook, H. H., 341
Cooperative Industrial Research, 151
Copper
    consumption of, 12, 27, 59, 65, 72, 84, 114, 115, 166, 218, 232, 300-1, 308, 312, 316, 340
    production of, 7, 12, 23, 57, 59, 64, 65, 71, 84, 112, 119, 132, 137, 147, 148, 166, 204, 216, 217, 231, 235, 288-9, 306, 310, 314, 330, 348
Corn
    acreage of, 211, 214, 323
    acre-yield of, 214, 323
    broom, 111, 344
    canned, 12, 58, 72, 113, 218, 231, 300-1, 308, 312, 316, 341
    production of, 12, 55, 70, 85, 111, 149, 203, 208, 209, 210, 211, 230, 284-5, 305, 309, 313, 327
Cotton
    acreage of, 211, 214, 323
    acre-yield of, 214, 323
    consumption of, 12, 58, 65, 72, 84, 114, 115, 119, 166, 204, 218, 232, 292-3, 306, 311, 315, 334
    production of, 12, 55, 65, 68, 70, 85, 111, 147, 148, 149, 166, 208,

INDEX

209, 210, 211, 230, 284-5, 305, 309, 313, 327
woven goods, 114, 344
Cotton Production and Distribution, 327, 334, 338
Cottonseed
  cake and meal, 12, 37, 58, 64, 71, 113, 130, 218, 232, 296-7, 307, 311, 315, 338
  oil, 12, 58, 64, 71, 83, 84, 113, 130, 172, 218, 231, 239, 298-9, 307, 311, 315, 338
Coverage of series, 17-22, 25, 116

Davis, J. S., 24
Day, E. E., 200, 201, 202, 205, 208, 262-3, 265, 266, 267, 268, 269, 272, 274, 275, 276, 277, 278, 279, 280, 322
Decadence, industrial, 66, 122-3, 158-62
Director of the Mint, *Annual Reports*, 147, 331, 339, 340
Douglas, P. H., 240, 270
Drawers (see Shirts and drawers)
Drills, grain, 114
Dun's Review, 242
Durand, E., 280

Earnings, real, 234, 240, 241, 324
Eckler, A. R., 62, 258
Epstein, R. C., 134

Failures, business, 240, 241, 242, 324
Farm Value, Gross Income and Cash Income from Farm Production, 18
Fertilizers, 113, 345
Fibers
  hemp, production of, 111, 159, 160
  jute, imports of, 12, 14, 15, 58, 65, 72, 114, 218, 232, 294-5, 307, 311, 315, 334-5
  Manila hemp, imports of, 12, 14, 15, 58, 72, 80, 114, 218, 232, 294-5, 307, 311, 315, 335
  minor, imports of, 12, 14, 52, 58, 72, 85, 113, 218, 232, 294-5, 307, 311, 315, 335
  sisal, imports of, 12, 14, 15, 58, 71, 113, 218, 231, 296-7, 307, 311, 315, 336
Fish, total, 12, 15, 36, 55, 70, 77, 85, 111, 208, 230, 263, 268, 272, 274, 288-9, 305, 310, 313, 330, 351
Fisheries, Bureau of, 330
Fishery Industries of the United States, 1929, 348
Flaxseed
  consumption of, 12, 36, 59, 65, 72, 84, 115, 166, 183, 219, 222, 232, 298-9, 307, 311, 315, 338, 350
  production of, 12, 55, 65, 70, 111, 166, 208, 210, 230, 286-7, 305, 309, 313, 329
Flour, 12, 22, 58, 72, 85, 114, 219, 224, 232, 298-9, 307, 311, 315, 339
Fluorspar, 12, 57, 70, 76, 112, 216, 230, 290-1, 306, 310, 314, 332
Foreign and Domestic Commerce, Bureau of, 326, 334
Foreign Crops and Markets, 343
Frasch, Herman, 156

Gas, natural, 12, 22, 57, 70, 112, 126, 216, 230, 292-3, 306, 310, 314, 333
Gemeinfassliche Darstellung des Eisenhüttenwesens, 147
Geological Survey, 21
Givens, M. B., 62, 119
Glass
  plate, polished, 113
  window, 114
Glover, J. W., 43, 105
Gloves and mittens, knit, 113, 345,
Gold
  consumption of, 12, 59, 72, 84, 114,

166, 218, 231, 239, 298-9, 307, 311, 315, 339
monetary stock of, 240, 241, 242, 324
production of, 12, 57, 59, 64, 71, 85, 112, 137, 141, 146, 147, 166, 216, 224, 231, 235, 239, 288-9, 306, 310, 314, 331
Graton, L. C., 138, 142
Growth, law of, 169-173
Growth, rates of
agriculture, 55, 56, 60, 62, 66-9, 91-2, 263-5, 305
construction, 56, 58-60, 263, 268, 308
corrected for cyclical factor, 38-42
defined, 37-8
fisheries, 56, 62, 263, 268, 305
interdecade correlation of, 86-95
manufactures, 56, 58-60, 62, 66-8, 263, 267-8, 306-8
measurement of, 34-44, 50-1, 262, 347-9
mining, 56, 57, 60, 62, 66-8, 93-4, 263, 266-7, 306
total production, 263, 269-70
trade, 56, 60-1, 62, 263, 268, 308
transportation, 56, 60-1, 62, 268, 308
variability of, 49-79
Gypsum, 12, 57, 71, 112, 216, 222, 230, 290-1, 306, 310, 314, 332

Harlan, C. L., 329
Harrows, other than disk, 113
Hay
acreage of, 211, 214, 323
acre-yield of, 214, 323
production of, 12, 55, 70, 85, 111, 203, 208, 209, 210, 211, 230, 284-5, 305, 309, 313, 327
Hearings on the Aluminum Company of America before the Committee on the Judiciary, 340

Hemp (see Fibers)
Hogs, 12, 14, 55, 58, 70, 76, 85, 111, 208, 230, 276, 286-7, 305, 309, 313, 329, 347
Honey, 111
Hop Crop of the United States, 1790-1911, 345
Hops, 111, 345
Hosiery, 114, 345
Hurlin, R. G., 62, 119

Industry
concept of, 15-6
structural changes in, 153-8
Ingalls, W. R., 335, 338
Iron
anthracite pig, 159
charcoal pig, 159, 160
ore, 12, 57, 71, 84, 112, 141, 216, 217, 231, 290-1, 306, 310, 314, 332
pig, 12, 59, 64, 72, 84, 100, 102, 104, 114, 119, 132, 147, 148, 204, 216, 218, 221, 232, 294-5, 307, 311, 315, 335
Iron and steel, rolled, 13, 15, 16, 59, 72, 84, 114, 115, 216, 218, 221, 232, 300-1, 308, 312, 316, 341

Jacob, K. D., 336
Jute (see Fibers)

King, W. I., 18-20, 200, 201, 322
Kondratieff, N. D., 177
Kreps, T. J., 349
Kuznets, S., 44, 45, 96, 142, 177, 247

Latham, Alexander & Company, 147
Laths, 114
Lead
antimonial, 12, 59, 71, 113, 191, 219, 231, 296-7, 307, 311, 315, 337
consumption of, 12, 59, 72, 84, 115, 166, 218, 232, 294-5, 307, 311, 315, 335

INDEX 359

domestic production of, 12, 14, 57, 71, 84, 112, 119, 132, 141, 147, 148, 166, 191, 204, 216, 217, 221, 231, 288-9, 306, 310, 314, 331, 348
total production of, 12, 14, 59, 71, 113, 191, 219, 231, 294-5, 307, 311, 315, 335
white, 12, 59, 72, 114, 219, 222, 224, 232, 300-1, 308, 312, 316, 340
Leith, C. K., 141
Liquors, fermented, 12, 51, 58, 72, 82, 88, 114, 218, 232, 292-3, 307, 311, 315, 334
Loaders, hay, 115, 345, 350
Locomotives, 10, 12, 23, 27, 60, 64, 71, 113, 169, 218, 231, 300-1, 307, 312, 316, 339, 349
Lumber
  consumption of, 114, 345
  production of, 111, 172, 262, 263, 268, 274, 345

Mackerel (see Cod and mackerel)
Manila hemp (see Fibers)
Mann, L., 68
Marketing of Crude Rubber, 336
Meats, all, 149, 265
Meeker, J. E., 28, 343
Meisner, M., 147
Merchant Marine Statistics, 326, 329, 330, 337, 343
Mercury, 12, 56, 57, 64, 71, 112, 137-8, 159, 160, 216, 230, 288-9, 306, 310, 314, 331.
Merrill, C. W., 221
Metal Statistics, 340
Milk, condensed and evaporated, 113, 344
Mills, F. C., 213, 240, 258, 267, 268, 276
Mineral Industry, 340
Mineral Resources of the United States, 18, 50, 131, 132, 137-8, 147,
326, 330, 331, 332, 333, 335, 337, 338, 339, 340, 344, 345, 346, 348
Mines, Bureau of, *Economic Papers*, 147, 330, 331, 332, 335
Mitchell, W. C., 31, 32, 33, 45
Mittens (see Gloves and mittens)
Molasses and sirup, 12, 55, 70, 111, 208, 210, 230, 284-5, 305, 309, 313, 328
Money in circulation, 240, 241, 324
Mowers, 113

Nails
  cut, production of, 159, 160, 161
  total production of, 12, 59, 72, 114, 218, 222, 225-6, 232, 298-9, 307, 311, 315, 338
National Fertilizer Association, *Proceedings*, 345
National Monetary Commission, 343
National Wealth and Income, 18
Newlin, J. A., 161
New York Stock Exchange, Year Book, 343
Nourse, E. G., 69

Oats
  acreage of, 211, 214, 323
  acre-yield of, 214, 323
  production of, 12, 55, 70, 85, 111, 149, 203, 208, 209, 210, 211, 230, 284-5, 305, 309, 313, 328
Ogburn, W. F., 96
Oils
  burning, 115, 116, 154-5, 344
  cottonseed (see Cottonseed oil)
  paraffin (see Paraffin oils)
Outlook for the Mackerel Fishery in 1931, 158

Paper
  boards, 113, 344
  fine, 115, 345
  newsprint and book, 113, 345

wrapping, 114, 346
Paraffin
  oils, 113
  wax, 113
Patents issued, 240, 241, 242, 246, 324
Pearson, F. A., 118, 200, 201, 202, 203, 205, 208, 240, 263-4, 265, 266, 269, 272, 274, 275, 278, 279, 280, 322
Perry, F. G., 257
Persons, W. M., 200, 201, 202, 205, 208, 262-3, 265, 266, 267, 268, 269, 272, 274, 275, 276, 277, 278, 279, 280, 322
Petroleum
  light distillates, 112, 115, 116, 154-5, 345
  production of, 12, 57, 64, 71, 83, 84, 110, 112, 119, 131, 147, 148, 156, 169, 191, 204, 216, 217, 224, 231, 290-1, 306, 310, 314, 331
Phosphate rock, 12, 57, 71, 84, 112, 183, 216, 231, 239, 290-1, 306, 310, 314, 331
Plows, walking, 114, 159, 160
Poor's Manual of Railroads, 342, 343
Population, 105, 123-6, 262-4, 269, 274, 279-80
Postage Rates, 342
Postage stamps, 11, 13, 23, 61, 73, 84, 117, 118-9, 169, 183, 220, 233, 235, 239, 302-3, 308, 312, 316, 342, 350, 351-2
Postal money orders, 11, 13, 61, 73, 117, 220, 223, 226, 233, 302-3, 308, 312, 316, 342
Postmaster General, *Annual Reports*, 342
Potatoes
  acreage of, 211, 214, 323
  acre-yield of, 214, 323
  production of, 12, 55, 70, 85, 111, 203, 208, 209, 210, 211, 230, 284-5, 305, 309, 313, 328
  sweet, production of, 111, 346
Prescott, R., 96, 154
Prices
  all-commodity, 240, 241, 324
  nonagricultural, 240, 241, 324
Production (see also Growth, Retardation, and Trend-cycles)
  comparison of United States with other countries, 145-50
  concepts of, 5-6
  defects of measures of, 22-7, 105, 255-61, 347-53
  indexes of: crops, 205, 263-5, 272, 274, 275-6, 322; manufactures, 205, 263, 267-8, 272, 274, 276-7, 322; mining, 205, 263, 266-7, 272, 274, 275, 322; total, 201, 263, 269,-70, 272, 273, 274, 277-80, 322; trade, 117, 262, 263, 268, 272, 274, 277
  measurable aspects of, 6-8, 50-1, 254-5
Pyrites, 12, 57, 70, 76, 112, 216, 230, 292-3, 306, 310, 314, 333

Railroad Gazette, 339
Rails
  consumption of, 13, 14, 17, 59, 71, 85, 107, 112, 115, 183, 218, 222, 231, 239, 302-3, 308, 312, 316, 341
  iron, production of, 159, 173
  production of, 10, 12, 15, 23, 59, 72, 114, 119, 166, 204, 218, 222, 231, 294-5, 307, 311, 315, 335-6
Railway Age, 339
Railways
  freight, 11, 13, 14, 16, 61, 73, 84, 117, 220, 223, 233, 235, 263, 268, 272, 274, 304, 308, 312, 317, 343-4, 349
  passenger-miles, 13, 61, 73, 84, 107, 117, 220, 223, 225, 233, 302-3, 308, 312, 316, 343
  ton-miles, 11, 13, 61, 73, 84, 117,

INDEX

119, 204, 220, 223, 225, 233, 235, 239, 302-3, 308, 312, 316, 342, 353
Raisins, 12, 55, 56, 60, 70, 76, 111, 191, 208, 210, 230, 286-7, 305, 309, 313, 329
Rakes, hay, 114
Retardation
  agriculture, 109-11, 119, 274, 275-6
  causes of, 120-69
  construction, 109, 110, 112-6, 119, 274, 277
  continuity of, 103-4, 107-8, 111-2, 113-5, 117, 272
  correlated with growth, 167-9
  defined, 100-1
  effects of, 150-3
  fisheries, 109-11, 119, 274
  forestry, 109-11, 119, 274, 275
  in technical progress, 141-5
  manufactures, 109, 110, 112-6, 119, 274, 276-7
  method of computing rates of, 98-9, 105
  mining, 109-10, 112, 119, 274, 275
  stage of, 101-3, 105-7, 111-2, 113-5, 117
  total production, 274, 277-9
  trade, 109, 116-7, 119, 274, 277
  transportation, 109, 116-7, 119, 277
  variability of rates of, 104-19, 162-7
Rice, 12, 55, 70, 80, 111, 130, 142, 157, 169, 208, 210, 230, 286-7, 305, 309, 313, 328
Rice Crop of the United States, 1792–1911, 328
Richter, F. E., 137
Rogers, H. O., 131, 141
Rubber, imports of, 12, 60, 65, 71, 80, 84, 115, 116, 154-5, 169, 218, 231, 239, 294-5, 307, 311, 315, 336
Rye, 12, 55, 70, 111, 203, 208, 210, 230, 286-7, 305, 309, 313, 328

Salt, 12, 57, 58, 71, 84, 112, 216, 231, 292-3, 306, 310, 314, 333
Secretary of the Treasury, *Annual Reports*, 242
Seltzer, L. H., 134, 135
Sette, O. E., 348
Shares traded, 13, 61, 73, 117, 169, 220, 223, 232, 304, 308, 312, 317, 343, 350
Sheep, 12, 14, 55, 58, 70, 85, 111, 208, 230, 276, 286-7, 305, 309, 313, 329, 347
Shelton, W. A., 336
Shingles, 113
Shirts and drawers, knit, 113
Shoes (see Boots and shoes)
Silk
  broad, 113, 344
  raw, imports of, 12, 14, 15, 58, 65, 72, 83, 114, 218, 232, 294-5, 307, 311, 315, 336, 350
  unmanufactured, imports of, 12, 14, 15, 58, 65, 72, 83, 84, 115, 169, 218, 232, 239, 300-1, 308, 312, 316, 340, 350
Silver
  consumption of, 12, 59, 72, 84, 114, 166, 219, 232, 300-1, 307, 312, 316, 340
  production of, 12, 57, 59, 71, 85, 112, 137, 146, 147, 166, 183, 216, 220, 231, 233, 235, 290-1, 306, 310, 314, 331
Silverman, A. G., 257
Sirup (see Molasses and sirup)
Sisal (see Fibers)
Slate Deposits and Slate Industry in the United States, 339
Slate, roofing, 11, 12, 13, 56, 60, 71, 103, 104, 113, 218, 222, 231, 298-9, 307, 311, 315, 338-9
Smith, B. B., 203
Snuff, (see Tobacco and snuff)
Snyder, C., 96, 117, 200, 201, 202-3,

204, 205, 260, 262, 263, 264, 265, 266, 268, 272, 274, 275, 278, 322, 341, 342, 343, 345, 350
Spirits, distilled, 12, 16, 51, 58, 72, 82, 88, 115, 118, 218, 232, 292-3, 306, 311, 315, 334, 350
Statistical Abstract of the United States, 326, 328, 329, 338
Statistical Report of Lake Commerce Passing Through Canals at Sault Ste. Marie, 342
Statistics Concerning Intoxicating Liquors, 334
Statistics of Meat Production, Consumption and Foreign Trade of the United States, 1900–1930, 149, 265, 347
Statistics of Railways in the United States, Annual Reports, 326, 342, 343, 344, 349
Steel, 12, 36, 59, 64, 71, 83, 84, 106, 113, 147, 148, 191, 216, 218, 221, 231, 296-7, 307, 311, 315, 336 (see also, Iron and steel)
Stewart, W. W., 277
Structural shapes, 113, 346
Sugar
 beet, production of, 12, 26, 55, 56, 58, 60, 70, 76, 80, 111, 126, 130, 172, 208, 210, 230, 284-5, 305, 309, 313, 327
 cane, production of, 12, 26, 36, 55, 56, 58, 70, 111, 208, 210, 230, 284-5, 305, 309, 313, 327
 maple, production of, 111, 159, 160, 345
 raw, consumption of, 12, 58, 72, 84, 114, 183, 219, 232, 294-5, 307, 311, 315, 336, 351
Sulphur, 12, 21, 56, 57, 58, 64, 70, 77, 80, 103, 112, 142, 156-7, 169, 216, 225, 230, 292-3, 306, 310, 314, 333
Sulphuric acid, 113, 346

Superintendent of New York State Department of Public Works, *Annual Reports*, 342
Superphosphate, 12, 14, 22, 60, 71, 113, 218, 231, 296-7, 307, 311, 315, 336
Switz, T. M., 151

Tarde, G., 96
Taussig, F. W., 65
Thompson, R. W., 161
Timoshenko, V. P., 205, 208, 263, 264, 272, 274, 322
Tin, imports of, 12, 59, 72, 84, 114, 115, 218, 232, 239, 296-7, 307, 311, 315, 337
Tin-plate, consumption of, 12, 59, 72, 84, 114, 172, 218, 232, 296-7, 307, 311, 315, 337
Tobacco
 consumption of, 12, 15, 58, 72, 83, 85, 115, 166, 218, 232, 300-1, 307, 312, 316, 340
 fine cut, production of, 159, 160
 raw, acreage of, 211, 214, 323
 raw, acre-yield of, 214, 323
 raw, production of, 12, 55, 68, 70, 85, 111, 149, 166, 208, 209, 210, 211, 230, 235, 286-7, 305, 309, 313, 328
Tobacco and snuff, production of, 12, 15, 58, 72, 114, 218, 232, 296-7, 307, 311, 315, 337
Tomatoes, canned, 12, 58, 72, 113, 219, 232, 300-1, 308, 312, 316, 341
Tonnage entered and cleared, 13, 61, 73, 84, 117, 118-9, 183, 220, 224, 233, 304, 308, 312, 317, 343, 349, 350-1, 353
Tower, W. S., 135, 136, 161
Townsend, C. H., 162
Trade, coastal, 11, 13, 14, 61, 73, 84, 117, 118-9, 183, 220, 233, 302-3, 308, 312, 316, 341, 350, 351

INDEX

Trend-cycles
  agriculture, 187-8, 204-5, 207-15, 313, 323
  amplitude of, 226-39, 272
  comparison of producers' and consumers' goods, 229, 233-4, 237
  comparison of production and consumption series, 235
  conformity to standard pattern, 206-26
  decils of, 183-93, 318-20
  defined, 48, 176-9
  in indexes of major industrial groups, 203-5, 322
  in indexes of total production, 199-203, 322
  medians of, 179-82, 193-6, 321
  nonagricultural series, 187-8, 215-26, 313-7, 324
  relation to business depressions, 247-52
  standard pattern of, 196-8, 241, 324
Trends, primary
  analysis of, 45-7, 49-69, 96-173, 262-81
  defined, 44-5
  measurement of, 45-6, 50-1, 97-101
Trends, secular
  analysis of, 47-8, 69-95, 174-252, 271
  defined, 30-4
  divergence of, 242-7, 325
  measured by exponential curves, 35-8
Tryon, F. G., 68, 131, 141, 333

Vegetable Statistics, 341
Vessels, 12, 60, 71, 80, 114, 119, 204, 218, 231, 296-7, 307, 311, 315, 337

Wardwell, C. A. R., 177
Warren, G. F., 118, 200, 201, 202, 203, 205, 208, 240, 263-4, 265, 266, 269, 272, 274, 275, 278, 279, 280, 322
Watkins, M. W., 134
Whale, 12, 14, 55, 56, 64, 70, 110, 111, 118-9, 137, 159, 160, 161-2, 173, 208, 230, 288-9, 305, 310, 313, 330, 348
Whalebone: Its Production and Distribution, 348
Wheat
  acreage of, 211, 214, 323
  acre-yield of, 214, 323
  production of, 12, 55, 70, 85, 111, 147, 148, 149, 203, 208, 209, 210, 211, 230, 286-7, 305, 309, 313, 328
Wheat Studies, 124, 147, 210, 328, 339
Whelpton, P. K., 62
Wigglesworth, H., 156
Wolf, J., 141, 143
Wolman, L., 18
Wood pulp, 113, 128, 346
Wool
  consumption of, 12, 58, 65, 72, 85, 114, 166, 219, 224, 232, 296-7, 307, 311, 315, 337
  production of, 12, 55, 60, 65, 70, 85, 111, 166, 208, 230, 276, 286-7, 305, 309, 313, 329

Yang, S., 183
Young, W. W., 118

Zinc
  consumption of, 12, 59, 72, 84, 114, 115, 166, 218, 232, 298-9, 307, 311, 315, 338
  oxide, 114, 224, 346
  production of, 12, 57, 59, 71, 84, 112, 119, 132, 147, 148, 166, 204, 216, 217, 231, 235, 290-1, 306, 310, 314, 332, 348

DATE DUE			
5.1 '63			
DEC 17 '69			
MAY 10 1975			
GAYLORD			PRINTED IN U.S.A